NEW
Historical Anthology
of
Music by Women

NEW
Historical Anthology
of
Music by Women

EDITED BY

James R. Briscoe

INDIANA UNIVERSITY PRESS

Bloomington and Indianapolis

This book is a publication of

Indiana University Press
601 North Morton Street
Bloomington, IN 47404-3797 USA

http://iupress.indiana.edu

Telephone orders   800-842-6796
Fax orders   812-855-7931
Orders by e-mail   iuporder@indiana.edu

© 2004 by James R. Briscoe

Cover illustration: "Elisabeth-Claude Jacquet de la Guerre" (ca. 1704), by François de Troy (1645–1730). The French art historian Dominique Brème recently identified this portrait, as reported by Françoise Getreau in the notes for Accord CD 205 782 (1997), "Ensemble Music of La Guerre." According to Brème, the painting was displayed at a painting exhibition at the Louvre in 1704 and identified in the catalogue as "Madame de la Guette" [sic]. La Guerre bequeathed the three portraits of herself that she owned to her nephews. In a post-mortem inventory, one listing appears to identify this painting, citing the composer's "large Flemish dual-keyboard harpsichord." The artist paints La Guerre at her height as composer, performer, and woman. We sincerely thank the owner of the portrait for authorizing its reproduction.

The paper used in this publication meets the minimum requirements of American National Standard for Information Sciences—Permanence of Paper for Printed Library Materials, ANSI Z39.48-1984.

Manufactured in the United States of America

Cataloging information is available from the Library of Congress.

ISBN 0-253-21683-4 (pbk. : alk. paper)

1 2 3 4 5 09 08 07 06 05 04

Contents

vi *Contents*

Contents   vii

Foreword

As I look back at that era a scant two decades ago, I can only describe it as the Dark Ages. When James Briscoe's *Historical Anthology of Music by Women* (HAMW) first appeared in 1987, musicological scholarship devoted to women had only begun to become visible. Carol Neuls-Bates's collection of source readings, *Women in Music*, had arrived in 1982, and Jane Bowers and Judith Tick had published *Women Making Music* in 1986; few biographies of female composers—with the notable exception of Nancy Reich's book on Clara Wieck Schumann (1985)—were yet available.

Of course, many view those times with nostalgia. The Culture Wars had not yet erupted within the genteel world of musicology, and methodological consensus still reigned; everyone knew which composers deserved to be studied as well as the proper questions to pursue. Indeed, some of my colleagues still made extensive use of Willi Apel's *Historical Anthology of Music* (HAM)—the comprehensive collection that had dominated the discipline and its undergraduate curricula for several decades. But those of us trying in the early 1980s to include female composers in our courses will recall mostly frustration, as we scoured our libraries in vain for scores (don't even ask about recordings!) to put before our students. Despite the increasing interest in women's history, the necessary musicological resources simply did not exist.

To his everlasting credit, Jim Briscoe persuaded Indiana University Press to publish HAMW—an expensive and risky enterprise with no guaranteed market. Only the most intrepid of presses will agree to print music, and this anthology presented scores by thirty-five composers familiar to only a handful of specialists. Moreover, given the almost complete absence of commercial recordings of music by women, Briscoe also had to assemble audiocassettes of performances to accompany the scores. His was a heroic venture by any standards, and he didn't even have the incentive of "special pleading" to keep him going.

Thanks to Briscoe's efforts, music by female composers began to appear on music history syllabi across North America and beyond. Instructors no longer had a ready excuse for their failure to present at least some of this music in their surveys, and whole courses devoted solely to women in music became part of the standard curriculum. We may have seen the last generation of music majors trained without at least some exposure to contributions by women.

But with this increased exposure in the classroom came a flood of new scholarship concerning women and recordings of their music by the very finest performing artists. It is a measure of the success of HAMW that it became dated so quickly. My own battered copy began to gather dust a few years ago as books, articles, scores, and CDs informed by more sophisticated methods appeared in ever greater numbers.

In this new edition of HAMW, Briscoe offers an indispensable resource for our own moment. First, he includes ten additional composers—Sappho, Dame Margot, Dame Maroie de Diergnau, Margaret of Austria, Barbara Strozzi, May Frances Aufderheide, Teresa Carreño, Florence Price, Elsa Barraine, and Augusta Read Thomas. Second, he has commissioned new biographical and critical essays by leading musicologists such as Thomas J. Mathiesen, Elizabeth Aubrey, Suzanne Cusick, Ellen Rosand, Mark Everist, and others, thus making the most recent interpretations of these women and their music easily available for the classroom. Third, he has changed the selections for several of the composers, in keeping with the focus of today's scholarship; thus, the entry on Hildegard includes the sequence "O virgo ac diadema" and the Ursuline antiphon "O rubor sanguinis"—compositions that correspond better to the questions now asked of Hildegard. Finally, *New Historical Anthology of Music by Women* (NHAMW) provides CDs of high-quality performances to supplement the scores and critical apparatus.

The decision to produce a new edition cannot have been easy for either Jim Briscoe or Indiana University Press. They persevered, however, and we will find ourselves in their debt for years to come in both the classroom and our scholarship. A comparison between the old and new tables of contents shows how far we have come since 1987. May the progress of women's history in musicology prove as significant over the course of the next sixteen years!

SUSAN McCLARY

Preface

When the *Historical Anthology of Music by Women* appeared in 1987, it contended with uneven previous research and a very limited discography of women's works. The authors of essays, many significantly updating their contributions now, performed spadework on music as yet little explored. Most works had to be recorded for the accompanying recordings for the first time, or virtually experimental recordings had to be republished. Scores required acceptance in the unequal state found at the time, and some eminent composers—Barbara Strozzi was notable—could not be represented because no usable modern score existed. Some scores appeared in manuscript or in uneven first editions. And yet, Indiana University Press, especially its music editor, Natalie Wrubel, determined that we must take a first step. It was requisite that we compile a collection representing the scope of women's creativity in music, and that we address it to a largely unknowing audience of performers, teachers, and students. We believed that people had to study and hear the music itself, and not simply hear about it.

The *Historical Anthology of Music by Women* was eagerly received as a breath of fresh air, as a unique point of departure. We have to remember that in 1987 Grout, Machlis, and other major textbooks contained no or only a fleeting reference to women composers—here two sentences on Clara Schumann, there some mere listing of Pauline Oliveros among avant-gardists. Not one music example of a score or recording was to be found in any leading text except those in Edith Borroff's general history. I sincerely thank the scholars and publishers who backed the idea from its inception in 1987, much as I recognize the admirable contribution of essays and score rights in 2004. It is right and healthy that a number of the essayists here are men, whereas previously the topic seemed a special case appropriate only for women scholars. We have come far since the jibes of the 1980s: "But you're not a woman. What interests you in that?" By contrast, and equally divisive, some critics faulted men scholars for "colonizing" when they considered music by women.

Turning to the present complete revision, one has only to observe that a wealth of basic references and specialized studies appeared beginning about 1980 and reaching a height after 1990, achieving a rightful chief attention today. Excellent monographs and many extended articles inform us about all composers seen here. Moreover, the ability to make new recordings and the opportunities for republishing existing, superior ones ensure the artistry of these recorded performances.

Authors of music history texts recognize not that including women is politically astute or fashionable, but that it is musically indispensable if one is to teach music history with integrity. That principle goes for performers as well. The musical public and our students now expect a comprehensive view. In that light the present anthology hopes to bring to fruition the aspiration of the 1987 anthology, and to extend it now to include the finest of today's scholarship.

The need for the *New Historical Anthology of Music by Women* is critical. Its strengths are an array of scores and composers expanded in number by one-fourth, specialist essays that are expertly informed and contain analyses of depth, and excellent recordings by leading artists. NHAMW is reinforced by two sources, Karin Pendle's *Women in Music: A History* and the series edited by Martha Schleifer and Sylvia Glickman, *Women Composers: Music through the Ages*. Both contain readings, and the latter contains scores, but neither is joined by a recording set. These, along with the Norton-Grove *Dictionary of Women Composers* and *The New Grove Dictionary of Music and Musicians* (second edition), are the first sources that should complement this book. If you are linked through a complete city or university library, or if you have purchased the link, you may consult Grove Online articles from both the latter two references: http://www.grovemusic.com.

Here is a collection of foremost compositions in all major genres, instrumentation, and structures of music composition. Essays written by leading specialists introduce the composers, and virtually all scores are recorded in the accompanying set of three compact discs. The anthology spans twenty-five hundred years of Western music history, from Sappho composing lyrics in Greece in 600 B.C.E. to Augusta Read Thomas writing chamber music for the third millennium. It is intended for music students, performers, and scholars who desire a knowledge of the leading women composers of Western concert music.

No discography is attempted now, but some recordings are suggested in the essays. Because libraries rarely lend recordings through Interlibrary Loan, and because recordings pass out of print quickly today, one is advised to begin a search for recordings not on hand by consulting Schwann and other current listings.

Researchers will need to consult databases such as Academic Search Elite, Art Index, Dissertation Abstracts, ERIC, Humanities Index, Grove Online, RILM (Music Literature), IIMP (Music Periodicals), and Music Index. Leads to monographs and periodical articles will be found there as well as in reference books dedicated to this literature. Essayists have included only specialized sources in their bibliographies that might not turn up in a normal search. Please see the General Bibliography for basic reference books.

Acknowledgments

I honor the artist Miriam Landman in particular by this writing, because she showed faith and offered essential support while this book was still an idea in the making.

I dedicate this collection to Anna, who for thirty years has realized by her artistry and her dedication Simone de Beauvoir's hope in *The Second Sex:*

> When we abolish the slavery of half of humanity, together with the whole system of hypocrisy that it implies, then the "division" of humanity will reveal its genuine significance and the human couple will find its true form.

NEW
Historical Anthology
of
Music by Women

Sappho
(ca. 612 B.C.E.)

THOMAS J. MATHIESEN

Sappho was born during the second half of the seventh century B.C.E., and by the time of her death sometime in the early sixth century, she had composed a substantial quantity of lyric poetry in many of the common genres of the day. Her fame as a poet and musician was so great that she came to be known as the "Tenth Muse" (*Anth. Pal.* 9.506).

Sappho probably lived in Mytilene on Lesbos (an island just off the western coast of modern-day Turkey) until she was exiled to Sicily around the turn of the century. In late antiquity, her poetry was collected in nine books, corresponding to the various meters she employed. Unfortunately, virtually all of her poetry is lost: only a single complete poem survives (see fragment 1 below; the poems are now known simply by their fragment numbers), together with some extended fragments and a large number of very short fragments (often only phrases) preserved in later authors' quotations from her work.

As a lyric poet (that is, a poet whose work is intended to be sung to the accompaniment of a lyre), Sappho is commonly associated with her contemporary Alcaeus and the somewhat younger Anacreon. Each of these poets makes frequent references to singing and to lyre-playing, and Sappho and Alcaeus are associated as well in vase paintings, as, for example, in a fifth-century red-figure kalathoid (a wine-cooler) that shows the two poets holding a special type of lyre with long arms, the barbitos (see Figure 1).

Because of the nearly inseparable relationships among poetry, singing, lyre-playing, and dance in ancient Greece, Sappho's importance as a musical innovator is well attested by the later Greek and Latin authors who are the sources for much of our knowledge of ancient Greek music history. According to Aristoxenus (fourth century B.C.E.), as quoted in a dialogue on music commonly but erroneously attributed to Plutarch (ca. 50–ca. 120 C.E.), Sappho invented the Mixolydian style—which the Plutarchean author describes as "impassioned"—and the later tragic poets learned the style from her. Aristoxenus's reference to the Mixolydian probably does not refer to a particular *tonos* as the *tonoi* came to be described by the Greek music theorists of his time and later (that is, as a kind of scale or tuning) but rather to a certain style created by the combination of poetic subject, rhythm and meter, characteristic melodic patterns, and type of instrumental accompaniment. This Mixolydian style, in Plato's mind, was associated with lamentation and accordingly banished from his ideal republic (*Rep.* 3.10); Aristotle had the same perception of the Mixolydian, but he believed that society might employ all the styles (*harmoniai*) at differing times and places and for various purposes (*Pol.* 8.5–7).

Figure 1. Sappho and Alcaeus with barbitos. Glyptothek, Staatlich. Antikensammlungen, Munich, Germany. Foto Marburg/Art Resource, NY.

Sappho's representation with the barbitos (see Figure 1), an instrument commonly associated with Dionysus (the god of wine, intoxication, madness, and ecstasy), certainly accords with her reputation for an impassioned poetic style, as does the tradition of attributing to her the invention of the pektis and magadis, two instruments (or perhaps two names for the same instrument) with multiple strings, possibly tuned in pairs at the octave, that would have been capable of playing highly complex melodies. In fact, a few lines later, in the same passage in which he banishes the Mixolydian, Plato also rejects instruments capable of playing the complex styles, including in this group the aulos (a complicated wind instrument with a single or double reed normally played in pairs) and stringed instruments such as the pektis and the trigona (a kind of triangular harp).

Much of Sappho's poetry was probably intended for solo performance, in contrast to choral lyric. While choral lyric could be arranged in the large structural units of strophe, antistrophe, and epode with complex metric patterns employing an artificial and formalized style of language, solo lyric typically used short stanzas with simple meters and the local dialect of the poet. Thus, Sappho's poetry, written in Aeolic dialect, was later described (e.g., by Marius Victorinus, *Ars gramm.* 6.161 Keil) as composed of four-line stanzas, the first three of which are comprised of eleven syllables and the fourth of which is shorter. This "Sapphic stanza," as it came to be called, influenced later poets such as Horace.

A relatively small number of notated melodies survive for ancient Greek poetic texts, but all of these are for later texts, in most cases much later, extending from the fifth century B.C.E. to at least the fourth century C.E. We know almost nothing about the performance practice of the surviving musical fragments, and even less for the music of the sixth and seventh centuries B.C.E. Nevertheless, a few points can be deduced about the music that may have formed the counterpart to Sappho's poetry. First of all, it is likely (though not absolutely certain) that the poetic rhythm of the verse was followed rather than altered by the music. In fragment 94, for example, the following pattern appears

THOMAS J. MATHIESEN

in the stanzas of lines 3–5 and 6–8 (× indicates a syllable of indifferent length, − a long syllable, and ◡ a short syllable): ×× − ◡◡ − ◡ − ‖ ×× − ◡◡ − ◡ − ‖ ×× − ◡◡ − ◡◡ − ◡ − ⦀, which can be expanded into the pattern of the "Sapphic stanza": − ◡ − × − ◡◡ − ◡ − − ‖ − ◡ − × − ◡◡ − ◡ − − ‖ − ◡ − × − ◡◡ − ◡⦙− ×⦙− ◡◡ − − ⦀, represented in fragment 1 (the third line—or period—was regarded by ancient critics and metricians such as Dionysius of Halicarnassus and Marius Victorinus as two lines, breaking at the caesura [⦙] following the ninth or eleventh position). If the melody tended to follow the pitch inflection of the Greek words, as often but not always happens in the surviving fragments, the contour might ascend for syllables with an acute accent, rise and fall on syllables with a circumflex, remain stable or fall on syllables without an accent, and fall on syllables with a grave accent. Thus, in fragment 94, the contour of lines 6–8 might look something like this (*a* indicates ascent, *c* indicates an up-and-down circumflex, *d* indicates descent, and *s* indicates a stable pitch): *d a s a s d a d* ‖ *a d a s d a d s* ‖ *a d c s d a s s a s d* ⦀. But this pattern would work only for lines 6–8, not for lines 3–5. In fact, if the same melody were used for each stanza, the relationship between text and melody could work for only one of the stanzas of a stanzaic poem (presumably the first), since we have no evidence that poets attempted to match the accentuation as well as the rhythm in every stanza. It is therefore quite possible that the melody would not have been constructed to follow the pattern of accentuation of any stanza but rather as a free and independent line. Finally, there is the matter of the accompanying instrument. Would the lyre double the vocal melody or play something else? Some evidence indicates that the older style of accompaniment involved no more than doubling the notes of the melody at the unison, but Archilochus, who was a generation or two earlier than Sappho, seems to have employed accompaniments below the vocal melody.

While we might compose an imaginary melody based on this uncertain array of evidence, it could be no more than that: imaginary. Moreover, in looking at the surviving melodies, we immediately see that the composers frequently violated the principles of rhythmic and pitch correspondence and were quite inventive in the construction of their melodies. Thus, if we applied the simple principles described above, composed an imaginary melody to a text for which we have a surviving melody, and then compared the imaginary and surviving melodies, it is unlikely that the resemblance would be more than slight.

But let us not be too disappointed. Although we have none of Sappho's melodies, we do have enough text to discern the euphony and charm of her language, the vividness of her imagery, the occasional musical allusions, and the recurring theme of love.

Translated Fragments

FRAGMENT 1 (= CAMPBELL FR. 1)

On the throne of many hues, Immortal Aphrodite,
child of Zeus, weaving wiles—I beg you
not to subdue my spirit, Queen,
with pain or sorrow

but come—if ever before
having heard my voice from far away
you listened, and leaving your father's
golden home you came

Sappho

3

in your chariot yoked with swift, lovely
sparrows bringing you over the dark earth
thick-feathered wings swirling down
from the sky through mid-air

arriving quickly—you, Blessed One,
with a smile on your unaging face
asking again what I have suffered
and why am I calling again

and in my wild heart which did I most wish
to happen to me: "Again whom must I persuade
back into the harness of your love?
Sappho, who wrongs you?

For if she flees, soon she'll pursue,
she doesn't accept gifts, but she'll give,
if not now loving, soon she'll love
even against her will."

Come to me now again, release me from
this pain, everything my spirit longs
to have fulfilled, fulfill, and you
be my ally.

FRAGMENT 51 (= CAMPBELL FR. 44), LINES 21–34

> . . . like gods
> . . . sacred gathering
> hastened . . . to Troy,
> the sweet melody of reed-pipe and [kithara] mingled,
> sound of castanets, the maidens
> sang a holy song, a silvery divine echo
> reached the sky, [laughter] . . .
> and everywhere through the streets . . .
> mixing bowls and drinking-bowls . . .
> myrrh, cassia, and frankincense together.
> The elder women all cried out "Eleleu,"
> and all the men shouted high and clear
> invoking Paion, the archer skilled in lyre,
> and they praised Hektor and Andromache, godlike.

Translations by Diane J. Rayor, from *Sappho's Lyre: Archaic Lyric and Women Poets of Ancient Greece* (Berkeley: University of California Press, 1991), 51–52 and 76–77. Used by permission of the University of California Press.

Further Reading

For the passages from Plato and Aristotle, see:
Treitler, Leo, ed. *Strunk's Source Readings in Music History*. Rev. ed. New York: Norton, 1998.

For further information on Sappho and editions and translations of her poetry, see:

Thomas J. Mathiesen

Campbell, David A., ed. and trans. *Greek Lyric.* Vol. 1: *Sappho and Alcaeus.* Loeb Classical Library. Cambridge, Mass.: Harvard University Press, 1982.

New Grove Dictionary of Music and Musicians. 2nd ed. S.v. "Sappho."

Sappho's Lyre: Archaic Lyric and Women Poets of Ancient Greece. Intro., trans., and ann. by Diane J. Rayor. Foreword by W. R. Johnson. Berkeley: University of California Press, 1991.

For further readings on ancient Greek music, see:

Mathiesen, Thomas J. *Apollo's Lyre: Greek Music and Music Theory in Antiquity and the Middle Ages.* Publications of the Center for the History of Music Theory and Literature, vol. 2. Lincoln: University of Nebraska Press, 1999.

New Grove Dictionary of Music and Musicians. 2nd ed. S.v. "Greece, §I: Ancient."

Kassia

(ca. 810–843 and 867)

DIANE TOULIATOS-MILES

The earliest woman composer for whom there is preserved music and the most important woman composer of medieval Byzantine chant is Kassia, who is also identified in manuscripts by other forms of her name (Kasia, Eikasia, and Ikasia). In addition to being a gifted composer and poet, she is an important historical figure of Byzantium. According to the chronicles of the Byzantine empire, Kassia, a beautiful and highly educated woman, was brought to the brideshow of Emperor Theophilos, where he would select his bride-to-be with the token of a golden apple. Theophilos first screened his candidates by testing their intelligence and wit. In a quick response that counteracted the emperor's question concerning the evil caused by women, Kassia displayed a mind far superior to his, which displeased and embarrassed the proud ruler. Although she captured Theophilos's heart, her greater wisdom and her response in defense of the honor of women lost her the opportunity to become empress. Hence, she is known to have founded, circa 843, a convent named after her outside the walls of Constantinople, and it is here that she spent the rest of her life and for which she wrote her music.

Kassia is mostly known as a composer of sacred poems with music, but she also wrote secular epigrams and moral sayings (many of which defend women's rights). She is credited with having written over fifty liturgical compositions—although some are of doubtful authorship, and the authenticity of some of her melodies has been questioned. Specifically, it has been debated whether Kassia wrote the music as well as the text for her liturgical poetry, but according to the tradition of the period, early hymnographers composed both text and music. Kassia also composed music to the text of other writers of the period.

The majority of Kassia's music falls under the category of the Sticheron, a lengthy verse chanted in various parts of the morning and evening office throughout the liturgical year. She also composed Kanons for the Dead, a Tetraodion, and a Troparion. In one of her most popular melodies, the Sticheron Idiomelon Doxastikon "Augustus, the Monarch," Kassia compares the rule of Augustus (27 B.C.E.–C.E. 14) with that of Jesus Christ. This melody was so well known during Byzantine times that it was documented in the chronicles of Byzantium. Besides the parallelism of textual themes, two verbal tenses are used to contrast the past and present accomplishments of the rulers; metrical rhyming schemes correspond to the parallelism in the music, for the melody consists of three phrases, each immediately repeated and followed by a fourth unrepeated phrase.

6

This melodic structure, *A A B B C C D*, is one of several sequence forms. Although it is difficult to prove that the sequence was invented by Kassia, at least her composition substantiates the use of the sequence form concurrently with the West, if not earlier!

Kassia's most famous composition is her Troparion "The Fallen Woman," which is sung in the morning office of Holy Wednesday. This hymn is about Mary Magdalene, a "fallen woman," who washed Christ's feet, anointed them, and wiped them with her long hair. The hymn is also considered to be pseudo-autobiographical. Having regretted not choosing Kassia for his bride, Emperor Theophilos later attempted to meet her to express his sorrow and love. Although Kassia avoided the emperor, in her heart she felt that she had returned his love and had become a "fallen woman." With the exception of verse eight of the poem, which is attributed to Theophilos, the melody and text are Kassia's. According to legend and documentation, Kassia was in the process of writing this composition when Theophilos made one of his state visits to her monastery. On seeing him unexpectedly, Kassia fled and left the unfinished poem on her desk. Her departure inspired Theophilos to write the verse "Thy feet, whereof when Eve in Paradise heard the sound, she hid herself for fear." Although this line is not consistent with the theme of a fallen woman, it was retained. It is perhaps this legendary incident that made the hymn so well known.

The setting of this chant is primarily syllabic with a few neumatic sections. The melody has an unusually wide ambitus of an octave and a fourth: c' to f". The linking device throughout this lengthy hymn is the motive B-A-G and its variants, which occur throughout the chant. Because of its fame, "The Fallen Woman" was arranged by many composers during Byzantine times as well as more recently.

Kassia's music displays her talent and originality as a poet and as a composer. Her poetry guides the structure of her musical compositions. Her compositions are far more original than most of her contemporaries'; otherwise, her music might not have been documented in the Byzantine chronicles of the time. Most hymnographers of the period were far less imaginative; their poetry was more verbose and their compositions were longer. They gave little attention to musical structure. Kassia's music is concise, and her texts are set syllabically. Her musical inventiveness and wit are demonstrated by the form of her compositions, which often parallels or contrasts with the text; by her poetic play with words; and in musical motives that symbolize and reflect the text, creating *musica reservata* long before it was used in the West. Much of her hymnography is written to defend women; hence, she has written hymns commemorating women saints, the Theotokos (Virgin Mary), and fallen women who redeemed their lives with their faith to the Lord. Historically, Kassia is important as the only hymnographer who wrote penitential hymns on "fallen women" (i.e., Mary Magdalene, Pious Pelagia, et al.), a subject that no male hymnographers deemed worthy of attention.

Texts of "Augustus, the Monarch" and "The Fallen Woman," translated from Byzantine Greek

AUGUSTUS, THE MONARCH

When Augustus became monarch upon earth,
  The multitude of kingdoms among men was ended.
And when Thou was incarnate of the Holy One,
  The multitude of divinities among the idols was put down.
Beneath one universal empire have the cities come,
  And in one divine dominion the nations believed.

Kassia

The folk were enrolled by the decrees of the emperor,
  We, the faithful, have been inscribed in the name of Deity.
    Oh, Thou our incarnate Lord,
    Great is Thy mercy, to Thee be glory.

Translation: H. J. W. Tillyard

Αὐγούστου Μοναρχήσαντος

Αὐγούστου Μοναρχήσαντος ἐπὶ τῆς γῆς
ἡ πολυαρχία τῶν ἀνθρώπων ἐπαύσατο
καὶ σοῦ ἐνανθρωπήσαντος ἐκ τῆς ἁγνῆς
ἡ πολυθεῖα τῶν εἰδώλων κατήργηται
ὑπὸ μίαν Βασιλείαν ἐγκόσμιον
αἱ πόλεις γεγένηται·
καὶ εἰς μίαν δεσποτείαν θεότητος
τὰ ἔθνη ἐπίστευσαν
ἀπεγράφησαν οἱ λαοί, τῷ δόγματι τοῦ
      Καίσαρος
ἐπεγράφημεν οἱ πιστοί, ὀνόματι
      θεότητος
σοῦ τοῦ ἐνανθρωπήσαντος Θεοῦ ἡμῶν
μέγα σου τὸ ἔλεος, Κύριε, δόξα σοι.

Byzantine Greek text of "Augustus, the Monarch."

THE FALLEN WOMAN

Lord, the woman fallen in many sins, seeing Thy Divinity,
Taking the part of myrrh-bearer, wailing bringeth to Thee myrrh
  against Thy burial.
Alas, she crieth, for that night is to me the wildness of sin, dusky
  and moonless, even the love of transgression.
Accept the springs of my tears, who with clouds partest the
  waters of the sea:
Bend to the groanings of my heart, who hast brought down
  Heaven by Thine ineffable humiliation.
I will kiss again Thy stainless feet,
I will wipe them then with the hair of my head—

*Thy feet, whereof when Eve in Paradise heard the sound, she
  hid herself for fear.*

The multitude of my sins, and the depths of Thy judgment who
  shall explore, Savior of souls, my Redeemer.
Forget not me Thy servant, Thou, whose mercy is infinite.

Translation by H. J. W. Tillyard

Κύριε, ἡ ἐν Πολλαῖς ᾿Αμαρτίαις

Κύριε, ἡ ἐν πολλαῖς ἁμαρτίαις
    περιπεσοῦσα γυνή,
τὴν σὴν αἰσθομένη Θεότητα,
    μυροφόρου ἀναλαβοῦσα τάξιν,
ὀδυρομένη μύρον σοι
    πρὸ τοῦ ἐνταφιασμοῦ κομίζει·
Οἴμοι, λέγουσα,
    ὅτι νύξ με συνέχει
    οἶστρος ἀκολασίας.
ζοφώδης τε καὶ ἀσέληνος,
    ἔρως τῆς ἁμαρτίας·
δέξαι μου τὰς πηγὰς τῶν δακρύων,
ὁ νεφέλαις στημονίζων
    τῆς θαλάσσης τὸ ὕδωρ·
κάμφθητί μοι
    πρὸς τοὺς στεναγμοὺς τῆς καρδίας,
ὁ κλίνας τοὺς οὐρανοὺς
    τῇ ἀφράστῳ σου κενώσει·
καταφιλήσω τοὺς ἀχράντους σου πόδας,
ἀποσμήξω τούτους δέ πάλιν
    τοῖς τῆς κεφαλῆς μου βοστρύχοις·
ὧν ἐν τῷ Παραδείσῳ
    Εὔα τὸν δειλινὸν
κρότον τοῖς ὠσὶν ἠχηθεῖσα,
    τῷ φόβῳ ἐκρύβη·
ἁμαρτιῶν μου τὰ πλήθη
    καὶ κριμάτων σου ἀβύσσους
τίς ἐξιχνιάσει,
    ψυχοσῶστα, Σωτήρ μου·
μή με τὴν σὴν δούλην παρίδῃς
    ὁ ἀμέτρητον ἔχων τὸ μέγα ἔλεος.

Byzantine Greek text of "The Fallen Women."

Further Reading

New Grove Dictionary of Music and Musicians. 2nd ed. S.v. "Kassia."

Touliatos, Diane. "Byzantine Women Composers." Available online at http://www.hellenist.org (contains the only existing picture of Kassia).

———. "Kassia (ca. 810–ca. 867)." In *Women Composer: Music through the Ages,* vol. 1: *Composers Born before 1599,* ed. Martha Furman Schleifer and Sylvia Glickman, pp. 1–24. New York: G. K. Hall, 1996 [inc. cat., facs., & transcrs.].

———. "Medieval Women Composers in Byzantium and the West." In *Proceedings of the VIth International Congress of Musicology "Musica Antiqua Europae Orientalis,"* pp. 687–712. Bydgoszcz, Poland, 1982.

———. *The Muses: Greek Women in Music from Antiquity to the End of the Byzantine Empire.* Forthcoming.

———. "The Traditional Role of Greek Women in Music from Antiquity to the End of the Byzantine Empire." In *Rediscovering the Muses: Women's Musical Traditions,* ed. Kimberly Marshall, pp. 111–23 and notes 250–53. Boston: Northeastern University Press, 1993.

———. "Women Composers of Medieval Byzantine Chant." *College Music Society Symposium* 24, pt. 1 (Spring 1984): 62–80.

Editions and Recordings

Touliatos, Diane, ed. *Kassia: Six Stichera.* Bryn Mawr, Pa.: Hildegard Publishing Co., 1996.

———. *Kassia: Thirteen Compositions.* Bryn Mawr, Pa.: Hildegard Publishing Co., 1999.

———. *Kassia: Her Complete Compositions.* Bryn Mawr, Pa.: Hildegard Publishing Co., forthcoming.

Kassia's "Using the Apostate Tyrant as His Tool." Transcription and Arrangement by D. Touliatos for the KRONOS String Quartet's *Early Music (Lacrimae Antiquae)* CD, 1997.

Augustus, the Monarch

Kassia, transcribed by Diane Touliatos

Source: Athens MS 883, fol. 97r. © Hildegard Publishing 2000, Diane Touliatos, ed. By permission of Theodore Presser.

The Fallen Woman
Lord, the Woman Fallen into Many Sins

Kassia, transcribed by Diane Touliatos

Plagal Mode IV

Ne - ha - gi - e Ký - ri - e e en pol - lais a - mar -

tí - ais pe - ri - pe - soú - sa gy - nē tin si - i - in

ai - stho - mĕ - e - nē Thĕ - ó - ti - ta mi - ro - fó - rou a - na -

la - voú - sa tá - xin o - di - ro - mé - nē mí - ron - soi pro tou en -

ta - fi - a - smou ko - mí - zei oi moi lé - gou - sa

ó - ti níx moi y - pár - chei oí - stros a - ko - la - sí - as zo - fó -

dis te - e ke a - sĕ - li - nos é - ros tis a - mar - tí - as

dé - xai mou tas pi - gás ton da - krí - on o ne - fé -

lais di - ex á - gon tis tha - lás - sis tŏ ý -

Source: Ambrosianae A 139, fols. 230r-v. © Hildegard Publishing 2000, Diane Touliatos, ed. By permission of Theodore Presser.

DIANE TOULIATOS-MILES

Hildegard von Bingen
(1098–1179)

MICHAEL KLAPER

The Benedictine nun Hildegard von Bingen was born in 1098 in Bermersheim, near Alzey in Rhine-Hesse; she died 17 September 1179 in her monastery at Rupertsberg. Hildegard was one of the most productive writers of the Middle Ages. Her vast literary output encompasses not only three major visionary works as well as theological, hagiographical, and medicinal writings, but also a collection of nearly eighty chants and a dramatic play, the *Ordo virtutum* (Play of Virtues), to be sung as a complete work. Hildegard's musical compositions are transmitted mainly in two sources, both probably copied during her lifetime. The earlier source (Dendermonde, St. Pieters & Paulusabdij, Ms. Cod. 9; datable between 1163 and 1175) preserves the chant collection only in a fragmentary state, although its original content can plausibly be reconstructed; the later one (Wiesbaden, Hessische Landesbibliothek, Hs. 2; apparently begun before Hildegard's death, but with later additions) is an edition of the author's opera omnia, transmitting the most comprehensive form of the chant collection known today. This collection is often referred to as Hildegard's *Symphonia armonie celestium revelationum* (Symphony of the Harmony of Celestial Revelations), a work that Hildegard cites as a composition dating from the 1150s. But it is doubtful that, in this connection, the title Symphonia actually means musical compositions, or that Hildegard initially conceived them as a poetic-musical cycle. Rather more plausible is that her compositional activities stretch over a period of more than two decades, and that her chants were not assembled together in a single collection until the 1170s—perhaps in an attempt to confirm the author's status as an extraordinarily gifted seer, inspired by divine authority.

According to the rubrics specifying the genre of the individual pieces in the two main sources of Hildegard's chants, her musical oeuvre comprises predominantly antiphons, responsories, hymns, sequences, and symphoniae (this last indication of genre seems to be unique in the twelfth century). One of the pieces entitled sequentia is "O virgo ac diadema" in honor of the Virgin Mary (see text below).

This piece is typical for Hildegard's sequences (and the genre in general) insofar as it consists of paired double versicles, in this case 1a/b, 2a/b . . . 6a/b (numbers indicating different melodic lines, letters indicating different textual passages connected with them). In "O virgo," however, this structure is mainly a musical one, because there is no evident parallelism between any two textual phrases sung to roughly the same melody—quite the contrary: the syllable count of the musically paired text segments differs from five to eighteen syllables. It is clear, therefore, that the music of each double versicle had to be altered for its repetition: One finds singular notes and whole melodic phrases left out or added, certain melodic turns contracted over one syllable or broken down into several syllables, and so on (moreover, the music of the end of versicle 6a and 6b is completely different). As regards melodic style, "O virgo" is not completely syllabic (a characteristic feature of the earliest sequences, some dating back to the ninth century) and in this respect has some similarities to some examples of the genre composed in the twelfth century. Rather untypical for this time is the textual style of Hildegard's sequence—which does not employ regular accent patterns and rhyme schemes, but is written in a highly artificial prose (Kunstprosa)—as well as its free handling of the double versicle structure. It is of interest, thus, that the text of "O virgo" is also transmitted in the Hildegard manuscripts as such, without any rubric and notation, in the context of her letters—perhaps an indication that "O virgo" had not been intended as a sequence from the outset.

In more than one respect, the Kyrie melody surviving among Hildegard's chants is unique: first, it is her only known composition based on a text that is omnipresent in the liturgy and not written by the author herself. Second, Hildegard's Kyrie is musically identical with the beginning of one of her lengthy chants, namely the responsory "O lucidissima apostolorum turba" for apostles (this is the only case in which two of Hildegard's compositions share substantial musical material). It is difficult to determine which of the pieces may have been written first. Kyrie eleison is an ancient litany characterized as part of the mass by its ninefold acclamations: Kyrie eleison (Lord have mercy; three times), Christe eleison (Christ have mercy; three times), Kyrie eleison (three times). As in many other Kyrie melodies of the Middle Ages, there is in Hildegard's melody a setting of the first, fourth, and sixth statement of Kyrie eleison as well as of the first Christe eleison. It is a well-shaped F melody, spanning the range of an octave (F/F) in the first articulation of Kyrie, of a tenth (D/F) in the second and the last one, and an even wider ambitus in the Christe (C/G = octave plus fifth). Some melodic phrases are heard (with differences) in more than one section, and the sixth Kyrie is an expanded repetition of the fourth. Clearly at work then are the principles of repetition, variation, and intensification. Since the repetitional structure of the Kyrie is not present in the responsory in the same way, one could argue that the former was based on the latter. By contrast, the Kyrie is Hildegard's only melody to expose a clear F tonality ("O lucidissima" begins and ends on G), and the musical material of the Kyrie seems alien within the modal framework of the responsory, and thereby may indicate that the material common to the two was taken over from the Kyrie.

It is a much-debated question if and how Hildegard's compositions might have been used in the liturgy, since precise indications of the liturgical placement of individual items are only seldom transmitted. This is the case, for example, with the antiphon "O rubor sanguinis," headed in both manuscript sources by the rubric "In evangelium antiphona."

"O rubor" belongs to a group of pieces written in honor of Saint Ursula and her companions, the legendary eleven thousand virgins. Of the other pieces of this group, two are responsories and eight are antiphons, five of which are connected by the rubric "Laudes"; furthermore, one of the remaining three antiphons is labeled "In evangelium antiphona" (as is "O rubor"). It is easy to see how this corpus of chants fits into the structure of the Divine Office of the monastic community. "Laudes" (Lauds) is the usual term for one of the canonical hours, the so-called morning prayer, during which five antiphons with their respective psalms are to be sung, as well as a further antiphon with the canticle Benedictus taken from Luke, whence the designation "In evangelium." Responsories are primarily used in Matins, also known as the Night Office, where they stand at the end of each nocturn. It seems probable, therefore, that Hildegard's chants honoring Ursula were meant to be used during the canonical hours on the feastday of the saint, although there are not enough chants for all liturgical positions (in the monastic cursus, for example, twelve responsories are needed for Matins), nor is the exact use of all Ursula chants determined (thus, the two antiphons following the final "In evangelium" antiphon might have been intended for the lesser canonical hours, but this is not made explicit). This notwithstanding, Hildegard's compositions for Ursula are most closely related to proper office compositions (historiae) for highly venerated saints by other authors. But whether this means that Hildegard's chants were regularly used in the liturgy is far from certain. To exemplify this last point: "O rubor sanguinis" is the only Ursula antiphon by Hildegard that has a conspicuous melisma both at its beginning (at O) and near its end (at num[quam]). This seems liturgically apt, because gospel antiphons are generally more ornate musically than antiphons sung with a psalm. By contrast, there exist many chants by Hildegard labeled "antiphona," which are musically exuberant (with a wide ambitus and lengthy melismas on more than just one or two syllables). It is quite possible that such antiphons were sung not during the canonical hours but during processions or as votive chants. The history of transmission of some of these chants, however, points in another direction: toward the possibility that the generically and liturgically ordered arrangement of Hildegard's chants could have been an afterthought, and that they may have been written down and codified not in order to make use of them, but to venerate them. Be that as it may, there are no indications of a reception of Hildegard's compositions beyond the cloister at Rupertsberg during the Middle Ages. Thus, the composer Hildegard is, to paraphrase Jürg Stenzl, largely a phenomenon of the music history of modern times.

Translated Texts

"O VIRGO AC DIADEMA"

1a. O branch and diadem of the king's purple, you who are in your enclosure like a breastplate:

1b. Burgeoning, you blossomed after another fashion than Adam gave rise to the whole human race.

2a. Hail, hail! from your womb came another life of which Adam had stripped his sons.

2b. O flower, you did not spring from dew nor from drops of rain, nor did the air fly over you, but the divine radiance brought you forth on a most noble branch.

3a. O branch, God had foreseen your flowering on the first day of his creation.

3b. And he made you for his Word as a golden matrix, O praiseworthy Virgin.

4a. O how great in its powers is the side of man from which God brought forth the form of woman, which he made the mirror of all his beauty and the embrace of his whole creation.

4b. Thence celestial voices chime in harmony and the whole earth marvels, O praiseworthy Mary, for God has greatly loved you.

5a. O how greatly we must lament and mourn because sadness flowed in guilt through the serpent's counsel into woman.

5b. For the very woman whom God made to be mother of all plucked at her womb with the wounds of ignorance and brought forth consummate pain for her kind.

6a. But, O dawn, from your womb a new sun has come forth, which has cleansed all the guilt of Eve and through you brought a blessing greater than the harm Eve did to mankind.

6b. Hence, O saving Lady, you who bore the new light for humankind: gather the members of your Son into celestial harmony.

Translation by Barbara Newman

MICHAEL KLAPER

O redness of blood, you who flowed from that height that divinity touched: you are a flower that the winter of the serpent's breath has never harmed.

Further Reading

Hildegard von Bingen. *Lieder: Faksimile Riesencodex (Hs. 2) der Hessischen Landesbibliothek Wiesbaden fol. 466–481v.* Ed. Lorenz Welker. Commentary by Michael Klaper. Wiesbaden: Dr. Ludwig Reichert Verlag 1998. English trans. Lori Kruckenberg. Illustrations, tables, and selected bibliography.

Williman, Joseph. "Hildegard cantrix. Überlegungen zur musikalischen Kunst *Hildegards von Bingen* (1098–1179)." In *Musik Denken: Ernst Lichtenhahn zur Emeritierung, 16 Beiträge seiner Schülerinnen und Schüler*, ed. Antonio Baldassarre, Susanne Kübler, and Patrick Müller, II/41: 9–34. Bern: Publikationen der Schweizerischen Musikforschenden Gesellschat, 1980.

O virgo ac diadema

Hildegard von Bingen

R ff. 471ᵛ – 472 (Sequentia de sancta Maria)
D ff. 156ʳ/ᵛ Incomplete

4a O quam mag-num est in vi-ri-bus su - is la-tus vi-ri de quo De - us

for - mam mu-li-e-ris pro-du-xit, quam fe-cit spe-cu-lum om - nis

or-na-men-ti su-i et am-ple-xi-o-nem om-nis cre-a-tu-re su - e.

4b In-de con-ci-nunt ce-les-ti-a or-ga-na et mi-ra-tur omnis ter-ra,

o lau-da-bi-lis Ma-ri - a, qui-a De-us te val-de a - ma-vit.

5a [O] quam val-de plan-gen-dum et lu-gen-dum est quod tris-ti-ci-a in

cri - mi-ne per con-si-li-um ser-pen-tis in mu-li-e-rum flu-xit.

5b Nam ip-sa mu-li-er, quam De-us mat-rem om-ni-um po-su-it,

vis-ce-ra su - a cum vul-ne-ri-bus ig-no-ran-ti-e de-cerp-sit,

et ple-num do-lo-rem ge-ne-ri su-o pro-tu-lit.

6a Sed, o au-ro-ra, de ven-tre tu-o no-vus sol pro-ces-sit

qui om-ni-a cri-mi-na E-ve abs-ter-sit et mai-o-rem be-ne-dic-ti-o-nem

per te pro-tu-lit quam E-va ho-mi-ni-bus no-cu-is-set.

6b Un-de, o sal - vat-rix, que no-vum lu-men hu-ma-no ge-ne-ri pro-tu-lis-ti,

col-li-ge mem-bra fi-li-i tu-i ad ce-les-tem ar-mo-ni-am.

O rubor sanguinis
In Evangelium

Hildegard von Bingen

Ant. O rubor sanguinis, * qui de excel — so illo flu — xi — sti, quod di — vinitas tetigit, tu flos es, quem hi — ems de fla — tu ser — pen — tis num — quam læ — sit.

Kyrie

Ky-ri — e * e — lei — son. Chri-ste e — lei- son. Ky-ri — e e — lei — son. Ky-ri — e e lei — son.

20   MICHAEL KLAPER

La Comtessa de Dia
(ca. 1175)

ELIZABETH AUBREY

The songs of the troubadours, poet-composers of what is now the south of France, revolve around the relationships between women and men, and their language— Old Occitan—is couched in stereotyped codes that are circumscribed by gender identity. The male is the lover who swears homage and obedience to his lady, eloquent in her praise or in censure if she rebuffs him. The woman is the beloved, distant and often unsympathetic, holding the power of joy or heartbreak over her lover. An overwhelming majority of the roughly twenty-five hundred extant songs of the troubadours are voiced by the man, so if a woman speaks, she does so in words created by a male author. In this sophisticated and controlled poetic system, women authors faced the challenge of maintaining the carefully structured social system of the poetry while giving expression to their own thoughts and feelings without the interpretive filter of a male author.

Fewer than fifty (some scholars put the number as low as twenty-three) songs were composed by women, the trobairitz, between about 1170 and 1260. About twenty women, most of them not yet securely identified historically, are named in the medieval manuscripts as authors. Four songs are the work of a shadowy woman referred to only as "la comtessa [countess] de Dia," and one of these, "A chantar m'er do so q'ieu no volria," is the only one by a trobairitz that survives with music.

A vida, or short biographical sketch, found in four thirteenth-century manuscripts reads in its entirety:

> The Countess of Dia was the wife of Lord Guillem de Poitou, a beautiful and good lady. And she fell in love with Lord Raimbaut d'Aurenga and composed many good songs about him. (Egan 28)

As with so many of the troubadours' vidas, often fictions created to provide a literary context for the songs, this account is difficult to reconcile with historical facts. If the Raimbaut d'Aurenga mentioned is the troubadour who died in 1173, then the "countess" would have been active in the third quarter of the twelfth century. One person who might meet this description is Beatriz, wife of Guillem I of Poitiers, count of Valentinois from 1163 to 1189. This Guillem held property in the diocese of Dia, a town in Provence on the Drôme River. But he was not the city's count, and his wife would not have been called "countess of Dia." Two other theories have been advanced, dating the trobairitz to a generation later. One contender is Isoarde, daughter of Count Isoard II of Dia, attested as the wife of Raimon d'Agout; her status as daughter of the count of Dia might have entitled her to the designation of "countess." A third possibility is found in a document of 1212 that mentions a "Beatrix comitissa" as witness to a legal transaction involving the widower of a daughter of Count Isoard II; this "countess Beatritz" may have been another of Isoard's daughters, sister of Isouarde. The latter two proposals date the career of the comtessa sometime after the death of the troubadour Raimbaut d'Aurenga in 1173, but it is conceivable that the "Raimbaut" mentioned in the vida was not the troubadour by that name but rather his great-nephew.

The comtessa's four songs are about love, fin' amors, the highest ideal of the troubadours. In them she expresses her desire for the affections of her beloved—a reversal of the male appeal to the lady in the songs of the troubadours. She thus places herself in the position of supplicant rather than that of the unattainable lady typically portrayed in the men's songs. In "A chanter m'er do so," the comtessa is passionate, swearing fidelity and honor, but appealing with anger and indignation to her beloved for a return of her love. She acknowledges her own high birth, but argues that this should give her an advantage in her suit with the equally noble object of her affections. This poem has an intricate metrical structure. The rhyme sound of verses 7 and 9, -ens, is the same in all stanzas, but the other verses end with a rhyme that changes from stanza to stanza (-ia, -enssa, -oilla, -ina, -atges).

The music of the troubadours, exclusively monophonic, does not survive in great quantity: only about one-tenth of the extant poems were provided with melodies in the surviving medieval sources, so it is not surprising that only one melody by a trobairitz was recorded. The melody of "A chanter m'er de so" has a small range and a simple neumatic texture that is typical of vernacular songs at the turn of the thirteenth century. It incorporates recurrent material, not only repetition of the first two phrases but also a cadential motive, sometimes varied, that ends nearly every phrase. The last verse repeats the music of verse 2, which gives the melody an overall rounded structure.

The comtessa's songs circulated in manuscripts from Occitania, Italy, and France, indicating her widespread fame. The single manuscript that preserves the melody (Paris, Bibliothèque nationale de France, f. fr. 844) is devoted mainly to the songs of the trouvères of the north, whose language was French, a sister language to the troubadours' Occitan. The French scribe modified the Occitan of the comtessa's song to make it more intelligible to his northern audience, but his changes corrupted the rhyme scheme of the first stanza. Significantly, one of these changes made the feminine word "amia"—"friend"—at the end of verse 2 into the masculine "amigs," which makes the verse one syllable too short. In the edition that follows, I have used the melody found in this manuscript but matched it with a text from the central Occitan tradition, which preserves the female identity of its author.

Questions of performance practice of medieval monophonic song continue to baffle scholars. The chief problems concern what rhythmic values to give to the notes (the notation in the manuscripts rarely gives clear indications), and whether to use instruments (such as fiddle, harp, or recorder) in accompaniment. None of the theories so far proposed is bolstered by enough convincing evidence to attract universal acceptance. Performance issues are explored in depth in Aubrey 1996 and Aubrey 2000.

Translation of "A chantar"

I must sing of what I'd rather not,
I'm so angry about him whose friend I am,
For I love him more than anything;
Mercy and courtliness don't help me

ELIZABETH AUBREY

With him, nor does my beauty, or my rank, or my mind;
For I am every bit as betrayed and wronged
As I'd deserve to be if I were ugly.

It comforts me that I have done no wrong
To you, my friend, through any action;
Indeed, I love you more than Seguis loved Valenssa;
It pleases me to outdo you in loving,
Friend, for you are the most valiant;
You offer prideful words and looks to me
But are gracious to every other person.

It amazes me how prideful your heart is
Toward me, friend, for which I'm right to grieve;
It isn't fair that another love take you away
Because of any word or welcome I might give you.
And remember how it was at the beginning
Of our love; may the Lord God not allow
Our parting to be any fault of mine.

The great valor that dwells in your person,
And the high rank you have, these trouble me,
For I don't know a woman, far or near,
Who, if she wished to love, would not turn to you;
But you, friend, are so knowing,
You surely ought to know the truest one,
And remember what our agreement was.

My rank and lineage should be of help
To me, and my beauty and, still more, my true heart;
This song, let it be my messenger;
Therefore, I send it to you, out in your estate,
And I would like to know, my fine, fair friend,
Why you are so fierce and cruel to me.
I can't tell if it's from pride or malice.

I especially want you, messenger, to tell him
That too much pride brings harm to many persons.

Bruckner, Shepard, and White, *Songs of the Women Troubadours*, 6–9; reproduced by permission

Further Reading

Aubrey, Elizabeth. *The Music of the Troubadours.* Bloomington and Indianapolis: Indiana University Press, 1996.
———. "Non-liturgical Monophony: Introduction" and "Non-liturgical Monophony: Occitan." In *A Performer's Guide to Medieval Music*, ed. Ross W. Duffin, 105–14 and 122–33. Bloomington and Indianapolis: Indiana University Press, 2000.
Bruckner, Matilda T. "Fictions of the Female Voice: The Women Troubadours." *Speculum* 67 (1992): 865–91.
Coldwell, Maria. "Jougleresses and Trobairitz: Secular Musicians in Medieval France." In

Women Making Music: The Western Art Tradition, 1150–1950, ed. Jane Bowers and Judith Tick, 39–61. Urbana: University of Illinois Press, 1986.

Dronke, Peter. *Women Writers of the Middle Ages: A Critical Study of Texts from Perpetua (d. 203) to Marguerite Porete (d. 1310)*. Cambridge: Cambridge University Press, 1984.

Egan, Margarita, trans. *The Vidas of the Troubadours*. New York and London: Garland, 1984.

Monier, Janine. "Essaie d'identification de la comtesse de Die." *Bulletin de la Société d'archéologie et de statistique de la Drôme* 75 (1962): 265–78.

Paden, William D., ed. *The Voice of the Trobairitz: Perspectives on the Women Troubadours*. Philadelphia: University of Pennsylvania Press, 1989.

Pattison, Walter. T. *The Life and Works of the Troubadour Raimbaut d'Orange*. Minneapolis: University of Minnesota Press, 1952.

Pollina, Vincent. "Troubadours dans le nord: Observations sur la transmission des mélodies occitanes dans les manuscrits septentrionaux." *Romanistische Zeitschrift für Literaturgeschichte* 9 (1985): 263–78.

———. "Melodic Continuity and Discontinuity in A chantar m'er of the Comtessa deDia." In *Miscellanea di studi romanzi offerta a Giuliano Gasca-Queirazza per il suo 65° compleanno*, ed. A. Cornagliotti et al., I: 887–95. Alexandria: Edizioni dell'Orso, 1988.

Editions

Bruckner, Matilda Tomaryn, Laurie Shepard, and Sarah White, eds. *Songs of the Women Troubadours*, 6–9 (text and translation). New York: Garland, 1995.

Kussler-Ratyé, Gabrielle. "Les chansons de la Comtesse Béatrix de Dia." *Archivum romanicum* 1 (1917): 161–82 (text).

Van der Werf, Hendrik. *The Extant Troubadour Melodies*. 21* (first stanza and music). Rochester, N.Y.: Author, 1984.

A chantar m'er de so q'ieu no volria

La Comtessa de Dia

1. A chan - tar m'er de so q'ieu no vol - ri - a,

2. tant me ran - cur de lui cui sui a - mi - a,

3. car eu l'am mais que nuil - la ren que si - a;

4. vas lui no.m val mer - ces ni cor - te - si - a

5. ni ma bel - tatz ni mos pretz ni mos sens,

6. c'a - tres - si.m sui en - ga - na - da e tra - hi - a

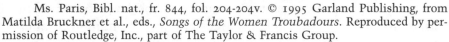

7. com degr' es - ser s'ieu fos de - sa - vi - nens.

Ms. Paris, Bibl. nat., fr. 844, fol. 204-204v. © 1995 Garland Publishing, from Matilda Bruckner et al., eds., *Songs of the Women Troubadours*. Reproduced by permission of Routledge, Inc., part of The Taylor & Francis Group.

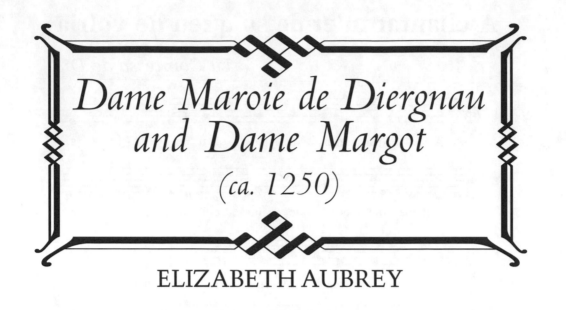

Dame Maroie de Diergnau and Dame Margot
(ca. 1250)

ELIZABETH AUBREY

As with the troubadours, there were women composers among the northern trouvères, although the tiny number of attributions to troveresses in the manuscripts suggests that their numbers were fewer. Like the trobairitz, only a few are identifiable as historical figures. Scholarship on the women trouvères has been hampered by the persistent notion that women were not composers of the Old French songs whose texts speak in the female voice. Part of the problem lies in the fact that medieval scribes attributed many of the feminine lyrics to male authors. Additionally, some scholars have been misdirected by the outdated view, with roots in late-nineteenth-century prejudices, that songs composed by women ought to be characterized by gentler, more emotional or delicate language than those of men, and that the forceful language and rational tone found in the surviving songs in a female voice could not have originated with women composers.

These objections to the existence of the troveresses are widely discredited now, and the corpus of songs that speak from the woman's perspective, including not only those that are ascribed to women in medieval sources but also the numerous anonymous ones, is receiving long overdue attention. The many unattributed songs whose subjects are feminine are of particular interest, because it seems likely that at least some of them were composed by women who either did not insist upon or were not given credit for their work.

Among troveresses about whom some historical information is known, by far the most distinguished personage is Blanche de Castille, wife of Louis VIII and mother of Louis IX of France. Others include the Duchesse de Lorraine, possibly Marguerite de Champagne, the daughter of Thibaut IV, and Dame de Gosnai, who was listed as a member of the important puy (trouvère confraternity) of Arras in the thirteenth century.

The "Dame Maroie" in the jeu-parti included here, "Je vous pri, dame Maroie," is probably the same as the "Maroie de Diergnau" to whom is ascribed a love song that survives with only one stanza. Diergnau was a castle outside the walls of Lille in northern France. Maroie de Diergnau also has been identified as the object of a song by Andrieu Contredit d'Arras, who sent his greetings to "the valiant Marote" of Diergnau in the envoi to his song Bonne, belle et avenant. He was active in Arras, about twenty-five miles to the southwest of Diergnau, until the middle of the thirteenth century, so Maroie's career probably unfolded around the same time.

The "Dame Margot" of "Je vous pri" may have been one of the judges of poetry mentioned in a jeu-parti between Jehan le Cuvelier and Jehan Bretel, also active in the puy of Arras, which places her within the same locale as Dame Maroie. She also has been suggested as the "Margot" of an acrostic in the song "Mais ne avris ne prinstens" of Perrin d'Angicourt, who sent his composition "to Metz," where "my beauty" resides (Doss-Quinby et al., 28).

The jeu-parti was a poetic genre in dialogue form, usually a debate on a question of love or other courtly topic. The two contestants alternate stanzas. The opening speaker describes a dilemma and suggests two contrasting resolutions, and then allows his or her opponent to choose which of the two positions to defend. The language is often blunt and playful, suitable to a game of words played by skilled protagonists in a leisured setting. Usually the two participants call for a decision at the end, to be rendered by a designated judge who may be another poet-composer, often a woman. The puy at Arras in particular fostered the jeu-parti.

Authorship of this and other dialogue genres often is difficult to establish. Where the two speakers are known trouvères or troveresses who had opportunity to meet in person, it is reasonable to suppose that what is written down in the manuscripts represents the exchange of stanzas that actually took place at some time. Many of the jeu-partis, however, refer to one of the speakers only by a vague title such as "Dame," "Seignor," or "Suer" (sister), or by first name only (e.g., "Lorete" or "Pierre"). Others seem to be debates between two persons who could not have known each other because of distance in time or place. In such cases, authorship by either a male or a female is impossible to establish, but there is no reason to suppose that the author could not have been a woman, and there are many reasons to believe that it was. In the case of "Je vous pri," it is plausible that Maroie and Margot were women whose paths actually crossed and who both participated in the creation of this song.

About one hundred jeu-partis in Old French survive with music, and a number of them, including "Je vous pri," are found with two different melodies in different manuscripts, not an uncommon occurrence in the trouvère repertoire. The edition that follows gives the text and melody as they are given in a manuscript produced before 1278 in the region where both women resided, ms. 657 of the Bibliothèque municipale in Arras. The other melody is found only in an Italian manuscript copied a few decades later, and thus might be a less reliable source for the song.

The melody of "Je vous pri" stays within the range of a sixth except for the briefest touch of high F in the middle of verse 11. The only musical repetition is of the first two verses, repeated in the next two verses. Otherwise the melody is through-composed, with a neumatic texture that flows in undulating waves through small steps, broken only by a prominent leap of a fifth halfway through, from verse 7 to verse 8 ("Mais cil est de tel maniere / Ki l'aime ke sa proiiere"). The style of the melody easily lends itself to a conversational performance of the rapidly unfolding exchange of arguments.

As with the troubadours, questions about performance practices remain unanswered, particularly those of rhythm and the use of instruments. Thorough discussion of the problems is found in Aubrey 2000.

Translation of "Je vous pri" (Doss-Quinby et al., *Songs*, 74, 76–77)

I	II
I entreat you, Lady Maroie,	Lady Margot, it is well worth
To debate against me.	Judging the truth fairly.
A woman, innocent and tranquil,	Since love governs them to such an extent
Is loved dearly and faithfully,	That they dearly love each other,
And loves dearly in return,	Each with a loyal heart, I say

This you should know with certainty;
But the one who teaches her is such
That his desire
He dares not avow,
Thus it can never come to pass
That he will ever admit it to her.
Now, please answer me truthfully,
Should she reveal her feelings
Or should she remain silent?

III
—You are going astray,
Lady Marote, I believe.
A grave mistake a lady makes who courts
Her beloved first. Why

Should she demean herself thus?
If he lacks courage,
I do not think it proper
That she should then solicit his love,
Rather, she should conceal her feelings
And suffer Love's pains

Without ever disclosing them;
For a woman should have such high
     merit
That no word should come from her
That could diminish her worth.

V
—Lady Marote, one is free
To act the fool; but I cannot concede
That any lunatic, man or woman,
Devoid of reason, can possess Love's joy.
Uphold no longer, as you have,
That a lady should entreat her beloved;
Because, if that is her habit,
She does herself such a disservice
That one must hate her because of it.
She should find other means to her end:
She should endeavor through her knowl-
     edge
To be able frequently to see him,
Speak to him, and sit by him;
Better that she limit herself to that.

That if he does not have the courage
To tell her he holds her dear,
She should not be proud,
Rather, she should obey
Her heart and speak
To let love appear.
Since she is incapable of it.
She should accomplish it,
If she wants love's joys.

IV
—Lady Margot, I really thought
You understood something
Of love; I had
Rendered a judgment to you, but I see
     clearly
That you argue against me
Wrongly. I promise you this:
True love will never be perfect
Unless struck by a little madness.
No one can partake of it
Without madness, so she should make
     known
Her desire to him.
Madness is necessary

To preserve good love
If one wants to enjoy its pleasures.

VI
—You know little about love,
Lady Margot, from what I see.
A woman is mad who grants her favors
In exchange for money,
Because there is no love in her;
But when two hearts are seized
By a love that is not deceitful,
It is perfectly right
To express one's desire
To one's beloved out of longing,
Lest one fall into despair.

Better it is to live in joy
For having pleaded than to languish now
For having been silent and then die.

Further Reading

Aubrey, Elizabeth. "Non-liturgical Monophony: Introduction" and "Non-liturgical Mo-
     nophony: French." In *A Performer's Guide to Medieval Music*, ed. Ross W. Duffin,
     105–14 and 134–43. Bloomington and Indianapolis: Indiana University Press, 2000.

Coldwell, Maria. "Jougleresses and Trobairitz: Secular Musicians in Medieval France." In *Women Making Music: The Western Art Tradition, 1150–1950*, ed. Jane Bowers and Judith Tick, 39–61. Urbana: University of Illinois Press, 1986.

Doss-Quinby, Eglal. "Rolan, de ceu ke m'avez/Parti dirai mon samblant: The Feminine Voice in the Old French jeu-parti." *Neuphilologus* 83 (1999): 496–516.

Dronke, Peter. *Women Writers of the Middle Ages: A Critical Study of Texts from Perpetua (d. 203) to Marguerite Porete (d. 1310)*. Cambridge: Cambridge University Press, 1984.

Gally, Michèle. "Disputer l'amour: Les Arrageois et le jeu-parti." *Romania* 107 (1986): 55–76.

Lavis, Georges. "Le jeu-parti français: Jeu de réfutation, d'opposition et de concession." *Medioevo Romanzoi* 16 (1991): 21–128.

Petersen-Dyggve, Holger, ed. *Onomastique des trouvères. Annales Academiae Scientiarum Fennicae* B 30, l. Helsinki: Suomalaisen Tiedeakatemian Toimituksia, 1934. Repr. Bibliography and Reference Series, 488. Music History and Reference Series, 4. New York: Burt Franklin, 1973.

Stewart, Michelle F. "The Melodic Structure of Thirteenth-Century Jeux-Partis." *Acta Musicologica* 51 (1979): 86–107.

Tyssens, Madeleine. "Voix de femmes dans la lyrique d'oïl." In *Femmes, mariages-lignages, XIIe–XIVe siècles: Mélanges offerts à Georges Duby*, 373–87. Brussels: De Boeck Université, 1992.

Editions

Doss-Quinby, Eglal, Joan Tasker Grimbert, Wendy Pfeffer, and Elizabeth Aubrey, eds. *Songs of the Women Trouvères.* 74–78 (text, translation, and music). New Haven, Conn., and London: Yale University Press, 2001.

Långfors, Arthur, Alfred Jeanroy, and Louis Brandin, eds. *Recueil général des jeux-partis français.* 2 vols. II: 171 (text). Paris: Champion, 1926.

Tischler, Hans. *Trouvère Lyrics with Melodies: Complete Comparative Edition.* 15 vols. XI: No. 1005 (text and music). Corpus Mensurabilis Musicae, 107. Neuhausen: American Institute of Musicology, 1997.

Je vous pri, dame Maroie

Dame Margot and Dame Maroie de Diergnau

MS. Arras, Bibl. mun. 657, fol. 141v-142

Je vous pri, da - me Ma - roi - e,

Ke res - pon - dés con - tre moi.

U - ne da - me simple et choi - e

Est bien a - me - e de foi,

Et ele ai - me bien au - si,

Ce sa - ciés vous tout de fi;

Mais cil est de tel ma - nie - re

Ki l'ai - me ke sa proi - ie - re

N'o - se pas ge - hir,

Et si ne puet a - ve - nir

Ke ja li fai - ce sa - voir.

S'or me vo - liés di - re voir,

S'en doit e - le des - cho - vrir,

U e - le s'en doit ta - sir?

MS. Arras, Bibl. mun. 657, fol. 141v-142. Reprinted from Eglal Doss-Quinby et al., eds., *Songs of the Women Trouvères*. New Haven, Conn.: Yale University Press, 2000.

ELIZABETH AUBREY

Margaret of Austria
(1480–1530)

MARTIN PICKER

Margaret of Austria, one of the most important political figures in sixteenth-century Europe, was born in Brussels, capital of the Netherlands. She was the second of two children of the Habsburg archduke of Austria, Maximilian (later Emperor Maximilian I), and Mary of Burgundy. Mary died in a hunting accident in 1482, and in an effort to involve his family in the affairs of France, Maximilian negotiated Margaret's betrothal to the French dauphin (later Charles VIII), sending her to be raised as a princess at the French court.

Until the age of thirteen, Margaret's education was entirely French. However, Maximilian and Charles had a falling out, and in 1493 Margaret, rejected by her fiancé, was returned to Maximilian, who sent her to live with her brother Philip the Fair, heir to the title of Duke of Burgundy, in Mechelen. In 1495 Maximilian, attempting yet another grand political liaison for his offspring, arranged for the betrothal of Philip and Margaret to children of the Spanish monarchs Ferdinand of Aragon and Isabella of Castile.

Within months of Margaret's marriage in 1497, her husband, Juan, died suddenly, and Margaret gave birth to a stillborn child. In 1499 she returned to the Netherlands. Maximilian's plan bore fruit, however, when in 1500 Philip's bride, Juana, gave birth to a son, Charles, heir to the Spanish kingdoms and Habsburg lands, which he would later rule as King of Spain and Holy Roman Emperor Charles V.

In 1501 Maximilian arranged for his daughter's marriage to Philibert le Beau, Duke of Savoy. At Philibert's court at Pont d'Ain, Margaret discovered and began to exercise her extraordinary political abilities. Coincidentally, in 1504 both Philibert and Queen Isabella died, leading to Margaret's assuming power in Savoy and to her brother's becoming King of Castile. However, the series of family disasters that had already begun to plague Margaret's life continued unabated. In 1506 Philip died in Spain, and his distraught widow (known to history as Juana the Mad) proved incapable of ruling. Ferdinand of Aragon assumed the regency of Castile for his grandson Charles, and Maximilian assigned guardianship of Charles and his sisters to Margaret, who again took up residence in Mechelen, where she reconstituted the dispersed court of Burgundy. Many courtiers from Savoy joined her there, forming the nucleus of a highly cultivated, French-oriented circle.

Margaret acted as Charles's regent in the Netherlands until he attained his majority in 1515. In the following year Ferdinand of Aragon died and Charles was proclaimed King of Spain. Simultaneously governing both Spain and the Netherlands proved awkward for the young king, and in 1518 Charles asked Margaret to serve again as his regent in the

Netherlands. Following Maximilian's death in 1519, Charles succeeded his paternal grandfather as emperor (1520), and Margaret continued to administer the Netherlands in his name. In 1529 she negotiated the Treaty of Cambrai with her cousin and childhood friend Louise of Savoy, sister of Philibert le Beau and mother of the French king Francis I, thereby resolving the long quarrel between the Empire and France. In 1530 Margaret died after a botched surgical operation. Widely mourned, she was recognized as one of the most remarkable women of her time.

Margaret had received instruction in music and the arts as a child. Her court poet Jean Lemaire, who was to follow her from Savoy, referred to her talents in a literary portrait of her, La Couronne Margaritique, written in 1504–1505:

> Besides feminine work of sewing and embroidery, she is excellently skilled in vocal and instrumental music, in painting and in rhetoric, in the French as well as the Spanish language; moreover, she likes erudite, wise men. She supports good minds, expert in many fields of knowledge; and frequently she reads noble books, of which she has a great number in her rich and ample library, concerning all manner of things worth knowing. Yet not content merely to read, she has taken pen in hand and described elegantly in prose as well as in French verse her misfortunes and her admirable life.

In 1506 Lemaire wrote a poem about Margaret, "Les Regretz de la Dame Infortunée," describing her grief after the death of her brother. Her misfortunes are a constant theme in poems by and about her. She chose for herself the sobriquet "La dame infortunée," and many portraits throughout her life show her in mourning clothes.

At the time of her death, Margaret owned a library of almost four hundred volumes, mostly in manuscript (printing was still in its infancy), acquired in France, Savoy, and the Netherlands through inheritance, gift, and commission, and dealing with a broad range of subjects, including literature, religion, ancient and medieval history, and music. Many of her manuscripts were decorated with miniatures by skilled painters. Some volumes have been lost, but about one-third of those listed in early inventories remain today in the Royal Library of Belgium in Brussels. Among the volumes devoted to music are books of sacred polyphony by leading masters, as well as secular songbooks and a book of dances. Most of these books were written specifically for Margaret or her court.

Two of these manuscripts are chansonniers containing mainly French songs, a small one acquired in Savoy and a larger one made for Margaret in the Netherlands around 1516 that contains miniatures, including her portrait as well as coat of arms as princess of Austria and Burgundy and Duchess of Savoy, and many floral decorations featuring daisies (marguerites in French). This larger manuscript, now in the Royal Library, includes musical settings of poems by Margaret and her courtiers, many of which contain personal references to Margaret's life and experiences and often reflect her sorrows and disappointments. Only one composer is cited by name (Josquin Desprez), but others can be identified from other sources, while many pieces remain anonymous. Pierre de la Rue, Margaret's and Charles's court composer, is responsible for the largest number of works by known composers in the manuscript. However, one anonymous composition found there uniquely is stylistically unlike any other work in it, and is of special interest because its text, a lament on the death of Philip the Fair, identifies its author as "the most unfortunate daughter of the emperor" and the deceased as "my brother Philip." Presumably the author of these words is Margaret.

This work belongs to a type of song called "motet-chanson," a modern term referring to a work combining a text in French sung by one or more of the upper voices with a Latin one placed in the tenor or bass. Such songs were composed in the later fifteenth and early sixteenth centuries by many composers and are usually found in collections of chansons rather than motets. This work is for three voices and is in two sections. The cantus and tenor sing the French text "Se je souspire et plaingz," while the bass sings "Ecce iterum novus dolor accedit!" The full texts are translated below.

MARTIN PICKER

Musically, this composition stands apart from other compositions of the early sixteenth century because of its free-flowing counterpoint and almost total avoidance of imitation. Its melodic and harmonic styles are archaic, harking back to the French manner of the mid-fifteenth century in avoiding cadences, recurrent motives, or symmetrical phrases. The only full cadence occurs at the very end of the piece. The form of the piece, and to some extent its melodic design, is determined by its union of the two texts. The Latin text in section 2 paraphrases the biblical verse "O vos omnes" (Lamentations 1: 12), and is set to the Gregorian chant to which those words are sung in Holy Week. The personal nature of the text and the musical skill Margaret is known to have possessed, as well as the idiosyncratic nature of the music itself, point to her as poet-composer of the work rather than to any professional writer or musician in her service. In sum, the conception and execution of this work is likely to have been the responsibility of Margaret, with or without assistance, and is consistent with her conservative tastes, literary accomplishments, and known musicianship.

Text Translation

Cantus and tenor:

(1.) Thus I sigh and lament, saying "Alas, aymy!" And in fields and plains I grieve for my sweet friend. He was chosen above all, but by death proud destiny has taken him from me, the sad unfortunate one.
(2.) My songs are full of sorrow; I have neither a good day nor half. You who hear my laments, have pity on me!

Bass:

(1.) Behold, again a new sorrow comes! It was not enough for the most unfortunate daughter of the Emperor to have lost her dearest husband; bitter death must steal even her only brother. I mourn thee, my brother Philip, greatest King, nor is there anyone to console me.
(2.) O ye who pass this way, attend and see if there is any sorrow like my sorrow!

Further Reading

Picker, Martin. *The Chanson Albums of Marguerite of Austria.* Berkeley and Los Angeles: University of California Press, 1965.

Se je souspire / Ecce iterum

Margaret of Austria (?)
Martin Picker, editor

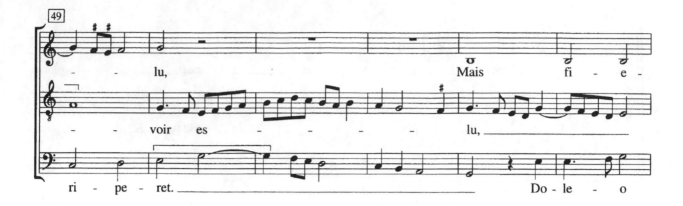

MARTIN PICKER

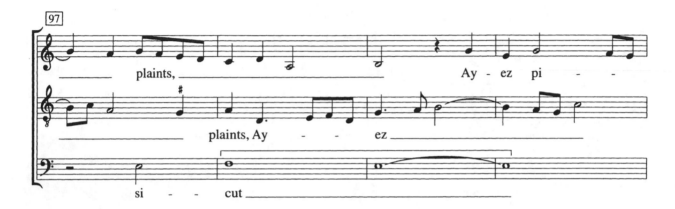

MARTIN PICKER

Anne Boleyn
(ca. 1501, ?Blicking, Norfolk–19 May 1536, London)

JANET POLLACK

Anne Boleyn, the unfortunate second wife of King Henry VIII of England, may very well have been a composer as early biographical sketches of her life proclaim, although no work has been proven to be by her hand. This lack of documentation has not deterred the imagination of composers and writers, and Anne has been linked with music in various ways ever since her execution on 19 May 1536. She was the subject of Ippolito Pindemonte's "Enrico VIII ossia *Anna Bolena*" and Alessandro Pepoli's "Anna Bolena," and the heroine of Gaetano Donizetti's immensely popular opera *Anna Bolena*. Anne's tragic downfall is a subject ripe for opera, but her involvement with music is more personal, and evidence suggests that Anne herself was an able musician capable of composing a piece of the quality of the song "O Deathe, rock me asleepe," presented here. The intense sadness of the lyrics and music, and the mention of imprisonment, "guiltlessness," and an inability to challenge destiny closely reflect Anne's own personal circumstances as she awaited her execution in the Tower of London.

Anne Boleyn, although born in England of relatively common stock, lived at the French court from age twelve to sixteen after her father received the position of ambassador to France under Henry. From all accounts she received the finest education, and one typical of noble women at court. Music instruction within court society was often on a high level, and typically involved study in notation, sight singing, and the playing of an instrument. A Frenchman wrote in 1522 of Anne's skills in dancing and music. Viscount Chateaubriant wrote in his memoirs that Anne Boleyn, "Besides singing like a syren, [and] accompanying herself on the lute, . . . harped better than King David and handled cleverly both flute and rebec." Other accounts suggest that she may have studied keyboard with the organist Henry Bredemers. Court expense accounts confirm that she did indeed own a virginals. From these contemporaneous accounts one sees Anne as an intelligent, vivacious, talented women and an accomplished performer.

The writing of poetry intended for musical performance was also common among courtly women, and John Milsom has recently reminded us that the poem "Defyled is my name" was attributed to Anne Boleyn and set to music by the English composer Robert Johnson (ca. 1500–1560). With her level of education and musical accomplishments, Anne Boleyn would have been able to commit her songs to paper, if convention permitted. The musicologist Karin Pendle points out that "the early modern period was one in which anonymous creativity by both men and women of European nobility was encouraged." This all-pervasive attitude is one possible explanation for the lack of surviving music bearing Anne's name. Pendle also points out that "improvised songs by women . . . [were] so common as to deserve no particular attention in contemporary sources." The improvisatory quality of "O Deathe, rock me asleepe" may further explain why no composer's name appears on the manuscript. One also must consider the fact that musical talent ran in Anne's family, for her daughter, Queen Elizabeth I, was known to be accomplished on the virginals and lute.

Anne Boleyn's interest in vocal polyphonic music was serious, and a manuscript collection of French motets and chansons copied in France (GB-Lbl 1070) bears her coat of arms. Anne presumably performed from this collection along with her female friends in her private chamber. Noble women at this time were often responsible for financing court performances and encouraging composers, and it is likely that, as Queen of England, Anne encouraged the performance of Continental works at the Tudor court. From her time at the French court Anne came into contact with Continental repertories, and her compositions—if she did indeed write music—would have had a cosmopolitan flavor. "O Deathe, rock me asleepe," with its English-style false relations (C-sharp against C and G-sharp against G) combined with the French treatment of a ground, is just what one would imagine of Anne.

"O Deathe, rock me asleepe" comes down to us in a number of manuscripts and in several different musical settings. The poem, attributed to Anne, enjoyed some degree of long-standing notoriety, for it is mentioned in Shakespeare's *Henry IV* (Part 2, II.iv.211), and later in John Hawkins's *History*. The voice and lute version reproduced here is from the article in the periodical *Concerto* listed below, although a version in G minor is published in the Royal Collection by Novello and Company. The recording accompanying this anthology is pitched in G minor and not the notated A minor, for reasons of lute tuning. The poem, literate and effective, is set to music that sensitively captures the pathetic words. The phrase "let passe my wearye giltles ghost," for instance, is set monotonously on the pitch B, as if the music had lost its will to stray far from tonic A, the note just below; whereas "Lett thye sound my deathe tell" is set to a steeply descending melodic line E down to G, creating a melodic contour that could be thought a musical emblem for sudden death. A six-note ostinato (or ground) heard at the outset conveys a sense of urgency in its repetition and inevitability in its incessant return to tonic A. In its brevity and insistence, the ground evokes the knelling of bells mentioned in the refrain at the end of each of the four stanzas. This six-note figure gives way to a more steeply descending three-note one (in mm. 44–52), a French tendency in ostinato compositions noted previously by Edith Borroff. It is worth mentioning that in London at the time the clanging and jangling of bells was a common sound. Cathedrals had up to seven bells in their steeples early on, and English composers appear to have been fascinated by the clamor and the musical potential of the repeated figures suggested by the tolling. Sarah Cobbold and David Wulstan have noted that certain passages in the masses of Tye and Sheppard, for instance, resemble "six-bells tolling," and bell sounds were frequently the subject of popular grounds (typically on two-note ostinati) from the fifteenth century on. "The Great Bells of Osney" and "Let's Have a Peal" are two well-known examples.

The keyboard version in the Royal Collection is but one of several surviving settings of "O death." Claudia Knispel has recently pointed out that a manuscript copied between 1608 and 1615 (London, British Library, Ms. Additional 15117) contains the lute-song "O death, rock me asleepe" (fol. 3v), the version reproduced here. The manuscript contains twenty-seven lute-songs in all, twenty-two of which are in G and five in A. "O death" is one of the five lute-songs in A minor. Composers represented include John Dowland, Diomedes Cato, Richard Allison, and Robert Johnson, and pieces range from a technically easy "Alamine" and "Curranto" to the "Psalms of David in Meter" to selections copied from John Dowland's 1603 *The Third and Last Booke of Songs or Aires*. The lute-song is similar in most respects to the keyboard arrangement: the triple meter, the opening six-note ground, and the tune itself are nearly identical, only the key is A minor rather than G minor, and chord voicing varies.

Additional settings of "O Deathe, rock me asleepe" are found in two manuscripts, one compiled about 1560–1590 (Add. MSS 30480–84), and the other originating in the household of Edward Paston sometime before 1670 (Add. MSS 18936–39). In both these manuscripts the poem is set as a consort song (solo voice and four viols), with the voice singing a tune somewhat different from the lute and harpsichord versions, and the meter is duple rather than triple. The melodic contour of emotionally charged words such as "Let the sound my death tell," however, shows a similar downward sweep. A striking difference can be seen on "Let pass my weary guiltless ghost," where the static quality is spoiled by a change of pitch on "guiltless ghost."

Further Reading

Brett, Philip. "Consort Songs." In *Musica Britannica*, vol. XXII. London: Stainer and Bell, 1967.

Knispel, Claudia. "Abschied von dieser Welt: Ein Lautenlied von Anne Boleyn?" *Concerto: Das Magazin für Alte Musik* 14, no. 129 (December 1997–January 1998): 25–29.

Strickland, Agnes. *Lives of the Queens of England*. Vols. 4-5. Philadelphia: Lea and Blanchard, 1849–1851.

Recordings

"O Deathc." In *Songs in Shakespeare's Plays*. James Bowman, counter-tenor, and James Tyler, lute. Archiv Producktion Stereo, 2533 407.

———. In *The Pleasures and Follies of Love*. Jennifer Lane, mezzo-soprano, and Hanneke van Proosdij, organ. Kock International Classics 2001, 3-7527-2 HI.

O Deathe, rock me asleepe

Anne Boleyn (attributed)

Reprinted from the periodical *Concerto* No. 129, Dec./Jan. 1998/99, pp. 26–27. Ed. by Claudia Knispel from Ms, Add. 15117, fol. 3v, British Library (Music).

JANET POLLACK

Anne Boleyn

43

Maddalena Casulana
(ca. 1540–ca. 1590)

BEATRICE PESCERELLI WITH
JAMES R. BRISCOE

Maddalena was probably called Casulana because she was born at Casola d'Elsa (Casula) near Siena. However, as Thomas W. Bridges states in *Grove*, there is little evidence linking her to any locale except Vicenza. Casulana received her earliest musical education and experiences in Florence. She began her career as a composer in 1566, when she published four madrigals in four voices in the first book of the anthology *Il desiderio* and a fifth in four voices in the third book of *Il desiderio*. In Florence, Maddalena Casulana had connections with Isabelle de' Medici, daughter of the Grand Duke of Tuscany Cosimo I. She dedicated her first book of madrigals *a 4* to Isabella in 1568, a publication that appears to be the first printed work by a woman in the history of European music. In the same year the renowned composer Orlando di Lasso conducted her five-voice composition *Nil mage iucundum* during the festivities in Munich surrounding the marriage of Wilhelm IV of Bavaria to Renée of Lorraine. Casulana's music for this work has not survived, but the text, by Nicholas Stopius, is extant.

In 1570 Casulana published a second book of madrigals *a 4*, dedicating it to Anonio Londonio, a magistrate of the city-state of Milan. Of all her known madrigals, this set alone survives intact. In that same year Antonio Molino, a merchant and actor in Venice, dedicated his *Dilettevoli madrigali* to Casulana, stating that he had studied music with her. Three poems are also included in her praise. Her activities between 1570 and 1582 are not known. However, during this period Maddalena lived in northern Italy, where she seems to have married one Mezari: in the publication of her first book of madrigals *a 5*, which appeared in 1583, the composer's name is shown as Maddalena Mezari "detta Casulana." The previous year Giambattista Crispolti described a banquet in Perugia involving a performance when "The famous Casulana . . . sang with lute some divine music."

The last of Casulana's known works is a madrigal in three voices, which appeared in the 1586 anthology *Il Gaudio*, but the work is lost. "Di Mezarii," apparently her married name, appears in a variant form on the title page of her last extant publication, *Di Maddalena Mezari detta Casulana Vicentina, Il primo libro de madrigali a cinque voci* (1583). However, the catalogue of the Venetian editor Giacomo Vincenti, in a publication of 1591, mentions another collection presently unknown: a first and second book of madrigali spirituali (sacred, devotional madrigals) in four voices.

Maddalena Casulana was fully aware of her exceptional position as a woman composer in the sixteenth century. In the dedication of her first book of madrigals to another woman, Isabella de' Medici, she declared proudly the desire "also to show the world (as much as is possible in the profession of music) the vain error of men that they alone possess intellectual gifts, and who appear to believe that the same gifts are not possible for women." According to various witnesses, Maddalena was a talented singer and an able lutenist. Her talents as a composer and performer were appreciated by such contemporary poets and musicians as Antonio Molino, Giambattista Maganza, Orlando di Lasso, and Filippo di Monte. It was di Monte to whom she dedicated her 1586 madrigal in three voices.

Thomas Bridges, in his *Grove* article, finds "skill and originality in the handling of harmony and dissonance. She used chromatic alteration and unexpected harmonic juxtapositions daringly and experimented with dramatic contrasts of register and passages in falsobordone style. . . . She illustrated contemporary poetry with an arsenal of word-painting devices."

The madrigal presented here, "Morte—Che vôi?—Te chiamo?," is the sixth work in the second book of madrigals *a 4*, published in Venice by Gerolamo Scotto in 1570. The words are by Serafino Aquilano, whose texts had been set to music beginning earlier in the century. Casulana's choice of Aquilano (an esteemed friend of Josquin Desprez) as a poet testifies to her uncommon literary interests.

The composer seems to have been attracted to the dramatic form of the dialogue, which she exploits ably in the musical structure by distributing the questions and answers throughout the several voices. She alternates the voices polyphonically in the first section, bringing them together only in the final verse. The exclamations "Sì fa!" ("Yes, have done!") and "Non fa!" ("No, have done!") inspired a musical interpretation using the corresponding notes B (si) and F (fa). At measure 17 "sì fa" is set to B and C; and immediately thereupon in the alto "non fa" is set to E and F. As with other madrigalists in this generation of Luca Marenzio, a quieter moment in Casulana calls for a homophonic and unperturbed treatment, such as measures 10 and 16 with "shall my heart reign." However, the struggle with metaphorical death, "sì fa, non fa" at measure 16 and following, is set with a fragmentation of voices.

Text Translation

Death, you whom I call, behold, for I draw near.
Take me and complete thereby all that remains of my sorrow.
You cannot do so?
Since, in you, no longer shall my heart reign,
Yes . . . no . . . have done!
Then restore that which life can no longer destroy.

Further Reading

Bowers, Jane. "The Emergence of Women Composers in Italy, 1566–1700." In *Women Making Music: The Western Art Tradition, 1150–1950*, ed. Jane Bowers and Judith Tick. Champaign-Urbana: University of Illinois Press, 1986.
Pescerelli, Beatrice, ed. Preface to *I madrigali di Maddalena Casulana*. Florence: Olschki, 1979.

Madrigal VI
Morte—Che vôi?—Te chiamo

by Serafino Aquilano

Maddalena Casulana

Reprinted from *I madrigali di Maddalena Casulana*, ed. Beatrice Pescerelli. © Casa Editrice Leo S. Olschki, Florence, 1979. Newly notated by Seth Berrier.

Francesca Caccini
(1587–after 1641)

SUZANNE CUSICK

One of the first women to enjoy a fully professional career as a salaried musician, Francesca Caccini (18 September 1587–after June 1641) was both one of the most admired virtuosa singers and one of the most prolific composers of her generation. In her twenty-eight years of service to the ruling family of Tuscany in central Italy (1607–1627 and 1633–1641), she composed music for at least fifteen theatrical works performed at court, as well as an unknown amount of vocal chamber music. Very little of her music survives. The thirty-six songs and duets gathered in her *Primo libro delle musiche* (1618), the published score of her balletto-opera *La liberazione di Ruggiero dall'isola d'Alcina* (1625), and a few isolated songs in manuscript and print anthologies represent but a slice of a compositional output that was reported to include some three hundred titles as early as 1614. Highly valued by her patrons as a composer and performer, Caccini was evidently equally valued as a teacher and coach. Her pupils ranged from artisan-class girls whose parents hoped they would find work as court musicians to the children of Tuscany's royal family, the Medici. Her training of other women for court service is known to have included lessons in singing, instrumental performance, and composition.

The daughter of two singers, the much-praised virtuosa Lucia Gagnoletti (d. 1591) and the better-known singer and composer Giulio Caccini (1555–1618), Francesca Caccini was described by a contemporary as a girl "of the sharpest intelligence" who studied Latin, Greek, rhetoric, languages, and math as a child. She showed a special gift for the critical exegesis of Latin poetry, a special passion for geometry, astrology, and "the occult sciences," and so strong a bent toward philosophy that "had she been allowed. . . . like Asteria [a woman pupil of Plato's] to attend public lectures in male clothing, she would have equaled or surpassed the women who are learned in that profession." According to the same contemporary, she first learned music "as a pastime, and to please her father." Mastering harp, theorbo, harpsichord, lute, and guitar, able to play well any stringed instrument that she touched, as an unmarried girl Caccini was known to overwhelm her listeners with the wit, literary acumen, and affective power of her song. Looking to take advantage of Caccini's energetic intelligence and passion for study, Grand Duchess Christine de Lorraine of Tuscany channeled both toward a musical career by arranging that the girl be taught counterpoint and ornamentation. Caccini quickly mastered both, producing compositions that were "admired, sought, and prized by the best professionals, and by princes." The Grand Duchess also organized Caccini's 1607 marriage to the handsome but impoverished court musician Giovanni Battista Signorini, a precondition to her hiring as a salaried musica of the court. For the next thirty years Caccini's career would intertwine with that of the Grand Duchess, their fortunes' interdependence sustained by mutually satisfactory relations of clientelism more than by direct commissions. A contralto who sang much more often in chamber settings than onstage, Caccini is known to have sung in Rome, Paris, Turin, Milan, Padua, Verona, Venice, Genoa, Parma, Modena, and Bologna, always astounding her listeners. But her work centered on her frequent performing, composing, and teaching presence among the women and children of Tuscany's ruling family, among their elite women companions the *dame* and *donne*, and in certain of Florence's convents.

After her first husband's death in December 1626, Caccini remarried almost immediately to the amateur musician and instrument collector Tommaso Raffaelli. A sixty-five-year-old bachelor and a member of Lucca's minor nobility, he was described at the time as "a gray-bearded Ganymede, but attractive." At the time of her second marriage, Caccini arranged to place her daughter, Margerita Signorini (b. 1622), in service to the Medici when she reached the age of nine. But when Raffaelli died in 1630, Caccini reneged on her promise, negotiating her own return to Medici service as her daughter's teacher. After a long delay caused by several epidemics of plague, in late 1633 mother, daughter, and Caccini's young son, Tommaso Raffaelli (b. 1628), returned to Florence, where Francesca again served primarily among the women and children of the court, counting among her likely pupils Princes Gian Carlo and Leopoldo and Princess Anna, as well as the teenage Grand Duchess Vittoria della Rovere. Through the 1630s Francesca managed from a distance the agricultural property and investments in the silk trade that her son would eventually inherit as his father's estate. Caccini remained in Florence, in Medici service, until her daughter began her novitiate in the Franciscan Monasterio di San Girolamo sulla costa in 1641: Caccini's release from Medici service is dated 8 May that year. Her letter to Roman prince Paolo Giordano Orsini requesting six weeks' lodging in his palace while she pursued "very pressing business" in Rome, dated 18 June 1641, is the last known trace of Francesca Caccini's life; the place, date, and cause of her death remain unknown.

The spiritual madrigal *Maria dolce Maria* comes from Caccini's *Primo Libro delle Musiche* (1618). Published in the composer's thirtieth year, the *Primo Libro* represented Caccini's claim to her role as the new maestra of her father's virtuosic craft (singer-composer and, as she wrote in a 1618 letter, "maestro [teacher] to many"). Including thirty-two solo songs and four soprano/bass duets, the *Primo Libro* was the largest and most internally diverse collection of monody published in Italy in the 1610s. Its table of contents and meticulous rubrics direct users toward "spiritual" and "temporal" repertoire, and organize the songs according to poetic genre. The book's unusual scope and inclusiveness suggests that Caccini meant it to participate in the encyclopedic urge fashionable among some Italian poets. This breadth is notably manifest in her colleague Michelangelo Buonarroti il giovane's gigantic, all-inclusive multiple-day comedy on city life, *La fiera*, and Giambattista Marino's gargantuan poetic romance *L'Adone*. Internal evidence strongly supports the notion that Caccini also intended her *Primo Libro* as a document more of her teaching work than of her performances. Performance occasions can be identified for several monodies contained therein, including two songs from the 1614 comedy *Il Passatempo*, one from the 1611 *La Tancia*, and the setting of a poem that had been commissioned for an aristocratic woman's profession as a nun at Santa Maria degli Angeli. However, none of the songs Caccini published can be linked definitively to her own known performances.

The first of eleven songs to poems by Michelangelo Buonarroti il giovane that Caccini chose to publish in the *Primo Libro, Maria dolce Maria* immediately follows a recitative soliloquy (on poetry by Andrea Salvadori) that explicitly articulated the constraining paradoxes by which women's self-expressive speech was all but strangled into silence by early modern social convention. Heard as a response to that soliloquy, *Maria dolce Maria* can be understood as teaching its performer a way of coming to voice that would dodge social opprobrium: the song itself is born of the performer's increasingly ecstatic response to the inspiriting power of the word, the name of Christ's Virgin mother. Ecstasy erupts first as vocal ornaments that fill and then expand the intervallic space to which Caccini had assigned the word "Maria," as if the word itself bore a pure sonic energy that sought release. As the singer's hands explore the accompaniment's ever wider harmonic range, that sonic energy in the throat builds toward release into an untrammeled vocality on the words "io canto": there, a delicious passaggiot suspends the poem's linguistic momentum to indulge a full enactment of song itself. The goal of Caccini's *Maria dolce maria*, however, is not the liberation of song from speech but the performance of the two in equilibrium: her singer returns from ecstasy to a clear enunciation of the poem's last lines made musically memorable by melodic sequence, a tight motivic relationship between vocal and bass melodies, and the support of a harmonic phrase that sweeps through the vastly widened tonal space (two adjacent hexachords) to which her inspiriting utterance of the Virgin's name had led her.

Caccini's one surviving stage work, *La Liberazione di Ruggiero dall'isola d'Alcina* (Florence: Cecconcelli, 1625), was conceived for a single performance at the Medici palace known as Villa Imperiale during Carnival, 1625. That performance was in turn part of a season intended to celebrate the visits of Archduke Carl of Styria and Crown Prince Wladislaw of Poland, to seal an alliance by the public betrothal of the twelve-year-old Medici princess Margherita to her twenty-five-year-old cousin Wladislaw, and to justify the authority to negotiate both sexual and diplomatic alliances of Florence's two co-regents, Archduchess Maria Maddalena of Austria and her mother-in-law, Grand Duchess Christine de Lorraine. Court functionary Ferdinando Saracinelli's libretto gave a surprisingly gynecentric spin to the well-known episode from Ariosto's *Orlando furioso* on which it was based, the "liberation" of a lovesick knight from his infatuation with a sorceress who seduced others by surrounding them with pleasure. Focusing his plot on the struggle between two sorceresses for control of the young man's destiny, Saracinelli ensured that the show could be received as an allegory by which one woman's ability to channel others' real or metaphorical sexuality toward reproductive couplings would restore social order to the stage.

Further Reading

Alexander, Ronald James, and Richard Savino. *Francesca Caccini's* Il primo libro delle musiche *of 1618: A Modern Critical Edition of the Secular Monodies.* Bloomington, Ind.: Indiana University Press, 2004.

Cusick, Suzanne G. "Of Women, Music and Power: A Model from Seicento Florence." In Ruth Solie, ed., *Musicology and Difference: Gender and Sexuality in Music Scholarship,* 281–304. Berkeley: University of California Press, 1993.

———. " 'Thinking from Women's Lives': Francesca Caccini after 1627." *Musical Quarterly* 77 (1993): 484–507.

Harness, Kelley. "Amazzoni di Dio: Florentine Musical Spectacle under Maria Maddalena d'Austria and Cristina di Lorena (1620–30)." Ph.D. diss., University of Illinois, 1996.

Maria, dolce Maria
from *Il Primo Libro*

Francesca Caccini, transcribed by Carolyn Raney

Transcribed by Carolyn Raney. Used by permission.

Francesca Caccini

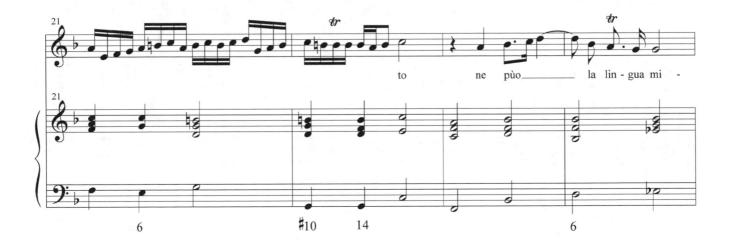

SUZANNE CUSICK

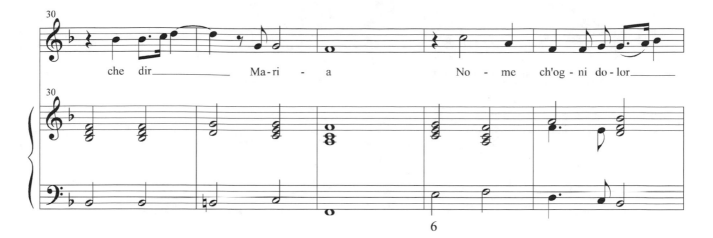

che dir_____ Ma - ri - a No - me ch'og - ni do - lor_____

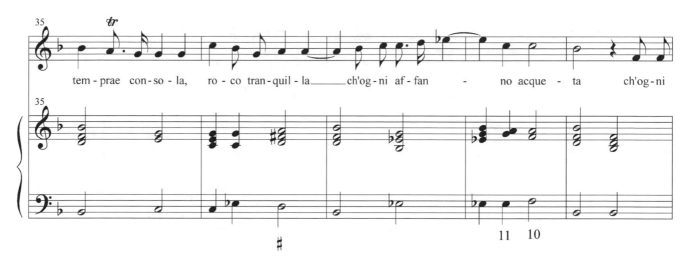

tem - prae con - so - la, ro - co tran - quil - la_____ ch'og - ni af - fan - - - no acque - ta ch'og - ni

cor fa se - re - - no, ch'og - ni cor fa se - ren'_____ ogn' al - - - - ma liet -

ta, ch'og-ni cor fa se-re — — no, ch'og-ni cor fa se-re — — no ogn'

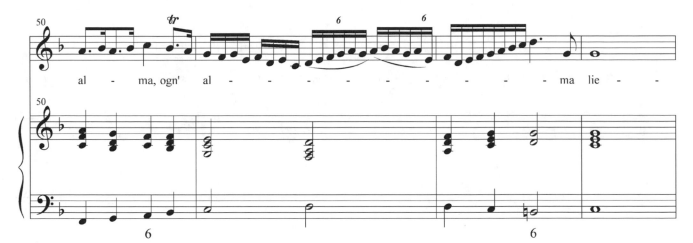

al — ma, ogn' al — — — — — — — — — ma lie —

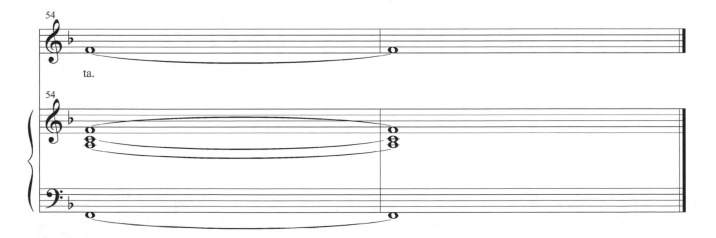

ta.

SUZANNE CUSICK

Aria of the Shepherd
from *La Liberazione di Ruggiero*

Francesca Caccini
edited by Doris Silbert

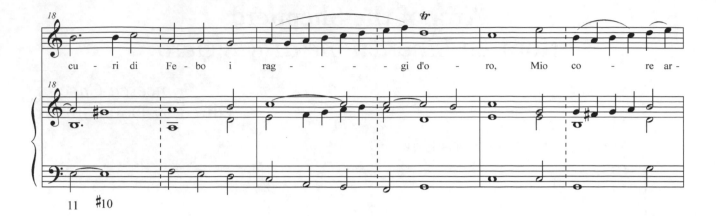

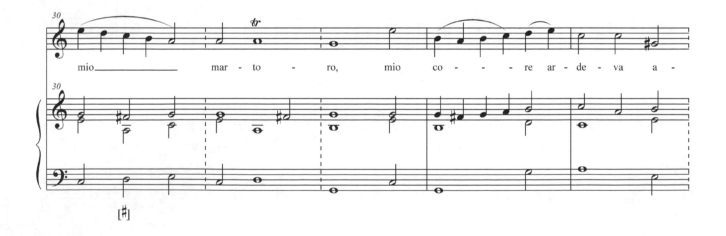

SUZANNE CUSICK

Ritornello, di flauti come sopra [meas. 1] *Segue il medeslmo Pastore* [meas. 42]

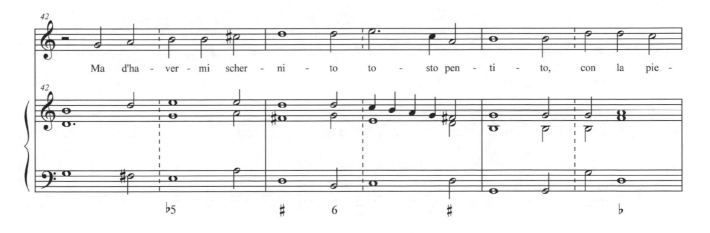

tà   di   lei   mi   sa_____na_il pet - - - to,   ond'

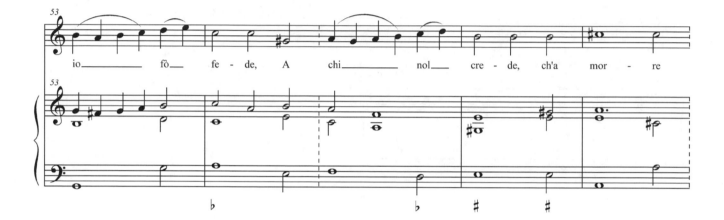

io_____ fò - fe - de,   A   chi_____ nol___ cre - de,   ch'a   mor - re

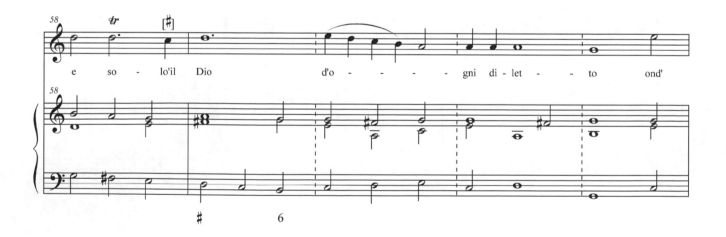

e   so - lo'il   Dio   d'o - - - - gni di - let - - to   ond'

Suzanne Cusick

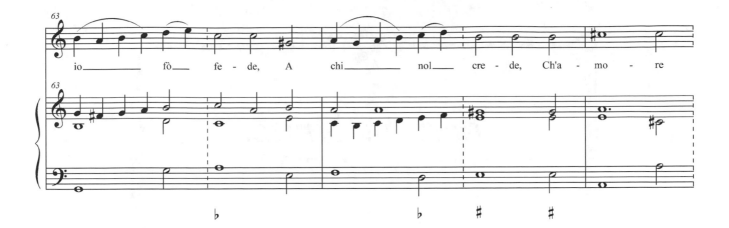

io____ fò____ fe - de, A chi_____ nol____ cre - de, Ch'a - mo - re

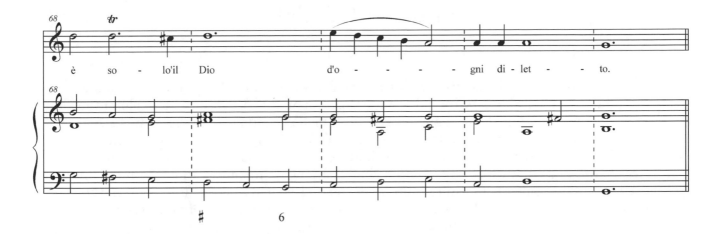

è so - lo'il Dio   d'o - - - - - - gni di - let - - to.

Ritornello di flauti come sopra [meas. 1]
Ruggiero

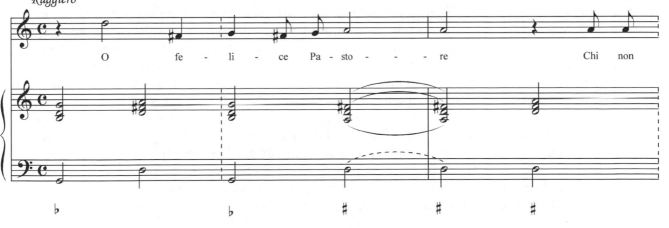

O   fe - li - ce Pa - sto - - - re   Chi non

Barbara Strozzi
(1619–1677)

ELLEN ROSAND

The singer and composer Barbara Strozzi was born in Venice in 1619 and died in Padua in 1677. She was the adopted (probably natural) daughter of the Florentine expatriate writer Giulio Strozzi and his servant Isabella Garzoni. Her father, who became an important librettist during the infant years of public opera, was a founding member of several academies, including the leading Venetian academy of the period, the Accademia degli Incogniti. This group included among its members all of the most important intellectuals of the time, from Venice and elsewhere. Like Giulio Strozzi, they were all prolific writers, of novels, romances, poetry, historical and religious tracts, academic discourses, and opera librettos. Through her father, Barbara thus had the opportunity to become acquainted with the leading figures in Venetian cultural life. (One of her father's aristocratic friends, Giovanni Paolo Vidmann, to whom he dedicated one of his opera librettos, fathered her three children [Glixon, 1999].) He also encouraged her musical activities, by arranging for her to study with the most famous composer of the day, Francesco Cavalli, and by founding an academy specifically to display her gifts as a singer, the Accademia degli Unisoni, which met at their house and where she performed regularly during the mid- to late 1630s. (A striking portrait of her by the painter Bernardo Strozzi, no relation, dating from the late 1630s, gives an idea of what she might have looked like at the time of these performances.) Giulio also provided texts for two volumes of songs dedicated to her by Nicolo Fontei (Opp. 1 and 2, published in 1635 and 1636), which she performed at Unisoni meetings. Giulio's most extraordinary intervention on behalf of his daughter's career, however, was to supply the texts for her own first publication, a volume of Madrigali for from two to five voices of 1644.

Indeed, whereas singing was a fairly common activity for a woman during this period, composition, certainly published composition, was not. It was clearly thanks to her father—his material support, social connections, and vision—that Barbara Strozzi could actively pursue such a career. Her Op. 1 was followed over the course of the next two decades by at least seven further publications, all but one of them devoted to arias and cantatas for solo voice. She seems to have preferred the role of miniaturist, and does not seem to have written any operas, although a few of her texts were apparently drawn from opera librettos by her father and may have been performed on the stage.

Her total published output, of more than one hundred solo vocal works, marks her as one of the most prolific contributors to secular chamber music of the seventeenth century, comparable to well-known composers such as Luigi Rossi, Giacomo Carissimi, and Antonio Cesti, all of whom were active in Rome. Unlike their music, however, which survives mainly in manuscript, virtually all of Strozzi's known music was published, a testament to the active printing industry in Venice, which encouraged the publication of aria and cantata collections for general use, and which thereby guaranteed Barbara's reputation as a composer. It presumably also contributed to her livelihood, through sales and dedications.

All of Strozzi's publications were dedicated to prominent aristocratic patrons, most of whom were foreigners. These included Vittoria della Rovere (Op. 1), Emperor Ferdinand III of Austria (Op. 2, 1651), and Francesco Caraffa, Prince of Belvedere (Op. 6), as well as two other women, Anna de' Medici, Archduchess of Austria (Op. 5, 1655), and Sophie, Duchess of Brunswick and Luneberg (Op. 8, 1664). The single Venetian dedicatee, Nicolò Sagredo (Op. 7, 1659), an important government official at the time, was subsequently elected doge. Although no copy of Op. 4 survives, good evidence suggests that it resembled her other publications, and that it was published in 1655 and dedicated to Carlo II, Duke of Modena (Glixon, 1997).

With the exception of the Madrigali of Op. 1, nearly all of her music was scored for solo soprano and can probably be associated with her own performances. (The dedications of several of the volumes refer to such performances.) Many of the texts, in addition to those by Giulio Strozzi, were evidently written expressly for her. Some of them convey a woman's point of view or feature her name as an adjective, while others directly address the dedicatee of the volume. As indicated by their title pages, five of the known volumes contain secular music (pieces called *arietta, aria,* and *cantata*), while one, Op. 5, is a collection of fourteen Italian motets. But the titles were not binding on the actual contents of the volumes, which also include pieces called *lamento* and, in one case, *serenata*. The distinctions between these terms, however, for Strozzi as for most of her contemporaries, are not always clear.

The *arietta* was evidently a short aria, usually in simple strophic form. At the other end of the spectrum, "cantata" designated a lengthy, varied work of several sections and a mixture of vocal styles: recitative, arioso, and aria, responding to textual distinctions between open-ended narration and more formal lyricism. The "lamenti" and "serenata" fit within this category. Between these two extremes, pieces called "aria" were often strophic, and frequently enclosed by a refrain at beginning and end, though some are extremely long and complex multisectional forms that resemble cantatas.

Most of the texts belong to the category of poetry made famous by the "poet of the marvelous," Gimbattista Marino: precious love lyrics filled with conceits, ironic and lachrymose by turns. Strozzi's music perfectly matches the emotional contrasts of this poetry by means of unpredictable melodic, rhythmic, metric, and dynamic shifts: from recitative to arioso, from syllabic to exaggerated melismatic text setting, from free melodic unfolding to rigid sequential patterning.

The full range of her style is well illustrated in her single serenata from Op. 8, one of her longest and most varied compositions, and one of very few to utilize strings. The anonymous text, comprising multiple sections in a variety of meters, is delivered by an unhappy lover in the presence of his sleeping beloved. In a paroxysm of self-consciousness—a kind of *Erwartung avant la lettre*—it alternates narrative description of the night scene, of his own feeling and actions, and of the imagined reaction of his beloved, with direct address and lyrical outpouring of emotion, which culminates in a grand lament of farewell based on a descending tetrachord ostinato, accompanied by strings. Seven contrasting vocal movements alternate with some six different three-part ritornellos that either echo preceding material or anticipate what follows. Only one of these movements, in the center of the work, actually qualifies as a formal aria, with two numbered stanzas of four lines. But even this formality is undermined by the fact that the stanzas end differently. In the first case, a reprise of the opening ritornello calmly separates the stanza from three lines of recitative poetry, set in arioso style. In the second, the stanza leads directly into passionate recitative, without a break. It is as if the emotions of the character/performer (poet and musician together) cannot be bound by form. Unable to wait for the ritornello, they burst into recitative: "isfogatevi, spriggionatevi, miei sospir." The most regular movement of all is the lament of resigned farewell that closes the work. It consists of seven statements of the ostinato: two in an opening ritornello, two for voice and strings, and one for strings alone, culminating in a grand fourfold statement of the ostinato for voice and strings together. This lament finally anchors the work, providing a solid, effective resolution to the previous emotional and formal turmoil.

Many aspects of Strozzi's compositional style, as exemplified in this piece, reflect the singer-composer in the act of performing, even improvising. The absence of strict structure in the poetry, mostly a succession of rhymed quatrains, leaves the composer (or singer) free to vary the setting according to the expressive needs of the text. The numerous performance indications, too, for trills, dynamics, and tempo reveal the singer in the composer. The passionate, extravagant, irregular, almost mannered quality of her music allows us to imagine the sound of her voice.

Op. 8 of 1664 is Strozzi's last surviving publication. She lived another thirteen years, however, and her career as a composer did not necessarily end then. Indeed, documentary evidence shows that it continued, at least for another year (Glixon 1997). Nor do we know when she stopped singing. Unlike many other singers, though, whose voices were buried with them, Strozzi's is preserved in her publications, at once the frozen records of her performances and testament to a successful career as a composer. Although very few exemplars have survived (in most cases only one, in one case none), it is thanks to those publications that Strozzi has made her mark in the historiography of the seicento cantata.

Further Reading

Glixon, Beth. "New Light on the Life and Career of Barbara Strozzi." *Musical Quarterly* 81 (1997): 311–35.

———. "More on the Life and Death of Barbara Strozzi." *Musical Quarterly* 83 (1999): 134–41.

Rosand, Ellen. "Barbara Strozzi, Virtuosissima Cantatrice: The Composer's Voice." *JAMS* xxxi (1978): 241–81.

———. "The Voice of Barbara Strozzi." In *Women Making Music: The Western Art Tradition, 1150–1950,* ed. J. Bowers and J. Tick, 168–90. Urbana and Chicago: University of Illinois Press, 1986.

Hor che Apollo

Barbara Strozzi
Randall Wong, editor

Note: The bass realizations of this edition are in no way meant for actual performance; they are merely one possible and plausible way of interpreting the largely
unfigured bass. The actual performance realization is up to the interpreters, the performance circumstances, and most importantly, what instrument(s) are
accompanying the voice and their idiomatic realization.

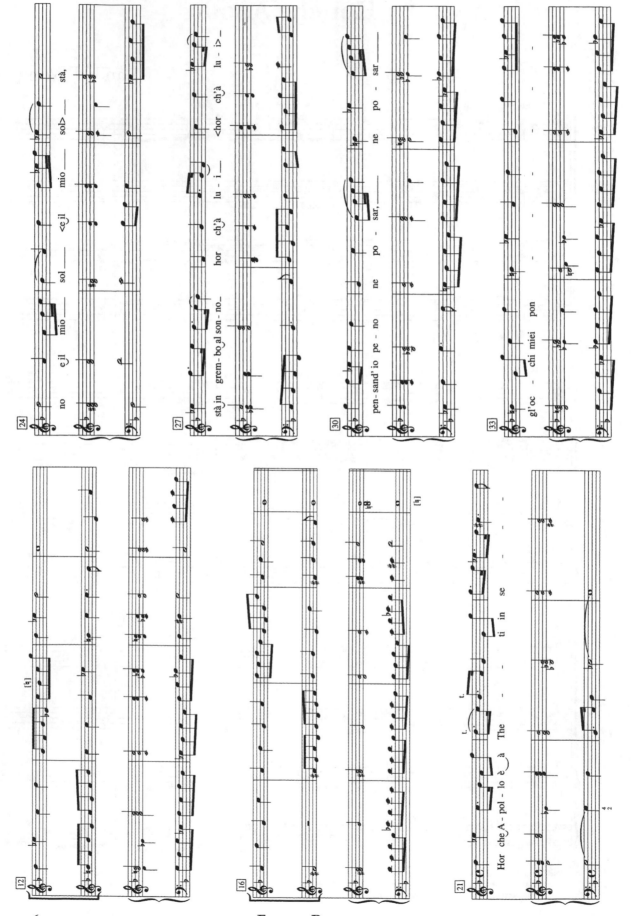

ELLEN ROSAND

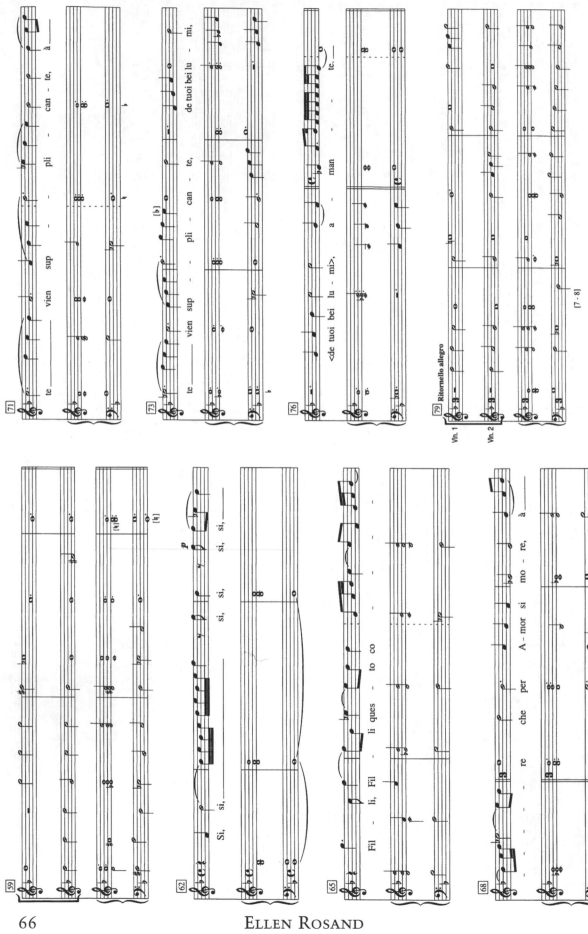

ELLEN ROSAND

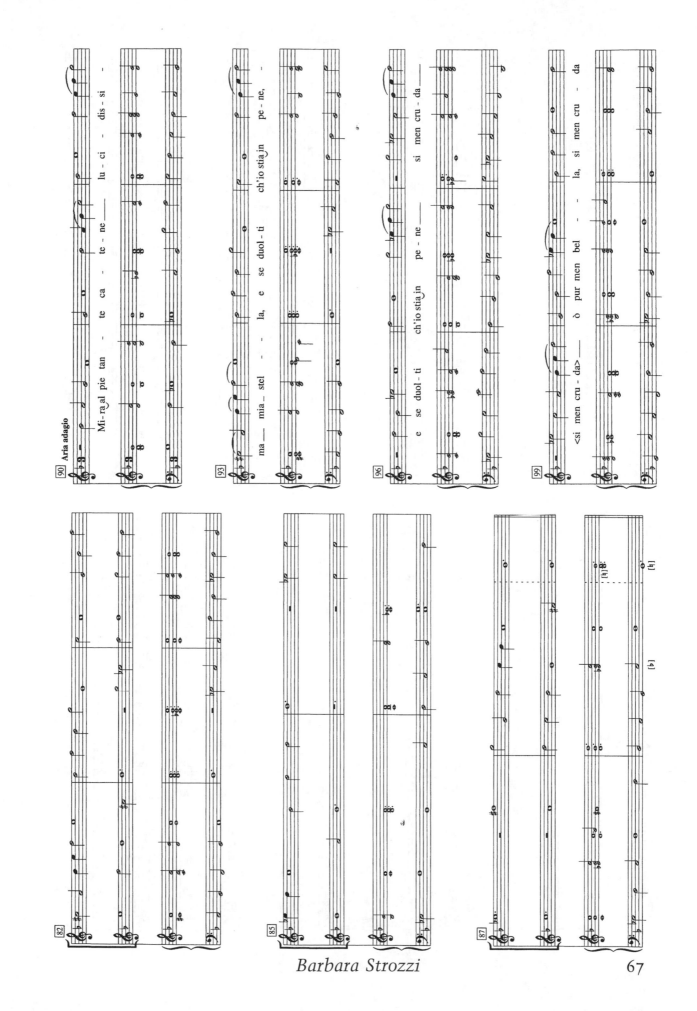

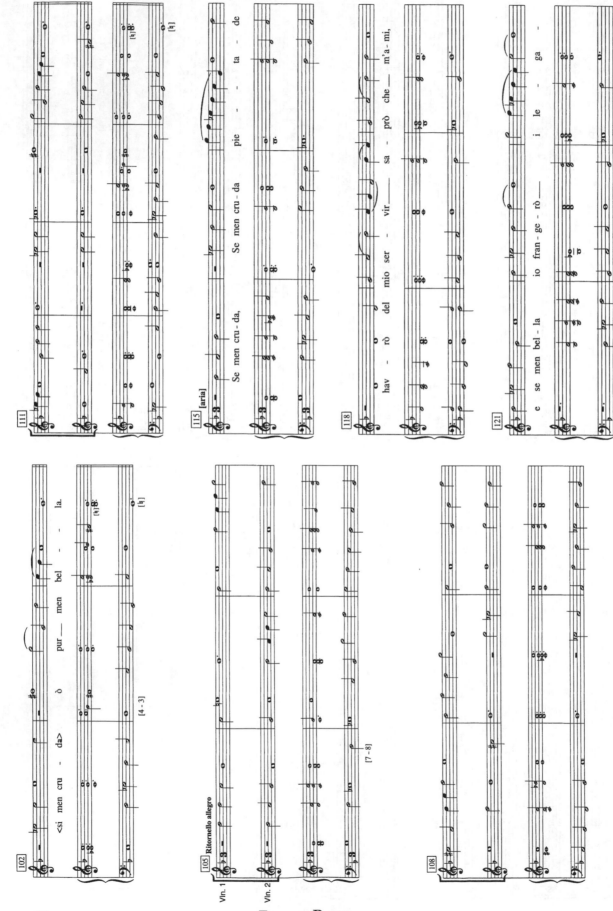

ELLEN ROSAND

Isabella Leonarda
(1620–1704)

BARBARA GARVEY JACKSON

Isabella Leonarda was born in Novara, Italy, into a family of minor nobility. Little is known of her early life or her musical studies. Isabella took her vows at age sixteen, and she and some of her sisters were nuns in the convent of Sant'Orsola in Novara. Isabella may have been a student of Gasparo Casati, chapelmaster of the Novara cathedral from 1635 to 1641, since her earliest known compositions appeared in a volume of Casati's sacred concenti in 1640.

From the prefaces and title pages of the twenty volumes of music she subsequently published, it appears that Isabella served her order as an administrator—madre (Mother Superior) by 1686, madre vicaria in 1693, and consigliera (Counselor) in her last years. In a document of 1658, her duties are given as music teacher, clerk, and madre in the congregation. Since the Ursulines were a teaching order, it is possible that there was a school attached to the convent, but little is known of either the institution or its musical life. Many records were probably lost when the convent was closed in 1811. Two motets by Isabella Leonarda were dedicated to musical nuns of her own convent, and two to nuns of other congregations. These nuns were probably singers, and the works may reflect their singing skills.

Leonarda's publications include more than two hundred works, all for church use, although only about a quarter of them are settings of liturgical texts. Her first published Mass was in Op. 4 (1674), together with several psalm settings. Op. 18 (1696), from which the following Kyrie and Crucifixus are drawn, contains three Masses. Leonarda also set litanies, Magnificats, Marian antiphons (she had a special devotion to the Virgin and used a double dedication for each volume of her works—to the Virgin and to a human patron), responsories, a hymn, and a sequence. Most of her works were settings for one to four voices (often with concertato violins) of nonliturgical religious texts, many of which she may have written. They express a passionate religious devotion, usually to the Virgin. Op. 16 (1693) is entirely devoted to sonate da chiesa ("church sonatas")—eleven trio sonatas and one solo sonata for violin and organ continuo. It is the first known publication of instrumental sonatas composed by a woman to survive complete.

In accordance with regional practice, Leonarda set only the Kyrie, Gloria, and Credo in her Masses, and not the Eucharistic portions of the Ordinary. Her style, which is similar to that of other north Italian contemporaries, is marked by an intense personal identification with the religious text. For example, in the Crucifixus portion of the Credo, she marks a change of tempo of character in the middle of the sentence "Crucifixus etiam pro nobis." The word "Crucifixus" is adagio and mournful in spirit, but the phrase "etiam pro nobis" is abruptly marked spiritoso, joyfully responding to the thought that the sacrifice was for us. The alternation continues, with text repetitions of the joyful phrase. Leonarda sometimes indicates dynamics—"et sepultus est" is marked piano. After the concluding words there is a meditative adagio Sinfonia, the last phrase of which is also marked piano.

In recent years there have been many recordings of works by Leonarda, making her the most frequently heard woman composer of her era.

Text and Translation

Kyrie eleison.	Lord have mercy on us.
Christe eleison.	Christ have mercy on us.
Kyrie eleison.	Lord have mercy on us.
Crucifuxus etiam pro nobis	He was crucified also for us
Sub Pontio Pilato passus	under Pontius Pilate suffered
Et sepultus est.	and was buried.

Further Reading

Carter, Stewart Arlen. "The Music of Isabella Leonarda (1620–1704)." Ph.D. diss., Stanford University, 1981.
Giegling, Franz. "Leonarda, Isabella." *Die Musik in Geschichte und Gegenwart* VIII (2001): 634.
New Grove Dictionary of Music and Musicians. 2nd ed. S.v. "Isabella Leonarda."

Modern Editions and Recording

"Ave Regina Caelorum" for SAT soli, mixed chorus (SATB), and continuo. Ed. Stewart Carter. Nine Centuries of Music by Women series. New York: Broude Bros., 1980.
Messa Prima from Opus 18 for four voices with violin (1696). Ed. Barbara Garvey Jackson. Fayetteville, Ark.: ClarNan Editions, 1981.
Music for the Mass by Nun Composers. *Messa Prima* from Opus 18, Isabella Leonarda.
Schola Cantorum of the University of Arkansas, Jack Groh, conductor. Leonarda LPI-115, 1982.
Sonata Duodecima from Opus 16 (1693) for violin and continuo. Ed. Barbara Garvey Jackson. Baroque Chamber Music Series, no. 16. Ottawa: Dovehouse Editions, 1983.
Selected Compositions. Ed. Stewart Carter. Recent Research in Music of the Baroque. Madison, Wis.: A-R Editions, 1988. Includes two concerted liturgical settings, four motets, and two sonatas.
Solo Motets from the Seventeenth Century, iv–v, Novarra I–II. New York, 1987–1988. (Facsimile, with introduction by A. Schnoebelen.)

Kyrie and Crucifixus

(from the *Credo*) of *Missa Prima*, Op. 18

Isabella Leonarda

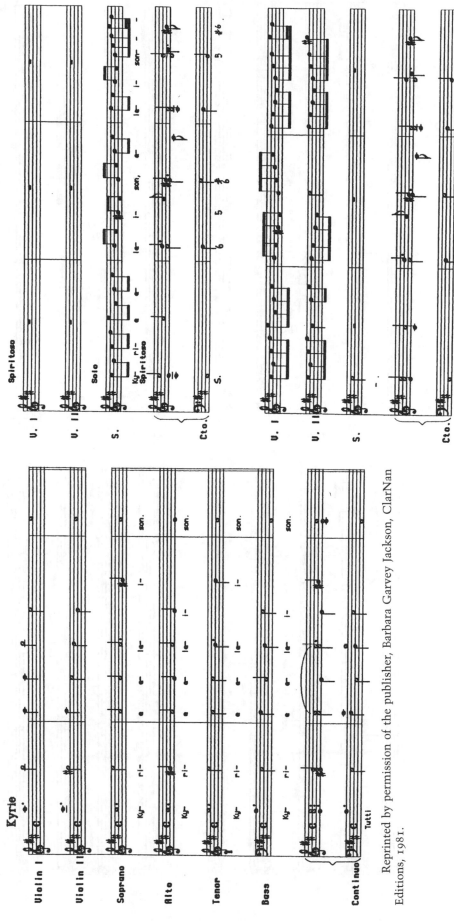

Reprinted by permission of the publisher, Barbara Garvey Jackson, ClarNan Editions, 1981.

Isabella Leonarda

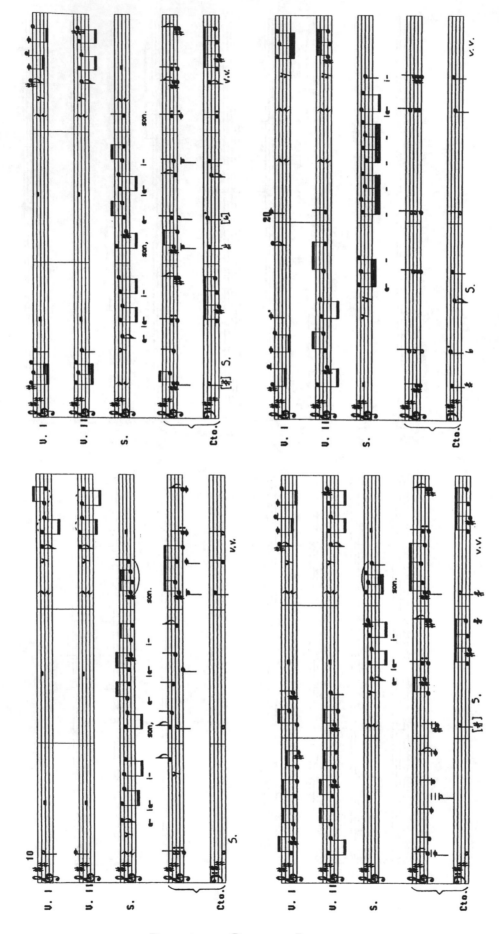

Barbara Garvey Jackson

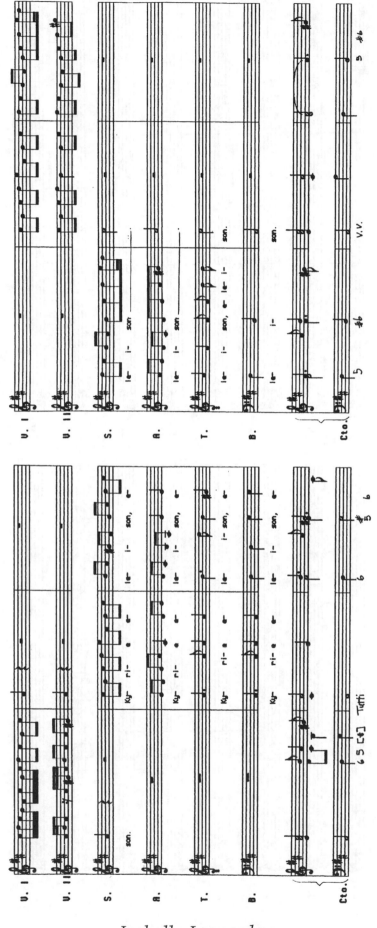

Isabella Leonarda

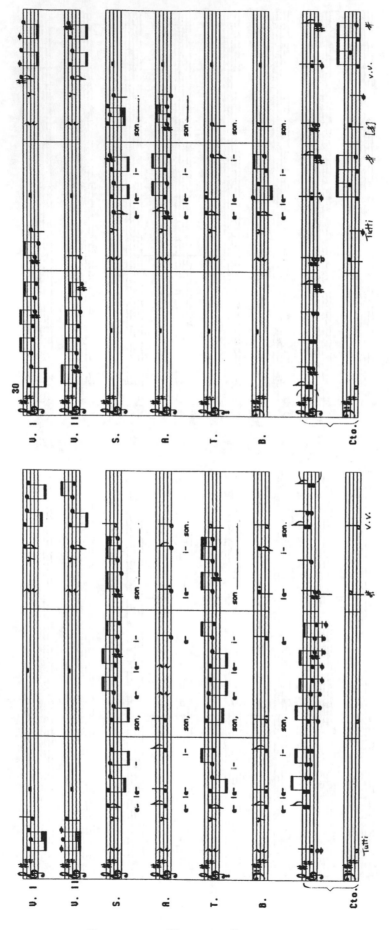

BARBARA GARVEY JACKSON

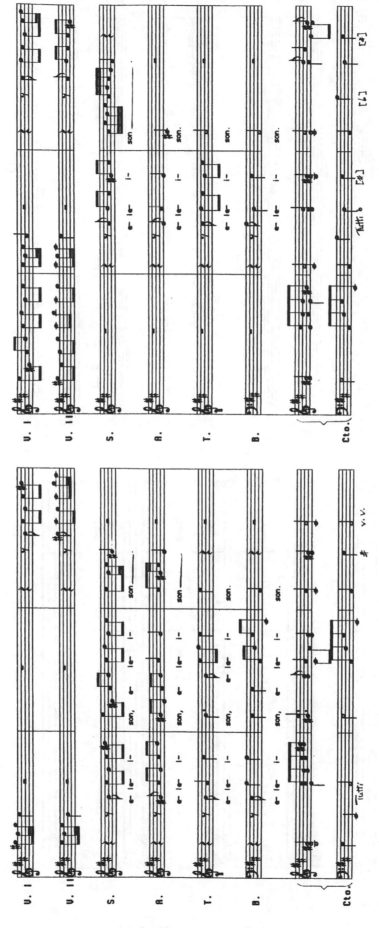

Isabella Leonarda

75

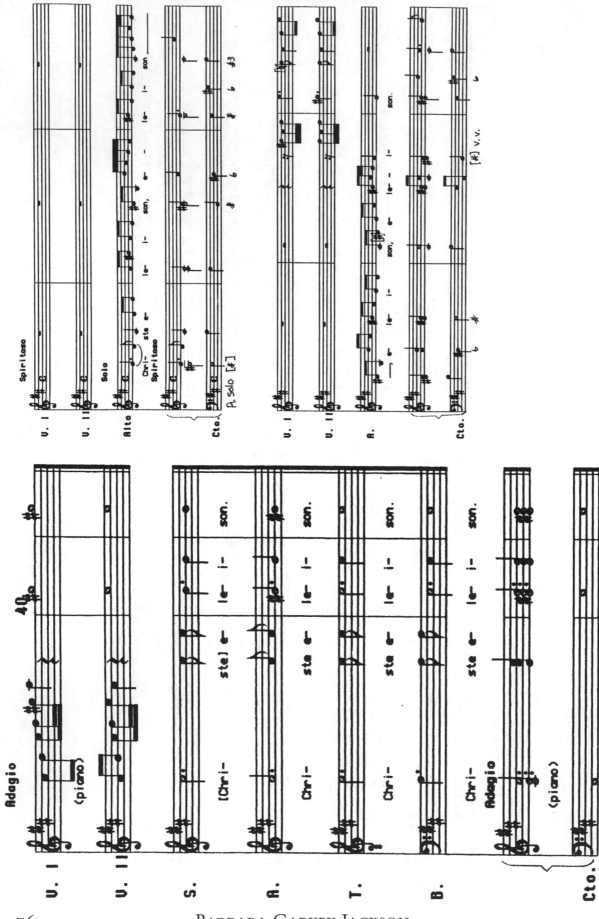

Barbara Garvey Jackson

Isabella Leonarda

77

BARBARA GARVEY JACKSON

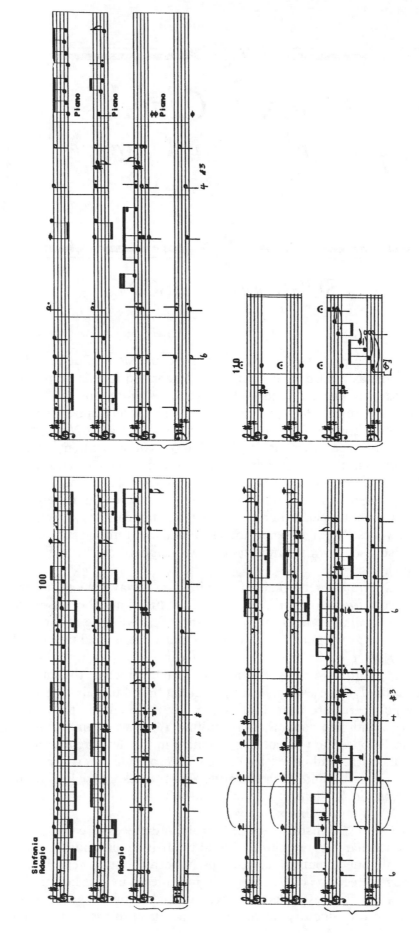

Isabella Leonarda

Elisabeth-Claude Jacquet de la Guerre (1665–1729)

SUSAN ERICKSON

The French composer Elisabeth-Claude Jacquet de la Guerre achieved recognition at an early age as a harpsichord virtuoso, celebrated for her improvisations. She attracted the notice of Louis XIV, enjoyed his continued protection, and dedicated most of her compositions to him. Her early education was closely supervised by Mme. de Montespan, the king's mistress; she also came into contact with Mme. de Maintenon, who was known for her commitment to education for young women. Elisabeth was descended from a noted family of harpsichord builders and musicians and in 1684 married the Parisian organist Marin de la Guerre. Their only son, said to be a prodigy like his mother, died at the age of ten. Marin de la Guerre died in 1704, and thereafter Elisabeth remained active as a public performer until her retirement in 1717. At the time of her death in 1729, she was still remembered and esteemed as an important public figure, and her music was discussed by the important lexicographers of the eighteenth century (Walther, Hawkins).

Jacquet de la Guerre is a remarkable figure in several ways: she wrote and published works in almost every form popular in France in her time, and she was instrumental in introducing the new Italian style of music to France. She was one of the first women to compose in such a wide variety of genres and to be fully recognized for her achievements in a field generally reserved for men. One of her earliest works was the five-act opera *Céphale et Procris*, the first work by a woman to be performed at the Paris Opéra. Modeled after the tragédie lyrique established by Jean-Baptiste Lully, it received high praise in the form of a poetic tribute from Lully's son, Louis de Lully, and was published in 1694. Her early trio and solo sonatas, from around 1695, were among the first of that genre composed in France. She was equally a pioneer in the new French cantata. Her two books of biblical cantatas, published by Ballard in 1708 and 1711, are noteworthy for their unusual subject matter and Italianate style. Other works, now lost, include a ballet, *Les Jeux à l'honneur de la victoire* of 1691, and a Te Deum, written to celebrate the recovery of Louis XV from smallpox in 1721.

Jacquet de la Guerre published a set of harpsichord pieces as early as 1687. She was one of the few French harpsichord composers to publish a collection in the seventeenth century, and the only one to publish collections in both the seventeenth and eighteenth centuries. The 1687 collection consists of thirty-four pieces in four key groups (she never used the word "suite"). These works are distinguished from her subsequent collection by the presence of an introductory movement, in addition to the usual allemande, courante (always a pair of courantes), sarabande and gigue, and chaconne, minuet, gavotte, and cannaris. All the introductory movements are examples of the unmeasured prelude, a form that uses white notes of no fixed value, sometimes interspersed with black notes of varying values to indicate harmonic or melodic direction. One finds this type of writing in the works of a few other seventeenth-century French composers, such as Louis Couperin, and even in the keyboard suites of later composers such as Handel. The importance of these preludes lies in what they may tell us about Jacquet de la Guerre's own improvisations.

When she published her double collection of violin sonatas and keyboard suites in 1707, Jacquet de la Guerre established herself as an important figure in the emerging production of violin sonatas in France. In taking up the sonata, a turn-of-the-century Italian import, she was showing the most innovative side of her creative personality. Some distinguishing features of her writing in these sonatas include a pervasive use of bimodality both at the level of movements within a sonata and within a movement or section, bass lines that frequently exceed the traditional role of support and allow the gamba to become a partner with the violin and occasionally a soloist in its own right, and the frequent use of an aria or slow movement as a concluding movement. While any one of these features may be found in the works of others, they all appear in these sonatas to an unusual degree, and could explain the "originality" of Jacquet de la Guerre's music that appealed to audiences in 1707.

The other part of the 1707 publication consists of fourteen movements for harpsichord solo that make up two suites, in D and G. "La Flamande et son double" in d minor, reproduced below, is actually an allemande with a varied repeat of each section. Its broad compass and abundant ornamentation follow the great tradition of the French clavecinistes, established by Chambonnières and developed by François Couperin and others. The concluding Chaconne is an expansive and virtuoso set of variations.

Jacquet de la Guerre also wrote a volume of cantatas on traditional mythological subjects; it was dedicated to the Elector of Bavaria and published by Foucault, probably after 1715. (Her previous works had been dedicated to Louis XIV, who died in that year.) A short comic duet for soprano and bass, "Le Raccommodement comique de Nicole et Pierrot," is included in the collection. The composer explains in the score that there are just three cantatas (rather than the customary six), because each one is longer than usual. All three cantatas are scored for soprano and continuo, with symphonie.

Semelé is the first of the three cantatas and is included here in its first modern edition. It is based on the Greek myth of Semelé, mistress of Zeus and mother of Dionysus. When Semelé insists on knowing the identity of her lover, Zeus appears in the form of a thunderbolt, and Semelé dies. She is later rescued from Hades by her son, and her return to Earth is associated with the yearly return of spring. The three airs of Semelé, all in da capo form, are on a larger scale than those typically found in the cantatas of Jacquet de la Guerre's contemporaries. The composer explains in her preface that they may be performed separately if desired. The recitatives are typically French, in that frequent meter changes accommodate the rhythm of the speech. The instruments, violin and continuo (with the suggestion of flute in the second air, "Quel triomphe"), are used in independent instrumental numbers and interludes. In certain recitatives and one air, they provide contrast and intensify the expression of the text.

A word about the edition is in order. The symbol "x" that appears in both the vocal and upper instrumental lines is original with the Foucault print and has been retained here. In virtually all cases, a short trill seems to be intended. Clefs have been modernized for the convenience of modern performers. In the original source the French violin clef (first line G clef) was used for the violin part, and the bass line frequently moves into a C clef to avoid the use of ledger lines.

Text Translation

NARRATOR: Jupiter had made an indiscreet oath, to grant any wish to a faithful lover. Semele doubts the rank of her lover, and this doubt torments her; she aspires to see him in his immortal glory; but Love, out of pity for her, averts the moment of so fatal a pleasure! Semele, however, laments, frets. She complains of waiting overlong.

SEMELE: Can one not live in your bonds without suffering the pains of a mortal? Love, you promised a thousand gifts, but one finds none at all in your chains. A heart that has let itself be charmed must sacrifice all to its flame. My lover, if he were able to love, would foresee the desires of my soul.

NARRATOR: But what astonishing noise bursts forth in the air. What devastation; the thunderbolt roars, the sky opens, and the lightening flashes announce to me the master of the world.

SEMELE: What a great display, what a spectacle for me; forgive me, I was wrong to doubt your faithfulness. What triumph, what victory flatters my ambitious heart. Is anything equal to my glory? I will enjoy the fate of the gods. I do not wish mystery to hide the happiness of my fetters; let all know that I was able to please the greatest god of the universe. Ah! What sudden conflagration terrifies me, I see this palace catch fire; Ah! Heaven! I feel myself consumed; Jupiter, what is the fate of your mistress! One desire has led me to the final misfortune. What terrible torment, I succomb, I die.

NARRATOR: When Love binds us in his most engaging knots, let us not mix with his fires the ardour of a vain glory, let us not divide his desires. Splendour, supreme grandeur, were never a blessing. It is in a tender bond that one finds supreme happiness. Splendour, supreme grandeur are of no importance.

Further Reading

Barroff, Edith. *An Introduction to Elisabeth-Claude Jacquet de la Guerre.* Brooklyn, N.Y.: Institute of Medieval Music, 1966.

Bates, Carol Henry. "The Instrumental Music of Elisabeth-Claude Jacquet de la Guerre." Ph.D. diss., Indiana University, 1978.

Cessac, Catherine. *Elisabeth-Claude Jacquet de la Guerre: Une Femme Compositeur sons le Regne de Louis XIV.* Arles: Actes Sud, 1995.

SUSAN ERICKSON

La Flamande and Chaconne et son double
from Suite in D minor for harpsichord

Elisabeth Jacquet de La Guerre

La Flamande

Reprinted from *Pièces de Claveçin*, © Editions de l'Oiseau Lyre, Les Remparts, Monaco, 1965.

Elisabeth-Claude Jacquet de la Guerre

[segue]

(*) 🎵 dans l'original

SUSAN ERICKSON

Double

SUSAN ERICKSON

Chaconne

Elisabeth-Claude Jacquet de la Guerre

87

SUSAN ERICKSON

5.º Couplet

On reprend le 1.er Couplet 𝄋

Elisabeth-Claude Jacquet de la Guerre   89

Semelé

Cantata for voice, violin, and continuo

Elisabeth Jacquet de la Guerre
continuo realization by Robert Samson Bloch

From *Cantates françoises*. Paris: Foucault, n.d. (PN Vm7. 161). Reprinted by permission of the Bibliothèque nationale, Paris, Département de Musique, Mme Catherine Massip, Directeur. First modern edition by Susan Erickson and Robert Bloch. Continuo realization by Robert Bloch. New edition for this anthology.

SUSAN ERICKSON

Elisabeth-Claude Jacquet de la Guerre

91

SUSAN ERICKSON

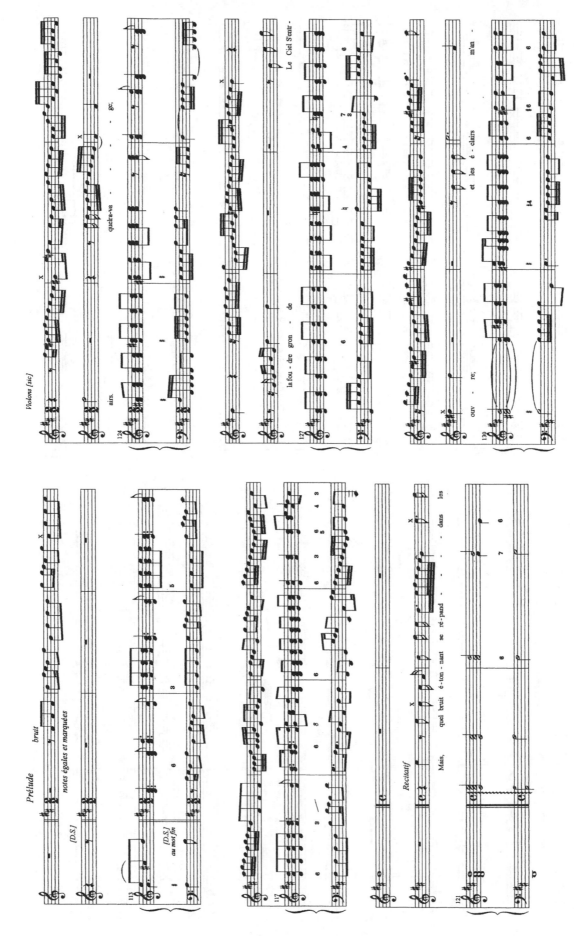

Elisabeth-Claude Jacquet de la Guerre

93

SUSAN ERICKSON

Elisabeth-Claude Jacquet de la Guerre

Elisabeth-Claude Jacquet de la Guerre

97

Susan Erickson

Maria Margherita Grimani (fl. ca. 1713–1718)

BARBARA GARVEY JACKSON

Seven women are known to have composed oratorios and other dramatic works that were performed in northern Italy or Vienna between 1670 and 1724. Among the works performed at court in Vienna were two oratorios and a dramatic work (which may have been staged) by Maria Margherita Grimani.

Nothing is known of Grimani's life except the dates of these performances. It is not even certain that she was ever resident in Vienna; the manuscript score of *Pallade e Marte* is inscribed "April 5, 1713, Bologna." An important family of Venetian aristocrats bears the name Grimani, but it has not been possible to establish a definite relationship between them and the composer. It may be significant that one Pietro Grimani was the ambassador negotiating an alliance with Emperor Charles VI in 1713, the very year the composer's works began appearing in Vienna. We do not even know whether Maria Margherita was a nun or whether Grimani was her maiden name or her married name.

Pallade e Marte, an "opus dramaticum" for two singers, was performed on the name day of the emperor in Vienna on 6 November 1713. Later the same year Grimani's oratorio *La Visitazione di Santa Elisabetta* appeared, and two years later her *La Decollazione di S. Giovanni Battista* was heard. *La Visitazione* was revived in 1718, the last time her name appears in Vienna.

All Grimani's surviving works are for soloists and orchestra. Like other oratorios and similar works of the early eighteenth century, they used da capo arias, often followed (if they are continuo arias) by short orchestral ritornelli as interludes. The recitatives are all secco, that is, with only a figured bass accompaniment. Several arias are performed with concertante instruments, and some are accompanied by string orchestra. The works open with sinfonie in several movements, as in the score presented here. An ensemble of soloists often appears at the conclusion; typically, there is a vocal duet at the end of *Pallade e Marte*.

Pallade e Marte, from which the following three-movement Sinfonia is drawn, is the shortest of Grimani's works (sixty-five pages of manuscript). It is set for soprano and alto, with solo cello, oboe, theorbo, strings, and continuo, the same scoring (except for the theorbo) as in *La decollazione*. The vocal soloists sing alternate arias: Pallas is accompanied by the strings, and Marte responds along with cello obbligato, theorbo, and continuo. Pallas then answers with strings, a continuo aria with orchestral ritornello for Mars follows, Pallade sings with oboe obbligato, and then comes the closing duet. The aria types are typical of the Italian and Viennese oratorios of the period, as cultivated by

Alessandro Scarlatti and others, and they are similar to those used by the other contemporary women composers whose music survives.

The movements of the opening sinfonia are appropriately short for a work of this scale. The listener will notice the three-movement sinfonia form of fast–slow–fast, which will be followed by later compatriots such as Giovanni Battista Sammartini, in his works from about 1720–1740. As Neal Zaslaw (1989) observes, the sinfonia of this type might also occur in church, its movements being played between movements of the Proper. Like Sammartini, Grimani retains the string orchestra of the Baroque ripieno concerto, but she also prefers the tuneful nature of the early Classic.

Further Reading

Eitner, Robert. "Grimani, Maria Margherita." *Quellen-Lexikon* IV (1959): 378–79.
Klein, Rudolph. "Grimani, Maria Margherita." *Die Musik in Geschichte und Gegenwart* V (1994): 922–23.
New Grove Dictionary of Music and Musicians. 2nd ed. S.v. "Grimani, Maria Margherita."
Zaslaw, Neil. *The Classical Era.* London: Macmillan, 1989.

Recording

Women's Orchestral Works. The New England Women's Symphony.
Sinfonie [sic] (1713) by Maria Grimani. Concertmaster, Jean Lamon. Galaxia Women's Enterprises, 1980. The jacket notes incorrectly state that the longer work which the Sinfonia introduced has been lost and that no figured bass is indicated.

Sinfonia
from *Pallade e Marte*

Maria Margherita Grimani

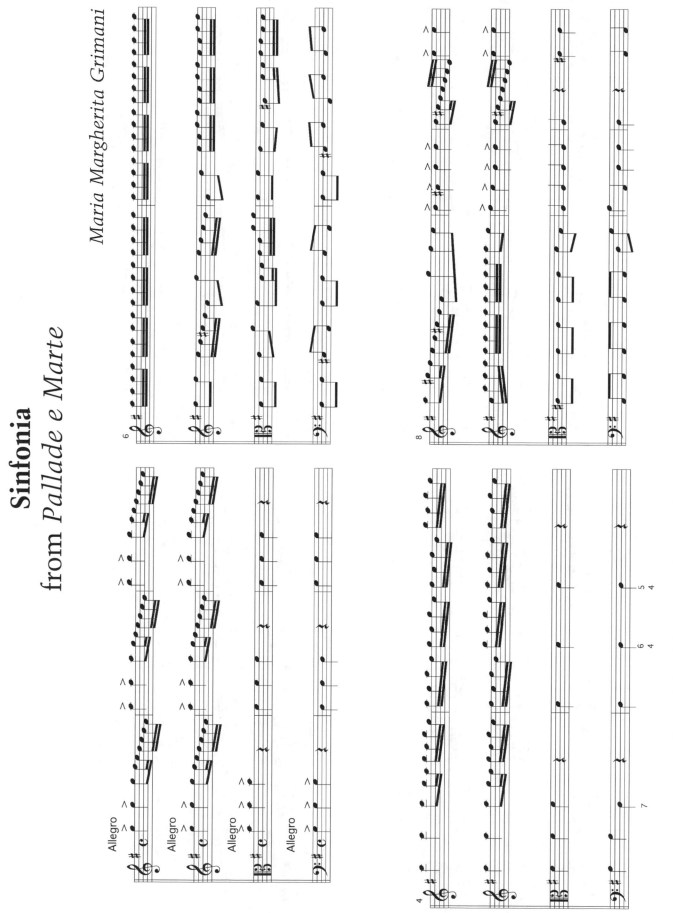

By permission of the Oesterreische Nationalbibliothek, Vienna. First modern edition for this anthology.

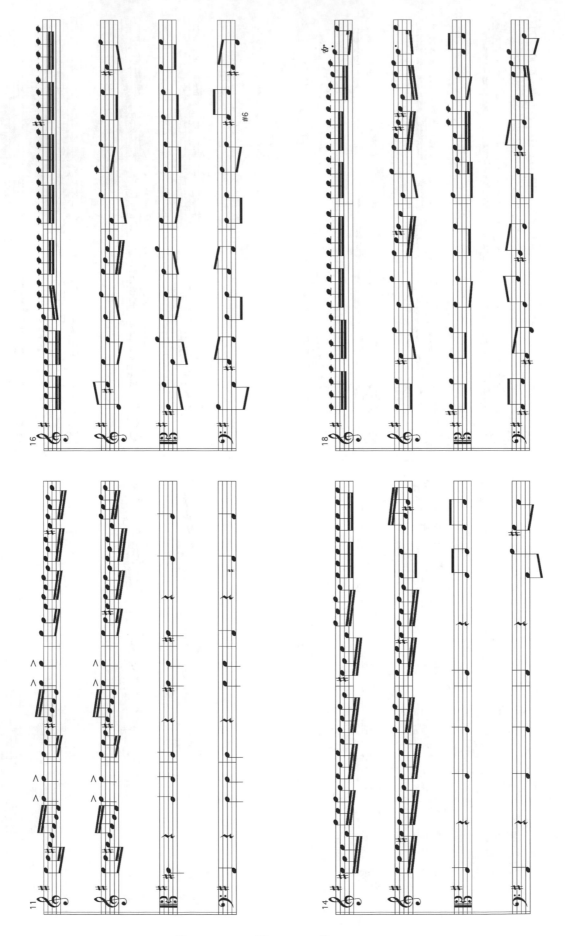

BARBARA GARVEY JACKSON

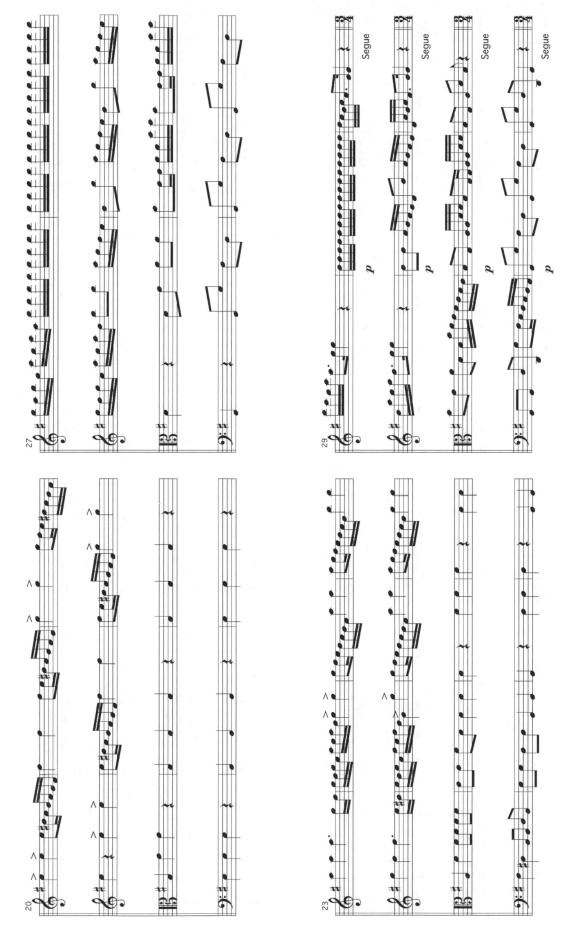

Maria Margherita Grimani

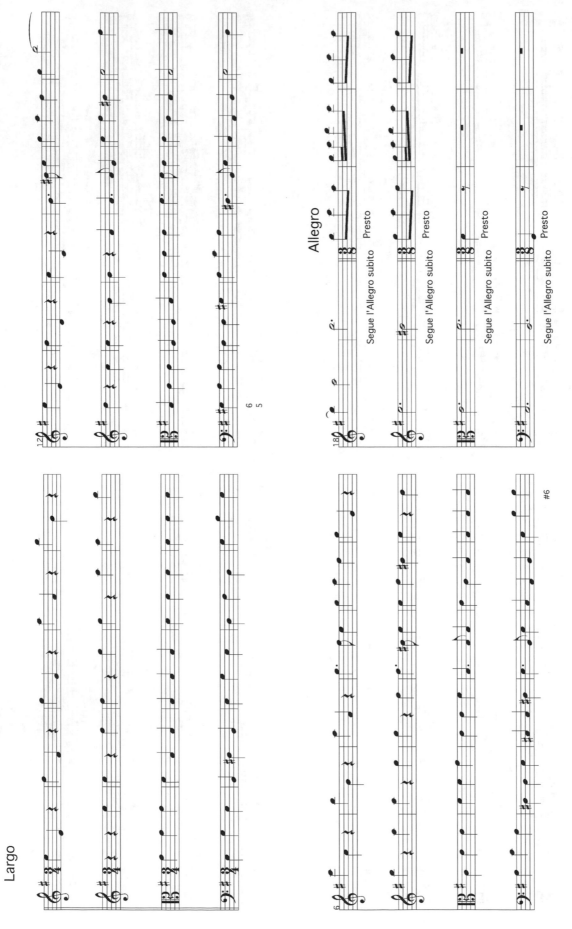

BARBARA GARVEY JACKSON

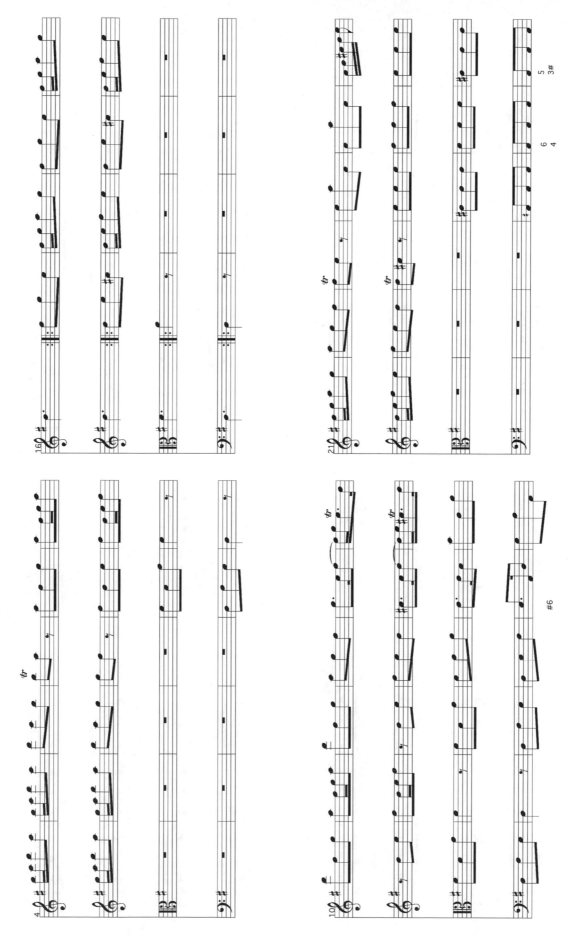

Maria Margherita Grimani

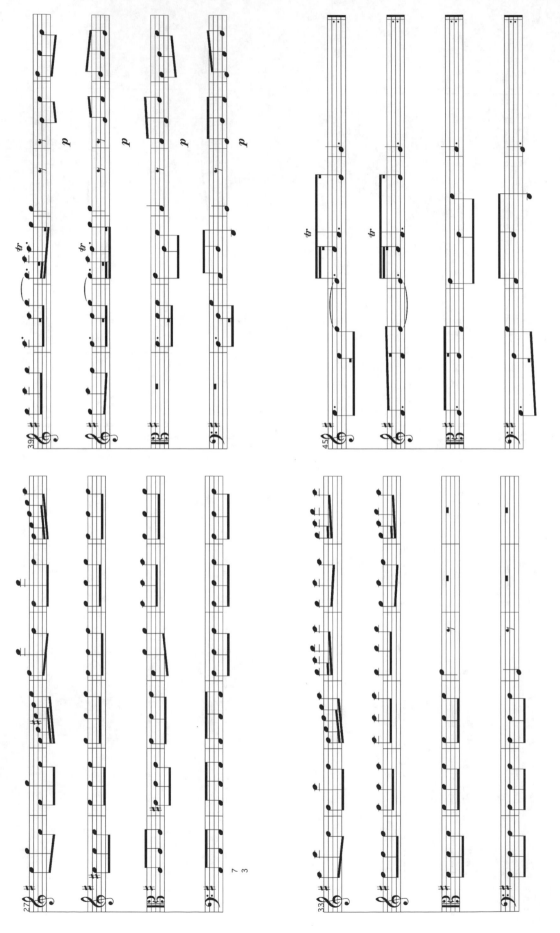

BARBARA GARVEY JACKSON

Anna Amalie, Princess of Prussia (1723–1787)

JILL MUNROE FANKHAUSER

Anna Amalie was born 9 November 1723, the twelfth child and sixth daughter of the soldier-king Frederick Wilhelm I and Queen Sophie Dorothea, his first cousin. There had been fourteen births, but the first two children died in infancy, making their third child, Frederick, heir to the throne. Anna Amalie was born during a highly dynamic period of Prussian history. The reigns of Anna Amalie's father and brother transformed Prussia from a relatively inconspicuous eastern European country into a highly militarized bureaucracy that took its place among the great western European countries. A century later, by 1871, Prussian organization made possible the unification of Germany, the most powerful industrial state in Europe. The priorities of Frederick Wilhelm I became the defining characteristics of "Prussianism." He was an absolutist who held the idea of devoted service to the state supreme over individual happiness, and he centralized governmental administration in order to focus the country's resources on the military, which was inordinately large (eighty thousand men, or 4 percent of the population). Through numerous wars his son Frederick II later expanded Prussian territories, earning the title "Frederick the Great."

In education Frederick Wilhelm I began reforms that, in the nineteenth century, made Prussia the outstanding education model for other European countries as well as for the United States. The ostensible goal was mass literacy, but its emphasis was on lay Bible reading and a rigid control of the most private chambers of the individual's heart and soul. This spirit of Pietistic, absolutist, and militaristic control manifested itself nowhere more destructively than in the relationship between Frederick Wilhelm I and his children.

Royal children at this time were generally taught by governesses and tutors, but Frederick Wilhelm forbade his children to study Latin, literature, or the arts. He put little Frederick in uniform at the age of five. He ordered his family as well as the nation to suffer a Spartan existence. The royal children were forbidden not only intellectual and artistic pursuits, but also the physical comforts, entertainments, and pleasures enjoyed at the other royal courts of Europe. They often left the table hungry or were forced to eat food that did not agree with them, so fanatical was this king in his aim to sacrifice everything to the military. Prince Frederick's liberal education was nurtured by his tutor only in secret. He met with his musicians on hunting trips and heard concerts in the forest or in a cave.

There may have been many reasons that led Frederick Wilhelm to make life unbearable for his family. He may have suffered from gout; he may have suffered repeated agony owing to the disease now known as porphyria, the hereditary condition that afflicted King George III; he may have drunk too much in an attempt to numb his pain.

But whatever the reasons, he flew into rages that severely disrupted family life with their excessive violence and cruelty. He frequently used his cane on those who annoyed him, and no one annoyed him as much as the sensitive Crown Prince Frederick, whose personality was so different from his own.

While Queen Sophie Dorothea was in a position to mediate, reconcile, and heal differences between the father and his children, she did not do so. In fact, her behavior may have sown the seeds of discord and widened the rift. At times she encouraged the children to act in secret against their father's orders, but at other times she would report their transgressions to him, which further inflamed his anger and increased the abuse he heaped upon them. For comfort young Frederick ran not to his mother but to his older sister Wilhelmina, with whom he had already formed a defensive alliance by the time Anna Amalie came into the world.

Anna Amalie was only six years old when, in 1730, her brother attempted to flee from the abject misery of his daily life. He planned to escape from Prussia with a close friend who was probably his lover, Lieutenant Hans Hermann von Katte, but the king found out about the plan. Frederick Wilhelm was so incensed that he nearly put his own son to death, but instead imprisoned him for desertion of the army and had Katte beheaded in the courtyard below his son's cell. No one was spared the father's severity. In one of his rages he dragged Anna Amalie across the room by her hair. Writers such as Voltaire and Macaulay have remarked upon his cruelty. Fear and chaos reigned in the household, augmented by incessant crass political and sexual intrigues.

At first, when it was noticed that young Frederick, Wilhelmine, and Anna Amalie showed exceptional talent and interest in music, they were given instruction in harpsichord, flute, and violin. Anna Amalie probably had her first music lessons from her brother. But by 1730 their father refused to allow them to study music.

In 1740 the old king died, and Crown Prince Frederick ascended the throne. From this time on, Frederick made music abundantly available at court. Anna Amalie could now openly and formally study music. She took lessons with Gottlieb Hayne, the cathedral organist; she heard the Italian operas of Johann Adolf Hasse and Karl Heinrich Graun; she was surrounded by many other composers and musicians, including Johann Gottlieb Graun, Franz Benda, Johann Friedrich Agricola, the theorists Friedrich Wilhelm Marpurg and Johann Philipp Kirnberger, Carl Philipp Emanuel Bach, and Johann Joachim Quantz. It was Quantz the flautist who at first taught Frederick to play flute, and later became the king's most highly paid musician. Anna Amalie took a special interest in J. G. Graun, a violinist in Frederick's orchestra. She neatly copied out his compositions, especially his symphonies, many of which show the newly developing sonata form. Musicians and musicologists have these pieces available because of her work.

As an enlightened despot, Frederick II numbered Voltaire among his friends. He spoke French, and he filled his court with music. He extended religious toleration to include all Christian sects. However, he was also his father's son and a Prussian soldier. When Anna Amalie fell in love with Friedrich, Freiherr von der Trenck, a soldier from a military family, her brother found the liaison unacceptable. He had Trenck arrested and put in prison for ten years. Frederick may have regretted this act later, for he seems to have been uncomfortable in his sister's company, but at least he did not force her into an unwanted marriage, much as he had been forced. Instead, she held the office of Abbess of Quedlinburg, although she was able to live in her own house in Berlin.

Frederick also ruled musical life with an iron hand, controlling all aspects of musical activity and limiting it strictly either to the operas of Hasse and K. H. Graun or to instrumental music that contained prominent parts for solo flute and that were composed either by Frederick himself or by Quantz. Frederick's preferred instrumental style was a homophonic rococo style modeled on the solo violin concerti of Vivaldi or Tartini: galant in allegros and Empfindsamer in adagios. Musical taste at court seemed to come to a standstill. The contrapuntal Baroque music of J. S. Bach reminded the atheistic Frederick too much of church. By contrast, Frederick failed to appreciate the compositions of C.P.E. Bach, perhaps the greatest musical genius at court, who incorporated something from the literary Sturm und Drang movement into his compositions. In hindsight, the music of C.P.E. Bach pointed to classicism, which Frederick deemed decadent. But Frederick's relative neglect of this great musician was at least partially overcome by Anna Amalie, who recognized his talent and appointed him her Kapellmeister von Haus aus in 1767.

During the whole of Frederick's reign, both music and music theory flourished in Berlin. There Anna Amalie held soirées attended by the artists, musicians, and intellectuals of this capital city and from all of Europe. Included may have been Marburg and Johann Friedrich Reichardt. In this way, Anna Amalie furthered the musical and cultural life of the city at a time when most concert music was heard in the salons of private homes. Harpsichord and organ were fashionable as home keyboard instruments in these years during the early development of the piano, and at the age of thirty-five Anna Amalie had an organ built in her home. She began the serious and systematic study of composition and counterpoint with Kirnberger, a student of J. S. Bach, and she retained him as her court musician for twenty-five years until his death in 1783. Kirnberger used portions of two of her compositions, including her oratorio *Der Tod Jesu*, as models of counterpoint in his *Kunst des reines Satzes* (1779); the composer J. G. Naumann praised her work. Music was the greatest joy of Anna Amalie, and she spent her entire day composing and practicing in order to be able to express, as she says in her letters, the tenderest and noblest passions of the soul.

Anna Amalie collected music and left to posterity a library of enormous value, particularly rich in eighteenth-century music, above all that of J. S. Bach. It contains 680 items and is housed under its own name, the Amalienbibliothek, in Berlin. Modern musicologists will appreciate that this collection was compiled by a broad-minded woman in an environment that judged Bach's style to be outdated.

Anna Amalie's compositions include trios, marches, chorales, cantatas, arias, songs, fugues, several exercises in counterpoint, and the piece presented here: the Adagio first movement of her Sonata in F for Flute and Basso Continuo. Frederick's (and Quantz's) sonatas also followed the scheme Adagio–Allegro–Presto. Quantz had devoted a chapter to the art of playing an adagio in his celebrated method book on playing the flute, and many, including Charles Burney and the historian Carlyle, praised the king's sensitive performances of adagios.

In this selection, an elegant and graceful melody for flute rests on its harmonic pedestal. The first two phrases are four measures each in length, but subsequent phrase lengths later vary seductively. The opening motive, a rising stepwise passage, full of hope and promise, descends in measure three in coquettish syncopation. The second theme (m. 23) contains triplets, lending the piece a pleasing rhythmic variety. Several features of this piece are suggestive of sonata form: of the three iterations of the first theme, for example, the middle one (m. 33) is in the dominant. The second theme appears originally in the dominant, and both themes recapitulate in the tonic. The most poignant moment in the harmony occurs in measure 21, where Anna Amalie uses a chain of secondary dominants to arrive at the dominant, surprising us on the way with a deceptive resolution to the V7/ii. The closing sequential passages and the echo in measure 14 seem especially playful and idiomatic to the flute.

Further Reading

Goldsmith, Margaret. *Frederick the Great*. New York: Albert and Charles Boni, 1930.
Helm, E. E. *Music at the Court of Frederick the Great*. Norman: University of Oklahoma Press, 1960.

Adagio
from Sonata for Flute and Continuo in F

Anna Amalia von Preußen

Anna Amalie, Princess of Prussia

JILL MUNROE FANKHAUSER

Marianna von Martines
(1744–1812)

KARIN PENDLE

Marianna von Martines, Austria's most prolific woman composer of the last half of the eighteenth century, was born into an upper-class family headed by a father who served as maestro di camera (master of ceremonies) at the papal embassy in Vienna. Home to Mozart, Haydn, and Beethoven, Vienna also saw premieres of operas by Salieri and Cimarosa, Singspiels by Andre and Dittersdorf, chamber music by Boccherini, and more. Thus Martines was able to study and socialize with her era's most illustrious musical figures without ever having to leave home. Although one surely cannot speak of gender equality where music was concerned, Martines's talent, her skills, and her class (she was independently wealthy and a member of the minor nobility) contributed to her status as a member of Vienna's elite, a prominent hostess and guest in the salons of her day, and a respected performer and composer. Although few of her fabled two hundred compositions were published during her lifetime, the nearly seventy extant works reveal an ambitious and well-tutored hand. From large-scale symphonic Masses and multi-movement motets for chorus and orchestra to single arias on Italian texts, Martines produced music of high quality that was admired not only by her Viennese contemporaries but also by prominent figures in Italy and Germany.

Marianna von Martines (christened Anna Katharina) caught the attention of Pietro Metastasio, Vienna's court poet and a resident in her family home, who observed her musical talents when she was still a child. It was Metastasio who arranged for singing lessons from opera composer Niccolo Porpora and harpsichord lessons from the young Joseph Haydn, another tenant in the Martines home. Then came studies of composition with court composer Giuseppe Bonno and, informally, with Johann Adolph Hasse. By the time she was in her twenties she was writing grand sacred works for chorus and orchestra and her three keyboard sonatas. A list of her works, along with locations of their manuscripts, is available in Irving Godt's article "Marianna in Italy."

Martines wrote her masterpiece, the motet *Dixit Dominus*, in 1774 as a response to the Accademia Filarmonica of Bologna, which the year before had elected her to membership, the first woman to be so honored. In April of 1773 Martines herself had made bold to address Bologna's distinguished teacher and writer on music, Padre Giovanni Battista Martini, requesting that she be considered for membership in the Accademia. Although she forwarded the score, a large work for chorus, soloists, and full orchestra, to Padre Martini within a year of her election, there is no record that the work was ever performed. A modern score is available from A-R Editions, part of its series Recent Researches in the Music of the Classical Era.

Meanwhile, in Vienna Martines had become a prominent figure in the city's musical life. Each Saturday she opened her home to guests who came to listen to and perform music, some of it undoubtedly her own. Haydn and Mozart were at times among the guests, the latter perhaps to perform his four-hand piano sonatas with his hostess. Clearly Martines had acquired an excellent reputation as a keyboard artist, first on harpsichord, later on piano. Two of her sonatas had been published in 1765 in an anthology of harpsichord music; later, fitted out with dynamic markings and shadings specific to the piano, they reappeared in Emil Pauer's collection *Alte Meister: Sammlung wertvoller Klavierstucke des 17. und 18. Jahrhundert*.

The Sonata in A, a three-movement work, is written with a sure hand in a style that reveals Martines's own facility at the keyboard and the influence of her teacher, Haydn. The first movement, a sprightly Allegro, is reproduced here. It opens with distinctive motifs that are stated, expanded upon, then recalled in a different order and a more concise manner. The dotted rhythm that marks the initial A major theme soon gives way to triplet figuration as the music moves to the dominant. Here several identifiable ideas emerge (see mm. 4, 6, 8, and 12). Although each idea has a different shape, it resembles the others in character; the motifs are joined together by recurring scalar fragments that lend a feeling of energy and forward motion to this section of the work. The style is that of the rococo, with its homophonic texture and its agréments, a style already dated by the 1760s. The second half of the movement presents the themes of the first in new combinations, in a working-out that is largely sequential. At measure 25, material from measures 6–8 returns, this time in the tonic. A restatement of the movement's opening theme (m. 29) is followed by ideas from measures 9–13, but in A rather than E. Although the movement shows traces of sonata-allegro principles, it lacks clarity of definition. The second movement, a rather melancholy Adagio in A minor, features a melody that is clearly in the Empfindsamer Stil of the mid-eighteenth century. An appealing minuet in A major concludes the sonata.

Charles Burney, who met Martines in 1772, speaks of her as a respected composer and performer. Yet the style in which she still composed and performed, as represented by this sonata along with her works for solo voice, was already dated. Metastasio's remark to Burney is often quoted: "E perduta la scuola; non si trova questa maniera di cantar; domanda troppo pena per i professori d'oggi di" (The training is lost; one no longer finds this sort of singing; it demands too much trouble for today's teachers).

Martines wrote what is apparently her final composition, a solo cantata "Orgoglioso fumicello," in 1796. A decade later she established a singing school in her home that trained singers of professional caliber. She continued to be part of Viennese musical life, and last appeared in public on 27 March 1808 at a performance of Haydn's *Creation*. She died on 13 December 1812. In later years her reputation would be sullied by the strong words of Caroline Pichler, whose salon had competed with that of Martines, and whose memoirs (written in 1844) cast Martines's abilities as a composer in a critical light. However, the modern editions of Martines's music that have appeared in recent years allow us to see for ourselves the beauty of her music and the skill that she brought to each work.

Further Reading

Burney, Charles. *The Present State of Music in Germany, the Netherlands and United Provinces.* 2 vols. 2nd ed., corrected. London: T. Becket, J. Robson, and G. Robinson, 1775.

KARIN PENDLE

Fremar, Karen Lynn. "The Life and Selected Works of Marianna Martines (1744–1812)." Ph.D. diss., University of Kansas, 1983.

Geiringer, Karl. *Haydn: A Creative Life in Music.* Rev. ed. Berkeley and Los Angeles: University of California Press, 1968.

Godt, Irving. "Marianna in Italy." *Journal of Musicology* 13 (1995): 538–61.

———. "Marianna in Vienna: A Martines Chronology." *Journal of Musicology* 16 (1998): 136–58.

———. "Marianna Martinez, Accademia Filarmonica Onorata." *Studi e materiali per la storia dell'Accademia Filarmonica 1773* 6 (1994): 3–9, i–xii.

———. "Mozart's Real Joke." *College Music Symposium* 26 (1986): 27–41.

Jackson, Barbara Garvey. "Musical Women of the Seventeenth and Eighteenth Centuries." In *Women and Music,* 2nd ed., ed. Karin Pendle, 97–144. Bloomington: Indiana University Press, 2001.

———. *"Say Can You Deny Me": A Guide to Surviving Music by Women from the Sixteenth through the Eighteenth Centuries.* Fayetteville: University of Arkansas Press, 1994.

Newman, William S. *The Sonata in the Classical Era.* 3rd ed. Chapel Hill: University of North Carolina Press, 1983.

Scholes, Percy, ed. *An Eighteenth-Century Musical Tour in Central Europe and the Netherlands: Dr. Burney's Musical Tours in Europe.* Vol. 2. London: Oxford University Press, 1959.

Modern Editions

"Alfin fra le tempeste," aria for soprano and orchestra. Ed. Shirley Bean. In *Women Composers: Music through the Ages,* ed. Sylvia Glickman and Martha Furman Schleifer, vol. 4: *Composers Born 1700–1799, Vocal Music,* 69–92. New York: G. K. Hall/Gale Group, 1998.

Dixit Dominus for SSATB choir, soloists, and orchestra. Ed. Irving Godt. In *Recent Researches in Music of the Classical Era,* vol. 48. Madison, Wis.: A-R Editions, 1997.

In Exitu Israel de Agypto for choir, soloists, and orchestra. Ed. Conrad Misch. Kassel: Furore, 1993.

Concerto for Piano and Orchestra in A Major. Ed. Rosario Marciano. Kassel: Furore, 1977.

Mass No. 1 in C Major for SATB choir, soloists, and orchestra. Ed. Shirley Bean. Fayetteville, Ark.: ClarNan Editions, 1998.

Miserere for SATB choir and organ continuo. Ed. Shirley Bean. Fayetteville, Ark.: ClarNan Editions, 1996.

Quarta Messa for choir, soloists, and orchestra. Ed. Conrad Misch. Kassel: Furore, 1993.

Sinfonia in C Major for orchestra. Ed. Shirley Bean and Karen Fremar. Fayetteville, Ark.: ClarNan Editions, 2002.

Three Sonatas for Keyboard. Ed. Shirley Bean. Bryn Mawr, Pa.: Hildegard 1994.

Two Arias for Soprano ("Se per tutti ordisce amore" and "Per pieta bell' idol mio"). Ed. Shirley Bean. Fayetteville, Ark.: ClarNan Editions, 1995.

Recordings

Composition: Piano Music for Women Composers. La Ma De Guido 37. ASIN: B00000FYNY.

Eighteenth-Century Women Composers. Barbara Harbach, harpsichord. Gasparo Records 272. ASIN: B000025YJJ.

Haydn, Martinez and Auenbrugger. Monica Jakuc, piano. Titanic 214. ASIN: B000000117X.

Women Composers & the Men i[n] Their Lives. Leanne Rees, piano. Fleur de son 57939. ASIN: B0000479BH.

Allegro
from Sonata in A for piano

Marianna von Martines

Reprinted from *Alte Meister, Sammlung wertvoller Klavierstücke des 17. und 18. Jahrhunderts*, No. 60. Ed. E. Pauer. Leipzig: Breitkopf und Härtel [1868–85]. Public domain.

Karin Pendle

Karin Pendle

Maria Theresia von Paradis (1759–1824)

HIDEMI MATSUSHITA

The Vienna-born pianist and composer Maria Theresia von Paradis was the only child of Josef von Paradis and his wife, Rosalia Maria Levassori della Motta. Her father was the Imperial Secretary and Court Councilor to Empress Maria Theresia, after whom she was named. However, the empress did not serve as her godmother, as was widely believed. At the age of three, she lost her eyesight, possibly because of an ocular disorder. Despite treatment from some of Vienna's leading physicians, including Dr. Anton Mesmer, her blindness became permanent. Her affliction, however, did not affect her sense of hearing, memory, or musical abilities, and by the age of eleven she sang Pergolesi's *Stabat Mater* and accompanied herself on the organ. This impressed the empress, who granted her a stipend for a broad music and general education. She studied piano with Leopold Kozeluch, singing with Vincenzo Righini, theory with Karl Frieberth, singing and composition with Antonio Salieri, and, later, composition with Georg Vogler. Several leading composers of the time began composing works specifically for her. Salieri dedicated his only organ concerto to the fourteen-year-old Paradis in 1773. It is believed that Mozart's Piano Concerto in B flat Major, K. 456 (1784), and Haydn's Clavier Concerto in G major, H. XVIII:4 (1781?), were written for her as well.

At sixteen, Paradis performed as a pianist and singer in various Viennese salons, palaces, and concert halls. An idolizing public often called her "The Blind Enchantress." In 1783, she undertook a three-year concert tour of Europe, accompanied by her mother and a family friend, the librettist and inventor Johann Riedinger. Their stops included Linz, Salzburg, Frankfurt-am-Main, Bonn, Stuttgart, Mannheim, Munich, Bern, Geneva, Lyon, Paris, London, Brussels, Amsterdam, Hamburg, Berlin, and Prague. During this extended tour, Paradis started composing. Riedinger invented a composition board that enabled her to write without paper. Her most significant composition during the tour was the *Zwölf Lieder auf ihrer Reise in Musik gesetzt* (Twelve Songs Set to Music upon Her Journey); this set of Lieder was published by Breitkopf in Leipzig at the end of her tour in 1786. Of the twelve songs, the eighth, "Morgenlied eines armen Mannes" (Morning Song of a Poor Man), has become her best-known lied. The text of "Morgenlied" and two other lieder in this set are by Johann Timotheus Hermes, from his *Sophiens Reise von memel nach Sachsen* (1769–1773). Sturm und Drang characteristics, popular during this period, are found in "Morgenlied"; they include the emotional text (translated below), use of a flat minor key (G minor), quick changes to the relative major and vice versa (mm. 10–11, 15–16), contrasts of forte and piano (mm. 1, 18–19, 21–22, 23–24), and restless syncopated sixteenth-note figures in the piano part (mm. 4–9, 19–24). The song is set strophically, in a three-part form consisting of a contrasting period, repeated phrase, and two one-part phrases, the latter with an extension and coda.

After returning to Vienna from her tour, Paradis concentrated on composing large-scale works from 1786 to 1797. Compositions during this period include two piano concertos, three cantatas, three operas, and a setting of Gottfried Bürger's lengthy ballad *Lenore.* Both piano concertos are now lost. Out of the three cantatas (one in honor of the death of Emperor Leopold II, one celebrating the recovery of her father from illness), her only extant cantata is *Deutsches Monument Ludwigs des Unglücken* (1792), a mourning cantata in memory of King Louis XVI of France.

Paradis, despite her blindness, composed at least three and possibly five operas. Her first, *Ariadne und Bacchus,* with libretto by Riedinger, was performed in 1791–1792 at the Laxenburg Schlosstheater in Vienna. Her second opera, a Singspiel called *Der Schul-kandidat,* premiered at the Marinelli Theater in Vienna in 1792. Each opera had a run of about six performances. However, her third major opera, *Rinaldo und Alcina* (1797), was even less successful; only two performances were given, both in Prague.

Because of this failure, Paradis composed less after 1800 and instead put her effort into music education, especially for young girls. In 1808 she started her own music school, where she taught until her death in 1824. Her students began giving regular Sunday concerts in November 1809 that drew praise from the public and critics alike. Paradis also contributed to the education of the blind and assisted Valentin Haüy, a teacher and humanitarian, in the formation of the first major school for the blind in Paris.

Although it is not apparent in "Morgenlied," Paradis experimented with modulations to remotely related keys, reflecting the teachings of Abbé Georg Vogler, with whom she studied in Paris in 1784. For example, in her later Piano Fantaisie of 1808 (dedicated to Vogler), Paradis chooses G major, F-sharp minor, G major, C minor, B-flat major, and G major as the keys for the main sections, and within each section are unusual modulations, such as G major to A-flat minor and back to G major in the final measures.

Because only a few of her works have survived, it is difficult to judge Paradis as a major composer. The long-attributed "Sicilienne" is a spurious work, probably composed by Samuel Dushkin, its purported "discoverer." Dushkin likely modeled the "Sicilienne" after the second movement of Carl Maria von Weber's *Sonata Progressive* No. 1, Op. 10.

However, Paradis's accomplishment should not be judged solely on her existing compositions, but on her life's achievements. First, her struggle to overcome blindness, surviving disastrous treatments and triumphing over her condition by means of education, is an inspiration to handicapped and disabled people. Second, her ability to learn inspired the founding of a school for the blind. Third, inventors created original devices (such as Riedinger's compositional board) specifically for Pardis's use that also have benefited others. Finally, she opened and operated her own music school, geared especially toward young women. Paradis undoubtedly inspired other female musicians to survive as virtuosa musicians in the otherwise male-dominated world of concert music of the early nineteenth century. Thus, Maria Theresia von Paradis was more than a blind female composer; she was also a humanitarian who made significant contributions to the education of the blind and gave encouragement to other women to become musicians.

Text Translation

Art thou waking me for pain anew,
Day, whom my longing called,
When in my small room slept my wife,
And my baby, quietly?
Touch only me, you sorrows new,
Please protect my woman's heart,
Wake her late thou misery morn,
Oh! Thy recent glance was pain.

Just gently rest; the pain of life,
Infant, ne'er will touch you too, too late;
You will feel how fruitlessly
My pain for thee doth plea.
Soon shall attack thy naked limbs
Each raging storm so gruesomely,
Soon hunger will again thee plague,
Which my wife can never still.

Slumber, girlfriend of my youth,
Feel not the need that frightens me,
She is here 'cause diligence and virtue
No more protect me as they did;
I cannot save my child and wife,
God of grace that thou canst do,
Give them happiness and draw the chains,
Which press me, ever firmer 'round.

Quietly I want to tread
On rugged paths of accustomed pain,
And also now for bread and blessings
I plead with thee for child and wife.
They awaken—oh your teasing,
Infant mine, it stabs me through,
These, oh so deeply driving pains
Truly, Lord, they pain thee too.

Modern Edition

Paradis, Maria Theresia von. *Zwölf Lieder auf ihrer Reise in Musik gesetzt.* Fayetteville, Ark.: ClarNan Editions.

Morgenlied eines armen Mannes

Johann Timotheus Hermes

M. Th. Paradis.

Reprinted from *Denkmäler der Tonkunst in Oesterreich* 54 [1920]: 99–11. Public domain.

HIDEMI MATSUSHITA

Schonet doch des Weibes
Jedes Wetter grausam

Herz, schonet doch des Weibes Herz, Weck' sie
an, je - des Wet - ter grau - sam an, Bald quält

spät, qual-vol - ler Mor - gen, Ach ihr letz - ter Blick war
dich der Hun - ger wie - der, Den mein Weib nicht stil - len

Schmerz, ach ihr letz - ter Blick war Schmerz.
kann, den mein Weib nicht stil - len kann.

3.
Schlummre, Freundin meiner Jugend,
Fühl die Not nicht, die mich schreckt,
Sie ist da, weil Fleiß und Tugend
Mich nicht mehr wie vormals deckt;
Ich kann Kind und Weib nicht retten,
|:Gott der Gnaden, das kannst du,:|
Mach sie glücklich, und zieh Ketten,
|:Die mich drücken, fester zu.:|

4.
Ich will still auf rauhen Wegen
Des gewohnten Jammers gehn
Und auch heut' um Brot und Segen
Für mein Kind und Weib dich flehn.
Sie erwachen— o dein Scherzen
|:Säugling, wie durchdringt es mich,:|
Diese allertiefsten Schmerzen
|:Wahrlich, Herr, sie jammern dich.:|

Maria Theresia von Paradis   125

Maria Agata Szymanowska
(1789–1831)

NANCY FIERRO

Born in Warsaw, Poland, on 14 December 1789, Maria Agata Szymanowska was destined to become the first Polish pianist of stature. Her playing won her the title "Royal Pianist of the Court of Russia" and the admiration of Field, Hummel, and Schumann. Her many piano compositions, published during her lifetime, presage the Romantic style and are significant in the history of Polish music before Chopin.

The daughter of Barbara Lanckoronska and the middle-class merchant Franciszek Wolowski, Maria exhibited a precocious talent at an early age. With scant keyboard instruction, the young girl would seat herself at the spinet and entertain family guests, playing improvisations on her own themes or accompanying her mother's singing. This early hearing of singing may explain her lifelong desire to imitate the flowing legato of the human voice on the keyboard. Between 1798 and 1804, she studied piano with Antoni Lisowski and Tomasz Gremm. Josef Elsner, Franciszek Lessel, John Field, and Karol Kurpinski may occasionally have advised her. Otherwise, it appears that Maria was largely self-taught.

In 1810, the young pianist made her debut in Warsaw and then traveled to France for her first Paris concert. In the summer of that year she married a wealthy landowner, Josef Szymanowski (no known relationship to composer Karol Szymanowski). They had three children, Helena, Celina (who later married the poet Adam Mickiewicz), and Romuald, who died in his youth. By 1815, Szymanowska was in great demand for public concerts, but her frequent appearances were offensive to her husband as he sought to protect his social status. Josef's continued disapproval caused Maria to separate from him in 1820 and take her three children with her. She supported herself through her concerts and by giving lectures on piano technique. As a performer and published composer, she began regular appearances throughout eastern and western Europe, returning intermittently to her beloved Warsaw. After playing in St. Petersburg in 1822, she was nominated "First Pianist to the Russian Court," an appointment confirmed with gifts of pearls, gold, diamonds, and sapphires.

The years 1823–1827 were a time of enormous success for her. Her performances in western Europe commanded huge audiences and high ticket prices. Reviews praised her masterful technique, keen musicality, wide dynamic span, and extraordinary cantabile style. She was called "the Queen of Tones" (Mickiewicz) and "the feminine Field" (Schumann). Not all critics agreed. Some criticized her extensive use of rubato. Her competitor, the young Felix Mendelssohn, thought that her success was simply due to her personal charm. Among her admirers was the seventy-four-year-old Goethe, who fell in love with her and later alluded to her in his "Aussöhnung" verses.

Szymanowska made an impact not only as a concert artist but as a composer. Nearly all her compositions—about 110 pieces, including 20 songs with piano accompaniment, chamber works, and a large body of piano music—found immediate publication. Breitkopf and Härtel in Leipzig and publishers in Paris, Warsaw, St. Petersburg, Moscow, Kiev, and Odessa released her works. The piano pieces, approximately 90 miniatures, include nocturnes, waltzes, polonaises, minuets, marches, mazurkas, and concert etudes. Although simple and modest in form, her works hold a significant place in the history of nineteenth-century Polish piano music. She was the first to introduce the concert etude and nocturne into Poland (*Grove*). Her etudes, *Vingt exercises et préludes* (Breitkopf and Härtel, 1820), explore new technical possibilities later developed by Chopin. The *Nocturne in B flat Major*, reproduced here, is more personal and expressive than her earlier compositions. With this work (published posthumously in 1852), Szymanowska takes a step forward in the development of the nocturne between Field and Chopin.

Szymanowska designed the *Nocturne in B flat Major* as an enlarged song form with a coda. The music opens in a pensive mood with an eight-bar vocal melody fashioned in two phrases. This basic melody returns throughout the composition in more and more embellished versions. A gentle barcarolle accompaniment supports the melodic line and provides an expressive counterfoil. Later, the left-hand figures grow to encompass more than three octaves. She contrasts the opening cantilena with two fantasy sections, one scored more dramatically in the darker parallel minor. The second section has a more nationalistic character and explores color possibilities of the mediant key. After a final return of the opening melody in octaves, Szymanowska closes with an extended coda highlighting the bell-like tones of the piano's upper register.

In 1828, Maria withdrew from the concert stage and settled into her permanent home in St. Petersburg. She turned her attention to raising her children, giving piano lessons, performing occasionally in aristocratic circles, and devoting herself to long-delayed projects. One of these activities was collecting manuscripts of her compositions and binding them into a single album. This album, now housed in the Jagiellonian Library in Krakow, was intended as a gift for her two daughters and contains locks of her hair encased in a small dome of glass attached to the cover.

Szymanowska always enjoyed wide social contacts. Her salon in St. Petersburg became a gathering place for prominent artists, musicians, poets, and friends. Good wishes, watercolor paintings, music, poems, and other memorabilia cram her autograph albums and attest to the many admirers and friends whom she met on her tours or who visited her salon. Contributors include Glinka, Pushkin, Beethoven, Cherubini, Liszt, and Clara and Robert Schumann. All regarded her as a gifted, attractive, and remarkable personality. On the afternoon of 23 July 1831, Szymanowska suddenly fell ill with cholera. She died early in the morning on 25 July and was buried in St. Petersburg.

Nocturne in B-flat

Maria Szymanowska

NANCY FIERRO

Maria Agata Szymanowska

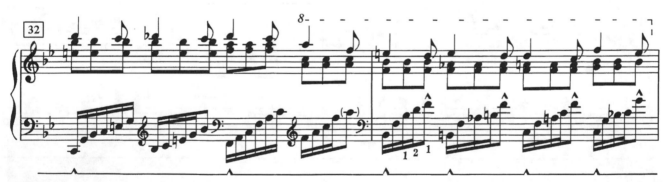

Nancy Fierro

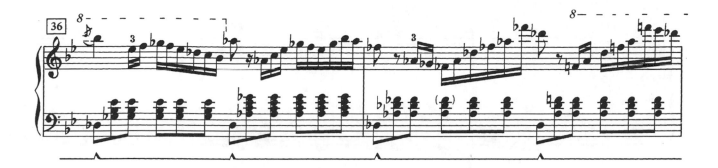

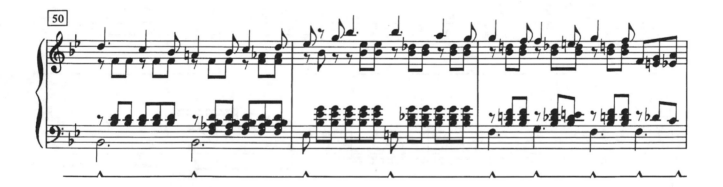

NANCY FIERRO

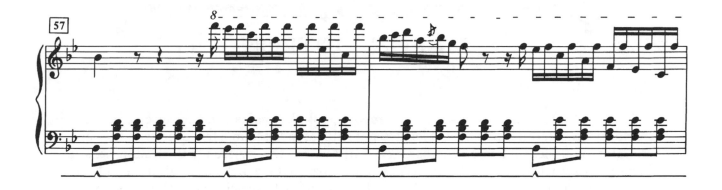

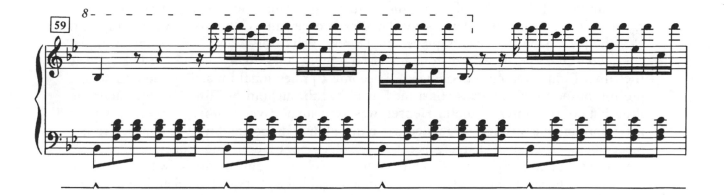

ⓒ The left hand arpeggio should be played before the beat with the right hand chord played on the beat.

Maria Agata Szymanowska

Fanny Mendelssohn Hensel (1805–1847)

MARCIA J. CITRON

Fanny Hensel was a prolific composer, a skilled pianist, and a respected leader of a flourishing Berlin salon. The elder sister of Felix Mendelssohn, Hensel grew up in a culturally sophisticated home, where from an early age she was exposed to the leading artistic and intellectual figures of the day. These formative contacts helped instill in her a keen, discriminating mind and a knowledge and love of poetry. Heinrich Heine, the author of the text of Hensel's song "Schwanenlied," was a frequent visitor to the Mendelssohn household, and Fanny may have heard some of his poems even before they were published.

Fanny and Felix shared a common music education and developed an unusually close sibling relationship. They stimulated each other musically and intellectually, and each helped shape the other's pieces-in-progress. Felix's oratorio *St. Paul*, for example, completed in 1837, benefited from his sister's input. Like many women of her class at the time, Fanny was not encouraged to become a professional musician. Nonetheless, a prolific outpouring of pieces continued unabated throughout her life. Her husband, the Prussian court painter Wilhelm Hensel, was very supportive; and her brother, on whose good opinion she strongly depended, encouraged her composing but was opposed to her pieces being published. Largely because of Felix's negative attitude, only a very small percentage of her compositions—which number well over four hundred—were published. Almost all appear within eleven opus numbers, published between 1846 and 1850. Since the 1980s, many more works have been published, and many have been recorded.

Hensel composed almost exclusively in the genres associated with women and their domestic environment: lieder and piano pieces. Many of these pieces, as well as her forays into orchestral and choral works, were presented at her lively Sunday musical gatherings, or Sonntagsmusiken. Hensel herself was a leading participant, playing the piano as soloist or as part of the ensemble. Except for a large charity concert in 1838, she did not perform in public, in accordance with her family's attitudes about woman's proper role. Thus her celebrated private gatherings provided her with a needed forum for her various musical activities.

Hensel's first published compositions, three lieder, appeared under her brother's authorship in his Op. 8 (1827); three more followed in his Op. 9 (1830). Unfortunately, we do not know the reason for this camouflage, although it was not an uncommon practice among women composers. The first piece issued under Hensel's own name was a lied that appeared in an anthology that appeared in 1837. With the exception of an isolated lied published two years later, it was not until the last year of Hensel's life that her pieces reached the public in printed form, and this time in a spate of seven publications rather than as isolated works. "Schwanenlied" is the first song in Op. 1, *Sechs Lieder für eine Stimme mit Begleitung des Pianoforte* (Six Songs for One Voice with Piano Accompaniment). The collection appeared in the summer of 1846 and provided Hensel with the great satisfaction of finally seeing an entire volume published under her own name.

"Schwanenlied," with a text by Heinrich Heine, resembles a lullaby. In its clear separation of melody and accompaniment, it is akin to the style of many *Songs without Words*, for piano solo, some composed by Hensel and some by Mendelssohn. Formally it is simple, like most Hensel settings, consisting of two strophes with the second slightly modified. That slight modification proves significant, however, for it fashions the climax of the song. Occurring in the middle of the second strophe, it is effected by an extension on the word "Fluthengrab" (depths of the river), a turning point for the carefree swan and the drama of the poem. The song gains much of its affective character as a lament from the interval of a descending third, which permeates the vocal line. Overall, Hensel has successfully captured the bittersweet quality of Heine's text. A brief piano postlude concludes each strophe.

Text Translation

A star falls down
From its twinkling height,
It is the star of love
That I see falling there.
So much falls from the apple tree,
From the white leaves;
The teasing breezes come
And urge on their game.

The swan sings in the pond,
And paddles up and down,
And singing more and more gently,
He disappears into the depths of the river.
It is so quiet and dark,
Scattered is leaf and blossom,
The star has flickered into dust,
The swan song has faded away.

Further Reading

Citron, Marcia J. *Letters of Fanny Hensel to Felix Mendelssohn.* Stuyvesant, N.Y.: Pendragon Press, 1987.
———. "The Lieder of Fanny Mendelssohn Hensel." *The Musical Quarterly* 69 (1983): 570–93.
Reich, Nancy. "The Power of Class: Fanny Hensel." In *Mendelssohn and His World*, ed. R. Larry Todd, 86–99. Princeton, N.J.: Princeton University Press, 1991.
Tillard, Françoise. *Fanny Mendelssohn.* Trans. Camille Naish. Portland, Ore.: Amadeus Press, 1996.

Recording

Fanny Hensel, Opus 1. Leonarda LPI 112.

Schwanenlied

Fanny Mendelssohn Hensel

Marcia J. Citron

Fanny Mendelssohn Hensel

Clara Wieck Schumann
(1819–1896)

NANCY REICH

Clara Schumann, a peer of Franz Liszt and Sigismund Thalberg on the concert stage, was an exceptionally well educated musician. As a child prodigy, she was as renowned for her compositions as for her celebrated virtuoso career. Her creative work was praised by the "new romantic" composers—Mendelssohn, Chopin, and Liszt—as well as by the man who later became her husband, Robert Schumann. Other admirers included Johann Wolfgang von Goethe, Louis Spohr, and Gasparo Spontini.

From her letters to friends, there is evidence that Clara Schumann found composition a source of great pleasure; and she declared more than once that only a composer could achieve true immortality. Yet she herself had grave doubts about her role as a composer; she was more comfortable in the world of the interpretive artist. The ambivalence she displayed was due in part to the social attitude toward women composers and was certainly influenced by her position as the wife of a creative genius.

From our vantage point, she might not rank with her husband and his friends and contemporaries Frédéric Chopin and Felix Mendelssohn, but their esteem of her work was sincere. Both before and after their marriage, Robert Schumann encouraged and supported his wife's work: theirs was a true musical union. She and Robert exchanged musical ideas; they studied scores of Bach, Beethoven, Haydn, and Mozart together; he urged her to compose, to preserve her autographs, and to catalogue her work; he wrote to publishers on her behalf and published two of her works as supplements to *Neue Zeitschrift fur Müsik*, the music journal he edited. After his death in 1856, she stopped composing and devoted herself to performing piano works she respected; her time was also occupied with the supervision of her seven children, teaching, and editing the music of Robert Schumann.

Until her marriage, just before her twenty-first birthday, the young pianist wrote only works for performance at her own concerts, events that were carefully planned by Friedrich Wieck, her teacher-manager-father. Almost all of the 182 programs she gave between 1828 and 1840 boasted at least one work by the young Clara Wieck. But beginning in 1839, the year before Robert Schumann's "song year," she and her husband-to-be began reading poetry, with an eye to eventual musical settings. Her first published musical works after she married Schumann were three songs in a collection entitled *Zwölf Lieder aus F. Rückert's Liebesfrühling für Gesang und Pianoforte von Robert und Clara Schuman*, brought out in Leipzig by Breitkopf and Härtel in 1841. (The collection is often referred to as Op. 37/12—Robert's Op. 37 and Clara's Op. 12.) There was no indication in the first edition as to which songs were Clara's, but Robert, who enjoyed the confusion of the critics, noted on the flyleaf of his copy that numbers 2, 4, and 11 were hers. Autographs in Zwickau and Berlin attest to her authorship.

Clara Schumann's first song in the collection, "Er ist gekommen in Sturm und Regen," is an impassioned setting of Rückert's poem about a woman in love. Most striking is the virtuoso piano accompaniment that sweeps upward, emulating both the storm and the rain and the surging agitation of the woman. Calm is finally restored in the third verse as the singer, moving stepwise, is reassured about the permanence of their love. The postlude reminds us again, however, of the turbulence that love may bring before it fades quietly away. In her Scherzo, Op. 14, published in 1845, Clara Schumann recalled the stormy figured piano accompaniment and the reiterated motive, "Er ist gekommen."

Text Translation

Er ist gekommen in Sturm und Regen
   He has come in storm and rain
Ihm schlug beklommen mein Herz entgegen.
   My anxious heart beats to meet his own
Wie konnt' ich ahnen, dass seine Bahnen
   How could I suspect that his paths
Sich einen sollten meinen Wegen.
   Would unite with mine.

Er ist gekommen In Sturm und Regen
   He has come in storm and rain,
Er hat genommen mein Herz verwegen
   With daring he has taken my heart
Nahm er das meine? Nahm ich das seine?
   Did he take mine? Did I take his?
Die beiden kamen sich entgegen.
   The two hearts drew nearer to each other.

Nun ist gekommen des Frühlings Segen.
   Now spring's blessings have come
Der Freund zieht weiter, ich seh es heiter
   My friend goes forth, I do not grieve
Denn er bleibt mein auf allen Wegen.
   For he remains mine with every step I take.
Denn er bleibt mein auf allen Wegen.
   For he remains mine with every step I take.

The *Trio for Violin, Cello, and Piano*, Op. 17, composed in 1846, is decidedly different from Clara Schumann's earlier works, which are mainly character pieces and virtuoso variations. Robert Schumann, obviously proud of his wife's works, submitted the Trio to Breitkopf und Härtel and arranged to have it published and ready for her birthday in September 1847. It was her first extended composition written in the traditional four-movement form, the fruits of her studies of the Classical masters and her personal experience performing the trio literature of Beethoven and Schubert. Published in 1847, the Trio received exceptionally favorable reviews. For example, one states, "The work is clear, something rarely seen; it demonstrates a calm mastery of the formal artistic medium that we would not have expected of a woman composer" (*Neue Berliner Musik-*

zeitung, 17 November 1847). The Trio is a polished effort, eminently playable, that enriches the repertoire for this combination of instruments.

Although the Trio is by far Clara Schumann's best-known work in an extended form, she had also composed a *Concerto for Piano and Orchestra,* Op. 7, between the ages of thirteen and sixteen, a remarkably innovative work in three contiguous movements. A *Sonata for Piano in G minor* was composed in December 1841–January 1842, soon after her marriage. Quite surprisingly, it was published only in 1991.

The movements of the Trio are marked Allegro moderato, Scherzo, Andante, and Allegretto. The first movement is presented here and is in clear-cut sonata form. The opening theme, a lyrical and melancholy eight-measure melody in G minor, is balanced in structure and regular in rhythm. It contrasts strongly with the second theme (m. 45), a syncopated descending motive in B-flat major. In the exposition, the violin and piano dominate, while the cello plays a supporting role. In the development section (after the double bar), however, the cello takes its proper place in the ensemble and, in a series of sequences and imitative episodes based on the first theme, engages in interchanges with the violin. The recapitulation, preceded by a long pedal on D, is almost literal, but with the second subject in the parallel major this time. Although this was the composer's first and only published work in this style and form, it is a polished effort, eminently playable, that enriches the repertoire for this combination.

After a hiatus of seven years, Clara Schumann took up her pen again for a birthday gift for her husband. Her *Variations on a Theme by Robert Schumann,* Op. 20, was written in June 1853 and published in November 1854, after she had met the composer Johannes Brahms. During the summer of 1854, the younger Brahms also wrote a set of variations (his Op. 9) on the same Schumann theme. Brahms quoted a theme from a childhood work by Clara Schumann (Op. 3) in his tenth variation, thus paying tribute to both husband and wife. In the coda of her Op. 20, Clara Schumann also quoted from her earlier work, and since the quotation does not appear in the 1853 autograph, it seems likely that she inserted the quotation after she heard Brahms play his Op. 9. Like Brahms and Clara herself in her Op. 20 Variations, Robert Schumann also refers to Clara's Op. 3 in his *Impromptus on a Romance by Clara Wieck.* The theme as it appears in Opp. 3 and 20 of Clara, in Robert, and in Brahms differs slightly from work to work. In Clara Schumann's Op. 20, it begins at measure 202 (thirty-six measures before the end) in the section treating the Robert theme simply again. It is heard in the tenor voice, on the pitches C-sharp, E, A-sharp, D-sharp, G-sharp, C-sharp, F-double sharp, G-sharp, G-double sharp, A-sharp, F-sharp, C-sharp, and so on. Robert Schumann places this theme in the top voice of his *Bunte Blätter.*

The theme of Clara Schumann's Op. 20 is based on Robert Schumann's *Bunte Blätter,* Op. 99, No. 4, a twenty-four-measure piece in simple ternary form composed in 1841 but published only in 1852. Robert Schumann's melody, presented in its entirety in Clara's Op. 20 but without designated repeats, appears in each of the seven variations with only slight modifications. Except for minor changes, this regularity applies to the structure and tonality as well. Only Variations 2 and 7 differ in form, and the entire piece, except for Variation 3 and the Coda, is in F-sharp minor, the key of the Robert Schumann piece. Unlike Clara Schumann's earlier sets of variations, Op. 3, Op. 8, and Op. 9, which are designed to please the public by displaying her dazzling technique, this work shows balance, proportion, and control throughout. Here the composer-pianist explores the theme by skillful changes in harmony, texture, motion, articulation, dynamics, rhythmic patterns, and coloration.

Further Reading

Chissell, Joan. *Clara Schumann, a Dedicated Spirit: A Study of her Life and Works.* London: Hamish Hamilton, 1983.

Kimber, Marian Wilson. "From the Concert Hall to the Salon: The Piano Music of Clara Wieck Schumann and Fanny Mendelssohn Hensel." In *Nineteenth-Century Piano Music,* ed. R. Larry Todd. New York: Routledge, 2003.

Current Recordings

Clara Schumann: Complete Works for Piano. Jozef de Beenhouwer, piano, three CDs. Includes all published and some unpublished music. Partridge 1129-2, 1130-2, 1131-2 (1990–1991).

Clara, Robert, and Johannes: Theme and Variations by Clara and Robert Schumann and Johannes Brahms. Veronica Jochum, piano. Pro Arte CDD 396 (1988). Released on Tudor 7028 (1997).

Clara Schumann Piano Concerto. Includes Piano Trio and Romances for Violin and Piano Op. 22. Veronica Jochum, piano; Colin Carr, cello, Joseph Silverstein, conductor and violin. Pro Arte CDD 395 (1998). Released on Tudor 788 (1992).

Clara Wieck-Schumann: Sämtliche Lieder. Isabel Lippitz, soprano, Deborah Richards, piano. Bayer Records, BR 100 206 (1992).

Completely Clara: Lieder by Clara Wieck Schumann. Korliss Uecker, soprano, Joanne Polk, piano. Arabesque Recordings CDZ6624 (1992).

Soirées Musicales: Clara Schumann. Veronica Jochum, piano. Pro Arte 1984. Released by Tudor CD 7007 (1996).

The Songs of Clara Schumann. Susan Gritton, soprano, Stephen Loges, baritone, Eugene Asti, piano. Hyperion CDA67249 (2002).

Er ist gekommen durch Sturm und Regen

Clara Wieck Schumann

op. 12 (Nr. 2)

Reprinted from *Clara Schumann: Sämtliche Lieder*, ed. J. Draheim and B. Höft (Edition No. EB 8558). © Breitkopf & Härtel, Wiesbaden, 1990.

NANCY REICH

Clara Wieck Schumann

145

in Sturm und Re - gen!

Ruhig

Nun ist ge - kom - - - men des Früh - - - lings

Ruhig

Se - - gen. Der Freund zieht wei - ter, ich seh' es hei - ter, denn

er bleibt mein auf al - len We - - gen, denn er bleibt mein auf al - len

NANCY REICH

We - - - gen. Nun ist ge-kom-men des Früh-lings Se-gen, der

Freund zieht wei-ter, ich seh' es hei-ter, denn er bleibt mein auf al-len We - - -

animato

Ped. ✲

gen.

p

dimin.

pp

Ped.

Allegro Moderato
from Trio in G minor for Piano, Violin, and Cello

Clara Wieck Schumann

Reprinted from the edition of 1847, Breitkopf und Härtel, Leipzig. By permission of Verlag Walter Wollenweber, Gräfelfing. Reprint 1972.

Clara Wieck Schumann

44

51

poco rit.

58

a tempo

64

NANCY REICH

Clara Wieck Schumann

Nancy Reich

Clara Wieck Schumann

142

148

154

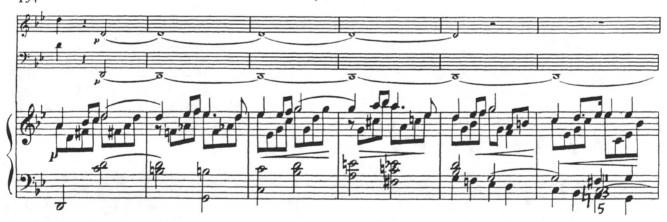

160

NANCY REICH

Clara Wieck Schumann

NANCY REICH

Clara Wieck Schumann

Nancy Reich

Clara Wieck Schumann

159

Variations on a Theme by Robert Schumann

Clara Wieck Schumann

Thema

Ziemlich langsam

Variation I

Variation II

Clara Wieck Schumann

NANCY REICH

Variation III

Variation IV

Clara Wieck Schumann

NANCY REICH

Variation V
Poco animato

Variation VI

Variation VII

Nancy Reich

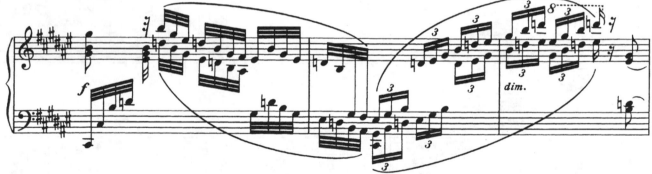

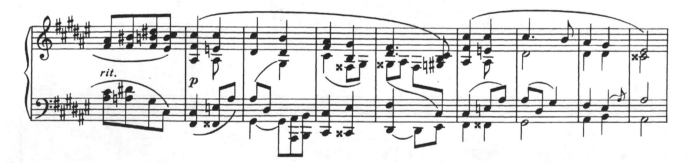

NANCY REICH

Clara Wieck Schumann

Louise Farrenc
(1804–1875)

CHRISTIN HEITMANN

TRANSLATED BY NICOLE-DENISE KADACH

Musical life in Paris during the nineteenth century was focused primarily on either the Opéra or salon music. Pure chamber and orchestral music, such as string quartets, trios, concertos, and especially symphonies, were called "serious music" (*musique sérieuse*) and were regarded as specifically German. New French orchestral works consisted almost exclusively of symphonic poems or overtures with a programmatic title and theme. Thus, Louise Farrenc (née Dumont) has to be considered an exceptional figure, both as a composer and a pianist and as a teacher, scholar, and editor of early music for keyboard instruments.

Louise Dumont was born in Paris in 1804. She was the product of a long artistic tradition, as both her father, Edme Dumont, and her brother, Auguste Dumont, were famous sculptors. Louise Dumont revealed a talent for both art and music from an early age. Her first piano and solfège teacher was Madame Cécile Soria, who had studied under Muzio Clementi. In 1819, at the age of fifteen, Louise Dumont began to study composition, harmony, and orchestration in Paris under Anton Reicha, a well-known teacher of composition and author of compositional textbooks. In all probability, Louise Farrenc took private lessons with him, as women were not allowed to take part in composition classes at the Conservatoire in Paris until around 1870. In 1821, Louise Dumont married the flutist and music publisher Aristide Farrenc (1794–1865) and temporarily suspended her composition lessons to travel to the north and south of France with her husband. Their marriage would appear to have been not only a personal partnership but also a fruitful union for work and studies; they supported each other, demonstrating concern and sympathy for each other's field of professional activities. Each of them also contributed toward the family's livelihood.

After returning to Paris, Louise Farrenc resumed her studies with Reicha, and had her first compositions for piano solo issued by her husband's publishing house in the 1820s. Their only child, Victorine Farrenc, was born in 1826; she started a promising career as a pianist but died at the young age of thirty-three in 1859. At the end of the 1820s and during the 1830s, the first concert reviews of Louise Farrenc as a pianist were to be found in Parisian musical journals. Subsequently, during the 1840s and 1850s, regular and numerous concert reviews followed annually, mostly featuring semi-private matinées or soirées, which were organized by Louise Farrenc herself and always included at least one of her own compositions in the program. The world première in 1849 of her Third Symphony Op. 36 by the esteemed Conservatoire orchestra, the Société des concerts du Conservatoire, was prominently noted. Likewise, the world premiere of her Nonet Op. 38 in 1850, in which the young but already famous German violinist Joseph Joachim took part, featured among the composer's outstanding successes.

In 1842 Louise Farrenc was appointed professor of piano for female students by the Paris Conservatoire. She was the first woman in Europe to retain the position of instrumental professor, and remained at the Conservatoire for a duration of thirty years until her retirement in 1873. Accounts speak of her as an excellent and committed instructor, and many of her students graduated with Premier Prix and later took up professional careers. Louise Farrenc also held private lessons not only for piano but also in composition. The names of her private students of the latter, however, remain unknown, with the exception of her nephew Ernest Reyer, who went on to become a successful composer of operas.

During the last few years of her life, from the 1860s until her death, Louise Farrenc appears to have stopped composing. She increasingly participated in her husband's research into early music instead, in particular that for keyboard instruments. Aristide and Louise Farrenc's extensive musicological research resulted in a historical anthology of keyboard instrument masterworks from the sixteenth to nineteenth centuries, *Le Trésor des pianistes,* which consisted of twenty-three volumes. Publication began in 1861 and was accompanied by concerts, so-called séances historiques, where the works published in the anthology were performed and discussed for the benefit of the audiences. The first volume of the *Trésor* includes introductory texts, such as a report on the editorial work for the anthology as well as treatises concerning the history of piano manufacture alongside passages pertinent to historical performance practice. By the time Aristide Farrenc died in 1865, eight volumes had been published. Louise Farrenc continued the editorial work and completed twenty-three volumes by 1872. The Farrenc interest, issuing an elaborate and detailed edition, and performing the works with the intention of fueling the revival of early music were novel concepts in the nineteenth century.

Louise Farrenc was awarded the Prix Chartier of the Académie des Beaux-Arts (forming part of the Institut de France) for her chamber music oeuvre on two occasions, in 1861 and 1869. She had not composed any new chamber music for several years. However, her last compositions were printed and published at the beginning of the 1860s: the Clarinet Trio Op. 44, the Cello Sonata Op. 46 (both in 1861), and the Flute Trio Op. 45 (in 1863). That Louise Farrenc was awarded the Prix Chartier must have been of particular significance to her, considering that women in the nineteenth century were allowed neither to become members of the Institut de France nor to take part in France's most prestigious composition competition, the Prix de Rome. Her works were performed in Paris up to her death in 1875. The Alphonse Leduc publishing company in Paris reissued a series of her chamber music and piano works in the years following 1875, but only rare performances occurred, leaving the composer to fall into oblivion for about a hundred years.

By composing chamber music for relatively large ensembles, including a nonet for wind and string instruments, a sextet for piano and five wind instruments, and orchestral works, Louise Farrenc not only turned her back on the musical mainstream of concert life in Paris, but she resisted the constraints of small-scale domestic music and songs (romances). This latter niche was accorded to women composers inside the socially sanctioned roles of the nineteenth century. The symphony did not represent a genre highly esteemed in France at that time. Nevertheless, Farrenc's symphonies were performed on several occasions during her lifetime, even though she was never allowed to organize and conduct concerts of her own orchestral works as she had done with her chamber music. The skillful instrumentation of her orchestral works can be seen above all in her independent treatment of wind instruments, and her instrumentation remains striking for today's listeners.

Farrenc's twelve chamber music works rank behind only the thirty works for solo piano in her oeuvre. From a compositional point of view, however, they are of far greater significance than the piano pieces. With the exception of the etudes, the piano pieces are mainly variation cycles and rondos on popular themes such as opera melodies, and thus they represent contemporary taste. Louise Farrenc ranked among the very few French composers in the tradition of "absolute music" in the mid-nineteenth century. She drew inspiration from Viennese Classicism even before that tradition became widely known in Paris. Prior to 1850, German Romantic compositions such as those by Robert Schumann or Felix Mendelssohn were hardly known in Paris.

From today's perspective, it is the extraordinary scoring in many of her works that is particularly remarkable. Both Piano Quintets Opp. 30 and 31 (1839 and 1840) were scored for double bass, as was the famous "Trout Quintet" by Franz Schubert, although Louise Farrenc probably did not know the "Trout." The Nonet Op. 38 for flute, oboe, clarinet, French horn, bassoon, violin, viola, violoncello, and double bass (1849) had few precedents, among them works by Louis Spohr and Georges Onslow. Works scored for piano, flute, oboe, clarinet, French horn, and bassoon were completely unknown before Louise Farrenc's Sextet Op. 40 (1852). By contrast, the composer drew on a long and rich tradition in writing her Piano Trios Opp. 33 and 34 (1841, 1844) and Opp. 44 and 45 (1854, 1856). Yet Op. 44 for piano, clarinet, and violoncello and Op. 45 for piano, flute, and violoncello deviated from the piano trio norm of piano, violin, and cello.

The Trio Op. 45 for piano, flute, and violoncello was composed between 1854 and 1856 and performed in several concerts before its publication in 1863. It was Louise Farrenc's last piano trio and well represents the style of her chamber music. Its structure of four movements (the first an allegro movement in classical sonata form: andante, scherzo, and, finally, presto), the independence of each instrumental part, its compositional technique, and its thematic approach rediscovered the line from Beethoven's piano trios.

The energetic opening to the first movement, given below, is extraordinary (mm. 1–8). Its tempo is more rapid than the main part of the movement (mm. 9 ff.). In the further course of the movement, the main ideas (*idée mère* was the term used by Louise Farrenc's teacher Anton Reicha; first *idée mère* mm. 8–28; second *idée mère* mm. 56–85) are more reticent in both character and expression than the transitional, "less important" passages of a more buoyant and lively nature. The opening section, because of its chordal, chiseled character, forms a contrast to the main part, which starts softly and melodiously. Both remain closely associated in their motivic treatment. The eighth-note rhythm in measures 2, 4, and 5 strikes the listener with its rests on the accented beats, and it figures importantly as the movement progresses in the accompaniment (mm. 16 ff. or mm. 52 ff.) and in thematic passages (mm. 66 ff., flute and piano; or mm. 70 and 72, cello).

The creation of new figures by modifying previous motifs is an important means of inner continuity, while the music develops still further. A second eighth rest is added in the eighth rhythm at measure 13, and ties occur to develop measure 66 and after. The duple values in measures 13 ff. change to legato at measures 36 and 103. The dotted quarter and tied eight of measure 10 becomes the subject matter of a dialog between the cello and the flute from measure 16. In the concluding part of the exposition, this melodious motif becomes an outstanding contrast to the dramatic sixteenth-note figures (mm. 99–102). The music is subdued by a tranquil reduction to chord repetitions when the exposition ends at measure 106.

In the development section (mm. 107–91), these means of development recur and are further varied. From measures 133 to 156, the second main idea reappears and can be heard thrice, played each time on a different instrument in differing keys. Another striking motive seems to be new: the brief figure of ascending sixteenth notes in measures 113 ff. is also elaborated upon in the development section (mm. 131 ff. and mm. 164 ff.). The important characteristic of this motive, however, is again the rest on the accented beat. The eighths are amalgamated into groups of sixteenth notes; thus the sixteenth figure is also related to the rhythm used in measure 2, from which it had been derived.

Further Reading

Farrenc, Aristide, and Louise Farrenc. *Le trésor des pianistes.* 23 vols. Paris, 1861–1872. Reprint, New York: Da Capo, 1978. With a foreword by Bea Friedland.

Friedland, Bea. *Louise Farrenc, 1804–1875: Composer, Performer, Scholar.* Ann Arbor: UMI Research Press, 1980.

Hoffmann, Freia. Foreword to the Work Edition of Louise Farrenc, Piano Trios No. 3 Op. 44 and No. 4 Op. 45. In *Kritische Ausgabe der Orchester- und Kammermusik sowie ausgewählter Klavierwerke,* vol. II/5. Wilhelmshaven: Noetzel Verlag, 2000.

Allegro deciso
from Trio in E minor for flute, cello, and piano

Louise Farrenc

à Mr. Louis DORUS.

Reprinted by Da Capo Press of the second edition, Paris: A. Leduc, ca. 1890. Public domain.

CHRISTIN HEITMANN

Louise Farrenc 175

176176   CHRISTIN HEITMANN

Louise Farrenc

Christin Heitmann

Louise Farrenc

CHRISTIN HEITMANN

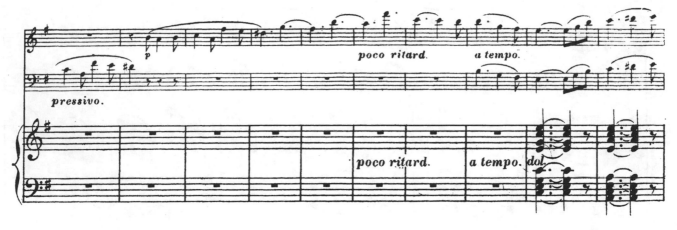

CHRISTIN HEITMANN

Louise Farrenc

CHRISTIN HEITMANN

CHRISTIN HEITMANN

Pauline Viardot-Garcia
(1821–1910)

MARK EVERIST

The long career of Pauline Viardot-Garcia covered most of the nineteenth century. It began with an education at the heart of the legendary Garcia family, and, as with the rest of her family, her early life followed the path of an international opera star. In her later career, she succeeded in carving out a musical and intellectual space for herself that placed her at the center of European musical thought; very few composers were left untouched by her influence. She lived long enough to have met both the librettist of *Don Giovanni* and the composer of *Pelléas et Mélisande,* and by the time of her death in 1910 she was established as a living monument to the music of the previous century.

Her family were all opera singers: Maria Malibran was her sister and Manuel Garcia her father; her mother and her brother, Manuel Garcia the younger, shared the same profession. Pauline was trained by members of her family, learned to play the piano in Mexico City while the family were on tour there, and continued her studies with Liszt. She also studied composition with Antoine Reicha. Her debut was much awaited, and there were obvious expectations for Malibran's younger sister. The latter died in 1836, and Pauline opened her singing career the following year at a concert given by her late sister's widower, the violinist Charles de Bériot. Her operatic career began in 1839 when she sang one of her sister's best-known roles, Desdemona in Rossini's *Otello,* in London and Paris. She married the director of the Théâtre Italien, Louis Viardot, in the following year. Between 1839 and her retirement from the stage in 1863, she sang all over Europe, enjoying success in London, Berlin, Dresden, and Vienna. Most remarkable was the fame she acquired in St. Petersburg, where she sang in the mid-1840s and where she met Ivan Turgenev for the first time, a meeting that developed into a complex relationship until the latter's death in 1883. To an extent, she mirrored her sister's career in participating in the emerging world of trans-European Italian opera, performing the same roles in cities in Russia, Austria, England, and Saxony. She was, however, already forging something of an idiosyncratic position for herself in the roles she chose to develop with most care; the roles of Donna Anna in Mozart's *Don Giovanni* and of Valentine in Meyerbeer's *Les Huguenots* were not in the same mold as those of Norma or Desdemona, although both her chosen operas were as much on the international opera circuit in the 1840s and 1850s as any bel canto work.

Perhaps the most remarkable absence from Viardot-Garcia's operatic itinerary was Paris. It was certainly difficult after Louis-Napoléon's coup d'état in 1851 for the wife of such a republican as Louis Viardot to work there, but the singer's greatest success was in one of the works that characterized the Second Empire: the role of Fidès in Meyerbeer's *Le Prophète*. The success of *Le Prophète* was matched only by that of Meyerbeer's earlier grands opéras, but benefited greatly from Viardot's creation of the role. She sang the part more than two hundred times as she followed the work's triumphant career all over Europe; Meyerbeer's only difficulty was finding someone who could replace her as the work developed its canonical status. The composer's recognition of the importance of Viardot-Garcia to the work was frequent and generous. Her second great success in Paris was in the Berlioz arrangement of Gluck's *Orphée et Eurydice,* which was premiered in 1859. Her retirement from the stage coincided with retreat to Baden-Baden. The Viardots had always kept a country house at Courtavenel along with their Parisian domicile in the rue de Douai, but abandoned both for the politically more tranquil grand duchy in the Black Forest. Here the family entertained not only artists and musicians but also diplomats and heads of state (Clara Schumann was more than once made aware of her relatively lowly status in her forays to play piano duets with Viardot-Garcia). The defeat of Napoléon III at Sedan cleared the way for a triumphal return to the rue de Douai and a new country house at Bougival (Courtavenel had in the meantime been demolished). Louis Viardot died in the same year as Turgenev, whereupon Viardot-Garcia moved to the Boulevard St.-Germain; she spent the last part of her life (1883–1910) there.

At all points in her career, Viardot-Garcia was an inspiration to composers: she was certainly an important prompt for Berlioz, and was closely involved in the compositional planning of Gounod's *Sapho* and Massenet's *Marie-Magdalene.* Her involvement in the composition of Meyerbeer's music for *Le Prophète* has been much overestimated, however. Although negotiations had been going on since 1841 (Léon Pillet at the Académie Royale de Musique wanted Rosine Stolz for the role), Viardot-Garcia had not seen a note of the score before 18 November 1848 and did not sing with the other soloists until 21 January 1849. Evidence of her influence over other composers lies in the works that were dedicated to her—compositions as different as Schumann's *Liederkreis* Op. 24 (1840) and Fauré's first violin sonata (1877). Her correspondence with Clara Schumann shows that the relationship was close but not without tensions, and she sang the premiere of Brahms's *Alto Rhapsody* as late as 1870, as well as taking part informally in performances of extracts from *Tristan.*

Viardot-Garcia's accomplishments as a vocal soloist and her influence on other composers were matched by her own creative work. Her songs number more than one hundred, and most are settings of texts with which she became familiar through her literary contacts (most notably Turgenev and her husband): Goethe, Mörike, Pushkin, Lermontov, Peth, and Turgenev himself. The other genre of composition to which she devoted herself was chamber operettas, the librettos to most of which were by Turgenev; of these, *Cendrillon* has recently been recorded complete. Compositional work was also directed into a number of other channels, one of which was important and successful, and today is understood as little more than a curiosity: in collaboration with Louis Pomey and Victor Wilder, Viardot-Garcia arranged a number of dance compositions for piano by Chopin, Schubert, and Brahms for voice and piano. Furthermore, she edited fifty Schubert Lieder in an important step in the reception of those works in the nineteenth century, and produced instruction manuals for singers that featured compositions from the past. In addition to setting texts by Ronsard and other early-modern authors, she arranged works by Handel, Jomelli, Haydn, and Marcello. This interest in the past was matched by her collection of musical autographs. Alongside manuscripts of the scherzo of Beethoven's String Quartet in Eb Op. 127 and Bach's Cantata for the twentieth Sunday after Trinity, *Schmücke dich, o liebe Seele,* BWV 180, Viardot-Garcia was the owner of the autograph of *Don Giovanni,* a possession that she honored by the elevation of a cult in its honor (and that of the composer and the work).

Viardot-Garcia welcomed only composers to the house on the rue de Douai and the villa at Baden-Baden, but was central to the lives of such literary figures as Alfred de Musset, Victor Hugo, Emile Zola, and the reluctant Gustave Flaubert. The two most important were Turgenev and her lifelong correspondent, Georges Sand. Sand was a critical figure in Viardot-Garcia's life, and an important point of comparison and contrast as a contemporary woman who developed a self-image that was equally successful to, but very different from, the one created by her friend. Sand effectively brokered Viardot-Garcia's marriage to Louis Viardot, and enshrined her as the fictional protagonist of her novel *Consuelo* of 1842. But it was Turgenev who colored her life more than any other literary figure. Modern views of the ménage à trois with Viardot-Garcia have sought to downplay the importance of Louis Viardot: the standard biography of the singer wrongly treats him as little better than a cuckolded buffoon. As a journalist with strongly republican sympathies, he collaborated on *Le Globe* alongside Sand, and on *Le National* and *La Revue Républicaine,* and was one of the founders of the *Revue Indépendente.* He was a prolific writer on artistic matters, and was the owner of a significant art collection, including Rembrandt's *The Butcher's Stall,* now in the Louvre. But his greatest contribution to letters was as a translator, in later years often in collaboration with Turgenev from Russian, but particularly from Spanish. It will never be known whether Turgenev's passion for Pauline Viardot-Garcia was ever physically reciprocated (nor can the paternity of her four children be definitively settled); this would not necessarily have been cause for the breaking of the other bonds that tied the ménage à trois together. The marital ties that connected Pauline and Louis were probably more cerebral than physical, and the former was more than willing to accept the great intellectual debt that she owed her husband. Turgenev benefited from Pauline's views on his poetry, and it seems that in later years he wrote little that did not receive her imprimatur. He sympathized with Louis's republican views as well as with his love of hunting; their literary collaborations were evident from published work. It is far from clear what intellectual benefit Pauline received from Turgenev, who seemed anxious to defer to her on most things. He certainly encouraged her to read Goethe while preparing Gluck's *Iphigénie en Tauride* and Shakespeare before Verdi's *Macbeth,* and he was clearly a stimulating reading partner, but this seems relatively little in comparison with the intellectual benefits that Turgenev apparently claimed in return.

Viardot-Garcia's career was marked by a successful manipulation of image, much of which she carefully engineered on her own or in collaboration with others. Her family models for how to negotiate the end of a successful operatic career were far from obvious. Her mother never achieved the stature of any of her children, and her sister died before her career had ended. Viardot-Garcia followed her brother's example in her inclusion of pedagogy as part of the suite of skills she cultivated in the second half of the nineteenth century, but taught at the Paris Conservatoire for only a few years in the early 1870s. Although the list of her pupils is distinguished, it is small and does not match up to the number of composers who held her in their debt. Viardot-Garcia's self image was crafted from the wide range of activities in which she excelled both before and after her retirement from the stage: composition, arrangement, teaching, performance, the nurturing of talent, and embryonic musicology. George Sand wrote to her in a letter of 1842 as follows: "You are the priestess of the ideal in music, and your mission is to proselytize, to make it understood and to lead recalcitrants to an instinct for, and a revelation of, the truth and the beautiful." The embodiment of Viardot-Garcia as the ultimate priestess of art and music—St. Cecilia—may be seen in the portrait by Ary Scheffer that adorned her Cavaillé-Coll organ in the house on the rue de Douai.

"Die Beschwörung" (Supplication) is by many accounts a very impressive composition that plays off a piano part that merges Brahmsian accompaniment figures with Wagnerian tremulandi against a melodic line that demands both control over line and vocal drama; it could have been written for Viardot-Garcia herself. It was published in

1865 as one of a set of twelve Pushkin settings. The poem is in three stanzas, and the music for the first recurs with changes only to local aspects of the text setting in the third. In the first and third stanzas the home key of F minor is subjected to Neapolitan inflection over a tonic pedal up to the point where the poetry alludes to the graves giving up their dead. Here the texture changes to a sinister tremulando that underpins the authorial cry "I wait to embrace you." Marked *molto expressione,* the middle stanza exploits the key of the subdominant major again over a pedal, this time its dominant. The modal shift on the word "Leiden" drags the music back to F minor and to the tremulandi that characterized parts of the music of the framing stanzas, and the loving recollection of the first three lines of the second stanza yields to the despair of the second half of the stanza and the poem as a whole.

Text Translation

O, if it is true that when night
Lulls all life to sleep,
And when moonlight's pallid gleam
Weaves among the tombstones;
O, if it is truly then
That graves yield up their dead,
It is then that I wait to embrace you
Hear me Leila! Come to me! Come home!

Emerge from your realm of shadows,
Just as you were before our parting,
Cold as a winter day,
Your face distorted with pain.
O come back, as a distant star,
As a breath, as a delicate sound,
Or in some more terrifying beauty,
It makes no difference. Come to me! Come home!

I cry to Leila not
To plumb the secrets of the grave,
    Nor to rebuke those who killed my love,
    Nor even because of the bitter despair
        Which tortures me.
        No, only to tell her that my
Stricken heart is still true;
Is still breathing . . . Come to me! Come home!

Further Reading

Borchard, Beatrix. " 'Ma chère petite Clara—Pauline de mon cœur': Clara Schumann et Pauline Viardot, une amitié d'artistes franco-allemande." *Cahiers Ivan Tourguéniev, Pauline Viardot, Maria Malibran* 20 (1996): 127–43.

Everist, Mark. "Enshrining Mozart: Don Giovanni and the Viardot Circle." *19th-Century Music* 25 (2001): 165–89.

Fitzlyon, April. *The Price of Genius: A Life of Pauline Viardot.* New York: Appleton-Century, 1965.

Marix-Spire, Thérèse. *Lettres inédites de George Sand et de Pauline Viardot, 1839–49.* Paris: Nouvelles editions latines, 1959.

Sieffert Rigaud, Yvette. "Pauline Viardot: Mythe et Réalité." Thèse d'État, Université de Rouen, 1991.

Die Beschwörung
from *Zwölf Gedichte von Pushkin* for voice and piano

Poetry by Aleksandr S. Pushkin

Pauline Viardot-Garcia
Catherine Sentman Anderson, editor

Pauline Viardot-Garcia

wahr   ist,   dass dann leer _____ die Grä- ber stehn die Tod - ten las - -

- sen,   er- wart' ich Dich, _____ er- wart' ich Dich, _____ Dich zu um-

fas - - sen.   Hör' Lei - la, mich!   Komm her!   Komm

her! _____ Komm her!

con molto espressione

Er - schein' aus dei-nem Schat-ten-

reich, ganz wie du warst vor un-serm Schei - den, dem kal-ten

Win - - ter-ta-ge gleich, das An - ge - sicht ent-stellt von

Lei - - den. O komm, ein fer - ner Stern, da - her, o

Pauline Viardot-Garcia 195

schwer mich Zwei - fel quä - - len..... Nein, zu sa -

- scen - - - do

- gen, dass treu, wie stets_____ mein Herz ge - schla - - gen, es jetzt noch

schlägt.... Komm her! Komm her!_____ Komm her! Komm

her!

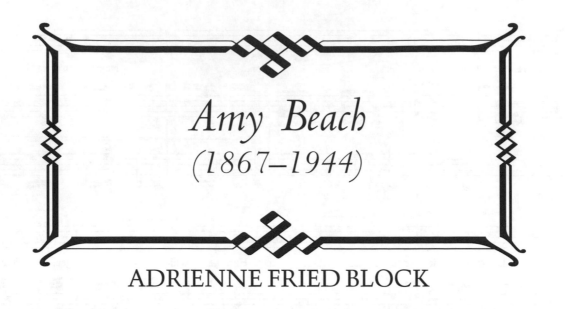

Amy Beach
(1867–1944)

ADRIENNE FRIED BLOCK

       Amy Marcy Cheney Beach (Mrs. H.H.A. Beach), an American-born and American-trained member of the Second New England School of composers, was the first woman in the United States to have a successful career as a composer of large-scale art music. She was prodigiously talented not only as a pianist but also intellectually, and was recognized in her lifetime as the dean of American women composers. She made her debut as a pianist in Boston at age fifteen. During the next two years she played recitals, and critics believed she would have a brilliant concert career. In 1885, a momentous year for her, Amy Cheney played for the first time with the Boston Symphony Orchestra, began a lifetime association with the music publisher Arthur P. Schmidt, and married the forty-three-year-old widower Henry Harris Aubrey Beach. Dr. Beach was a surgeon and society physician as well as an amateur singer, pianist, poet, and painter. He persuaded his bride to end her career as a performer and focus on composition, which she reluctantly agreed to do. For the next twenty-five years, she gave occasional concerts while composing more than half of her extensive oeuvre of over three hundred works.

       Dr. Beach died in 1910. A year later Amy Beach went to Europe to rest, to rebuild her career as a concert pianist, and to have her works performed and reviewed in Europe. After three successful years, she returned to the United States on the eve of World War I, already booked for the 1914–1915 concert season. From then on until she was seventy, she undertook annual winter concert tours, devoting her summers to composition.

       Beach's works list includes more than 115 songs, piano pieces, sacred and secular choral works with and without orchestra, a Mass with orchestra, a one-act opera, *Cabildo*, chamber music, a symphony, and a piano concerto. Almost all her compositions were published and were performed by leading artists and ensembles.

       The Piano Concerto in C-sharp minor, Op. 45, was composed in 1897–1899 and published in 1900; it brought together the two main strands of her musical life, performance and composition. While she was still at work on the orchestration, she received an invitation to give its first performance in April 1900 with the Boston Symphony Orchestra. I have suggested elsewhere that the concerto was—at least in part—autobiographical. Three of her own early songs, used as themes in the four movements of the concerto, have family connections. The "Scherzo," the second movement of the concerto and the one presented here, is a case in point. It is based on her song "Empress of Night," Op. 2 No. 1, a setting of a poem by her husband about the moon, a feminine symbol, and one that shines only with borrowed light. The song has a simple, almost unassuming vocal line and a lively, indeed overwhelming piano accompaniment, a strange reversal of roles. As "In the Twilight" shows, the song also given below, Beach knew very well how to write a supportive accompaniment. In the concerto, however, the accompaniment is transformed into a solo virtuoso role, a brilliant perpetuum mobile, and the accompanying orchestra has the quiet solo vocal line as its theme.

In 1921 Amy Beach spent her first of twenty annual residencies at the MacDowell Colony. One of the works she wrote that summer was "In the Twilight," Op. 85. On a poem by Henry Wadsworth Longfellow, it describes a stormy sea at night, and the dread that pervades the mood of a wife and son waiting in a lamplit cottage at the edge of the sea for a mariner's return.

Beach's lyrical gifts and sensitivity to language were apparent in her first published songs. In "In the Twilight," Op. 85, Beach set the stage with an accompaniment of restless figurations and ambiguous tonality. In the vocal line, however, she had to overcome the conflict between the looming tragedy and Longfellow's rhymed quatrains and galumphing iambic meter. This she did by means of long melodic arcs and expressive prolongations, at the same time varying phrase lengths and upbeat patterns. In a gesture recalling the final measures of Schubert's "Erlkönig," the piano ceases before the last phrase, leaving the singer alone to end on an unresolved leading tone.

In the Twilight

The twilight is sad and cloudy,
The wind blows wild and free,
And like the wings of the seagulls
Flash the white-caps of the sea.

But in the fisherman's cottage
There shines a ruddier light,
And a little face at the window
Peers out into the night.

Close it is pressed to the window,
As if those childish eyes
Were looking into the darkness,
To see some form arise.

And a woman's waving shadow
Is passing to and fro,
Now rising to the ceiling,
Now bowing and bending low.

What tale does the roaring ocean
And the night wind bleak and wild,
As they beat at the crazy casement
Tell to that little child?

And why do the roaring ocean
And the night wind wild and bleak
As they beat at the heart of the mother
Drive the color from her cheek?

Beach became interested in birdcalls as a child. At age eleven, when she was visiting San Francisco, the ornithologist E. R. Sill asked her to notate the song of the California lark, and he later published her transcription in a scholarly journal. Her continued interest in birdcalls can be seen in a number of works for piano and voice.

Beginning in 1921, Beach spent part of each summer as a Fellow-in-Residence at the MacDowell Colony. She produced a number of works her first summer, among then "A Hermit Thrush at Morn" and "A Hermit Thrush at Eve," which are probably her most inspired works using birdcalls. Both are based on "exact notations of hermit thrush songs in the original keys but an octave lower, obtained at MacDowell Colony, Peterborough, N.H." Her use of the calls in this set illustrates two techniques: In "A Hermit Thrush at Morn," the centuries-old decorative device of imitation; in the second, a relatively new one in which the birdcalls provide the melodic material out of which the entire piece is built. The poems quoted at the head of each piece stress the immanence of God in nature and Beach's own belief in the religious content of music, which on the one hand derives from Thoreau's and Emerson's transcendentalism and on the other looks forward to Messiaen.

In "A Hermit Thrush at Eve," scalar melodies in long ascending and descending sweeps suggest flight, while the chromatic, whirring triplets may represent the beating of wings. These passages introduce the birdcalls twice, while the entire piece is framed by a passage that makes a slow three-octave ascent. Its key is the darkest E-flat minor, an appropriate setting for the bird's evensong. The complete poem quoted at the head of the piece is by an American, John Vance Chaney (1848–1922): "Holy, holy! In the hush / Hearken to the hermit thrush; / All the air / Is in prayer."

In "A Hermit Thrush at Morn," reprinted here, the song of the thrush begins in measure 5 and becomes the motivic material for the Poco agitato sections, the second of which also presents the birdcall in the left hand. The descending second of the opening measure of the waltz accompaniment is also related to the song of the thrush, the principal notes of which are also a second, but ascending. This piece starts in the darker D minor and ends in the pastoral F major, suggesting the brightening at sunrise. The quotation at the head of the work is taken from "The Thrush's Nest" by the British poet John Clare (1793–1864). It begins: "Within a thick and spreading hawthorn bush / That overhung a mole-hill large and round, / I heard from morn to morn a merry thrush / Sing hymns to sunrise, while I drank the sound / With joy. . . ."

Further Reading

Beach, Amy. "Bird Songs." *The Designer* (May 1911): 7.

Block, Adrienne Fried. *Amy Beach, Passionate Victorian: The Life and Work of an American Composer, 1867–1944.* New York: Oxford University Press, 1998.

———. " 'A Veritable Autobiography'? Amy Beach's Piano Concerto in C-sharp Minor, Op. 45." *Musical Quarterly* 78 (Summer 1994): 394–416.

MacDonald, Claudia. "Critical Perception and the Woman Composer: The Early Reception of Piano Concertos by Clara Wieck Schumann and Amy Beach." *Current Musicology* 55 (1993): 24–55.

Recordings

Amy Beach: Empress of Night. Concerto for Piano and Orchestra in C-sharp Minor, Op. 45. Joanne Polk, piano, English Chamber Orchestra, Paul Goodwin, conductor. Arabesque AR Z6738.

Amy Beach. Cabildo: An Opera Premiere and Six Short Pieces. "In the Twilight," Op.

85, Charlotte Hellekant, mezzo-soprano, Christopher O'Riley, piano. Delos, DE 3170.

Mrs. H.H.A. (Amy) Beach, Piano Music. Virginia Eskin, piano. "A Hermit Thrush at Eve," Koch International Classics 3-73254-2H1. See also The AmericanVirtuoso, Alan Feinberg, piano. "A Hermit Thrush at Eve," Argo 436 121-2.

Amy Beach: A Hermit Thrush at Morn. Virginia Eskin, piano. Genesis Records GS 1054.

In the Twilight

Text by Longfellow

Amy Beach

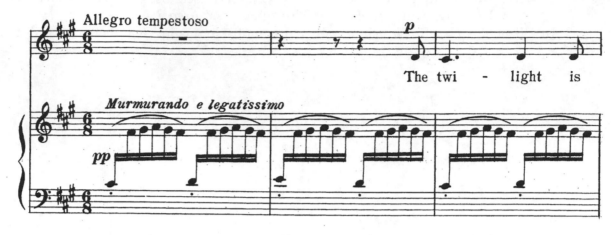

ADRIENNE FRIED BLOCK

And like the wings of sea - - gulls

Flash the white caps of the

sea.

But in the fish - - - er man's cot - - tage

There shines_____ a rud - - - di - er

poco rall.

light,_____

poco rall.

Ped.

Poco piu tranquillo *pp*

And a

ppp

Ped.

lit - tle face_____ at the win - - - dow_____ Peers

Ped.

pp

out_____

molto rit

in ___ to the

colla voce

     ADRIENNE FRIED BLOCK

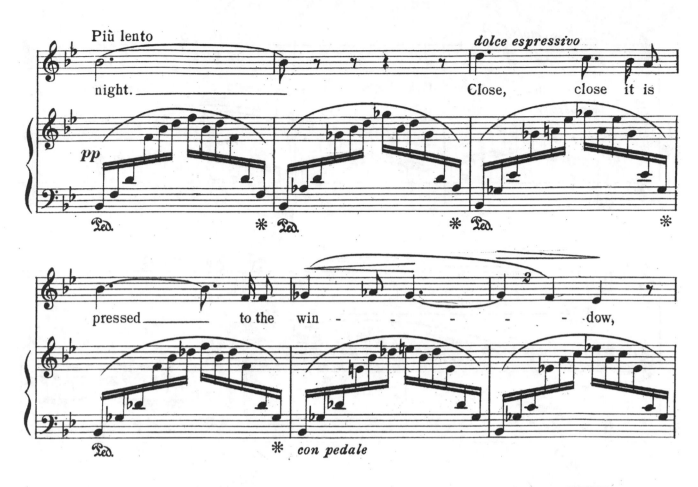

ADRIENNE FRIED BLOCK

to_____ and fro,_____ cresc.
Now

molto accel.

ri - sing to_____ the ceil -

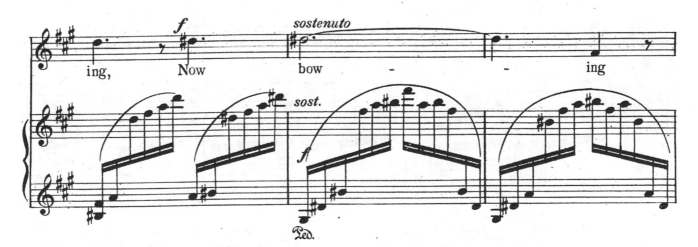

f *sostenuto*

ing, Now bow - - ing

and bend - - ing low._____

Adrienne Fried Block

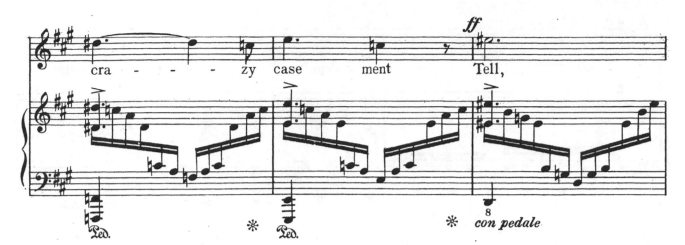

cra - - - zy case ment Tell,

tell_____ to that

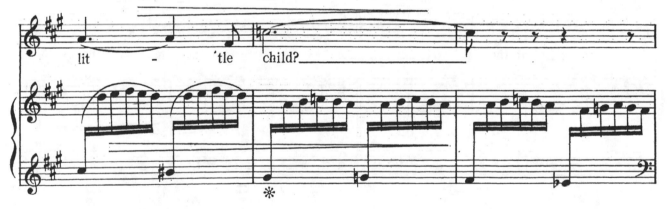

lit - 'tle child?_____

And why_____ do the

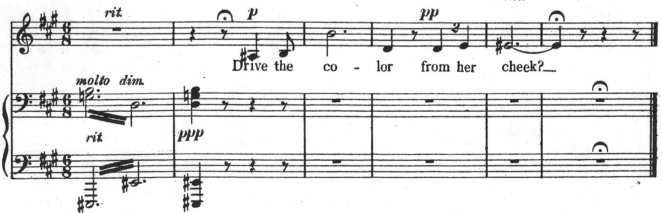

ADRIENNE FRIED BLOCK

A Hermit Thrush at Morn

Amy Beach

* These bird-calls are exact notations of hermit thrush songs, in the original keys but an octave lower, obtained at Mac Dowell Colony, Peterborough, N.H.

Reprinted with the permission of The MacDowell Colony. © 2004 The MacDowell Colony.

Amy Beach

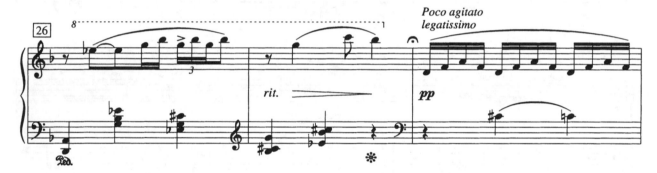

ADRIENNE FRIED BLOCK

melodia marcata

Amy Beach

ADRIENNE FRIED BLOCK

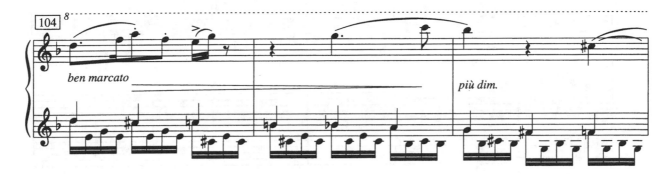

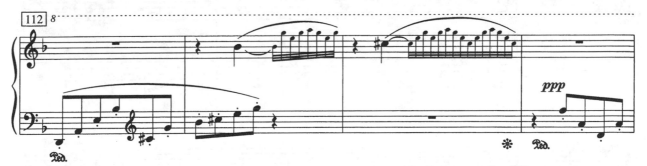

Scherzo
from Concerto for Piano and Orchestra

Amy Beach

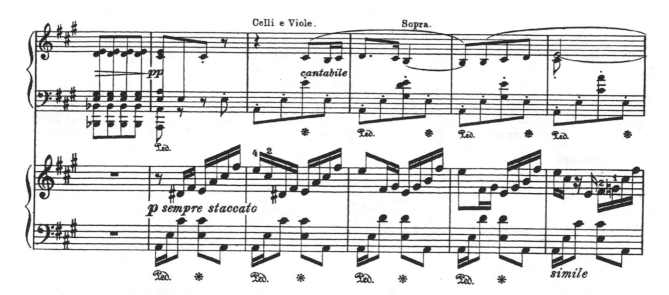

Amy Beach

B **Poco più animato.**

Amy Beach 221

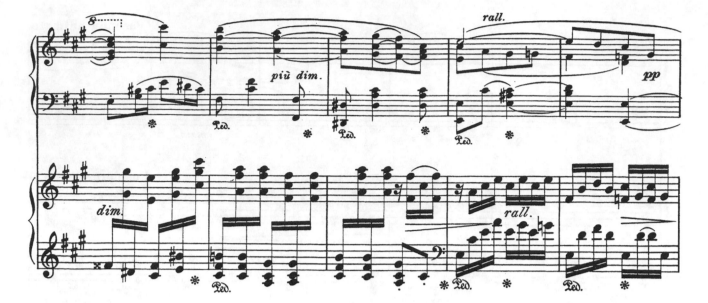

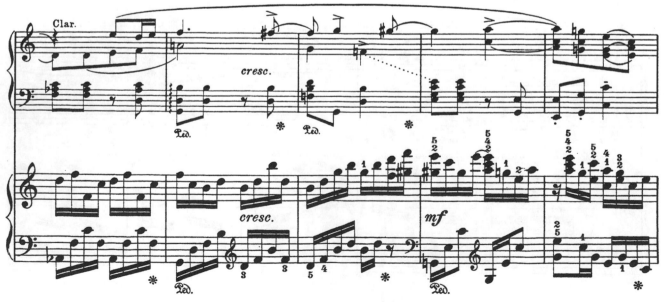

ADRIENNE FRIED BLOCK

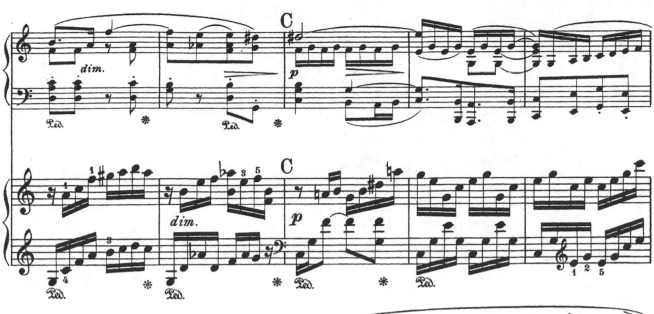

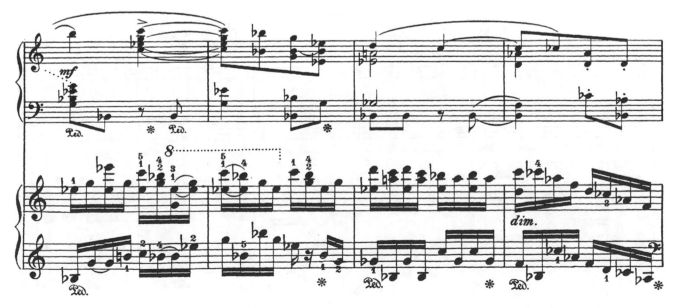

Amy Beach

ADRIENNE FRIED BLOCK

E **Poco a poco più animato.**

Amy Beach

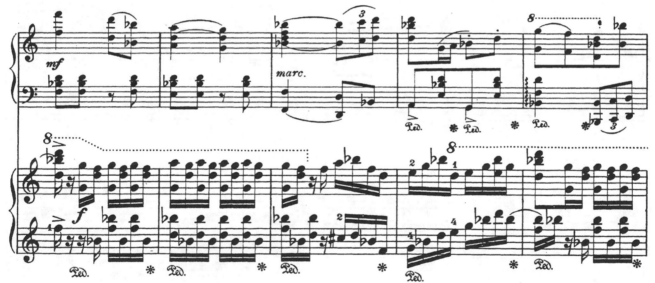

ADRIENNE FRIED BLOCK

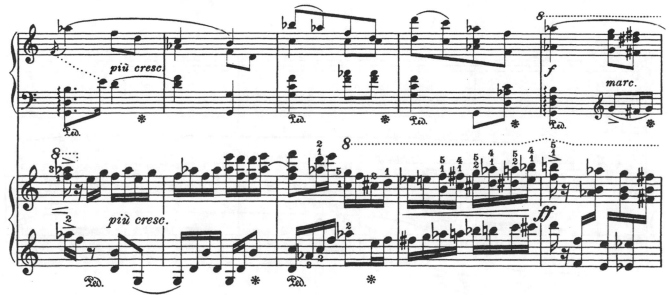

Amy Beach

ADRIENNE FRIED BLOCK

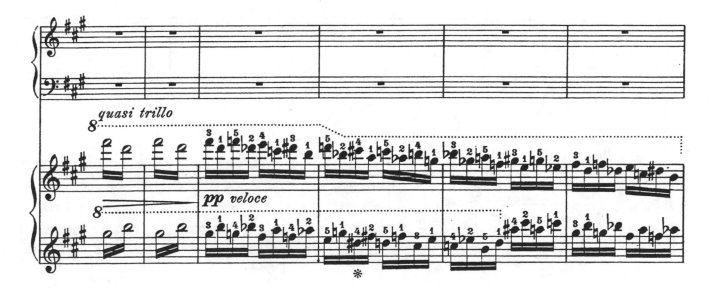

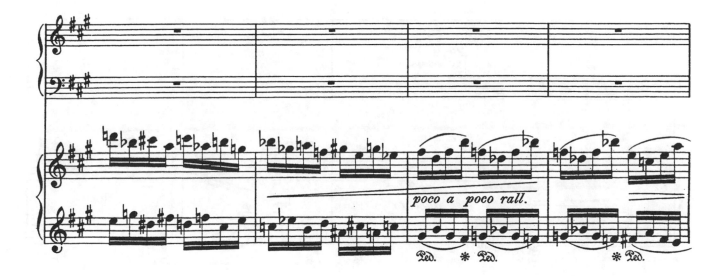

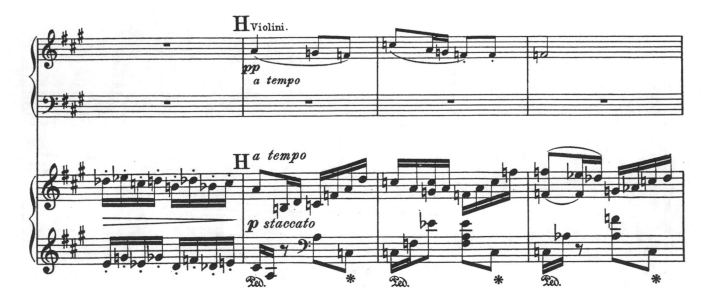

ADRIENNE FRIED BLOCK

Amy Beach

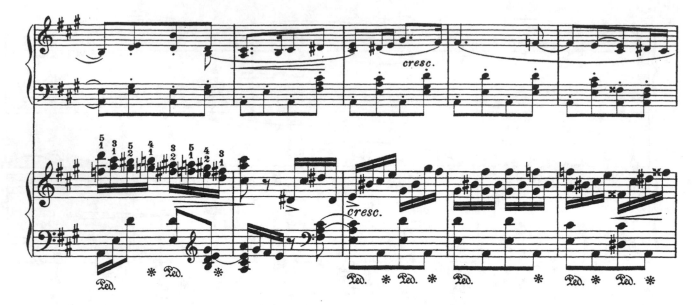

ADRIENNE FRIED BLOCK

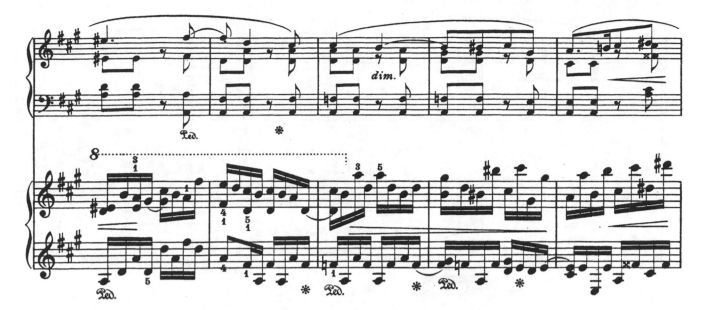

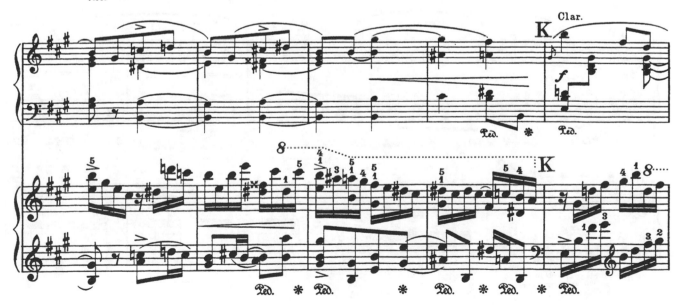

Amy Beach

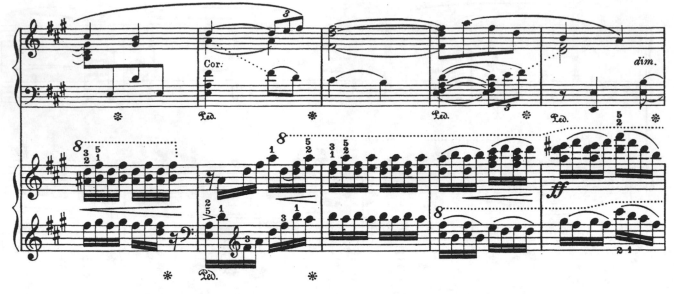

ADRIENNE FRIED BLOCK

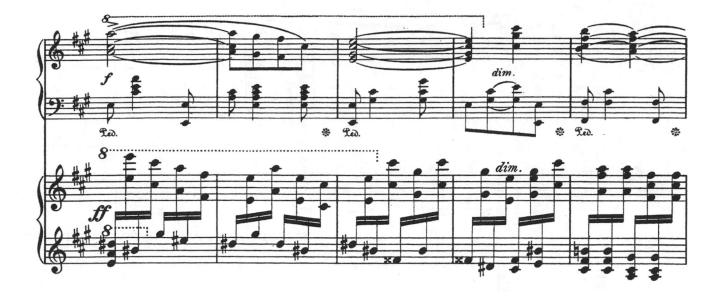

Amy Beach

ADRIENNE FRIED BLOCK

Teresa Carreño
(1853–1917)

LAURA BARCELÓ-LASTRA

María Teresa Gertrudis de Jesús Carreño García de Sena was born in Caracas, Venezuela, on 22 December 1853. A child prodigy, she received her earliest training in music at the hands of her father, Manuel Antonio Carreño. He was well known for his *Manual of Courtesy*, widely used in Latin America to teach manners to young people. At a very early age, he recognized his daughter's particular talent, and there are accounts of Teresita composing simple melodies at the piano before she was four years old.

Her family moved to the United States before Teresa was nine, looking for more opportunities for this child prodigy than Venezuela had to offer. As her father had already taught her all he could on the piano, he felt it was necessary for her to study under better teachers. While in the United States she became a touring artist, especially after her family went through some severe financial problems, and because she was the only one capable of earning money in a new land. In New York she met and played for Gottschalk, who would become one of the most important influences in her early life.

In 1866 the family moved to Europe. In Paris Teresa was admired by personalities such as Rossini, Liszt, Gounod, Berlioz, Saint-Saëns, and, most important for her, Anton Rubinstein, who would give her informal lessons whenever possible and would remain her friend for the rest of his life. She also studied harmony and counterpoint with Bazin. This would be her most prolific time as a composer. She began playing her own compositions in concert, and added those of her friend and pupil Edward MacDowell to her repertoire. Spreading the appreciation of MacDowell was perhaps one of Carreño's greatest contributions to American music.

After divorcing her first husband, violinist Emile Sauret, she returned to the United States and married Giovanni Tagliapietra, an opera singer. During this time, she explored her abilities in singing, an activity she truly enjoyed. She knew, however, that the piano would always be her primary medium. In 1885 she returned to Caracas, where she was welcomed as a national hero, but she felt disappointed with the way the Venezuelan elite frowned upon her lifestyle. The Venezuelan president, Guzmán Blanco, took particular interest in Teresa Carreño's artistry. He invited her to come back the following year to oversee the new opera season in Caracas. The enterprise was not as successful as she would have expected, and although the Venezuelan audiences loved Teresa Carreño the pianist, they disdained her work as an entrepreneur. This would be the last time she visited her homeland, although she always desired to go back.

Upon her return to Europe, she met another of the great pianists of the time, Eugen

D'Albert, who would eventually become her third husband. This relationship was perhaps the most relevant in her musical life, as D'Albert was able to help her structure her playing, teaching her to avoid excesses that were not liked by the German public. Despite its significance for her career, this marriage would last only two years.

After a bitter divorce, she found solace in her work. During a trip to America, she once again ran into her former brother-in-law, Arturo Tagliapietra, who had remained her unconditional friend after he helped her escape an abusive relationship with his brother Giovanni. In 1900 he joined her in Germany to become her assistant and manager, and it was then that she decided they should marry. He accompanied her on many of her tours, including trips to New Zealand, Australia, and South Africa. She had finally found some stability in her personal life, which had been far removed in gratification from the glamour of her life as a concert artist.

Her problems and migrant life were taking a toll on her. After the celebration of her fifty years as an artist, she felt she had nothing left to do. Her children, all grown by then, were still a financial responsibility. After her marriage to Arturo Tagliapietra, many of Carreño's friends had severed contact with her, including her brother Manuel, and she was outliving many of those who had remained loyal. In 1916 she went on another American tour, but her health was rapidly deteriorating. Teresa Carreño, whom Claudio Arrau described as "a goddess," died in New York on 12 June 1917. Her ashes were taken to Caracas in 1938, where they were laid to rest at the Panteón Nacional.

The piece included in this anthology is *Italian Sketches* Op. 33, No. 1, "Venise." It is in the form of a barcarolle, according to the *Grove Dictionary of Music and Musicians*, a piece that resembles the songs sung by Venetian gondoliers. Its most basic feature is the time signature 6/8, with a lilting rhythm that depicts the movement of the boat, and it was a popular form during the nineteenth century. The piece opens with a theme in G major that clearly sounds like a barcarolle. At the beginning of the second page, the second section appears where Carreño develops the opening theme, venturing into a more chromatic idiom. Note that except for the short cadenza on page three, the left-hand accompaniment keeps the quarter-/eighth-note pattern characteristic of a barcarolle. She does not, however, approach the extended harmony that was becoming widely used during her lifetime. After a short but virtuosic cadenza, the piece moves back to G major and to the opening theme.

Further Reading

Milinowski, Martha. *Teresa Carreño: "By the Grace of God."* New York: Da Capo Press, 1977.

Recordings

Chamber Works by Women Composers. Macalester Trio. VoxBox (1991).
Piano Music of Venezuela. Monique Duphil, Vicente Emilio Sojo, Federico G. Vollmer, and others. Electra (1889).
Solo Piano and Chamber Works (Obras para piano y música de cámara) by Teresa Carreño. Carmen Rodríguez-Peralta, ed. Artona (2000).

Venise
from *Italian Sketches* Op. 33, No. 1

Teresa Carreño

Teresa Carreño

LAURA BARCELÓ-LASTRA

Teresa Carreño

Laura Barceló-Lastra

Cécile Chaminade
(1857–1944)

MARCIA J. CITRON

Cécile Chaminade has always been famous as the composer of the *Concertino for Flute and Orchestra,* which she wrote for the Paris Conservatoire competition in 1902. In much of the twentieth century she was also known for her "Scarf Dance," a lilting character piece for piano. At the height of her fame, around 1900, Chaminade was wildly popular among aspiring piano students for such piano miniatures, and the enthusiasm in England and the United States far outstripped interest in her in her native country, France. In addition to regular visits to England beginning in 1892, when Chaminade performed piano works and *mélodies* (French lyrical songs), the composer-pianist made a triumphant visit to the United States in 1908, touring twelve cities from Boston to St. Louis. Her American fame extended to daily musical life as well, with many Chaminade Clubs thriving across the country. Family documents, for example, include inspirational material from the Chaminade Club in Brooklyn, New York, which celebrated its silver anniversary in 1923. In 1913 Chaminade became Chevalière of the Legion of Honor, the first woman composer so honored by the French government. With a changing musical climate, however, Chaminade's music fell into decline. She died in 1944, before the end of World War II, feeling passée and forgotten. After an initial effort by the family to revive her reputation, Chaminade's music was "rediscovered" in the 1980s by Gérard Condé, a journalist with the French newspaper *Le Monde.* Books by Marcia Citron and Cécile Tardif (the latter in French) have brought Chaminade's life and career into focus. Her music has been recorded with increasing frequency, and Anne Sofie von Otter's magnificent CD of *mélodies* issued in 2002 (DGG) is a real standout.

Chaminade was born in Paris in 1857 to a well-bred family. She began piano lessons with her mother. Prohibited by her father from attending the Conservatoire as a regular student, she received private lessons from several members of the faculty, including Félix Le Couppey and Antoine-Francois Marmontel. Near the family's suburban residence in Le Vésinet, Georges Bizet, the opera composer and a neighbor, predicted a bright future for the budding musician. Over her career Chaminade composed more than four hundred works. While piano miniatures and *mélodies* account for the lion's share, large-scale works for chamber groups and for orchestra populate the 1880s. Most of these pieces were reviewed, many of them favorably. We can see a Germanic influence in some, especially the *Concertstück* for piano and orchestra of 1888, the opening of which bears a striking resemblance to the start of Wagner's opera *The Flying Dutchman.*

With the death of her father in 1887, Chaminade felt a strong need to make a living through her music. She achieved it through the sales of published music and through tours to England and throughout the Continent. She met many members of royalty, and got along well, it is said, with Queen Victoria. Eventually Chaminade formed a long-term relationship with the Parisian publisher Enoch, who issued most of her pieces. In fact, Chaminade stands out among women composers because such a large proportion of her compositions originated expressly for the publishing market, and hence so many pieces exist as published works. In the next decades, some of her works were recorded. Artists of the caliber of tenor John McCormack and soprano Geraldine Farrar rendered her famous *mélodies* on disk. From 1908 to circa 1920, the composer herself recorded several pieces on piano rolls for the Aeolian Company.

Chaminade's music has attracted audiences and performers alike. Her character pieces for piano, some with fanciful titles such as "La Lisonjera" (The Flatterer) and "Scaramouche," exude an ease and elegance that make them suitable for intimate performance venues. They beautifully capture the mood of *la Belle Epoque.* The melodies are tuneful and memorable; the harmonies are mostly diatonic and avoid heavy chromaticism; the textures are clear and direct; and the forms are simple and often draw on dance or vocal idioms. These elements often led reviewers to single out "feminine" traits in her music, a characterization that usually meant a negative appraisal; either there was too much of this quality, or the critic found it missing when Chaminade's music displayed too many "masculine" traits. The musicologist Judith Tick, among others, has described the practice as a kind of "sexual aesthetics" that was applied to works by women in this period.

Chaminade's Piano Sonata, Op. 21, is her only keyboard sonata and was published in 1895. Its status as a large-scale instrumental work suggests that it was probably composed earlier, in the 1880s, when she was experimenting with large forms. It is dedicated to Moritz Moszkowski, a German composer and critic who would become her brother-in-law, and it is possible that he had a strong influence on the style of the work. Typical of the sonata genre, the work has three movements. The first movement is the weightiest and most complex; the second movement is a song-like Andante in ternary form; and the finale, previously published in *Six Etudes de Concert,* Op. 35 (1886), is a brilliant showcase for virtuosity. In contrast to her character pieces, Chaminade performed the Sonata only rarely in public. Perhaps she felt less comfortable with pieces of absolute music, which lack a descriptive title, or perhaps she believed that audiences had come to expect shorter and more tuneful pieces on her programs. Whatever the reason, the Sonata stands out in Chaminade's oeuvre and represents an important contribution to the sonata repertoire of the late nineteenth century.

The first movement, marked "Allegro appassionato," does not lie clearly in any traditional form. Instead, in the experimental spirit of many sonatas of the period, it combines several forms and procedures. Sonata form can be seen in the three-part scheme of the whole, the weight of the opening theme, and the strong recapitulation of this theme later on in the tonic key (m. 159). The movement moves at a leisurely pace, expansive in its presentation of material; this recalls the larger character pieces of Chopin, especially his ballades and scherzos. The first movement also incorporates fugue, beginning at measure 36, the subject of which becomes a kind of "second theme" developed in much of the movement, often in thematic transformation. This Lisztian device, in which a theme appears in another emotional guise, is especially noticeable in the middle section at measures 134–44. Although fugues are historically a Germanic feature, contemporary French composers such as Saint-Saëns, whom Chaminade knew well, were using the technique in their works. The piano writing in the movement is challenging in places, though not virtuosic as in the finale. At other times, especially when the tempo becomes less urgent ("Meno mosso," m. 134), the tone is relaxed, and one can glory in producing a rich sound. Harmonically the movement has a strong sense

MARCIA J. CITRON

of its tonic key, C minor. In fact, Chaminade seems to return to the tonic too many times and in unexpected places. The first theme is built up and then closed down in C minor, as in an ending gesture at measure 35. Then the fugue passage begins in C minor after a big break, as if starting a new piece. Even more surprising, the end of the first major structural section of the movement (m. 133), which feels dramatically like the end of a sonata-form exposition, ends in the tonic instead of in a contrasting key.

Indeed, this movement is unusual in that it does not establish a contrasting key area. It passes through and flirts with several keys, especially from measures 59 to 115, a large chunk of music, but never establishes one. This evasion led me to write a hypothetical analysis of the movement (in *Gender and the Musical Canon*, chapter 4) that suggests that the piece might avoid establishing a real second-key area because of its negative gendered connotations in nineteenth-century treatises that discuss sonata form. Beginning with the theorist A. B. Marx in 1845, first and second theme-groups were categorized respectively as masculine and feminine. The first, dubbed masculine, was described as assertive, rhythmic, and strong in its musical traits, while the second, labeled feminine, was characterized as delicate, lyrical, and nonassertive. Perhaps Chaminade's first movement avoids establishing a contrasting key and hence a second theme-group because it wishes to evade the gendered categories. If one major element is left out, in this instance the theme-group gendered "feminine," the gendered interplay and its associations of hierarchy are not engaged. A new narrative scheme is suggested, and perhaps this is one with which the composer (and her audience) might have been more comfortable. Of course, this is merely an analysis of possibility, one that offers an added perspective from which to view this rich work.

The movement ends with a grand flourish, similar to the gesture at measure 35 and measure 133. The nobility and length of the movement provide a fine opening to this wonderful sonata, a piece that deserves frequent performance in the piano repertoire.

Further Reading

Citron, Marcia J. *Cécile Chaminade: A Bio-bibliography*. Westport, Conn.: Greenwood Press, 1988.
———. *Gender and the Musical Canon*. Reprint Edition, with a New Introduction. Urbana: University of Illinois Press, 2000.
Tardif, Cécile. *Portrait de Cécile Chaminade*. Montréal: Louise Courteau, 1993.

Recording

Cécile Chaminade: Music for Piano. Gasparo GSCD-247. Enid Katahn, Piano (1994).

Allegro
Movement I from Sonata in C minor for piano

Cécile Chaminade

Original edition Paris, Enoch et Cie., 1895. Reprinted from *Cécile Chaminade, Three Piano Works.* Da Capo Reprint edition, 1979. Public domain.

MARCIA J. CITRON

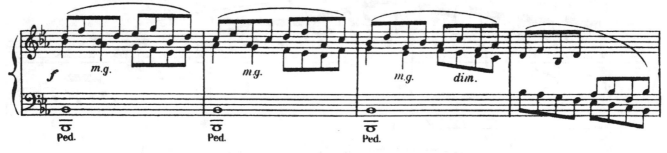

Marcia J. Citron

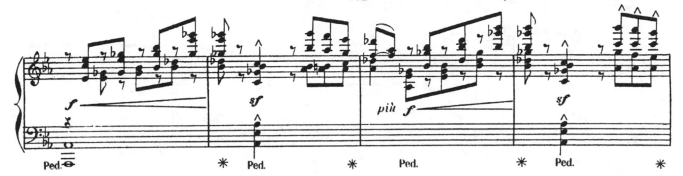

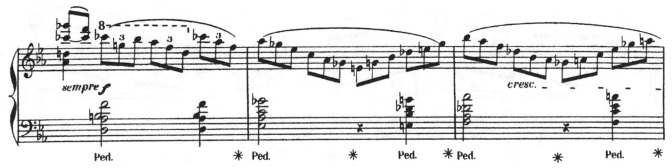

Cécile Chaminade

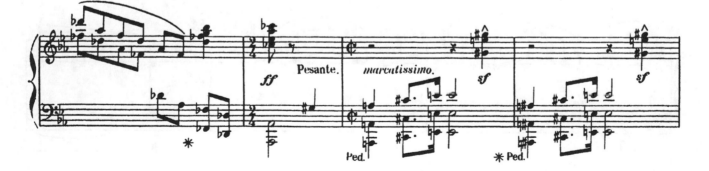

Marcia J. Citron

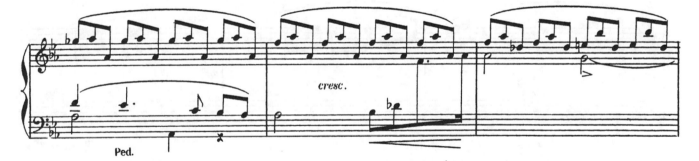

Cécile Chaminade

251

MARCIA J. CITRON

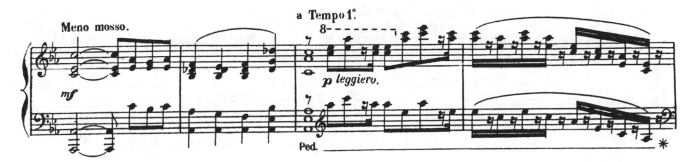

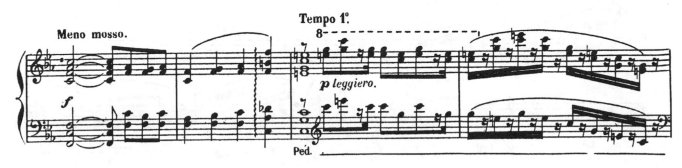

Cécile Chaminade

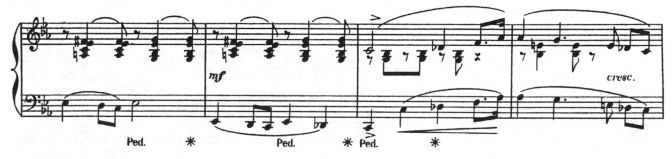

MARCIA J. CITRON

MARCIA J. CITRON

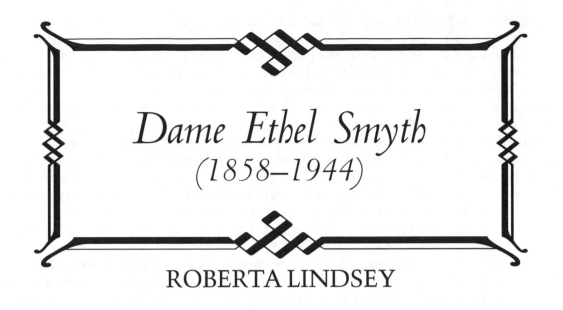

Dame Ethel Smyth
(1858–1944)

ROBERTA LINDSEY

Indomitable, Victorian-Edwardian, Lady, Composer, Writer, Suffragette, English, Nonconformist. All of these words describe Ethel Smyth. As a woman born in Victorian England, Smyth was expected to exhibit manners deemed proper by the rigid rules of English society. A young lady in an upper-middle-class family was educated in the genteel arts. She must know foreign languages, possess both artistic and musical skills for amateur entertainment, be well-read, "know how to darn stockings"—and eventually make a suitable marriage, one that might enhance her family's fortunes (St. John, 8). Ethel Smyth's father, a major-general in the British army, believed that all of his daughters would behave in an acceptable fashion. Her mother, distantly related to a baronet, quietly supported Ethel's decision to have a career as a composer. This career decision was difficult for her father to accept. Christopher St. John, in his biography of Ethel Smyth, relates that her father, believing that there was some impropriety on the part of well-known composer Alexander Ewing, brought his daughter's music lessons with the composer to an "abrupt end." Ethel reports her father's strange reaction upon hearing that his favorite daughter wished to be a composer: "It is not exaggeration to say that the life I proposed to lead seemed to him equivalent to going on the streets; hence the strange phrase he hurled at me, harking back in his fury to the language of Webster's or Congreve's outraged fathers: 'I would sooner see you under the sod' " (Smyth, 109). After months of tension, General Smyth finally allowed his daughter to travel to Leipzig with her brother-in-law, Harry Davidson, to attend what was considered to be the best musical conservatory in Europe. The terms of her father's capitulation were that he know the family with whom Ethel would be living, that she live within her allowance, and that she return home every summer for vacation.

The Leipzig Conservatory, founded in 1843 by Mendelssohn and some friends, is reported to have begun admitting women to its orchestration and composition classes in the 1870s. Pendle states, "It was assumed that the girls were studying to become performers or teachers rather than composers or conductors, and that they would limit their studies to voice, piano, or harp" (Pendle, 100). During Ethel Smyth's first and only year there (1877), she studied composition with Reinecke, conductor of the Gewandhaus concerts; counterpoint and general theory with Jadassohn; and piano with Mass. According to Smyth, "The lessons with Reinecke were rather a farce. . . . Jadassohn's classes, held in the Conservatorium, were at least amusing, but equally farcical as instruction; . . . Mass was a conscientious but dull teacher" (Smyth, *Memoirs*, 145). Not only did Smyth have disdain for her professors, but she also realized that the majority of students attended the Conservatory to "qualify for teachers' certificates" (Smyth, *Memoirs*, 146). Reportedly disgusted by the attitude of the students and professors, Smyth left the Conservatory to engage in private study with Austrian composer Heinrich von Herzogenberg, a close friend of Johannes Brahms (Fuller, Grove Online). Smyth remained in Europe for about ten years, returning home occasionally. The contacts she made during her stay in Europe proved invaluable for her future musical endeavors.

Smyth returned to England, where two of her orchestral pieces were performed to favorable reviews by the British press, which was "surprised to discover that E. M. Smyth was a woman" (Fuller, Grove Online). Her first large vocal and orchestral work was a Mass in D. This composition, included in Sir Donald Tovey's book on choral analysis, illustrated her dramatic abilities and her skill with handling large-scale forms. A friend from her Leipzig years, German conductor Hermann Levi, encouraged Smyth to write an opera after reviewing her Mass.

While it was not uncommon for a young composer to write a Mass, writing an opera presented a different type of challenge. Pendle notes, "England lacked a native tradition and an institutionalized structure for music making—it could boast only a few opera houses, very brief opera seasons, and a paucity of operas by English composers" (Pendle, 137). That Smyth would want to become an opera composer was unusual given the overall lack of support for English opera among British society. While operettas were acceptable for summer entertainment and for music halls, an opera required a larger orchestra, well-trained singers, extensive staging, and a suitable opera house for performance. Smyth persevered and composed six operas, *Fantasio, Der Wald, The Wreckers, The Boatswain's Mate, Fête Galante,* and *Entente Cordiale.*

Smyth's best-known opera is *The Wreckers.* The story was created after Smyth took a walking holiday with friends on the Cornwall coast. That such a rugged coastline and the wondrous stories told by the people of Cornwall should appeal to this English woman is not a surprise. Smyth was an intrepid outdoorswoman who enjoyed riding, walking, and various sports. She shared her experiences with Harry Brewster, who had written the libretti for her first two operas, and who was a friend from her continental days. Together they crafted the libretto for a third opera, which utilized as its background the practice of wrecking boats by moving lights to indicate false passages through dangerous seas. Looting the wrecks thereby ensured the survival of the community, a practice that existed for hundreds of years along the British coast. The Cornish coast, in particular, suggested this activity, as the land is too rocky to sustain crops. The members of the wreckers' community tended to keep an eye out for the most profitable venture and were even known for assisting the British navy during the Napoleonic wars. These wreckers knew the coastline and often prevented French spies from landing on the shore. However, there are also anecdotes that the wreckers may have aided French spies for a hefty price.

Smyth and Brewster's libretto is the tale of a young woman, Thirza, who is a preacher's wife. The preacher, Pascoe, is old, and Thirza has fallen in love with one of the young men in the congregation. She is horrified to learn that her husband, a man of God, is also the leader of the wreckers. He is one of the people responsible either for putting out the lights showing the safe passages through the rough waters around Cornwall, or for moving lights, causing the ships to falter. Once the ships run aground, the wreckers board them, steal from ship and survivors, and then kill the survivors. Then the wreckers leave the ship to the destructive forces of the sea and return to their communities. Thirza decides that she cannot be a part of this life and convinces the young man, Mark, that he must help her move the lights back into their proper position so that ships can safely navigate the churning waters. She and Mark are caught and brought before the Wreckers Committee—the law of the area. They are condemned to die by drowning in one of the many sea caves—similar to the one Smyth describes from her trip to the Scilly Isles, Cornwall:

> Some of the many smugglers' caves along that seaboard, the mouths of which are submerged at high tide, access being still possible by secret passages from the cliff above. The weirdest and most fascinating of them is the Piper's Hole in the Scilly Isles. On entering it, just above high water mark, you go downwards rapidly and alarmingly by an ever narrowing passage illumined by torches, which are stuck at intervals in rings in the wall; the passage suddenly bends sharp to the left, and you become aware, by the growling of boulders apparently only a few inches above your head, that you are under the sea; presently, to your great relief, the passage takes another turn, the rumbling ceases, and squeezing between two rocks at what seems to be the end of the cave, you behold an unearthly-looking little fresh-water lake, on which floats Charon's boat, while the waving torch of the guide reveals to you that the lake is full of goldfish (put there by the owner of that island, Mr. Smith-Dorrien) and that the goldfish are blind.
>
> Ever since those days I had been haunted by impressions of that strange world of more than an hundred years ago; the plundering of ships lured on to the rocks by the falsification or extinction of the coast lights; the relentless murder of their crews; and with it all, the ingrained religiosity of the Celtic population of that barren promontory, which, at the end of the eighteenth century, became the scene of Wesley's great religious revival! And I knew that these Cornish savages had come to believe that like the Israelites in the Old Testament they were God's Chosen People, whose right, nay, whose duty it was to plunder and extirpate less favoured peoples. And I learned too that Wesley had striven for ten years to wean his congregations from this hideous practice. (Smyth, *Memoirs*, 259–60)

The "romance" of the tales of survival against nature through the use of cunning and ingenuity was something understood by the people of this era. Nature and its glory represented a force that could not be fully tamed, but could instead be used to provide replenishment for the soul. (It was this very idea that inspired the great landscape architects to create public parks, such as Central Park in New York.)

The music for Smyth's opera, as shown in the following example, demonstrates the merging of her English musical tradition with her Germanic music training at the Leipzig Conservatory. A few of Smyth's melodies are reminiscent of the light operettas of Gilbert and Sullivan (Robertson, Opera News online). Her orchestration generates the necessary sound combinations to depict the rugged Cornwall coast, illustrating Kathleen Dale's statement that "She [Smyth] regarded the orchestra primarily as a medium for intensifying dramatic action or for evoking atmosphere" (St. John, 290).

Smyth's use of thematic material is similar to Wagner's leitmotiv, where the motive reflects a particular person, place, idea, or object. Such a motive is then used throughout the opera as a musical reminder to the audience. Pendle also notes that Smyth continues Wagner's tradition by not including clearly defined separations between numbers (Pendle, 139).

This example, the chorus of wreckers from the first act, demonstrates Smyth's ability to compose for the various voices. It also contains one of the major motives (found four measures after 33). This motive includes the intervals of a minor third followed by two major seconds. It first makes its appearance in the unison voices and then is echoed by the orchestra. The motive appears again fortissimo in the orchestra at 34. One measure after 34, Smyth's use of polyphonic texture is observed. Basses and tenors begin a passage that is repeated by the sopranos and altos. After incorporating a two against three pattern into the 6/8 meter two before 35, Smyth unites the choir in a homophonic hymn of ecstasy that a ship has foundered on the rocks. Another counterpoint passage is heard one after 36, with the altos and basses leading the tenors. The soprano entrance, four after 37, is combined with the altos over the tenor and basses separate melodies. It is possible to speculate that Smyth's polyphonic setting reflects the shouting of the wreckers to each other as they hurry through the storm down the cliffs to plunder the foundering ship.

The orchestration of this particular example replicates the surging power of the storm-tossed sea. The 6/8 meter invokes the power of the waves as they send a ship to the rocks. Tremolos are found in the treble part beginning one before 38 before switching to the bass at four after 38, where the main motive is once again heard in tenor and bass entrance.

Like her other operas, *The Wreckers* was not a commissioned work, and Smyth traveled from one major opera center to another seeking its production. The first performance was in Germany. The title and text were translated into German. Smyth objected to some of the cuts made by the conductor and removed the scores from the music stands before the second performance could occur.

Following the production of this opera, Smyth devoted two years to the British suffragette movement. During this time, she fully supported her friend Mrs. Pankhurst, leader of the cause. Smyth composed the music for a "March for the Suffragettes" and conducted a choral performance. This "March of the Women" was later incorporated into her fourth opera.

In her later years, Smyth suffered from illness and from deafness. A bout with influenza resulted in her "renunciation" of composing. Although Smyth stopped writing music, she did not stop writing; she authored ten books, mainly about her activities in the English arts and women's movement, and also providing a portrayal of English life during this time. Ethel Smyth was made a Dame Commander of the Order of the British Empire by the King of England in 1922 for her work as a composer and writer.

Further Reading

Collins, Louise. *Impetuous Heart: The Story of Ethel Smyth.* London: William Kimber, 1984.

Fuller, Sophie. "Smyth, Dame Ethel." In *The New Grove Dictionary of Music* Online, ed. L. Macy. http://www.grovemusic.com. Accessed February 2003.

Pendle, Karin, ed. *Women and Music.* Bloomington: Indiana University Press, 1991.

Robertson, Ruth. "Recording Review: Smyth The Wreckers." *Opera News* 59, no. 13 (March 18, 1995): 36.

Smyth, Ethel. *The Memoirs of Ethel Smyth.* Abridged and introduced by Ronald Crichton. Middlesex, UK: Viking Press, 1987.

———. *Impressions That Remained.* New York: Da Capo Press, 1981.

St. John, Christopher. *Ethel Smyth: A Biography.* London: Longmans, Green, and Co., 1959.

ROBERTA LINDSEY

Scene from act 1 of the opera *The Wreckers*

Dame Ethel Smyth

ROBERTA LINDSEY

Dame Ethel Smyth   263

ROBERTA LINDSEY

Roberta Lindsey

ROBERTA LINDSEY

May Frances Aufderheide
(1888–1972)

CAROLYNN A. LINDEMAN

One of the most successful and best-known women composers of ragtime, May Frances Aufderheide was from Indianapolis, Indiana. Ragtime flourished in many parts of the United States during its golden years (ca. 1896–1920), and Indianapolis was a major center for the development of white ragtime. Aufderheide made an impressive contribution to its development with her seven fascinating piano rags, two of which became best-sellers.

May Aufderheide was born on 21 May 1888, to John Henry and Lucy Deel Aufderheide. The family was middle class and of German heritage. Like many other young women of her generation, May took piano lessons. Playing the piano was considered a most worthy activity for young women of middle-class families, and it was studied, as was French, needlepoint, or any other "social grace." Her piano teacher was her Aunt May (May Kolmer), a professional musician in the Indianapolis area. While young May's piano studies focused primarily on classical music, she loved playing and composing popular music. It is said that she composed and played by ear.

In her late teens, Aufderheide became intrigued with piano rags. In addition to performing rags, she began improvising some of her own. It is not surprising that she decided to try her hand at composing. Rags were being showcased in the local five-and-dime stores by pianists–sales clerks, and interesting and exciting they were! Young women such as Aufderheide who were classically trained pianists were enticed to buy the sheet music and try this infectious music on their upstairs (or downstairs) parlor pianos. It did not take them long to discover that they, too, could compose rags of their own.

In 1908, at the age of nineteen, May Aufderheide published her first rag, entitled "Dusty." Considered the first major rag of the Indianapolis–Ohio Valley area, it was a big success and became one of her best-selling compositions. In fact, it was so commercially successful that her father decided to purchase the rights and start his own music publishing company, J. H. Aufderheide & Co., a sideline to his flourishing Commonwealth Loan Company.

The year 1908 was a significant one for May Aufderheide. Not only did she publish her first two rags, she also married Thomas M. Kaufmann, an architect from Richmond, Indiana. Her second rag of that year, "The Richmond Rag," must have been named in honor of her husband's hometown. Over the next several years she published five more rags: "Buzzer Rag" (1909), "The Thriller!" (1909), "A Totally Different Rag" (1909), "Blue Ribbon" (1910), and "Novelty Rag" (1911), along with several waltzes and at least eight songs. Her younger brother, Rudolph, was the lyricist for some of her songs, as were Earle C. Jones, J. Will Callahan, and Paul Pratt. All of her compositions were published by J. H. Aufderheide & Co., which also published the ragtime compositions of two other Indianapolis women composers, Julia Lee Niebergall and Gladys Yelvington.

Aufderheide's rags, like most, feature syncopated rhythms, duple meter, and a "ragged" (syncopated) melody line against a steady even eighth-note accompaniment pattern. Harmonically they stay close to the tonic, subdominant, and dominant in major keys. Aufderheide's rags are distinguished by the melodic chromaticism, open chords (especially for endings), syncopation, and pedal point that are prevalent in many of her compositions.

"The Thriller!" is the piano rag reprinted in this anthology. Like "Dusty," it was popular for decades in sheet music, piano rolls, and orchestrated versions. Apparently J. H. Aufderheide & Co. contracted the mechanical rights for these rags to six different piano roll companies. One was the Starr Piano Co. of Richmond, Indiana, while others were in more distant cities. This was considered an unusual marketing strategy for a small publishing company such as her father's.

"The Thriller!" is in three sections, with the following repetitions indicated in the score: AABBACC. The first section (A) touches upon the relative minor of the dominant, a feature of the classic rag style; a distinctive pedal point and "blue" thirds distinguish the second section (B); and in the third (C), a question/answer or call/response dialogue is featured between the right and left hands. This tossing of the melody back and forth contributes to the gradual build-up that results in the rag's dazzling finish. An abundance of melodic chromaticism is used throughout.

"The Thriller!" and "Dusty" lent themselves to jazz performances, although not all rags do. It is said that "Thirty-five years after their publication the great New Orleans trumpeter Bunk Johnson could play both from memory, so popular had they been with the early New Orleans jazz bands" (Blesh and Janis, 221).

Aufderheide published no new works after 1915 and apparently devoted the rest of her life to her family. Unable to have children of their own, she and her husband adopted a daughter. After several years of living in Richmond, Indiana, they moved back to Indianapolis, where Kaufmann tried to continue his career as an architect. Either his attempt to establish himself as an architect there was unsuccessful or he decided to make a career change. Shortly after moving to Indianapolis, he joined his father-in-law's prospering loan-brokering business. When Kaufmann retired from the family business decades later (1947), he and his wife and daughter moved to Pasadena, California. There they built a home called the "Rose Villa." It was on the grounds of the Huntington Sheraton Hotel and was designed by Kaufmann himself.

In 1958 May Aufderheide's daughter died, and her husband died a year or so later. May Aufderheide lived in the "Rose Villa" until her death on 1 September 1972. She is buried in a vault in the Mountain View Mausoleum in Altadena, California. After her death, the employees of the Huntington Sheraton Hotel were surprised to learn of her musical interest and talent. She apparently spoke little of her early composing and publishing career.

Aufderheide was fairly typical of the more than two hundred women composers who published rags during the ragtime era. She composed and published while in her twenties (some of her peers published into their thirties), and her composing career ended shortly after she married. Like the majority of women ragtime composers, she was white and a classically trained pianist, while ragtime in general was a black, male-dominated field. Her brief career accounts for the fact that she and many of her fellow women composers did not earn lasting reputations as composers. It was not until the ragtime revival of the 1970s that these women were rediscovered.

Regardless of how short-lived her musical career was, May Frances Aufderheide made a significant contribution to ragtime in the Indianapolis area with rags that were musical, interesting, and popular. Their quality and uniqueness are attested today with at least four of her rags reprinted in score form and six or more available on recordings. Her musical legacy lives on as we enjoy her music and properly credit her as a talented and noted woman composer of ragtime.

Further Reading

Blesh, Rudi, and Harriet Janis. *They All Played Ragtime.* New York: Random House, 1950.

The Thriller!

May Frances Aufderheide
Carolynn A. Lindeman, editor

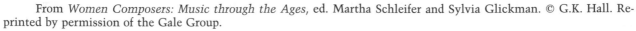

May Frances Aufderheide

273

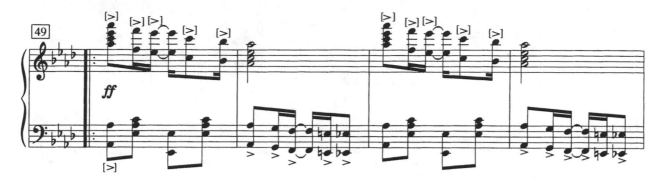

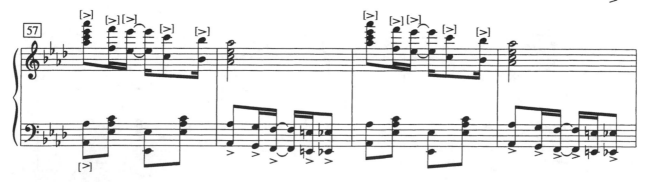

Carolynn A. Lindeman

Lili Boulanger
(1893–1918)

ANNEGRET FAUSER

The song "Demain fera un an" closes Lili Boulanger's song cycle *Clairières dans le ciel*, her first major composition after she won the Rome Prize in 1913. At that moment, she was nineteen years old and a celebrity in the musical world of Paris. Few musicians had ever won that prestigious prize at such a tender age. Besides, she was a beautiful young woman. What the public did not know, however, was that Boulanger had won this competition while fighting the illness that would eventually kill her at the age of twenty-four. Her frailty was a well-kept secret, protected by her family and friends. What the world saw was a child genius in the body of a fragile and beautiful princess.

Lili Boulanger grew up in a musical household, with both parents (Raïssa Mischetzky and Ernest Boulanger) and her sister Nadia trained or active as composers and performers. Her immense talent was recognized at the age of two, and she received a musical education from early childhood on. In 1895 she fell ill with bronchial pneumonia, after which her immune system was severely weakened. For the rest of her life, Boulanger was almost constantly ill, with either passing infections or outbreaks of her chronic condition of intestinal tuberculosis. Her frail health conditioned both her life, through the need for constant care, and her musical career, insofar as she had to rely on private lessons in composition and performance rather than a full musical education at the Conservatoire. In December 1909, after her sister Nadia gave up her attempts to win the Rome Prize, Lili decided to compete in her turn (her father, Ernest Boulanger, had won it in 1835). She prepared for the competition by studying privately with Georges Caussade, and, from January 1912, also with Paul Vidal when she entered his composition class at the Conservatoire for a short period. After an unsuccessful first attempt in the 1912 competition, she won the prize in July 1913 with the cantata *Faust et Hélène*. As a result, she was able to sign a contract with the Italian publishing house Ricordi, which offered her a decent annual income in return for the right of first refusal on publication of her compositions.

To compose a song cycle at that point in her career was a smart move: Boulanger could capitalize on her prize and ensuing fame with a substantial composition—one that could also be performed in its individual parts in the salons of Paris—while searching for a libretto that would allow her to conquer the most prestigious of all performance venues, the stage of the Paris Opéra. She wrote *Clairières dans le ciel* between December 1913 and November 1914, with revisions during the winter of 1914–1915. This was the first winter of World War I, which was probably why the publication of the song cycle was delayed until 1919, the year following both the end of the war and Boulanger's death.

The thirteen poems of the song cycle were taken from the Symbolist poet Francis Jammes's 1905 collection, *Tristesses*. With the exception of the penultimate song ("Je garde une médaille d'elle"), whose text is placed earlier in the collection, Boulanger kept Jammes's text order. Thus, the dramatic plot of the poetic cycle remains intact in Boulanger's condensed version in ways similar to the usual trimming of a poetic text to the bones of its plot, whether in song cycles such as Robert Schumann's *Dichterliebe* or in operas such as Claude Debussy's *Pelléas et Mélisande*. Dramatic cohesion was one of Boulanger's concerns as a composer, a trait visible not only in her text selection for *Clairières dans le ciel*, but also in her involvement in the preparation of the libretto for her opera *La princesse Maleine* (1912–1918).

Clairières dans le ciel traces the story of love lost, so common to the genre of song cycle after Franz Schubert's *Die schöne Müllerin*. In her final autograph copy of the cycle, Boulanger instructed her performer to sing "all these songs with the sentiment of invoking a past that has remained full of freshness." The comment was later omitted in the printed version, even though it offered a key to performance not only of the entire cycle, but especially of the final song. "Demain fera un an" is the only song whose text Boulanger altered, changing the dramatic direction of the cycle from Jammes's more cyclical organization to a more teleological one. Jammes ended "Demain fera un an" with a reminiscence to the collection's opening song, "Elle était descendue au bas de la prairie," thus referring his reader back to the beginning. Boulanger added a verse from the center of "Demain fera un an," right after Jammes's concluding recall of the opening verses of the collection

Plus rien. Je n'ai plus rien, plus rien quime soutienne.	Nothing. I have nothing left, nothing to support me.
Plus rien. Plus rien.	Nothing. Nothing.

With this one brief alteration to the poetic text, Boulanger thus moved the events from the continuous cycle of remembrance created by Jammes into a present in which the past is still fresh. Indeed, the present's nothingness gains sense only through invoking the past, as she instructed the performer.

Boulanger's setting of the cycle shows a composer finding her own voice. Her musical language reflects compositional concerns very much on a par with those of other composers of her generation, such as Arthur Honegger and Darius Milhaud, both a year older than Boulanger, and Francis Poulenc, who was six years her junior. Influences of Claude Debussy and Gabriel Fauré can be heard in the prosody, the motivic organization, and the harmonic language of the cycle, while the play with musical allusions—for example, Boulanger's reference to Tristan in "Si tout ceci n'est qu'un pauvre rêve," the sixth song of the cycle—is part of the French fin-de-siècle culture of sonic intertextuality. At the same time, however, characteristic elements of Boulanger's musical language begin to emerge in this cycle with her localized—and increasingly nonfunctional—use of harmony. It seems as if for Boulanger harmony was part of the musical surface rather than background, a color to clothe a musical structure derived from motivic and rhythmic relationships that form the structural skeleton of the piece. Whether in the use of Phrygian elements in "Je garde une médaille d'elle"—here both following and sublimating Fauré's use of the Lydian in his song "Lydia"—or in the highly chromatic sequence of seventh chords in "Parfois, je suis triste," Boulanger's use of specific harmonic modes and progressions remains localized. The overarching structure of the piece results here from (typically two-measure) cells that are employed as building blocks—see in particular "Si tout ceci n'est qu'un pauvre rêve"—to form a larger unit. I would argue that the poems—themselves often allusive in their use of poetic images and juxtapositions—offered a frame within which Boulanger could experiment with structural cohesion reached by means other than tonality, even though none of her compositions ever abandoned it entirely. In the remaining four years of her life, Boulanger's approach to the early-twentieth-century problems of organization, tonality, and structure in composition developed toward a less and less functional use of harmony and an increasing reliance on the developing variation of motivic and rhythmic cells. In her last work, *Pie Jesu* (1918), several passages are polytonal, while the use of extreme registers at the beginning of her setting of Psalm 130, *Du fond de l'abîme* (1910–1916), blurs the chords into low-register clusters.

All the works that I have mentioned so far are vocal. In part this is because of French composition training and the Parisian marketplace. Songs sold well in a world of bourgeois music-making, choral works had a wide group of possible users in amateur and professional choirs, and opera still was the most glamorous genre in France. But I would argue that for a young composer who tried her wings with new forms of musical-structural organization, the ready-made structure provided by the text offered an a priori framework that would allow her to experiment with the organization of the piece in purely musical terms. That this might have been the case with Boulanger can be seen in the few sketches that are surviving from the incomplete opera *La princesse Maleine*. In these sketches, Boulanger never seems to hesitate in the composition of vocal lines, which could best be described as hovering somewhere between the styles of Debussy and Dukas. This sureness, however, is contrasted with a much more experimental approach to the orchestra underneath. We can see in the sketches that Boulanger plays with various options for how to color specific chords in harmonic terms; her thematic organization and orchestration are much more fixed. Tonality thus seems to have been the unstable element in Boulanger's compositional process that could be manipulated to create the specific sonic quality needed at a given moment.

Boulanger also composed instrumental music. Very few pieces survive, mainly short works such as the light-hearted "Nocturne" (1911) and "Cortège" (1914) for violin or flute and piano, the theme and variations for piano (1911–1914), and the more developed character pieces "D'un matin de printemps" (1917–1918) and "D'un soir triste" (1917–1918). A symphonic poem (1915–1916) and a violin sonata (1912–1916) remained incomplete, although the latter—according to Nadia Boulanger—was close to being finished. That Boulanger was comfortable writing for the orchestra is obvious from her earliest works in this medium. Indeed, her manipulation of orchestral sounds was highly innovative, as both the *Vieille prière bouddhique* (1914–1917) and *Du fond de l'abîme* demonstrate.

When Boulanger died, only a handful of early pieces were published. Her music—so avant-garde when she wrote it between 1914 and 1918—was rarely performed and remained known only to a group of insiders that consisted mainly of Nadia Boulanger and her students. One member of this group, as Olivia Mattis has shown, was the young Arthur Honegger. He attended the first performance (1923) of Boulanger's Psalm 130, *Du fond de l'abîme*, and it appears that he also had access to the manuscript. The opening of this psalm is dramatic, colorful, and inventive, capturing the darkness of the text and the despair of its subject crying out from the depth of desolation in contrasting the cluster-like sonorities in organ, lower strings, and timpani with the dramatically upward-surging line in violins and wood instruments. In 1944, Honegger composed *Jeanne d'Arc au bûcher*, a piece whose opening shared not only the somber content of Psalm 130 in its text, but also the musical gestures so characteristic of Boulanger's psalm setting. But nobody knew the model for Honegger's striking opening. To all intents and purposes it was his, and his alone.

This intertextual reference—if such it was—was lost to an audience generally unaware of Lili Boulanger's work, for until recently she has been known mainly as a fragile girl whose life was cut short after two decades of dreadful suffering. The music behind the tragic legend of this child genius remained (and in part still remains) silent. The myth of a devout virgin overshadowed Boulanger's compositions for half a century and remained the hermeneutic key to her work until the 1990s. Autobiographical readings of works such as *Clairières dans le ciel*—whose subject is a fragile young woman who disappears mysteriously—or *La princesse Maleine,* an opera about a delicate princess who is brutally assaulted and killed by her fiancé's mother, are certainly tempting, given that Boulanger's life is often read as that of a frail young woman who died a gruesome death (witness, for example, Léonie Rosenstiel's detailed examination of medical treatment in her Boulanger biography). But such a reading devalues Boulanger's music as something similarly weak as her perceived persona as femme fragile. If she is viewed in the musical context of World War I and compared to her contemporaries, however, the picture changes radically. Suddenly Boulanger's music stands out as the works of a politically and culturally engaged composer whose musical language fits well in the context of her own and subsequent generations. While some of her works, in particular the Vieille prière bouddhique, show very Stravinskyian traits, her approach to compositional structure and harmonic color points to a composer fifteen years her junior: Olivier Messiaen. The fact that I have to invoke well-known male composers to convey the musical achievement of Lili Boulanger, the avant-garde composer, can (and should) be taken as a call to action. When her music is as widely played as that of other twentieth-century French composers such as Milhaud, Poulenc, and Messiaen, such comparisons will be obsolete.

Further Reading

Mattis, Olivia. "Lili Boulanger: Polytoniste." In *Lili Boulanger-Tage 1993, Bremen zum 100. Geburtstag der Komponistin: Konzerte und Veranstaltungen,* ed. Kathrin Moser, 48–51. Bremen: Callas Verlag, 1993.

Demain fera un an
from the song cycle *Clairières dans le ciel*

Lili Boulanger

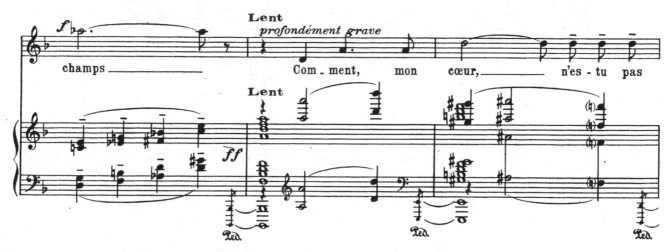

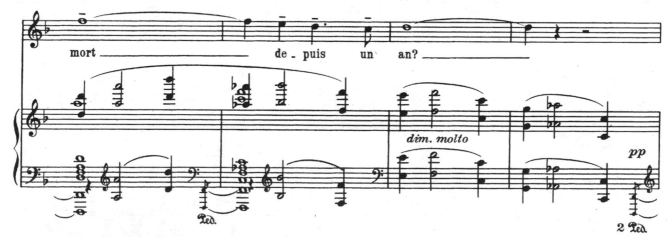

ANNEGRET FAUSER

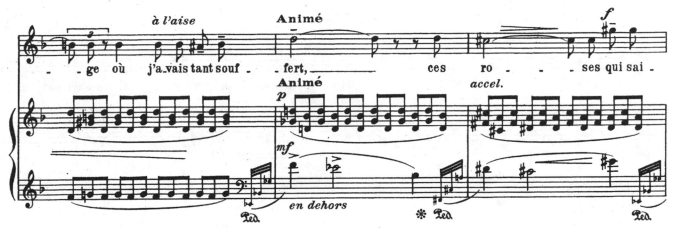

Lili Boulanger

ANNEGRET FAUSER

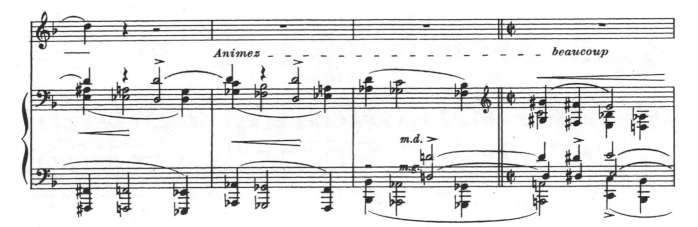

Lili Boulanger

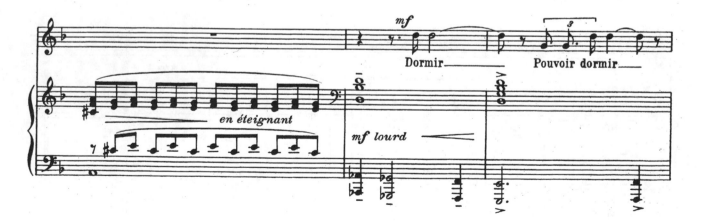

ANNEGRET FAUSER

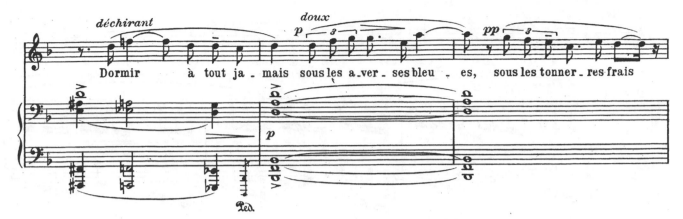

Dormir à tout ja_mais sous les a_ver_ses bleu_es, sous les tonner_res frais

Ne plus sen_tir. Ne plus sa_voir votre e_xis_

_ten_ce. Ne plus voir cet a_zur engloutir ces co_

_teaux dans ce verti_ge bleu qui mêle l'air à l'eau,

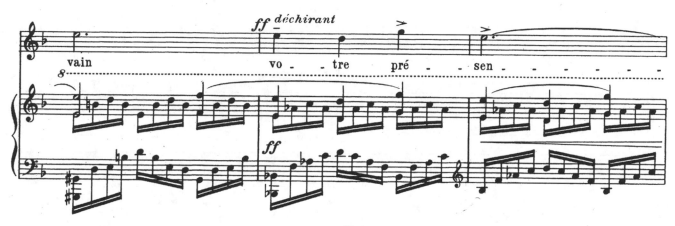

ANNEGRET FAUSER

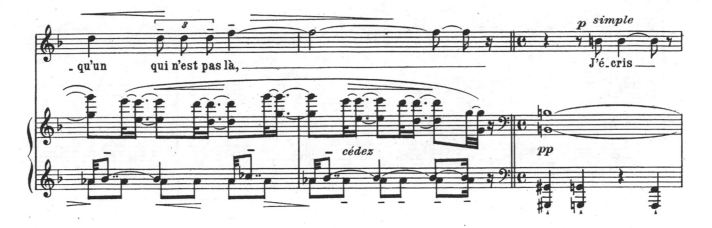

ANNEGRET FAUSER

Alma Mahler
(1879–1964)

SUSAN M. FILLER

Alma Mahler was the daughter of the artist Emil Schindler. During her long life she became a confidante of important men from many different fields of creativity, three of whom she married. In 1902 she became the wife of Gustav Mahler, who was then the director of the Vienna Opera and was also building a reputation as a major composer. He died in 1911, and four years later—after an affair with the artist Oskar Kokoschka—Alma married the architect Walter Gropius. The pressure of being separated from Gropius during his military service in World War I, combined with an affair with the young writer Franz Werfel, resulted in her separation and eventual divorce from Gropius. Alma and Werfel were married in 1929.

Alma's involvement with various men has resulted in her popular reputation as a *femme fatale*. This image is unfair, however, because it does not admit of her intellectual gifts. She was educated as a composer, studying counterpoint with Robert Gound and the blind organist Josef Labor and, at the turn of the century, composition with Alexander von Zemlinsky. In her autobiography she wrote, "Alexander von Zemlinsky was one of the finest musicians and . . . the teacher par excellence. His technical brilliance was unique. He could take a little theme, . . . squeeze it, and form it into countless variations."

While still a comparatively uneducated teenager, Alma began to compose music in many forms, including instrumental works. However, all of her surviving compositions are in the form of the lied, generally for medium voice and piano. Three books of songs were published: *Fünf Lieder* (Vienna: Universal Edition, 1910), *Vier Lieder* (Vienna: Universal Edition, 1915), and *Fünf Gesaenge* (Vienna: Josef Weinberger, 1924). In addition to these fourteen songs published during Alma Mahler's lifetime, two songs *Aus dem Zyklus* "Mütter" von Rainer Maria Rilke were published in 2000. A manuscript of the *Vier Lieder* (1915) survives in the collection of Henry-Louis de la Grange (Paris) and on film in the Toscanini Memorial Archive of the New York Public Library. No other sources for Alma Mahler's songs are known to exist. At the induction of the Third Reich in Austria in 1938, Alma and Franz Werfel left Vienna, leaving almost everything behind, including her manuscripts, which were destroyed when their house was bombed during World War II.

Alma and Werfel lived in France from 1938 to 1940. They were fortunate enough to escape when the Germans invaded France, and they moved to the United States. They lived in southern California near many of their friends, including Arnold Schoenberg,

Thomas Mann, and Bruno Walter. Werfel died in 1945; eventually Alma settled in New York, where she lived until her death in 1964 at the age of eighty-five. Of her four children (three daughters and one son), only her second daughter, Anna Mahler, lived to marry and have children. Her elder daughter by Mahler, Maria, and her son by Werfel, Martin, died in childhood; Manon, her daughter by Gropius, died of polio in 1935 at the age of eighteen.

In compositional style, Alma Mahler is something of a *Januskopf*. She had some affinity for the older piano style of Brahms and Liszt in her piano parts, which are demanding, with wide ranges, full harmonies, and equal partnership with the vocal parts. In other ways, however, her style looked forward to the harmonic dissonance and tight forms of the Second Viennese School. Credence is lent to Alma's description of Zemlinsky by comparison of her works with those of her fellow student Arnold Schoenberg.

The surviving songs show a decidedly modern taste insofar as the selection of texts is concerned: poems by, among others, Rilke, Otto Julius Bierbaum, Werfel, and Richard Dehmel. The last is a poet shared with Schoenberg, who was writing *Verklaerte Nacht* at about the same time Alma composed some of her early songs. Rarely, it appears, did Alma choose poems written before her own time; most of her poets were her contemporaries.

Performances of Alma Mahler's songs, initially rare, have increased in recent years; the most widely publicized have been by Lorna Myers and Suzanne Mentzer at the Ravinia Festival and by Eva Bruun Hansen in Copenhagen. There are now also several recordings of the composer's songs, most notably a CD of the complete songs in chamber orchestrations by Julian Reynolds, who conducted the orchestra of Brabant, Netherlands, with Charlotte Margiono as soloist. A more fully orchestrated version of the songs was also made by the British composers Colin and David Matthews, which has thus far not been recorded. The song "Der Erkennende," reproduced below, figures in all of the above live and recorded performances. The text is by Franz Werfel, whom she later married. In her autobiography she wrote:

> An episode in the summer of 1915 was the first cause of an upheaval in my life. . . . I bought the latest issue of a monthly called *Die weissen Blaetter,* and when I opened it I saw a poem: "Man Aware" ["Der Erkennende"] by Franz Werfel. . . . The poem engulfed me. It has remained one of the loveliest in my experience. I was spellbound, a prey to the soul of Franz Werfel, whom I did not know. . . . I set the poem to music, arbitrarily concluding halfway through the second stanza.

The following is a translation of the full text of Werfel's poem, of which Alma set only the first three stanzas:

Text Translation

Human beings love us and, unblessed,
They arise from table to lament us.
So we sit bowed over the cloth
And are indifferent and can deny them.

That which loves us, how we thrust it *away*!
And no sorrow will soften us callous ones.
That which we love snatches a place,
Becomes hard and no more reachable.

And the word that rules is: Alone!
When we impotently burn to each other.

SUSAN M. FILLER

One thing I know: Never and nothing is mine.
Mine alone to recognize that*

See the friend who portions your food,
Behind brow and countenance gathering together.
Where your glance hastens to meet him too,
A rock abides to bar the entry.

When I float through the range of the lamps
And evil wanderer, hear my steps,
Then I awaken and am close by,
And I myself am one who sneers, and an Other.

Yes, who descends to this position,
Where the solitary one severs and cleaves himself asunder,
That one himself dissolves in his hand
And nothing exists to fold him up.

In no more slumber is he embodied,
He always feels, while we sustain ourselves.
And the night of life, which remains to him,
Is inescapably a forest of mourning.

Further Reading

Filler, Susan M. "A Composer's Wife as Composer: The Songs of Alma Mahler." *Journal of Musicological Research* 4 (1983): 427–41.

———. *Gustav and Alma Mahler: A Guide to Research.* New York: Garland Publishing, 1989.

Mahler, Alma. *Mein Leben.* Frankfurt am Main: S. Fischer, 1960.

———. *Two Lieder.* Ed. Susan M. Filler. Bryn Mawr, Pa.: Hildegard Publishing, 2000.

———. *Vier Lieder.* New critical edition, ed. Susan M. Filler, Nadine Sine, and Juliane Urban. In *Women Composers: Music through the Ages.* Series Editors Sylvia Glickman and Martha Furman Schleifer. Boston: Gale Group, 2003.

Mahler-Werfel, Alma. *And the Bridge Is Love.* New York: Harcourt, Brace, 1958.

———. *Tagebuch-Suiten.* Ed. Antony Beaumont and Susanne Rode-Breymann. Frankfurt-am-Main: S. Fischer, 1997.

Schollum, Robert. "Die Lieder von Alma Maria Schindler-Mahler." *Oesterreichische Musikzeitschrift* 34 (1979): 544–51.

Urban, Juliane. "Die Lieder von Alma Mahler-Werfel geb. Schindler (1879–1964)." M.A. thesis, Freie Universitaet Berlin, 1994.

Werfel, Franz. *Das lyrische Werk.* Ed. Adolf D. Klarmann. Frankfurt: S. Fischer, 1967.

*Alma's setting ends here.

Der Erkennende

Alma Mahler

SUSAN M. FILLER

leicht bewegt (Tempo II.)

nei - nen.

Was uns

liebt, wie sto - ßen wir es fort und uns Kal - te kann kein Gram er -

espress.

wei - chen. Was wir lie - ben, das ent - rafft ein Ort, es wird hart und

rit.

Tempo I.

nicht mehr zu er - rei - chen.

molto rit.

Alma Mahler

293

Und das Wort, das wal-tet, heißt: Al - lein, wenn wir

macht - los zu ein - an - der bren - nen. Ei - nes weiß ich: nie und

nichts wird mein. Mein— Be - sitz al - lein,

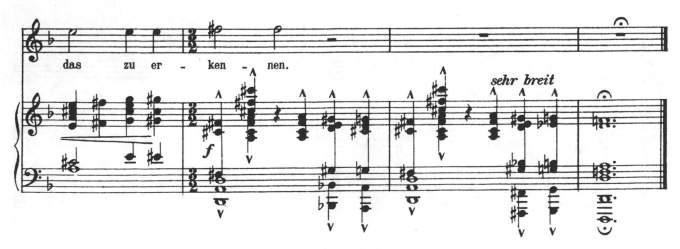

das zu er - ken - nen.

Susan M. Filler

Rebecca Clarke
(1886–1979)

BRYONY JONES

The meager entry on Rebecca Clarke in the 1980 edition of *The New Grove Dictionary of Music and Musicians*, which stated simply "Clarke, Rebecca b. Harrow, 2 Aug 1886. English viola player and composer, wife of James Friskin," summed up a typical attitude of indifference toward women composers prevalent throughout Western musical history. The fact that the entry on her husband also included several important details about Clarke—information that would have been far more appropriate under her own name—did nothing but add insult to injury for a composer who was one of the most significant English talents of her generation.

Clarke was born in Harrow, the eldest child of her Bostonian father, Joseph Clarke, and German mother, Agnes Helferich, into a household in which Victorian values were upheld. Joseph was a complex and domineering character capable of moments of appalling cruelty, and Rebecca's troubled relationship with him is detailed in her unpublished memoir. Her first music lessons were on the violin, and she studied at the Royal Academy of Music from 1903 until her harmony and counterpoint teacher, Percy Hilder Miles, proposed to her, prompting her father to withdraw her from the course in 1905. Later she studied at the Royal College of Music (RCM; 1908–1910), where she was one of the few female composition students of Sir Charles Stanford, England's foremost teacher of composition at that time. While at the RCM, Clarke gained two prizes in composition—an early indication of her talent. However, an argument with her father in 1910 resulted in her being thrown out of the family home, and, unable to finance further study, she was left with no choice other than to withdraw from the course. On leaving, however, she gained a place in the Norah Clench Quartet, the first of numerous professional chamber ensembles with which she performed throughout her career.

A regular visitor to the United States, Clarke was visiting her brothers in New York at the outbreak of World War II, and she was refused a visa to return to England. From then on, the United States was her home. In 1944, a chance meeting with the Scottish composer James Friskin, who had been a fellow student of Stanford at the RCM, renewed an old friendship, and the two married later the same year. After her marriage, Clarke's compositional output slowed considerably, and she completed her last work (other than revisions of earlier pieces carried out in the 1970s) in 1954. Friskin did not prevent Clarke from composing; indeed, he encouraged her to do so, but for various reasons she felt unable. She died in New York in 1979 at the age of ninety-three.

Clarke was an important figure in English musical history: she knew Vaughan

Williams and Holst, met Ravel (and told his fortune!), had viola lessons with the renowned violist Lionel Tertis, was present at the inaugural meeting of the Society of Women Musicians in July 1911, and played in Sir Henry Wood's New Queen's Hall Orchestra (she was one of the first six women admitted to the orchestra after auditions in 1913). She wrote songs for the distinguished tenor Gervase Elwes and the baritone John Goss, and as a chamber musician played with well-known performers such as Pablo Casals, Arthur Rubinstein, Guilhermina Suggia, Myra Hess, and the d'Aranyi sisters, spending much time traveling across Europe, America, and beyond, giving concerts. As a composer and violist she was extremely well respected in her day, and a concert of her works was held at the Wigmore Hall, London, in 1925. In addition to her skills as a composer and performer, Clarke wrote several articles for important music publications, as well as her memoir and extensive, though also unpublished, diaries.

Clarke is best known for her Viola Sonata (1919) and Trio (1921), but she actually completed more than one hundred works. She restricted her musical horizons to small-scale genres: chamber music, songs, and choral pieces. The majority, written from the late 1910s to the late 1920s, remained unpublished during her lifetime. Nevertheless, they show a remarkable consistency in quality, an individual voice, and an outstanding technical authority that is evident from the smallest song to the larger multimovement chamber pieces. Her Viola Sonata and Trio are the most expansive works of her career, and they did much to keep her name alive during a lengthy period when her absence from the pages of many music history books indicates that she was almost completely forgotten.

A renewed interest in Clarke's music began to gather pace in the 1970s, something which, fortunately, she lived to see. Today that interest is at an all-time high, and Clarke is at last beginning to receive the recognition she deserves: since 1998 much more of her music has been published for the first time, recorded, and issued on CD. She has a society named in her honor and a significantly longer entry in the second edition of *The New Grove Dictionary of Music and Musicians* (published 2001). Clarke was always extremely modest about her skills as a composer, but the attention she received during the early stages of her revival in the 1970s clearly caused her great pride. Now that her reputation has grown, it is only to be hoped that performances of her music will allow it to reach a wider audience.

Like her Viola Sonata of 1919, Clarke's three-movement Piano Trio (1921) was written as an entry for a competition held as part of Elizabeth Sprague Coolidge's annual festival of chamber music at Pittsfield, Massachusetts. Coolidge (1864–1953), who first met Clarke around 1916, was an important patroness of the arts and a supportive friend to many composers and performers. During the 1919 competition, Clarke's Viola Sonata caused a sensation when it tied for first place with a Suite by Ernest Bloch. When called upon to break the deadlock and declare a winner, Coolidge chose the Suite, but the judges demanded to know the identity of the runner-up (the competition had been anonymous), and many were surprised to discover that the composer was a woman.

In the 1921 competition, Clarke's Trio was also awarded second prize, losing this time to a work by the English violist and composer Harry Waldo Warner. Clarke's Trio was not performed at the festival, but was premiered by the Elshuco Trio during a private dinner party in New York on 12 February 1922. The first public performance was given on 3 November 1922 at the Wigmore Hall by Myra Hess (piano), Marion Hayward (violin), and May Mukle (cello). After disappointing rejections from several publishers, the Trio was finally published by Winthrop Rogers in 1928.

There are many similarities between the Viola Sonata and Trio, although the latter work is more complex harmonically and rhythmically and shows how Clarke's musical thinking had changed in the intervening two years. There are connections, too, with the other mature chamber works, in terms of harmonic language, the way the music is constructed, and even the use (or reuse) of specific thematic material. The 1918 work for viola and piano "Morpheus," for example, is in many ways a precursor to the Viola Sonata.

The basis of Clarke's compositional method is the transformation and repetition of motifs, and in the Viola Sonata and Trio, certain themes are also treated in a cyclic way. In the final movement of the Trio ("Allegro vigoroso"), Clarke introduces and transforms new motifs and cleverly combines these with themes from the first and second movements ("Moderato ma appassionato" and "Andante molto semplice") to create a satisfying sense of unity. A military-inspired figure used in all three movements provides another connection with the Viola Sonata and Rhapsody, in which similarly martial themes also make prominent appearances. Variously transformed repetitions of the Trio's "bugle-call" theme culminate in the third movement (given below) in a richly expressive piano solo.

A common rhythmic feature of much of Clarke's chamber music, noticeable in the Trio, is the simultaneous appearance of duplets against triplets, or triplets against quadruplets. The third movement of the Trio has a marked rhythmic flexibility, too, with familiar phrases extended and made irregular through frequent meter changes.

Most of the third movement is scored for all three instruments playing simultaneously, although in the other movements different combinations are used more often. Clarke exploits the full ranges and dynamic capabilities of the violin, cello, and piano, and creates different textural colors by using harmonics and pizzicato in the strings. Piano textures in the third movement vary from a single high melodic line and long, held chords to sweeping arpeggios divided between the hands. Swells in dynamic suggest the influence of Debussy.

Clarke's musical style is eclectic and distinctive, regularly combining "French" harmonic characteristics inspired by the music of Debussy and Ravel with chromatic, octatonic, and modal writing. It is worth noting, too, that her music is always meticulously constructed, a testament both to the lessons she had with Stanford and to a great deal of natural talent. The Trio is a remarkable work, of which Clarke was justifiably proud. It has been recorded several times and reissued by Da Capo Press (in 1981) and Boosey and Hawkes (in 1994).

Further Reading

Banfield, Stephen. "Rebecca Clarke." In *The New Grove Dictionary of Women Composers*, ed. J. Sadie and R. Samuel. London: Macmillan, 1994.
Curtis, Diane. *A Rebecca Clarke Reader*. Bloomington and Indianapolis: Indiana University Press, 2004.

Allegro vigoroso
Movement III from Trio for Piano, Violin, and Cello

Rebecca Clarke

Bryony Jones

Rebecca Clarke

BRYONY JONES

Rebecca Clarke

BRYONY JONES

Rebecca Clarke

BRYONY JONES

Rebecca Clarke

307

　　　　　　BRYONY JONES

Rebecca Clarke

Bryony Jones

Rebecca Clarke

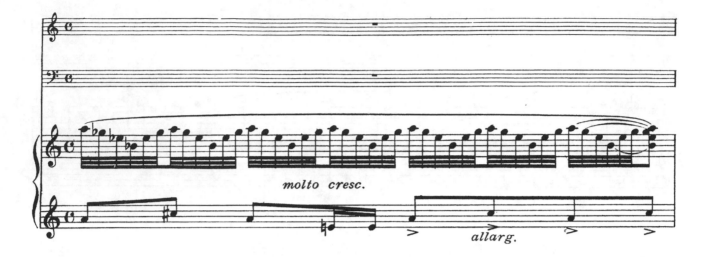

BRYONY JONES

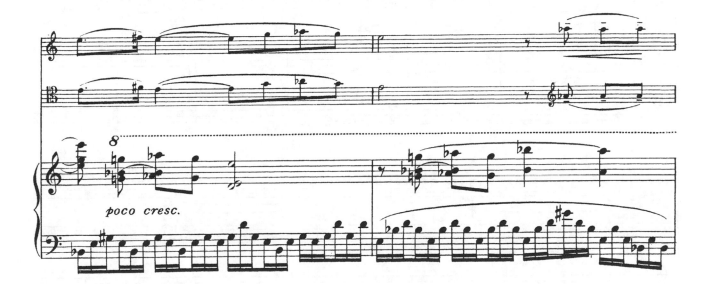

Rebecca Clarke

Tempo I

1921

Rebecca Clarke

Germaine Tailleferre
(1892–1983)

CAROLINE POTTER

If Germaine Tailleferre is known at all nowadays, it is because in 1917–1921 she was a member of the Nouveaux Jeunes, a loose association of composers grouped around Erik Satie, and then of Les Six, with Georges Auric, Louis Durey, Arthur Honegger, Darius Milhaud, and Francis Poulenc. But she continued composing almost until the end of her life, and many of her best works were written after the heyday of Les Six.

Tailleferre was something of a prodigy as both a pianist and a composer, and she had an excellent ear and memory. As a young woman, she often played her own Stravinsky ballet transcriptions in salons. She entered the Paris Conservatoire in 1904 despite great opposition from her father, who believed that institution to be a place of perdition comparable only to the red light district (Tailleferre, 12). However, she was encouraged by her mother, who introduced her to Eva Sauterau-Meyer, a solfège teacher at the Conservatoire who accepted Germaine as her pupil. Despite having to earn money by giving private lessons, as her father refused to support her, she won more first prizes at the Conservatoire than any other member of Les Six.

Tailleferre met Milhaud, Honegger, and Auric in 1913 in Georges Caussade's counterpoint class. Milhaud introduced her to contemporary composers; she eagerly devoured their music and came to detest the reactionary atmosphere of the Conservatoire. She was even expelled from Eugène Gigout's organ class for improvising in a style inspired by Stravinsky. Around this time, Tailleferre was torn between pursuing music or art, but the turning point came when a fellow Conservatoire student, a Swedish friend of Satie, told her of his plan to put on concerts at 6 rue Huyghens, a Montparnasse artists' studio. Satie had overheard Tailleferre and the pianist Marcelle Meyer practice her *Jeux de plein air* for two pianos (1917); when he discovered that Tailleferre was the composer, he allegedly kissed her, called her his "fille musicale" (Tailleferre, 26), and invited her to participate in a rue Huyghens concert. Young painters such as Picasso and Braque exhibited in this space, and Tailleferre developed friendships with many of the best-known Paris-based artists of the time. In an introduction to one of these concerts written in early 1918, Satie referred to the composers on the program as the "Nouveaux Jeunes," and some of these composers were subsequently baptized "Les Six" by the journalist Henri Collet in two articles in *Comoedia* in January 1920. Tailleferre remained close to her Les Six friends throughout her life, and always stressed the fun and camaraderie of the early 1920s, but she was never interested in group propaganda and never claimed that they adhered to a common style. For instance, she took no notice of their spokesman Jean Cocteau's belief that young musicians should draw inspiration from popular sources. She also struck up a friendship with Ravel (who advised her on orchestration), much to Satie's disapproval.

Tailleferre also took lessons from Charles Koechlin in both orchestration and composition at various times from 1916 to 1923. In later 1920 she began the Violin Sonata represented below, which has affinities with Koechlin's Viola Sonata (1915) in its large-scale four-movement plan and frequent bitonal clashes. Her Sonata was composed for Jacques Thibaud, whom she had met during a short visit to England in 1920, and with whom she had a brief relationship. Thibaud, accompanied by the pianist Alfred Cortot, premiered the work in June 1922 at the Théâtre du Vieux-Colombier in Paris. As is typical with Tailleferre, this work is essentially tonal (in the key of C-sharp minor), although chords may not resolve in the traditional manner, and she occasionally experimented with bitonality (following Stravinsky and Ravel's lead). Her fondness for modally inflected melodic lines is also evident in the first movement, as is her liking for thick piano textures, which she shares with Poulenc. The large scale of the sonata, together with Tailleferre's employment of traditional sonata form in the first movement, reveals that she viewed the work as a serious musical statement.

Tailleferre received many prestigious commissions in this period. Perhaps her most successful work of the 1920s was *Le marchand d'oiseaux* (The Bird Seller), a ballet composed for the Ballets Suédois, which was performed ninety-four times from its premiere in 1923 until the final Ballets Suédois season in 1925. The Ambache Chamber Orchestra gave the first modern performance of the work in 2002 in London. In her autobiography, published in the *Revue internationale de musique française* in 1986, Tailleferre amusingly recalls her attempts to demonstrate ideas for the choreography of the ballet: "In my enthusiasm and abandon, I started to dance, or rather run, from one end of the stage to the other, kicking up a cloud of dust with my shoes [. . .] it sounded like a cavalry charge! (Tailleferre, 31). The ballet is a charming example of the neoclassical style, drawing on traditional forms and dances and employing often acidulous harmonies with a distinctly modern twist.

One admirer of *Le marchand d'oiseaux* was the Princesse de Polignac, who had already supported Tailleferre by inviting her to St.-Jean-de-Luz in the winter of 1920 to write her Violin Sonata No. 1 in peace. The princess commissioned a Piano Concerto "because she had been impressed by the Scarlatti-like touches in [. . .] *Le marchand d'oiseaux*" (Cossart, 159–60) It is in a very similar style to the ballet—the outer, fast, movements are even in the same key as the ballet's overture—and the slow movement is one of her finest creations. Alfred Cortot, who performed the concerto in the United States as well as France, greatly admired the work, as did Stravinsky, who called it "honest music" (Tailleferre, 33).

Tailleferre decided to try to establish herself as a composer and teacher in the United States in the wake of this success. However, she was unable to find enough work to support herself and her elderly mother, and returned to Paris in May 1925. She returned to New York in 1926 and met the caricaturist Ralph Barton, who proposed to her on the evening of their first meeting. Unsure of her feelings and lacking confidence, Tailleferre asked friends for advice, and was persuaded to accept Barton's proposal. They married in Connecticut late in 1926 (Barton's fourth marriage), and a week later Tailleferre was introduced to Charlie Chaplin. Chaplin and Tailleferre enjoyed improvising at the piano together, and the movie star wanted her to return to Hollywood with him and write music for his films. But Barton refused to allow Tailleferre to pursue this idea (Tailleferre, 51). Although Tailleferre was attracted to Barton's charm and extensive French cultural interests, the marriage soon ran into difficulties. Serge Koussevitsky conducted her neoclassical Harp Concertino in 1927 (Tailleferre played the instrument), but her pleasure at

Germaine Tailleferre

hearing the work was marred by a fit of jealousy on the part of Barton, who made it clear that he would not tolerate being "Monsieur Tailleferre." The couple moved to France in 1927; Barton's manic-depressive tendencies came to the surface, and three years later he threatened to shoot the baby Tailleferre was carrying. This provoked a miscarriage, and Tailleferre was never to see him again, as he fled to New York and committed suicide in May 1931, a month after their divorce was pronounced.

By this time Tailleferre had married for a second time (her new husband was a lawyer, Jean Lageat) and had given birth to a daughter, Françoise. This marriage was to prove equally unsuccessful; there is evidence that her second husband beat her and their daughter and spattered her manuscripts with ink (Mitgang, 64). But in the 1930s she nevertheless wrote some of her best works, including the Violin Concerto of 1936, written in Switzerland for Yvonne Astruc and successfully transcribed as her Violin Sonata No. 2 in 1951. One of her happiest memories as a musician was her collaboration with Paul Valéry, with whom she wrote a cantata, *Narcisse,* in 1937, although her husband would constantly interrupt her work (Mitgang, 71). Also in the 1930s, she established herself as a film composer; her ability to write quickly to commission eased her constant financial worries, though it could be argued that this very facility and lack of self-criticism has harmed her reputation.

World War II greatly affected Tailleferre's career. She left France for the United States in 1942, escaping the Occupation, and wrote an informative article for the journal *Modern Music* about the pressures on French musicians, highlighting the appalling treatment of her Jewish colleagues and more mundane practical difficulties, which included a shortage of manuscript paper. In the United States she was cut off from her professional contacts, and she composed nothing more until her return to France in 1946.

In the early 1950s, she divorced Lageat and moved to the south of France, where she worked as an antique restorer in between composing commissions and concert tours with the baritone Bernard Lefort, who later became the director of the Paris Opéra. The duo visited London in November 1954, giving a recital at the Institut Français, where their program included works by all of the members of Les Six—excluding Tailleferre herself. Her seeming unwillingness to promote her music is surely another manifestation of the lack of self-belief that plagued her composing career. However, she later composed a concerto for Lefort to texts by the poet and playwright Jean Tardieu, a childhood friend whose mother had given her harp lessons. This work, *Concerto des vaines paroles,* was essentially a transcription of her large-scale *Concerto for two pianos, voice and orchestra,* which she wrote in 1933–1934. Perhaps because of time pressure, self-borrowing of this type was to become characteristic of Tailleferre from this period until the end of her career.

1957 was a vintage year for Tailleferre as a composer: she wrote an attractive Harp Sonata for the Spanish virtuoso Nicanor Zabaleta (whom she greatly admired), a work that harks back to her neoclassical style of the 1920s; a short opera, *La petite sirène* (based on Hans Christian Andersen's *The Little Mermaid*); and a lively *Partita* for piano, the outer movements of which are fizzing perpetuum mobiles, an idiom she often utilized. This rate of production is all the more extraordinary because 1957 was also a year of personal crisis; her daughter became estranged from her, leaving Tailleferre to bring up her granddaughter and step-grandson.

Tailleferre remained youthful in spirit until the end of her life, and although her works increasingly relied on self-borrowing, she also developed a new interest in composing for wind band, under the influence of her friend Désiré Dondeyne, then conductor of the Orchestre des Gardiens de la Paix. Having taught privately for many years, she accepted a part-time post as a pianist for children's dance classes at the Ecole Alsacienne (a private school near her final Paris home on rue d'Assas) in 1977, at the age of eighty-five. She worked there until shortly before her death, at the age of ninety-one, on 7 November 1983.

CAROLINE POTTER

Tailleferre was evidently determined to pursue her vocation as a composer despite dreadful personal crises, including her father's staunch opposition to her career and two failed marriages. But, in the words of her lifelong friend Madeleine Milhaud, she was "too honest, too upright" to promote her music aggressively (Mitgang, 93). Poulenc also referred to her "excess of modesty" (Poulenc, 337 note 9).

It is also fair to say that in her lifetime she suffered from prejudice against women composers, as many reviewers were unable to see beyond the fact that she was the only woman in Les Six. I believe that Tailleferre was more successful when handling large-scale musical forms—confounding the stereotype of the woman composer—which has perhaps not aided her posthumous reputation, as most currently available recordings are of smaller-scale works, which are more economically viable to perform and record. Although her output is undeniably uneven, her best works rank among the most attractive and successful composed by any member of Les Six, and they deserve to be far better known.

Further Reading

Buckland, Sidney, ed. and trans. *Echo and Chource: Francis Poulenc, Selected Correspondence.* London: Victor Gollanz, 1991.

Cossart, Michael de. *The Food of Love: Princesse Edmond de Polignac and Her Salon.* London: Hamish Hamilton, 1978.

Hacquard, Georges. *Germaine Tailleferre: La Dame des Six.* Paris: L'Harmattan, 1999.

Mitgang, Laura. "La Princesse des Six: A Life of Germaine Tailleferre." B.A. diss., Oberlin College, Ohio (n.d.).

Orledge, Robert. "A Chronological Catalogue of the Compositions of Germaine Tailleferre (1892–1983)." *Muziek en Wetenschap* 2, no. 2 (1992): 129–52.

Potter, Caroline. "Germaine Tailleferre (1892–1983): A Centenary Appraisal." *Muziek en Wetenschap* 2, no. 2 (1992): 109–28.

Shapiro, Robert. *Germaine Tailleferre: A Bio-bibliography.* Westport, Conn.: Greenwood, 1993.

Tailleferre, Germaine. "Mémoires à l'emporte-pièce." *Revue International de Musique Française* 19 (1986): 7–84.

Modéré sans lenteur
from Sonata in C-sharp minor for violin and piano

Germaine Tailleferre

Germaine Tailleferre

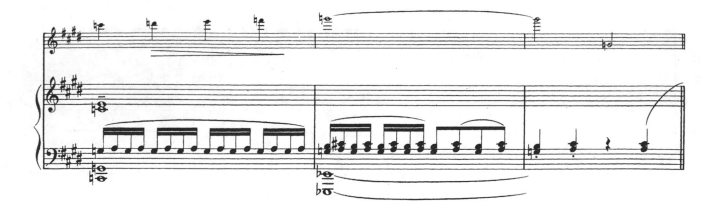

Caroline Potter

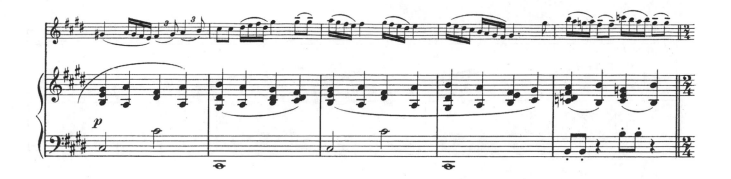

CAROLINE POTTER

Germaine Tailleferre

325

CAROLINE POTTER

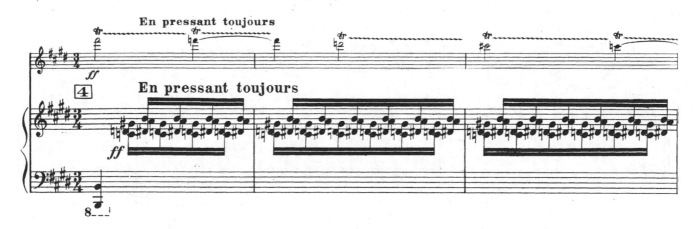

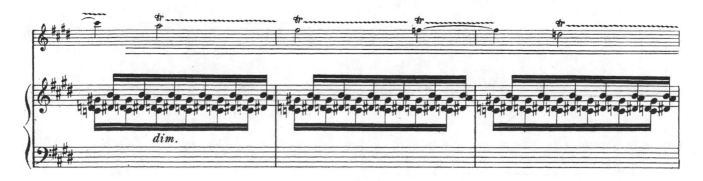

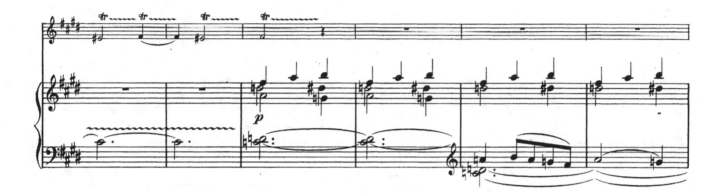

CAROLINE POTTER

CAROLINE POTTER

Ruth Crawford Seeger
(1901–1953)

SHARON MIRCHANDANI

Ruth Crawford Seeger, the first woman to win a Guggenheim Fellowship in composition, was a major composer in the American modernist movement of the 1920s and 1930s. She was also a pioneering advocate of American folk music in her work as a transcriber, editor, arranger, and music educator in the 1940s.

As a composer, Crawford belonged to the avant-garde of the 1920s and 1930s, referred to as the American Experimentalists or "Ultra-modernists." Others in this group include Henry Cowell, Carl Ruggles, and Edgard Varèse. Her reputation stems from a relatively small musical output of about fifteen major works composed between 1924 and 1936. The works are rich with original structural relationships, evoke strong emotion, and sometimes reflect social concerns. They include nine *Preludes for Piano* (Nos. 1–5 in 1924–1925; Nos. 6–9 in 1927–1928), *Music for Small Orchestra* (1926), *Sonata for Violin and Piano* (1926), *Suite for Five Wind Instruments and Piano* (1928–1928, rev. 29), *Five Songs to Poems by Carl Sandburg* (1929), *Suite No. 2 for Four Strings and Piano* (1929), four *Diaphonic Suites* for instrumental solos or duos (1930–1931), *Three Chants for Women's Chorus* (1930), *Piano Study in Mixed Accents* (1930), *String Quartet* (1931), *Three Songs to Poems by Carl Sandburg* for Contralto, Oboe, Piano, Percussion, and Orchestral Ostinati (1930–1932), and *Two Ricercare* for Mezzo Soprano and Piano (1930–1932).

Crawford's music can be divided into two style periods that correspond to the cities in which she primarily lived and composed: Chicago and New York. Her Chicago style is Expressionist, with its intensely emotional content and atonality, while her New York style is Constructivist, with its highly original and engrossing schematic forms. Her change in style may be profitably compared to that of the Second Viennese school.

Chicago

A Midwesterner and the daughter of a Methodist minister and his wife, Crawford was born in East Liverpool, Ohio, and raised in Jacksonville, Florida, where she received her early training in piano. In 1921 she entered the American Conservatory of Music in Chicago, intending to become a concert pianist and return home a "finished" musician. She soon changed her major to composition, and she received the Master of Music degree in composition in 1929. Adolph Weidig, a fine violinist and Berlin-trained composer, was her major composition teacher; some of her early works were performed at his annual student recitals.

In 1924 Crawford began to study piano with Djane Lavoie Herz, a noted interpreter of the music of the Russian composer Alexander Scriabin. Herz shared both Scriabin's music and his mysticism with Crawford. At the same time, as Crawford was developing her natural inclination toward dissonance and chromaticism, she met Henry Cowell and Dane Rudhyar through Herz. Her interest in dissonance and chromaticism was encouraged along with exploration in theosophy, transcendentalism, and eastern religious thought.

Crawford's interest in Scriabin's mysticism was characteristic of her. She was always able to accept a variety of approaches to God, and she enjoyed the process of seeking spiritual meaning more than relying on any one particular outlook. While in Chicago, Crawford sought spiritual insight in American Transcendentalism through the writings of Henry David Thoreau and Ralph Waldo Emerson. Her 1927 diary begins with descriptions of her summer spent at Dewey Lake with her mother, and on the first page she quotes a long passage from Thoreau's "Thoughts on Nature," underlining the portions she particularly liked. Crawford's reading of Thoreau and Emerson formed a foundation for her entire career. She frequently commented on the Soul or the Spirit in her diaries and expressed concern for society and a delight in nature.

Piano Prelude 2

Crawford composed her nine piano preludes in Chicago. Like Scriabin's piano preludes, Crawford's pieces emphasize quartal harmony and suggest an interest in alternative religious thought. Crawford labels passages in the music with the word "Mystico," and in her diary she wrote that one sounds like a human laugh and another was inspired by Lao-tse's *Tao.* Crawford's preludes are more freely structured than Scriabin's and more dissonant, with frequent seconds and sevenths. They use experimental pedal techniques, improvisatory-like melodies, symmetrical chord clusters, and ostinatos.

Prelude No. 2, Allegro giocoso, was performed in New York in 1925 by Gitta Gradova, a brilliant young pupil of Herz, and was described by the critic for the *New York Sun* as "sensational, pugnacious and curt." The basic material for the piece is found in the first chord, constructed of two perfect fifths separated by a minor second, and the opening melodic gesture of a tritone. The more romantic middle section (m. 21) uses thematic transformation in Lisztian style. Crawford achieves a sense of movement through strong contrasts of rhythmic patterns, and upper and lower registers of the keyboards.

"Rat Riddles"

Crawford spent the summer of 1929 at the MacDowell Colony in New Hampshire, where she composed her *Five Songs to Poems by Carl Sandburg.* In the fall of 1929, on the advice of Cowell, she moved to New York and began studying with Charles Seeger, who at that point in his eclectic career was a leading intellectual and theorist for American ultra-modern music. A 1927 entry in Crawford's diary stating that "Bach and Scriabin are to me the greatest spirits born to music" foreshadows her affinity for the dissonant counterpoint she adopted from Seeger. Her formal studies with Seeger lasted only about a year, but they were decisive in shaping her compositions for the remainder of her career (see Rao).

Crawford's strong interest in contrapuntal concerns is evident in her setting of Carl Sandburg's poem "Rat Riddles," which later became the first of *Three Songs for Contralto, Oboe, Piano, Percussion, and Orchestral Ostinati*. It was premiered in New York in April 1930 and received a number of performances in the next few years. The most important were in Berlin, at a concert conducted by Nicholas Slonimsky in March 1932, and in Amsterdam, at the festival of the International Society of Contemporary Music (ISCM) in June 1933. The *Three Songs*, along with Copland's *Piano Variations*, were chosen to represent the United States in competition at the 1933 festival of the ISCM in Amsterdam.

The concertanti section of "Rat Riddles" was completed in 1930, and the ostinati sections were added to the work by 1932. Crawford's dedication to heterophony is shown in her performance instructions published with the score:

> The concertanti section is complete in itself, and can be performed with or without the ostinati. The ostinati should be seated apart from the concertanti—if possible, at the rear of the stage. The concertanti and ostinati should, if possible, be rehearsed once or twice separately, in order that the independence of the two sections be understood by the players.

The ostinati section consists of twelve different chords presented in a rhythmic pattern that repeats eleven times (with slight variations), seldom coinciding with the concertanti parts (see detailed analysis by Joseph Straus).

The poem is a dialogue between a poet and a wise rat. The imagery of rat behavior allows the piano and oboe to "chase each other in the most surprising arabesques to a percussion accompaniment," as Charles Seeger later described this much-admired work. Crawford's careful attention to the formal aspects of the poem displays her literary sensitivity. She uses pitch repetition and intervals to correspond to related phrases and figures of speech and to Sandburg's characteristic alliteration. In keeping with the poem's mood, Crawford's vocal line is intended more as declamation than as lyrical melody. It interacts most with the oboe, which darts and scurries about. Oboe repetitions of D at key textual moments suggest extended tonality rather than avoidance of pitch centers. Describing the frequent tritones and sevenths, particularly noticeable in the piano and oboe, Charles Seeger related "its vicious little stabs of dissonance" to the composer's earlier Chicago period. The textural complexity and skillful handling of irregular rhythms is characteristic of her mature style.

String Quartet, Movements Three and Four

Crawford went to Europe in 1930–1931 on a Guggenheim Fellowship. She spent most of her year in Berlin and then traveled to a variety of European cities. Her String Quartet, completed in Paris in the spring of 1931, is her most famous composition, especially noted for its serial techniques. Although she was in Berlin when Arnold Schoenberg was teaching there, Crawford (who knew his twelve-tone method) never met him, did not consider herself a follower, and evolved her own methods. Movements 3 and 4 are presented here. Crawford's own 1948 analysis of these two movements is reproduced in Judith Tick's biography, and Tick, Joseph Straus, and Ellie Hisama have all analyzed the movements (see Further Reading).

When the Quartet was premiered by the Pan American Association of Composers in New York in 1933, the third movement, with its novel dynamic scheme, was immediately singled out for special praise. In 1949 Virgil Thomson described it as "striking for intensity and elevation. Consisting entirely of notes juxtaposed in slowly changing chords of high dissonance content, the piece seemed scarcely to move at all. And yet, it was thoroughly absorbing." Crawford's analysis describes its "heterophony of dynamics," in which "no high point in the crescendo in any one instrument coincides with the high point in any other instrument." Hisama offers a feminist interpretation of this movement as a reflection of Crawford's gender. She identifies two simultaneous "narratives": one of a dominant masculine voice leading to the climax (mm. 68–75) and one of a muted feminist voice (created by the "degree of twist" or number of voice crossings) that foils the climax with its cyclic organization.

In Crawford's analysis of the fourth movement, she refers to the first violin as "Voice I" and to the lower three instruments as "Voice II." Each voice systematically gains or loses a pitch at each successive entry. Voice I is free material that retrogrades at measure 60. Voice II is based on a ten-tone row, which is presented ten times on successive tones of the row. At measure 21 the row is transposed a whole step higher; at measure 60 it retrogrades with Voice I. Hisama argues for a feminist interpretation, based in part on the psychological contexts of the quartet, that designates Voice I as a female persona and Voice II as a male persona; in contrast, Straus suggests that a narrative that reverses those genders is equally plausible. Tick demonstrates how many details of the movement create "dissonance of mood."

In the fall of 1931, Crawford returned from Europe. She married Charles Seeger the following year. In 1935 they left New York for Washington, D.C., where both she and her husband began working for the Smithsonian as part of the New Deal program. She stopped composing; thereafter she transcribed, edited, and arranged folk songs for the rest of her life. In addition to providing more than two hundred transcriptions for John and Alan Lomax's *Our Singing Country*, she wrote a significant monograph, *The Music of American Folk Song*, intended as an introduction. At the time of *Our Singing Country*'s publication, the monograph was greatly shortened, and it was published in its entirety only in 2001, along with several shorter writings. Three major collections of Crawford's arrangements (*American Folk Songs for Children, Animal Folk Songs for Children,* and *American Folk Songs for Christmas*) are still used by music educators. The same attention to detail and appreciation of craft that Crawford showed in her composition comes across both in her scholarly writing and in her transcriptions and arrangements.

Crawford had many reasons to change from composition to folk music. After the Depression, disillusionment with avant-garde music was pervasive. In addition, she assumed primary responsibility for the couple's four children, born over a ten-year span, while contributing a large share of the family's finances. In 1939 Crawford composed a brief, largely tonal "American Fantasy for Orchestra," called "Rissolty, Rossolty," based on the folk tune. However, her 1952 *Suite for Woodwind Quintet* marks her true return to composition. Unfortunately she did not live long enough to produce more works. Crawford died of cancer in 1953, leaving behind a small body of exceptional works that show her extraordinary craft and her individuality as a modernist American composer.

Further Reading

Crawford Seeger, Ruth. *The Music of American Folk Song and Selected Other Writings on American Folk Music.* Ed. Larry Polansky with Judith Tick, with a Historical Introduction by Judith Tick and Forewords by Pete, Mike, and Peggy Seeger. Rochester, N.Y.: University of Rochester Press, 2001.

Hisama, Ellie. *Gendering Musical Modernism: The Music of Ruth Crawford, Marion Bauer, and Miriam Gideon.* Cambridge: Cambridge University Press, 2001.

Rao, Nancy Yunhwa. "Partnership in Modern Music: Charles Seeger and Ruth Crawford 1929–1931." *American Music* 15, no. 3 (Fall 1997): 352–80.

Seeger, Charles. "Ruth Crawford." In *American Composers on American Music*, ed. Henry Cowell, 110–18. New York: Frederick Ungar Publishing Co., 1962.

Straus, Joseph. *The Music of Ruth Crawford Seeger.* Cambridge: Cambridge University Press, 1995.

Tick, Judith. *Ruth Crawford Seeger: A Composer's Search for American Music.* New York: Oxford University Press, 1997.

Wilding-White, Ray. "Remembering Ruth Crawford Seeger: An Interview with Charles and Peggy Seeger." *American Music* 6 (1988): 442–54.

Selected Recordings

Ruth Crawford: American Masters Series. Includes Nine Preludes for Piano, Joseph Bloch, piano (1968). CRI 658 (1993) (remastering of LP recordings from CRI Archive).

Ruth Crawford Seeger: American Visionary. Continuum, Cheryl Seltzer and Joel Sachs, Directors. Three Songs for Contralto, Piano, Oboe, Percussion and Orchestral Obligati: "Rat Riddles." Musical Heritage Society, 513493M (1993).

Ruth Crawford Seeger: Portrait. Oliver Knussen, conductor; Reinbert De Leeuw, piano; Lucy Shelton, soprano; members of the Schönberg Ensemble; New London Chamber Choir. Includes *Three Songs for Voice, Piano, Oboe, Percussion, and String Orchestra:* "Rat Riddles," and *String Quartet 1931.* Deutsche Gramaphon, DG 449 925–2 (1997).

Seeger, Mike, and Peggy Seeger. *American Folk Songs for Children.* Rounder 8001 (1977).

———. *American Folk Songs for Christmas.* Rounder 0268 (1989).

———. *Animal Folk Songs for Children.* Rounder 8023 (1992).

String Quartet 1931. Arditti String Quartet. Gramavision R2 79440 (1989.)

Prelude no. 2 for piano

Ruth Crawford Seeger
Rosemary Platt, editor

[Throughout these preludes, accidentals affect only individual notes before which they occur.]

SHARON MIRCHANDANI

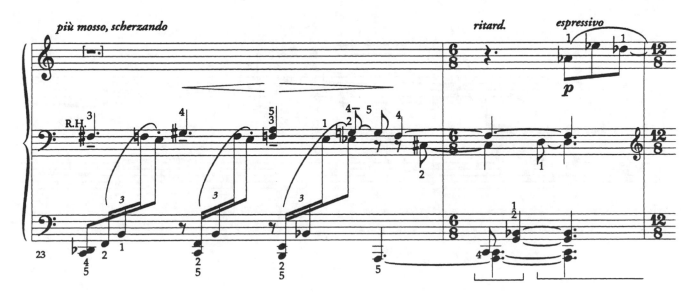

Ruth Crawford Seeger

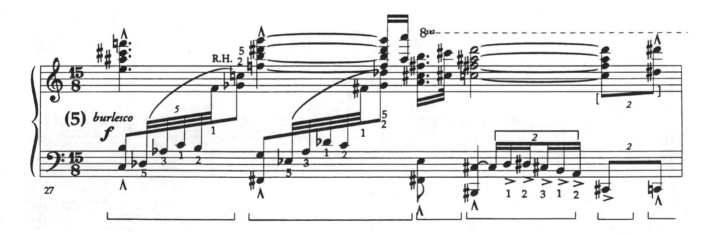

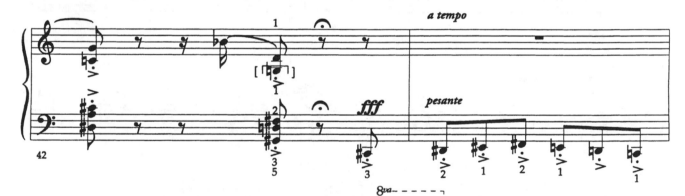

Autumn 1924

SHARON MIRCHANDANI

String Quartet 1931, Movements 3 and 4

Ruth Crawford Seeger

The dotted ties `- -_- -` indicate that the first tone of each new bow is not to be attacked;
the bowing should be as little audible as possible throughout.
The crescendi and decrescendi should be equally gradual.

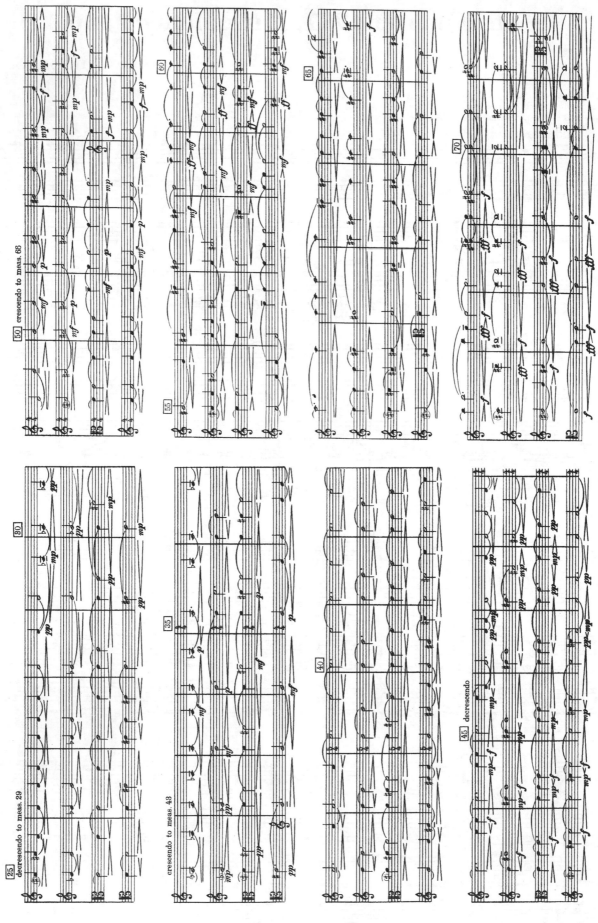

SHARON MIRCHANDANI

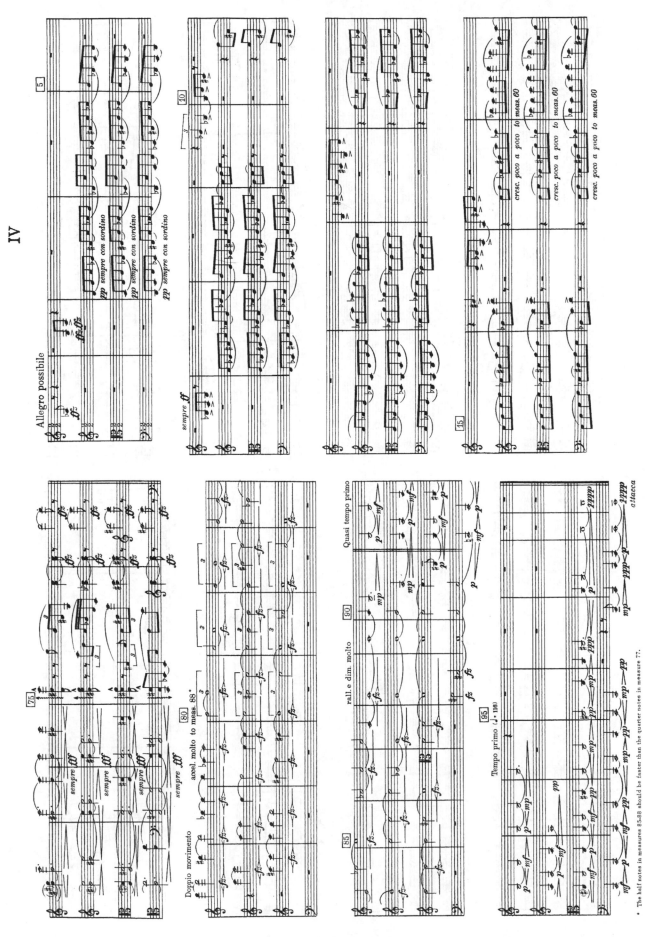

Ruth Crawford Seeger

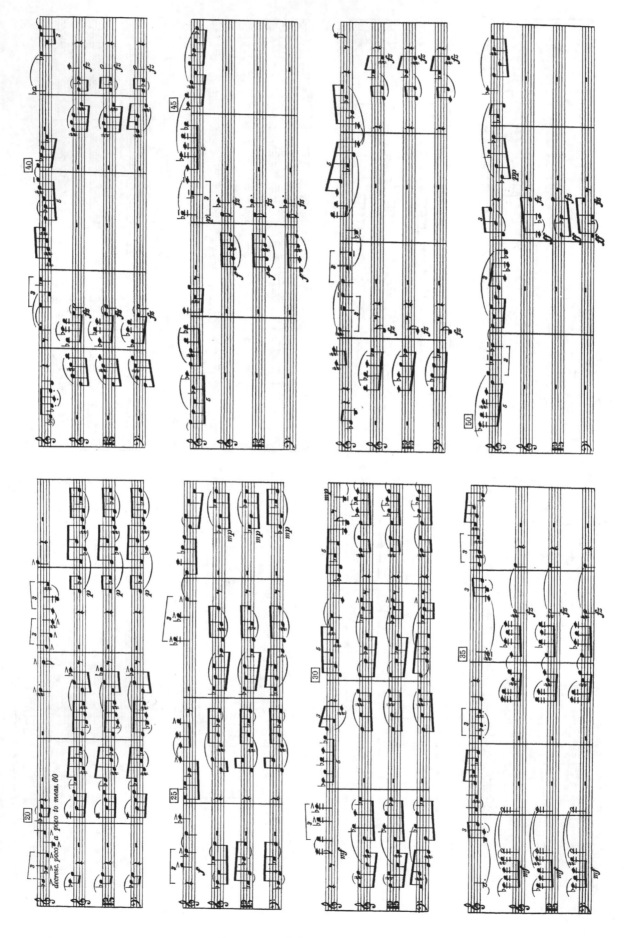

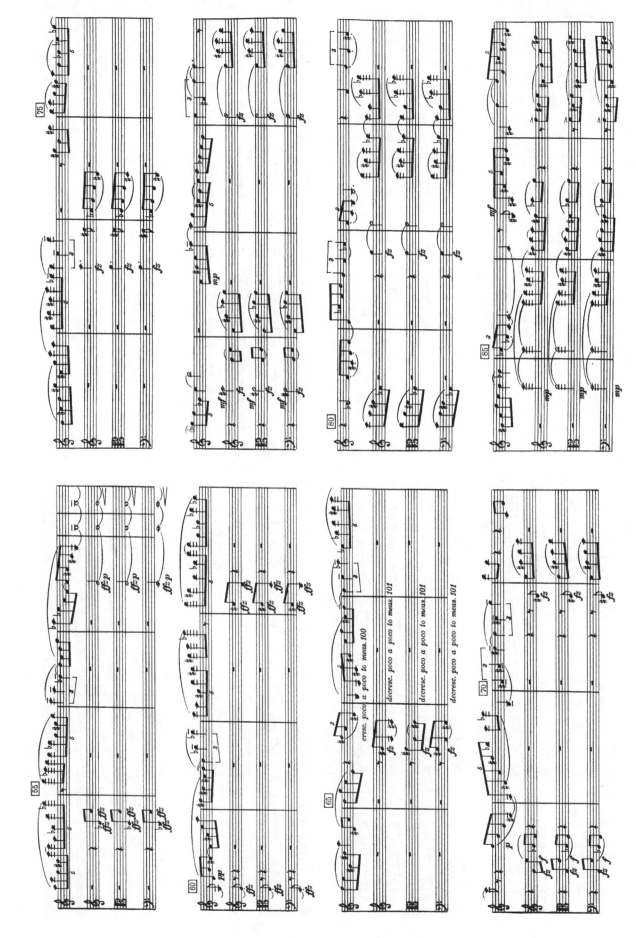

Ruth Crawford Seeger

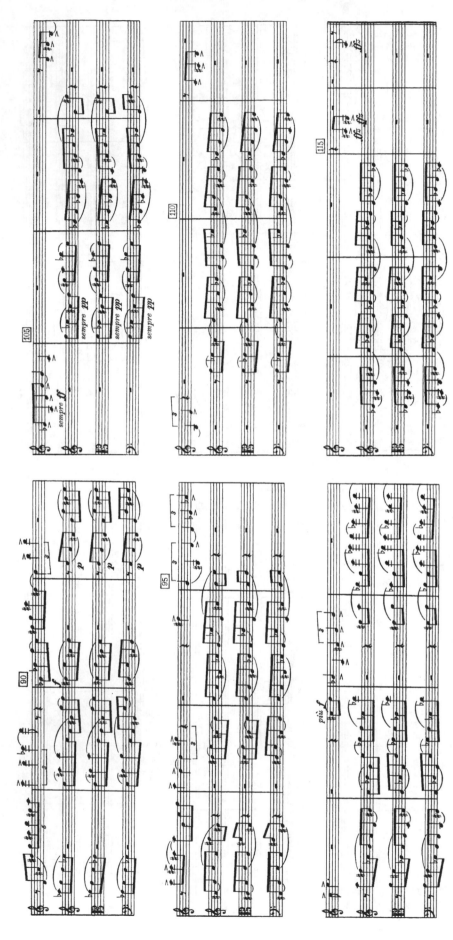
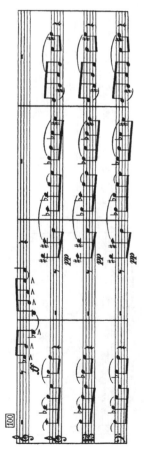

SHARON MIRCHANDANI

Rat Riddles

from *Three Songs for Contralto, Oboe, Percussion, and Orchestral Ostinati*

Ruth Crawford Seeger

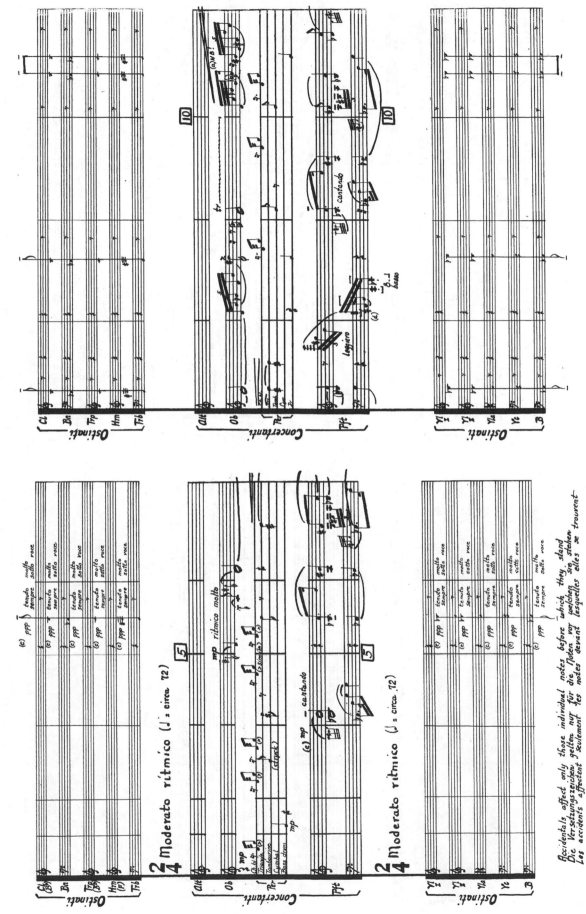

Ruth Crawford Seeger

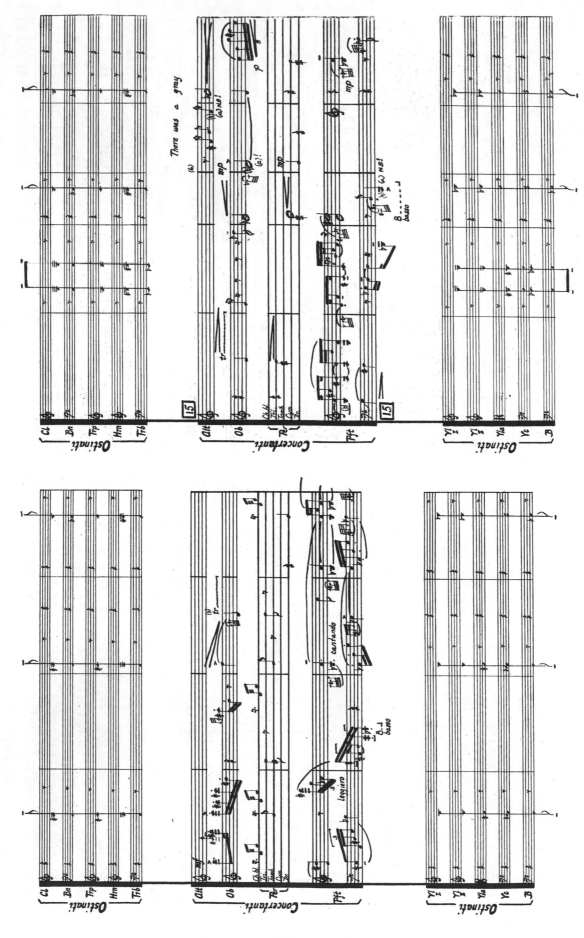

SHARON MIRCHANDANI

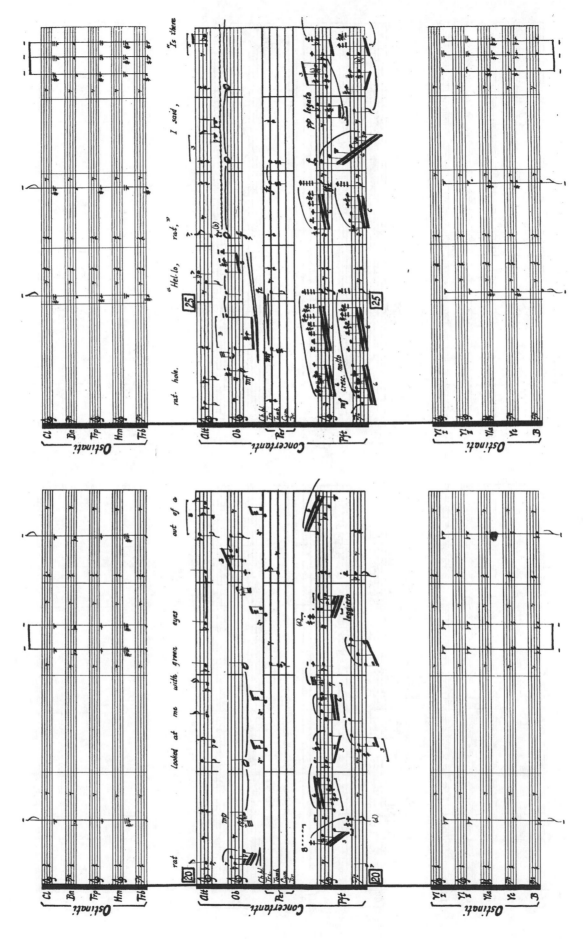

Ruth Crawford Seeger

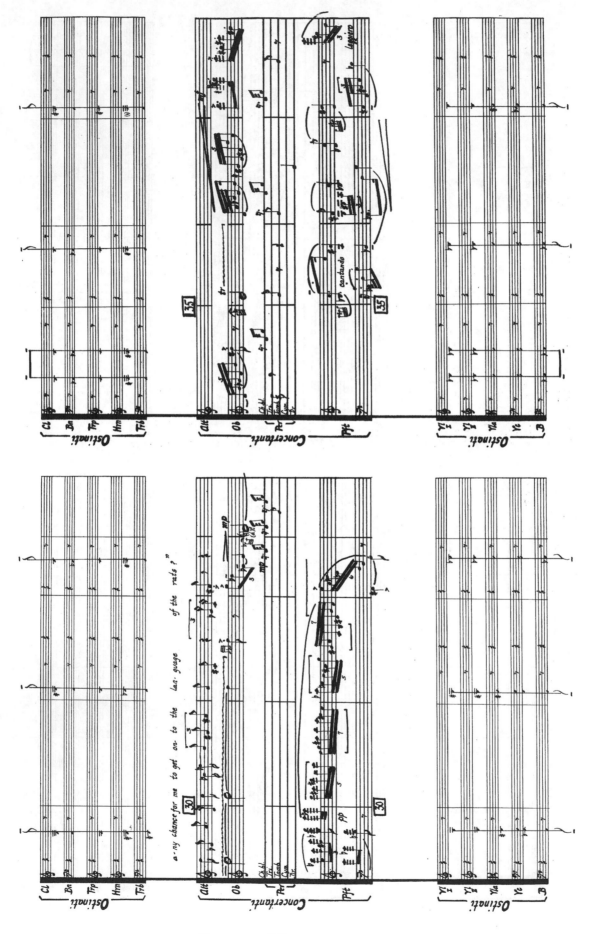

SHARON MIRCHANDANI

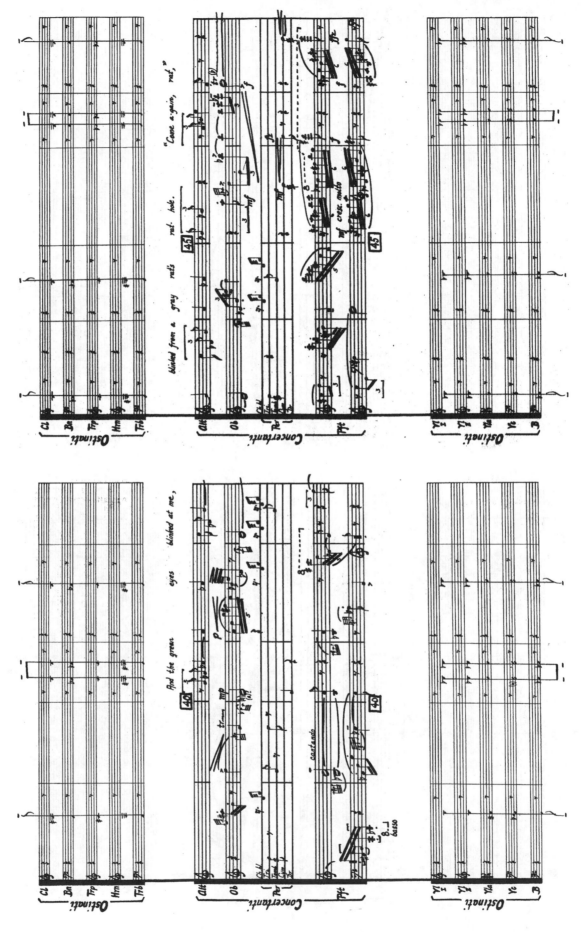

Ruth Crawford Seeger

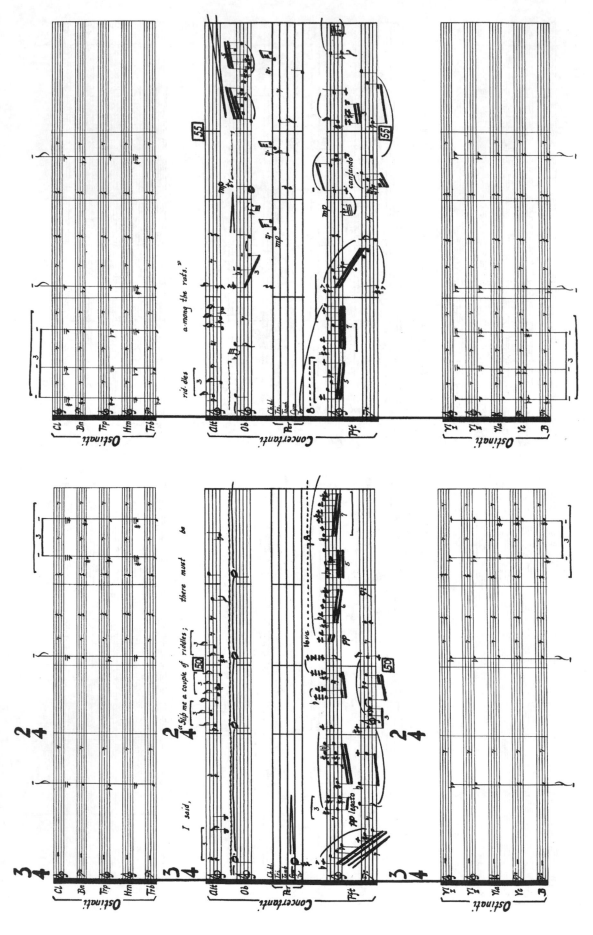

SHARON MIRCHANDANI

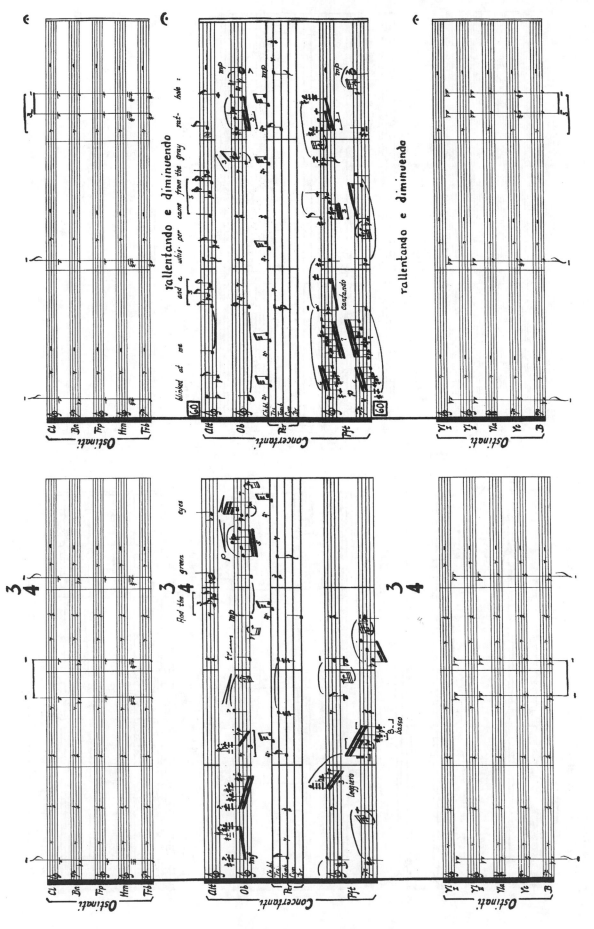

Ruth Crawford Seeger

355

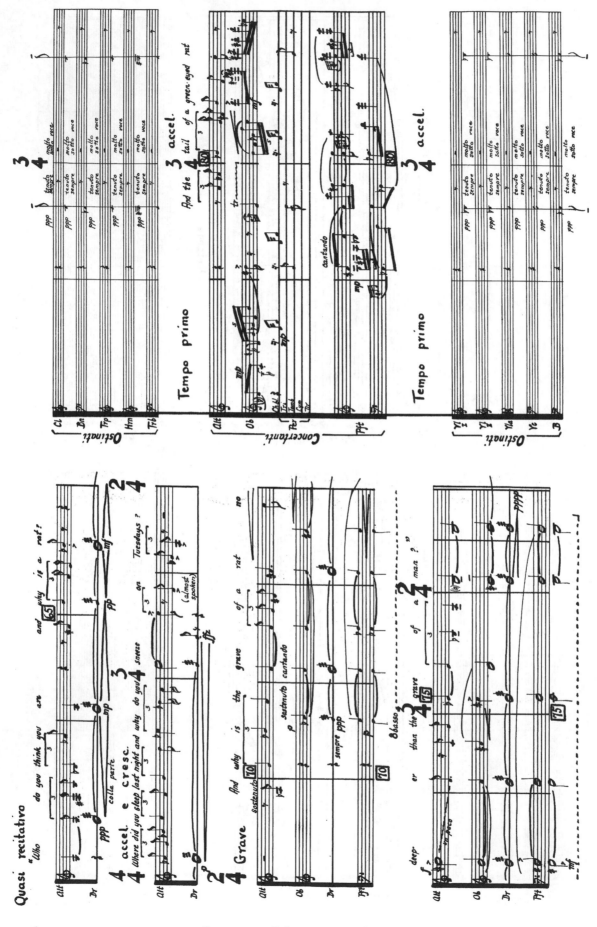

SHARON MIRCHANDANI

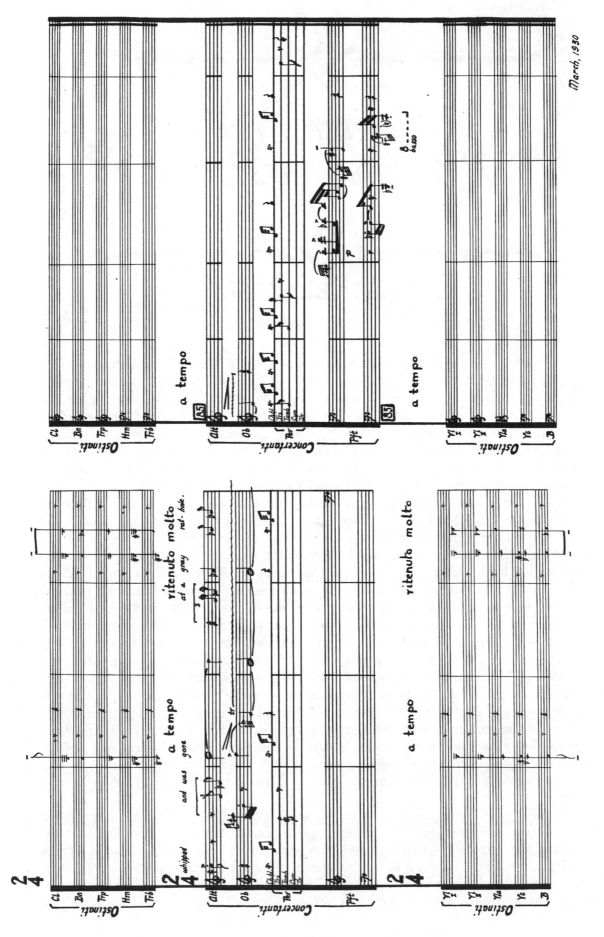

Ruth Crawford Seeger

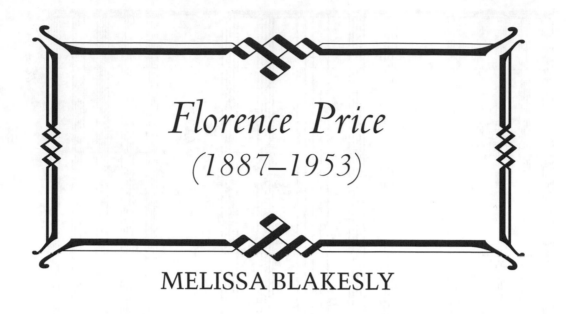

Florence Price
(1887–1953)

MELISSA BLAKESLY

Florence Beatrice Price (née Smith) was born in Little Rock, Arkansas, to a middle-class African-American family. She received her earliest musical training from her mother (a former elementary school teacher), and after graduating high school at the age of fourteen, she moved to Boston to study at the New England Conservatory. She studied composition there with Wallace Goodrich and Frederick Converse, and she also studied privately with George Chadwick (1903–1906). After earning an Artist's Diploma in organ and a piano teacher's diploma, she returned to Little Rock, teaching at Arkadelphia Academy (1906–1907) and Shorter College (1907–1910).

After a two-year period as the head of the music department at Clark College in Atlanta (1910–1912), Price returned once again to Little Rock, where she married and tried to focus on her composition. In 1927, with racial tensions continually increasing in Arkansas, the Price family moved to Chicago, where Florence studied at the American Conservatory, Chicago Musical College, the University of Chicago, and Chicago Teachers College. Price became nationally recognized as a composer in 1932, when she won the Wanamaker competition for her Symphony in E Minor, earning her the prestige of becoming the first African-American woman to win acceptance as a serious composer. With that status she joined William Grant Still and William Dawson as the first of a group of African-American composers who relied on European compositional models for their own works, while incorporating their own African-American cultural and musical heritage. Price's Symphony in E Minor is considered her most popular work and was performed by some of the finest American orchestras of the time, including the Chicago Symphony. Although the work is written within a more conservative European tradition, it is noteworthy for its incorporation of African-American musical elements, including the syncopated rhythms of the juba dance in the last movement and themes that emulate the style of spirituals in the second movement (without quoting any particular spiritual).

Florence Price's compositional style responds in part to a renaissance that was occurring within African-American communities around America. The concept was grounded in the belief that African-Americans were expected to be cultivated and "economically and socially prepared to enter an ideally integrated American Society" (Floyd, 4). This renaissance is often referred to as the Harlem Renaissance, even though the ideals promoted by the leaders found acceptance throughout the United States during the first decades of the twentieth century. Its goal was to "secure economic, social, and cultural equality with white citizens" (Floyd, 2); thus, the leaders of this movement felt that the music and poetry written by young African-Americans should seek to imitate European models but also reflect African-American experience. Price's music achieves these goals through the use of spirituals, characteristic dance rhythms, and melodies associated with African-American culture, which she embedded within classical forms and structures. Many of her works, which number more than three hundred, illustrate these traits of the musical Harlem Renaissance. Her compositions include art songs, arrangements of spirituals, works for chorus, four symphonies, piano and organ works, chamber works, and concertos for piano and violin.

Price's songs for solo voice are a perfect choice for analysis because as a group they are at once a reflection of the European art song tradition and a representation of African-American musical styles. The songs fall into two categories: settings or arrangements of spirituals and art songs that often set texts by black poets, some written in dialect. Several of Price's art songs are settings of poems by Langston Hughes, an important poet of the Harlem Renaissance and a writer whose works are very much an expression of black art within a European-influenced structure. The settings of spirituals seem to draw the most heavily on rhythmic elements present in African-American music and are an attempt to raise this genre to an art form on par with the European art song. For example, "I'm Workin' on My Building" relies on a mostly triadic melody that incorporates instances of syncopation and a somewhat modal accompaniment, lending the piece an African-American musical style. The setting is in call-and-response form and is rhythmically interesting for its emphasis on the second beat in several measures of the melody, while retaining the form and structure of a European art song (ABA form and a tonal melody).

The example included in this anthology, "Song to the Dark Virgin," belongs to the category encompassing art song settings of nondialectic poetry (the text is written by Langston Hughes). Price sets three stanzas, each of which begins with the same musical material, although successive stanzas deviate from the first after a few measures. The text alone is telling on at least two levels. The first is that of race, for the poem describes a dark virgin, probably of African heritage. The second level is that of gender, in that we have a male's perspective on gender (the author) and a female's musical interpretation of that text (the composer). In the text, the one word that seems to appear most often is "body," defining the virgin almost completely within the confines of her physicality. Particularly interesting are the ending phrases of the second stanza, which allude to the author's desire to hide the virgin's body: "Would that I were a garment, / A shimmering silken garment / That all my folds might wrap about thy body, / Absorb thy body, / Hold and hide thy body, / Thou dark one."

Price responds to the textual imagery with powerful music. The key of F minor immediately sets the tone, as does the rolling rhythm that accompanies the voice throughout. The second stanza reaches a higher and more intense climax than the first stanza, and the climax of each section appears near the mention of "body." The piece continues in this rather forceful way until the mention of "hide thy body," at which point the voice drops to among the lowest notes of the melodic line; the piano accompaniment is reduced to rolled chords separated by moments of silence or emptiness. This emptiness of chords may in some way signify the emptiness felt by the woman who is looked at as little more than a body, while the F-flat on the word "hide" is a metaphor whereby harmonic remoteness stands for emotional distancing. The second stanza culminates with a piano accompaniment fluctuating between C minor and B-flat minor, leaving the listener feeling empty and unsure about where the music will go. The third and final stanza continues much the same way as the opening one, but there is a feeling of fatigue after the constant emotional turmoil of the second stanza.

Further Reading

Floyd, Samuel, Jr. *Black Music in the Harlem Renaissance.* Westport, Conn.: Greenwood, 1990.

MELISSA BLAKESLY

Song to the Dark Virgin

Langston Hughes

Florence Price
Vivian Taylor, editor

Would that I were a gar - ment, A shim-mer-ing silk - en

gar - ment That all my folds might wrap a -

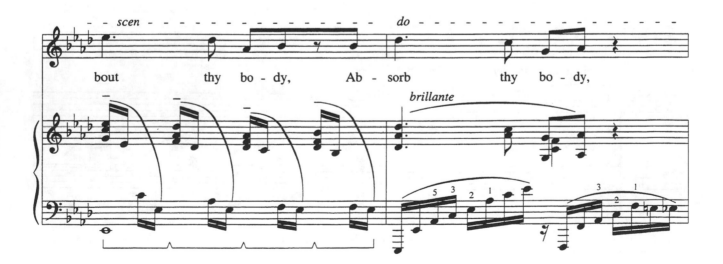

- scen - - - - - do bout thy bo - dy, Ab - sorb thy bo - dy,

MELISSA BLAKESLY

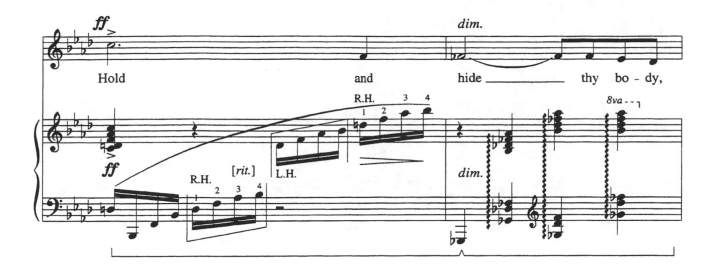

Hold and hide _____ thy bo – dy,

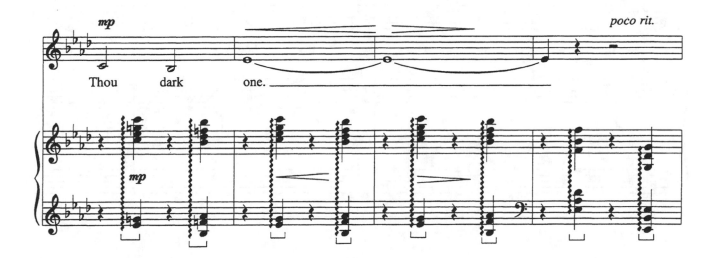

Thou dark one. _____

Tempo I

Would _____ that I were a flame, But

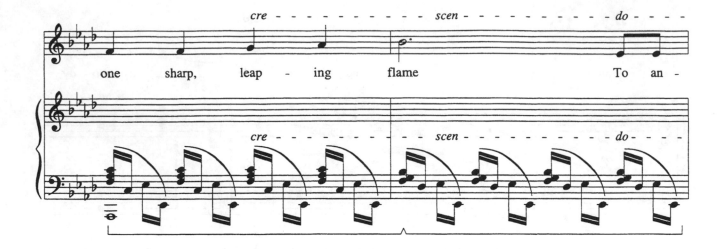

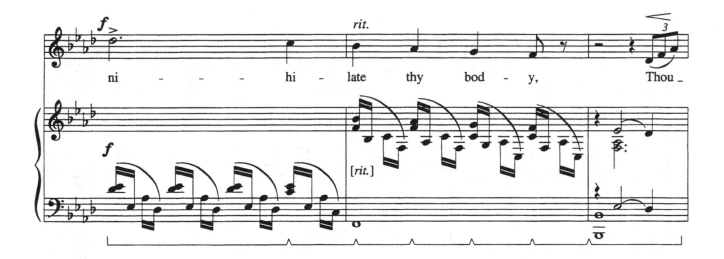

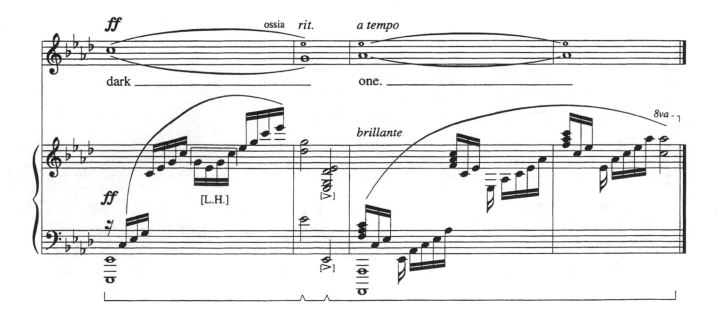

MELISSA BLAKESLY

Elsa Barraine
(1910–1999)

JAMES R. BRISCOE

Elsa Barraine contributed significantly to French music around 1950, after the neoclassicism of Les Six, Ravel, and Stravinsky had run its course. While her contribution is personal and clearly defined, it shares with La Jeune France important qualities. André Jolivet, Olivier Messiaen, Daniel-Lesur [Daniel Jean Yves Lesur], and Yves Baudrier called themselves "les quatres petits frères spiritualistes," turning like Barraine toward spiritual and human qualities while foreswearing the "mechanical and impersonal world" around them. In that frame of mind, Elsa Barraine rejected the cold ironies of the preceding generation as she also rejected serialism. Her music nonetheless responds to her near past, such as the music of Debussy, for Barraine is remarkably sensitive to instrumental color and offers a personal interpretation of classic forms and genres.

Parisian by birth, Barraine was the daughter of Alfred Barraine, the first cellist in the Orchestre de l'Opéra and a member of Conservatoire Orchestre. He and Mme. Barraine introduced Elsa to piano lessons at an early age. She studied composition at the Conservatoire with Paul Dukas, and took First Prizes in harmony in 1925 (at age fifteen) and in fugue and accompaniment in 1927. In 1929, at age nineteen, she gained the Premier Prix de Rome for her sacred trilogy *La vierge guerrière*, Joan of Arc. In a photo of Dukas's class that year, Barraine stands rather impishly among such classmates as Yvonne Desportes, Olivier Messiaen, Maurice Duruflé, and Claude Arrieu.

Thereafter she joined the French National Radio, working as pianist, sound mixer, and head of singing. No stranger to liberal causes, she fell in with the French Resistance during World War II, especially in the Front National des Musiciens. Already Elsa Barraine had exhibited anti-fascist values in her symphonic poem *Pogromes* (1933), and she demonstrated a clear voice of women's themes in the ballet *Claudine à l'école* (1950), based on the book by Colette. From 1944 to 1947 Barraine was Recording Director for the major firm Chant du Monde. In 1953 she joined the faculty of the Conservatoire National Supérieur de Musique de Paris as Professor of Analysis, teaching there until 1972. In that year the Ministry of Culture appointed her Director of Music, in which capacity she oversaw all French national lyric theaters. Clearly, then, Elsa Barraine was a survivor, one who weathered the storms of her nation's political turmoil while never losing her footing.

The music of Elsa Barraine wins over its listeners by a contrapuntal independence of line, virtuosity, and expressive intensity through motivic and rhythmic drive. It is accessible in tonal language and abandons tonality only once, and with particular expressive intent, in the *Musique rituelle* (1967) for organ, gongs, and xylorimba. The work is based on the Tibetan *Book of the Dead.* Three symphonies were composed, in 1931, 1938, and 1947, but it was the symphonic variations after Heine, *Harald Harfagard* (1930), that first introduced her to the public at large. The *comédie humaine* occupied Barraine in most of her works, and many have a program deriving from an emotion or psychological state: typical are *Avis* for chorus and orchestra on a text by Paul Eluard, *Hommage à Prokofiev* for harpsichord and orchestra, and *La nativité* for solo voices and orchestra. In the sphere of music theater, she composed the ballet *Le mur*, the film score *Pattes blanches*, incidental music on *Printemps de la liberté* (Springtime of Liberty) by J. Grémillon, and the *Suite astrologique* for chamber orchestra. There are a number of works for chamber ensembles and solo keyboard.

Ouvrage de Dame (Woman's Work) of 1937 is presented here. It is a suite of eight programmatic movements, all but the last portraying a feminine type and named after an imaginary woman. Their personalities may be understood from musical character, and Barraine reinforces the program by a tempo or expressive character prefacing each movement. They are Angélique (semplice), Berthe (allegro), Irène (sinueuse), Barbe (fugato burlesque), Sarah (vivacissimo), Isabeau (gently), Léocadie (sentimental old maid of olden times), and, in an abstract mode, the Finale (allegro).

The movements presented here in a score and recording are Berthe (II), Irène (III), Barbe (IV), and Finale (VIII). Movement I is a slow introduction that does not contain thematic material heard throughout the suite, despite a frank charm that prepares the entire composition. Immediately in Angelique, Barraine lyricizes in the oboe while she accompanies the line by sharp dissonance. The tonality of the suite *Ouvrage de Dame*, D, is established in Angélique just as competing tone clusters surround tonal functions. The second movement, Berthe, states the essential melodic material that will be varied in subsequent movements, although Barraine's melodic relationships are sometimes as adventuresome as her extended tonality. Measure 2 of the clarinet in Berthe, a long value followed by eighth and sixteenth values in disjunct motion, forms the first melodic cell. The figure of repetitive, mechanical sixteenth notes in measure 3, in the bassoon and horn, forms a second cell that will be varied widely. Measures 7–12 contain the fluctuating meters of Stravinsky. In the bassoon one hears another device of neoclassicism between the wars, a pedal tone that bears the tonality although it is surrounded by sharp dissonance.

The sinuous Irène calls on pan-diatonicism to establish the musical character, without placing tones in a hierarchy across the artificial scale grounded on E-flat, F-flat, and G but slipping chromatically. The easy rhythm of continual eighths coupled with even-paced quarter note lines enforces the mood of the sinuous Irène after measure 7. Barbe, movement IV, recalls the spirit, thematic basis, and central D tonality of Berthe (II). But here the first cell in Berthe (see m. 2 in that movement, a long followed by short values) is distilled to quarter notes, then eighths or dotted eighth and sixteenth. Barraine's mastery in instrumental timbre is particularly notable in this movement, where a counterpoint of sonorities is worth as much to the listener as that of tone and rhythm. Movements V–VII resemble III, Irène, in exploring a range of tonalities and variants on the melodic cells. The Finale, VIII, begins much like II, Berthe, reestablishing the extended tonality on D. It recalls the repeating sixteenth notes heard in Berthe but drives the first cell into the compressed form heard in Barbe (IV).

Elsa Barraine exhibits remarkable skills of the school following Les Six and Stravinsky in France, strong of itself but preparing for Boulez and Messiaen after 1950. She does so by an attention to tone color, motivic manipulation, and French transparency of texture. Her contribution to music is significant, and Elsa Barraine is a major force awaiting full discovery by performers and critics.

JAMES R. BRISCOE

Further Reading

Moulder, Earline. "Rediscovering the Organ Works of Elsa Barraine." *Women of Note Quarterly* (May 1995): 21–29.

———. "Jewish Themes in Elsa Barraine's Second Prelude and Fugue for Organ." *Women of Note Quarterly* (August 1995): 22–31.

Ouvrage de Dame

Theme and Variations for Flute, Oboe, Clarinet, Horn, and Bassoon

Elsa Barraine

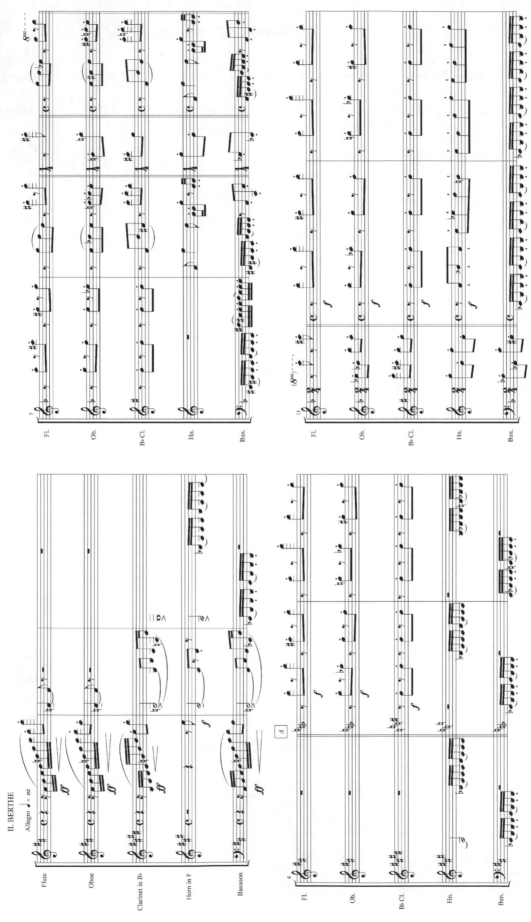

New edition for this anthology based on edition by Southern Music ca. 1950. Publisher no longer extant.

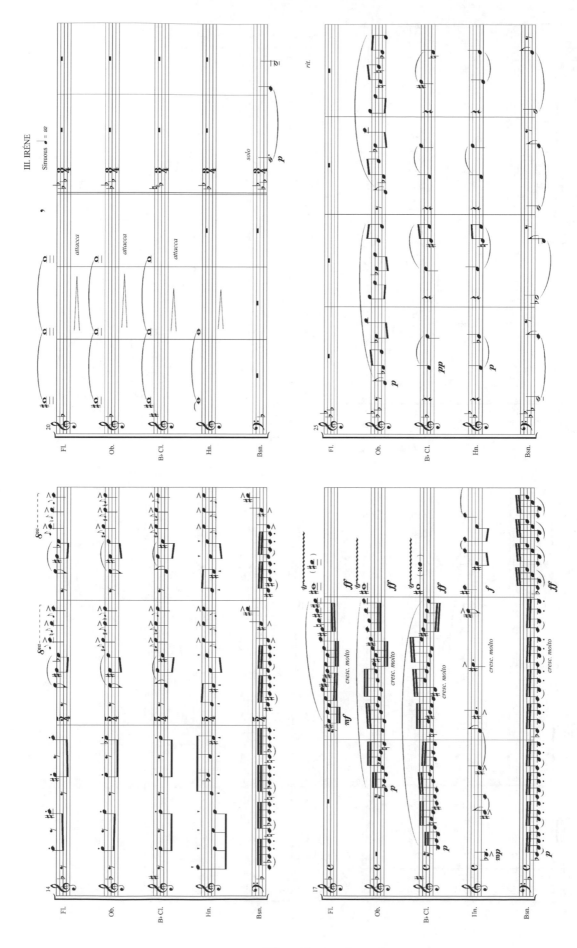

III. IRÉNE

Simoons ♩ = 82

attacca

Elsa Barraine

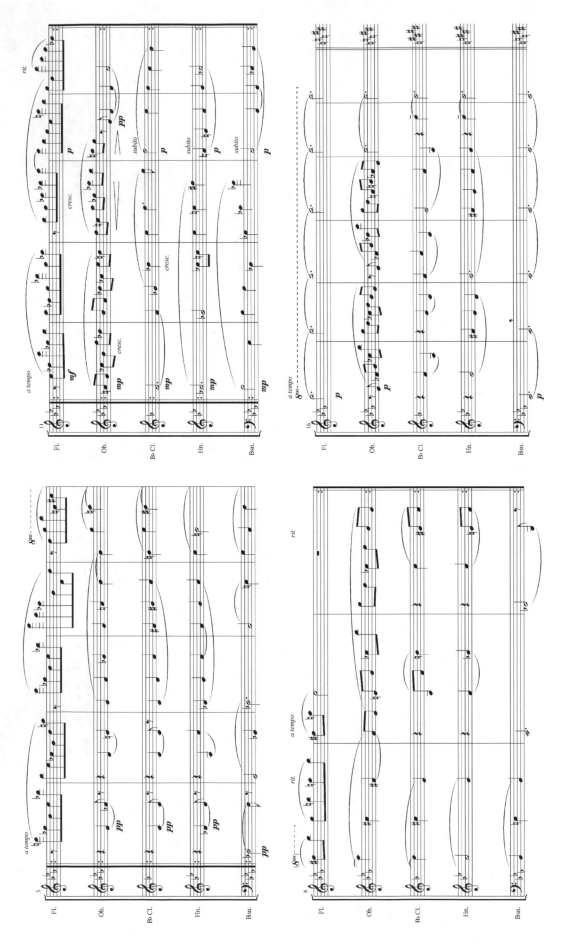

JAMES R. BRISCOE

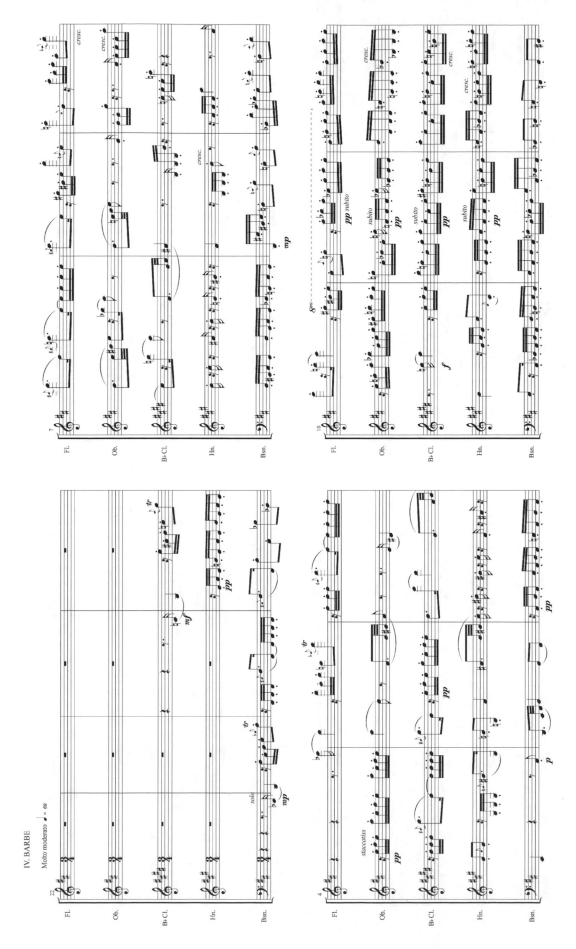

Elsa Barraine

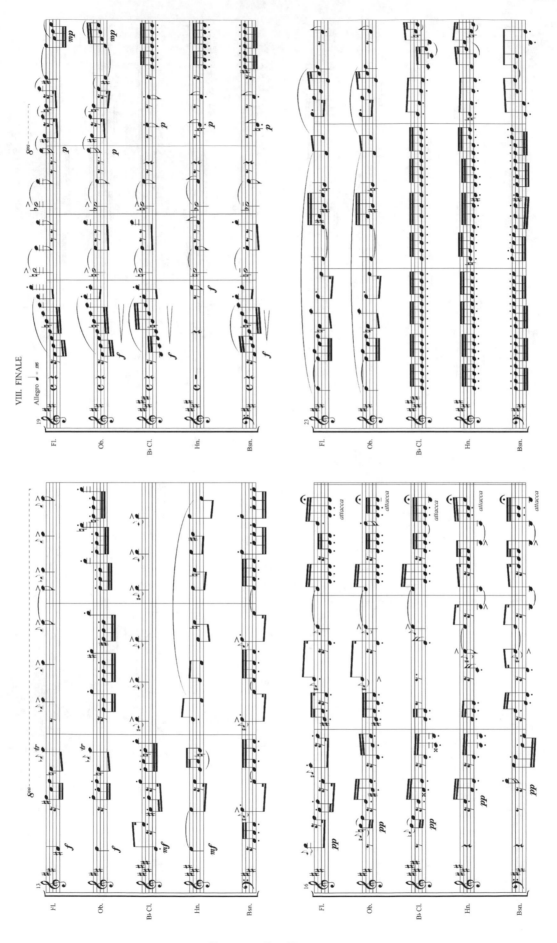

VIII. FINALE

JAMES R. BRISCOE

Elsa Barraine

373

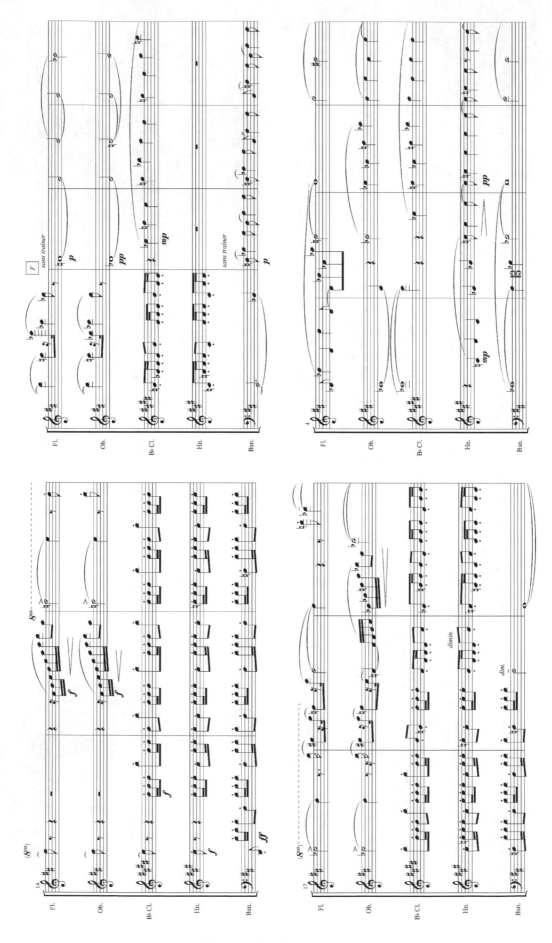

374　　JAMES R. BRISCOE

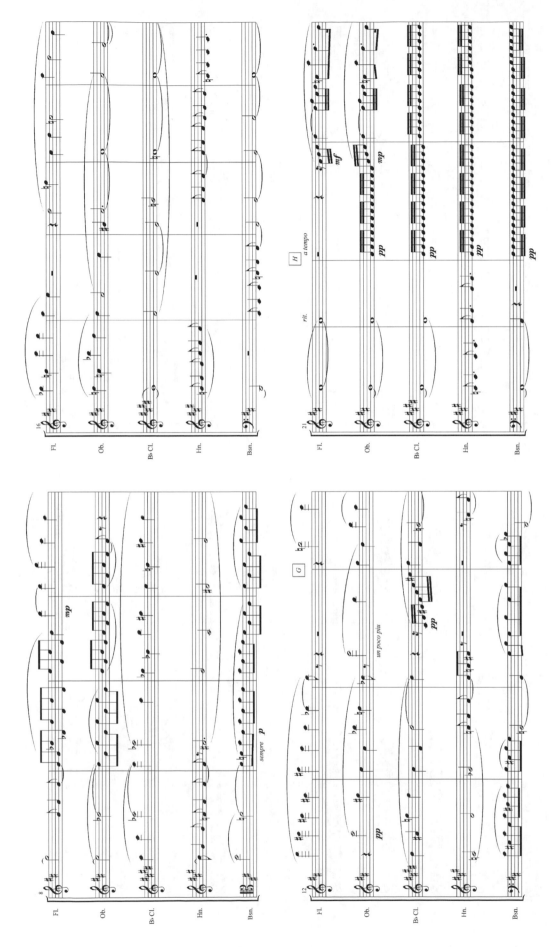

Elsa Barraine

375

JAMES R. BRISCOE

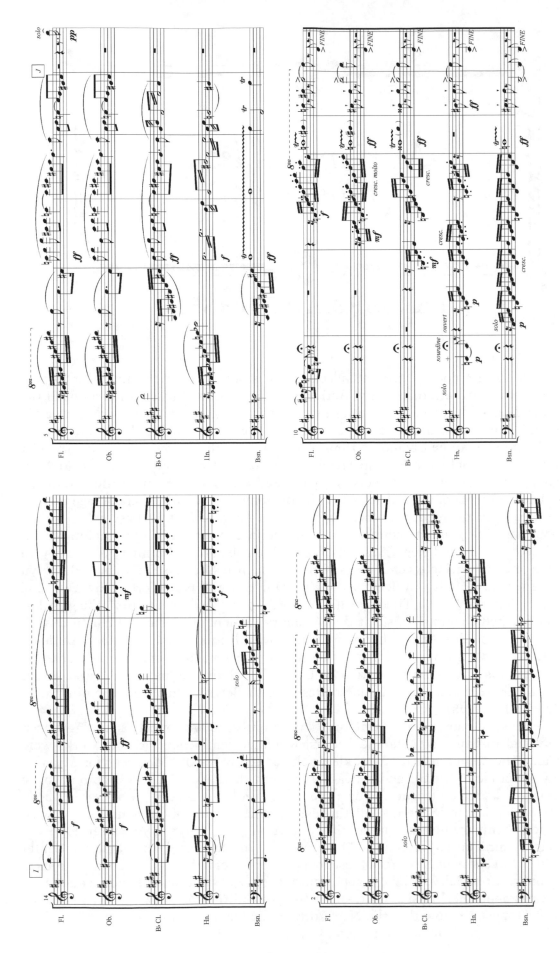

Elsa Barraine

377

Miriam Gideon
(1906–1996)

BARBARA A. PETERSEN

Without a doubt, Miriam Gideon ranks as one of America's foremost women composers of the twentieth century. Active as a composer and teacher nearly until the end of her life, she created more than seventy compositions in a career spanning six decades. Gideon was born in Greeley, Colorado (23 October 1906), but her family moved eastward, and she studied piano and music theory in both Boston and New York. Her academic degrees include a B.A. in French from Boston University (1926), an M.A. in musicology from Columbia University (1946), and a D.S.M. in composition from the Jewish Theological Seminary of America (1970). Some of her earliest encouragement to become a composer came from Martin Bernstein at New York University, where in the late 1920s she took graduate courses in music and intended to acquire a teaching certificate. Gideon considered Roger Sessions, with whom she studied from 1935 to 1943, to be her major composition teacher and strongest influence. She herself taught at Brooklyn College (1944–1954), City College of the City University of New York (1947–1955 and 1971–1976), and the Jewish Theological Seminary (1967–1991). In addition, she gave lessons and coached chamber music at the Manhattan School of Music and taught as well as in her private studio. Among her many honors was election to the American Academy and Institute of Arts and Letters (1975). She was the second woman composer to be named to the Institute. (Her good friend and neighbor Louise Talma was the first, a year earlier.) Gideon received honorary doctorates from the Jewish Theological Seminary and Brooklyn College (1981, 1983).

Gideon was honored on 5 April 1992 with a retrospective concert at the American Academy and Institute of Arts and Letters, where eleven of her chamber works were performed. The commemorative booklet included ten pages of "Messages for Miriam" from a wide circle of friends and colleagues. Among them were Milton Babbitt's words: "Miriam, a treasured colleague and dear friend for over half a century, has created a body of music which is one of the rare, distinguished achievements of our time." The Jewish Theological Seminary hosted a memorial concert on 4 June 1997, a year after her death at age eighty-nine on 18 June 1996. More recently (10 May 2002), the Graduate Center at the City University of New York presented an evening of her vocal and chamber music. As Gideon's centennial year (2006) approaches, there will doubtless be more concerts of and writings about her music. There are many possibilities for further study of her life and works, especially now that the New York Public Library houses the Miriam Gideon Papers. This collection includes numerous manuscripts in pencil or ink, a few sketches, published scores, personal and professional letters, poems, typescripts of librettos, concert programs, clippings, notes, journals, and other memorabilia.

Throughout her career, Gideon's concentration as a composer was on chamber music, especially works for voice and mixed ensembles. She also created nine choral works, both large and small, based on secular and sacred texts, between 1941 and 1984. Her thirty-minute works for the synagogue (*Sacred Service for Sabbath Morning* [1970] and *Shirat Miriam Shabbat* [1974], for the Friday evening service) are particularly notable. In the other larger forms, she created only two early orchestral pieces and two orchestral versions of vocal chamber works. She wrote her own libretto (after the play by Serafín and Joaquín Quintero) for an hour-long opera, *Fortunato* (1958), for five soloists and chamber orchestra. Gideon explained her concentration on music with text by saying, "I am moved by poetry and great prose almost as much as by music." She also admitted, "It takes me a long time to find the right texts" (Korall, 32, 33).

From the early conservative style of her *German Songs*, Op. 1 (1930–1937), which recall the musical and poetic worlds of Mendelssohn and Schumann, Gideon moved toward a more expressionistic style with strong elements of chromaticism and dissonance. Most of her works are on a small scale, with clear designs, and in a freely atonal idiom; they exhibit a harmonious balance of lyrical and dramatic elements. Without following any rigid compositional doctrine, she created a remarkably consistent body of works that fuse abstract ideas, poetic images, and subjective emotional experience. Milton Babbitt has cited "motivic saturation" as a salient feature of her works, especially from the 1950s through the 1970s. On a less technical level, Gideon's concerns have always been with "illuminating her inner feelings" and combining words and music into a meaningful whole. As she said on many occasions, she wrote not as a woman composer or a Jewish composer but as a composer, period. Of utmost importance is her declaration, "What I write has to mean something to me."

Gideon's interests extended to many languages, cultures, and periods, from ancient to modern. She set texts in several languages, sometimes within the same work: *The Condemned Playground* (1963) uses poems in Latin, English, Japanese, and French. In some works she set the poems in the original languages as well as in translation (*Songs of Youth and Madness*, 1977, or *Steeds of Darkness*, 1986). In others she used English translations of ancient originals (from the Japanese in *The Seasons of Time* [1969], and from the Greek in both *Voices from Elysium* [1979] and *Songs from the Greek for Pipes and Strings* [1989]). Some of her purely instrumental works also had prose or poetry as a source of inspiration, for instance, *Of Shadows Numberless—Suite for Piano* (1966), which drew on Keats's "Ode to a Nightingale." This is hardly surprising, since she was married for more than four decades to Frederick Ewen, a scholar, critic, and historian who specialized in European literature of the nineteenth century. Ewen once supplied poetry made to order when Gideon could not obtain permission to use the text she had originally set in the opening movement, *Mutterbildnis,* of her choral Spiritual Madrigals (later reworked for solo voice and ensemble as "The Resounding Lyre").

The text of *The Hound of Heaven* is drawn from an extended poem by Francis Thompson (1859–1907), an English poet and essayist known for his devout Catholicism. Whereas the poet was recording his reactions to specific disappointments in life (rejection from both the priesthood and the practice of medicine), Gideon selected verses that evoke the purification through suffering that underlies the Jewish experience. In crossing cultural boundaries, she created a poignant musical setting that emphasizes the suffering common to all humankind. *The Hound of Heaven* was commissioned by Lazare Saminsky (one of Gideon's early composition teachers) to celebrate the centenary of the founding of Congregation Emanu-El in New York City. It was first performed there on 23 March 1945. In this context, the choice of an overtly Catholic text may strike one as curious, but Gideon convincingly argued for the poem's relevance: it expresses "profound life experiences which mar, in order to make, the human being" (Gideon, in liner notes to CRI SD 286, reprinted with CRI CD 782).

Although it is the first in a series of eighteen works for voice(s) and small ensembles, *The Hound of Heaven* displays the most important stylistic features of Gideon's writing. She herself said that it was "probably the first piece written in what I would call my own style." As in most of her works in the genre, the vocal line may be taken by either a male or a female (medium) voice. The "mixed consort" of instruments, here oboe and string trio, is also a common characteristic. Lasting approximately seven minutes, *The Hound of Heaven* is atypical only in its being in a single movement; here the text is drawn from a single poem, whereas in most of Gideon's other chamber works there are separate movements for individual poems. Interludes such as the one in measures 62–86—or complete, if short, instrumental movements—occur in many of her chamber works to contrast with the surrounding passages with text.

The sinuous vocal lines, mainly syllabic text setting, fluctuating meters, and close interweaving of voice and instruments found in *The Hound of Heaven* are hallmarks of her later works as well. While avoiding exact doubling of the vocal line by a single instrument, Gideon often creates a subtle heterophony by having the singer's notes scattered among different instruments, or in different octaves. An example in *The Hound of Heaven* occurs at measures 51–54: notes doubling the voice are shared by violin or viola, then move to the oboe (m. 55). In this work she moves away from her earlier, rather traditional diatonicism toward her mature, freely atonal style. In a 1958 analysis of this work, George Perle wrote, "The texture . . . is strikingly personal, characterized by lightness, the sudden exposure of individual notes, constantly shifting octave relationships. . . . The larger melodic and harmonic components are generated from minimal basic cells in this way. This is a technique that imposes economy and the exclusion of irrelevancies—a technique that may be indefinitely expended and within which a composer may grow."

Further Reading

Ardito, Linda. "Miriam Gideon: A Memorial Tribute." *Perspectives of New Music* 34, no. 2 (Summer 1996): 202–14.

Gideon, Miriam. Miriam Gideon Papers. Music Research Division, New York Public Library.

Hisama, Ellie M. *Gendering Musical Modernism: The Music of Ruth Crawford, Marion Bauer, and Miriam Gideon*. Cambridge: Cambridge University Press, 2001. See especially pp. 163–64 on *The Hound of Heaven*.

Korall, Burt. "Miriam Gideon." *BMI News*, June 1963, 32, 33.

LePage, Jane Weiner. "Miriam Gideon." In *Women Composers, Conductors and Musicians of the Twentieth Century: Selected Biographies*, vol. 2, 118–41. New York: Scarecrow Press, 1983.

New Grove Dictionary of Music and Musicians. 2nd ed. S.v. "Gideon, Miriam."

Perle, George. "The Music of Miriam Gideon." *Bulletin of the American Composers Alliance* 7, no. 4 (1958): 2–9.

Petersen, Barbara A. *Miriam Gideon*. Brochure with work list. New York: Broadcast Music, 1980, with 1990 addendum.

———. "The Vocal Chamber Music of Miriam Gideon." In *The Musical Woman: An International Perspective*, vol. 2, ed. J. L. Zaimont, C. Overhauser, and J. Gottlieb, 223–55. New York: Greenwood Press, 1987.

BARBARA A. PETERSEN

The Hound of Heaven
for voice, oboe, and string trio

Francis Thompson

Miriam Gideon

A - cross the mar-gent of the

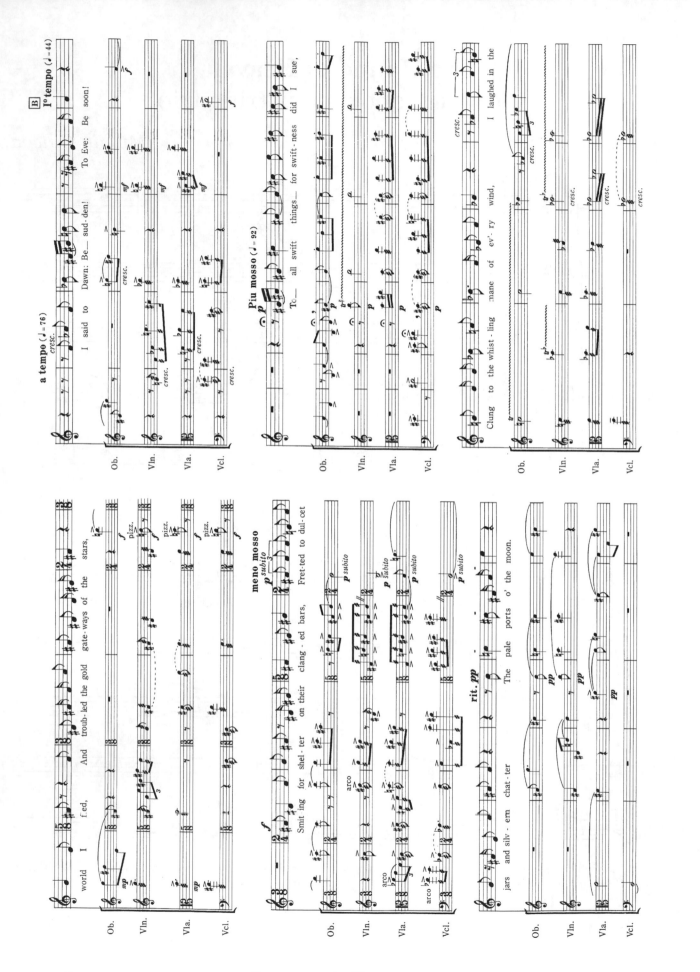

Barbara A. Petersen

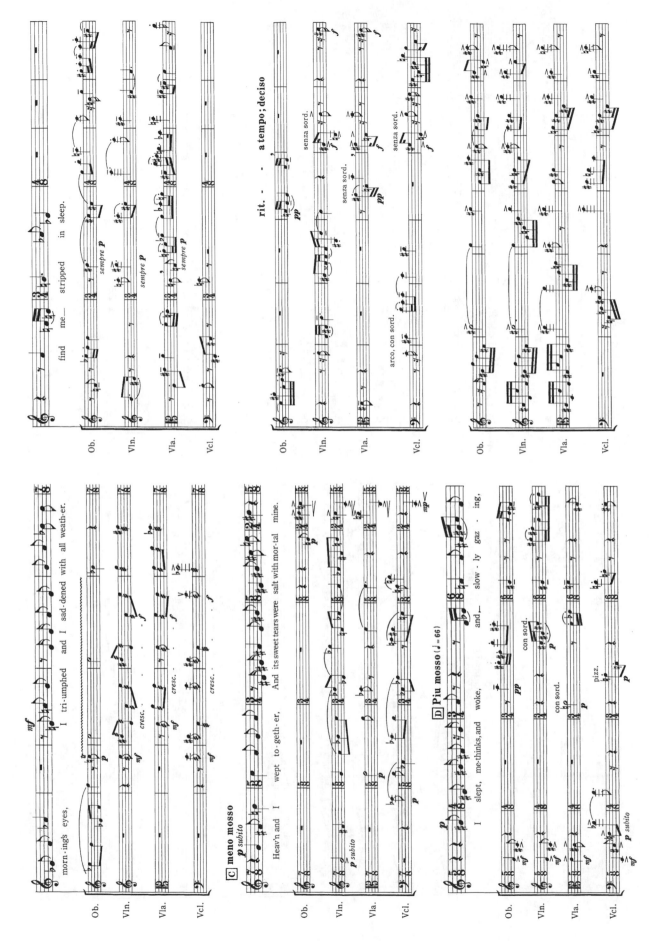

Miriam Gideon

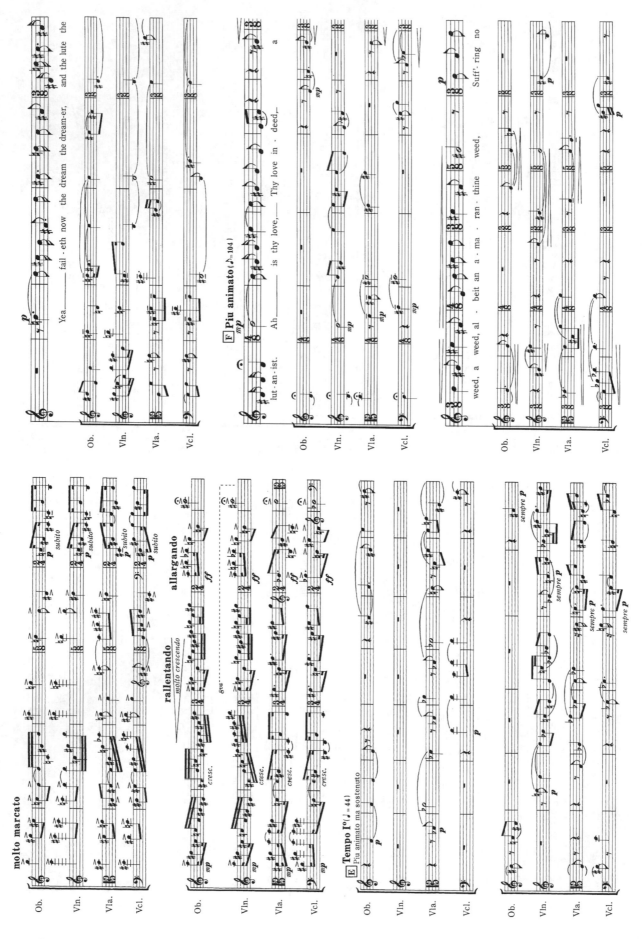

BARBARA A. PETERSEN

Miriam Gideon

Grażyna Bacewicz
(1909–1969)

JUDITH ROSEN

Virtually from the time of her birth in Łódź, Poland, Grażyna Bacewicz's life was tied to music. Her father was her first music teacher, and chamber music was often played at family gatherings. One older brother became a professor of music; her other brother was a composer. Her youngest sister was also exposed to music; she chose the field of literature and made her reputation as a poet, but she became the keeper of Grażyna's musical legacy. As a child, Grażyna played the violin and the piano, proclaiming that someday she would be a composer. Her first extant work was a march for piano composed when she was eleven. By her twelfth year she had composed a set of piano preludes.

In addition to her years at the Warsaw Conservatory, where she studied with Kazimierz Sikorski, among others, she pursued formal studies in philosophy at the university. These studies, combined with a wide interest in literature and world affairs, no doubt enriched her musical expression. Like many of her fellow students, Bacewicz followed the advice of Karol Szymanowski, whom she had met at the Conservatory, and pursued her studies in Paris in 1932 and 1934. This was a departure from the previous emphasis on a Germanic training. In addition to studying violin with André Touret and later with Carl Flesch, she attended composition classes with Nadia Boulanger. As an example of her artistry as a violinist, she received Honorable Mention in the first Wieniawski International Violin Competition (1935). It should be noted, however, that she was surpassed only by Ginette Neveu and David Oistrakh, who won the first and second prizes.

As was her compositional method in general, Bacewicz worked at a rapid pace during the next few years, completing a substantial number of works, including her first violin concerto. Neither her personal commitments (she married in 1936) nor her professional ones (she toured with the Polish Radio Orchestra as principal violinist from 1936 to 1938) lessened the intensity with which she composed.

The war years of 1939–1945 forced her to curtail a public musical life and brought difficult personal hardships as well as joys. She nursed her wounded sister and was forced to live in several places outside of Warsaw, but her daughter and only child was born in 1942. Nevertheless, her compositional output continued and her music was performed, albeit in private hearings. Among the works composed during this time was the *Overture for Orchestra* (1943), premiered at the first "Festival of Polish Music" held in Krakow just after the war.

At the end of the war, the family returned to Warsaw, and Bacewicz began to serve on numerous international juries for violin competitions. She became a member of the Polish Composers Union, which was founded a few months after the liberation. However, the introduction and popularizing of Polish music abroad, which had been a pledge of the Union, was not to be seen immediately. There were hopes as well for the opportunity for composers to enter into a period of complete creative freedom and musical thought, but neither did this occur. The decades just after the war saw Poland under socialist control, when artistic institutions were nationalized and creativity rigidly controlled. Nationalization did at least encourage the collecting and cataloguing of folklore. Thus, folk themes infused many, although not all, of the compositions of Bacewicz and her contemporaries, and such a contemporary musical language became the sanctioned idiom.

In about 1953 she began to withdraw from concertizing to devote even more time to composition. In 1954, at the height of great recognition, a serious automobile accident threatened her life. This may have influenced her decision to withdraw from the concert stage and devote all her energies to composition, which occurred by 1955.

The political and social unrest throughout these years erupted with the Polish working-class riots of 1956. This resulted in a more liberal Polish Communist Party and increased cultural freedom. The musical symbol of this new freedom was the first International Festival of Contemporary Music, known the world over as the "Warsaw Autumn." Its scope is evidenced by the composers whose works were presented, including Stravinsky, Schoenberg, Berg, Bartók, Shostakovich, Honegger, Prokofiev, Szymanowski, Lutoslawski, and Bacewicz. Festival audiences heard three of her compositions, and over the years "Warsaw Autumn" has programmed many of her works.

In the ensuing years, the long period of isolation from Western musical trends ended, and Polish composers were inundated by the musical avant-garde. Bacewicz, who by this time had found her own musical style and could not be classified as an innovator, nevertheless could not (nor did she desire to) ignore the musical avant-garde. Thus, subtle but perceptible changes in her artistic craft occur along three paths: departure from tonality, greater attention to instrumental color, and enrichment of rhythmical patterns.

Music critics have attempted to divide and even pigeonhole her oeuvre into specific time and stylistic frames. However, I see a gradual evolution of her idiom. Her early French neoclassical influences (as in the *Wind Quintet* of 1932, the first composition to win a prize) led to the development of her own neoclassical style, culminating in *Music for Strings, Trumpets, and Percussion* (1958). There followed an experimentation with modernist style, as in *Pensieri Notturni* (1961), characterized by tone color exploration and varied harmonic effects and techniques for string instruments. In this idiom, the Concerto for Orchestra (1962) is one of her frequently performed works.

Bacewicz's music thus is a result of multiple forces, both historical and musical, that surrounded her. Her talents speak eloquently through her works, which number more than two hundred. These include four symphonies; seven violin concertos; seven string quartets; five sonatas for violin and piano; concertos for piano, two pianos, viola, and cello; numerous vocal pieces; and works for chamber orchestra and for symphony orchestra. The excellence of her compositions has assured Grażyna Bacewicz a special place in the musical history of the twentieth century. They likewise illustrate what can be achieved in spite of or perhaps because of external circumstances.

It should be noted, moreover, that she did not think of herself as a "woman" composer; nor was she thought of as such by her colleagues. Rather, her achievements encouraged and validated a generation of women who followed her. The number of women in Poland who have continued the tradition of composition is extensive.

In addition to her dual careers as composer and violinist, she was an accomplished pianist. In 1953 she premiered her own Piano Sonata II in Warsaw under the auspices of the

Polish Composers Union. This was the sixth sonata, including those for violin and piano; she had written her first piano sonata in 1930 as student at the Warsaw Conservatory.

Like her compatriot Chopin, Bacewicz knew the full possibilities of the piano, made clear by the example given here. Although the first movement is in sonata-allegro form, Bacewicz (like Chopin in his second piano sonata) uses a short introduction (Maestoso) before stating the first theme (Agitato). Her two-measure introduction built on fourths, the first three eighth notes, calls for a resolution, which she culminates brilliantly by the cadence ending the movement. The second theme at measure 42 (poco meno) is rooted in a Polish folk tune. This movement is also marked by its abrupt change of tempos, meter, and toccata-like passages that add tension and motoric thrust to the music.

The musical attitude changes abruptly in the second movement (Largo), which begins with a chorale-like theme. Throughout the movement, there are harmonies suggestive of Gershwin and Ravel. A brief fugato is heard before a return to the first theme, which ends this movement. The last movement is a toccata based on an *oberek* (a fast Polish form of mazurka). It is everything a toccata should be and poses a challenge for the virtuosa pianist.

Like many other works of this most accomplished and prolific composer, the Piano Sonata II deserves to join the repertoire and to receive many more performances by today's performing artists.

Further Reading

McNamee, Ann K. "Grażyna Bacewicz's *Second Piano Sonata* (1953): Octave Expansion and Sonata Form." *Music Theory Online*, September 1993 (revised 1996).

Plaut, Linda Burian. "Musical Profile: Grażyna Bacewicz." *Women of Note Quarterly* 2, no. 3 (1994): 1, 3–5.

Rosen, Judith. *Grażyna Bacewicz: Her Life and Works.* Polish Music History Series, 2. Los Angeles: University of Southern California, 1984.

Schäffer, Bogusław. "Bacewicz, Grażyna." In *The New Grove Dictionary of Music and Musicians*, ed. Stanley Sadie, 772–74. London: Macmillan, 1980.

Shafer, Sharon G. *The Contribution of Grażyna Bacewicz to Polish Music.* Lewiston, N.Y.: Edwin Mellen Press, 1992.

Thomas, Adrian. "Bacewicz, Grażyna." In *The New Grove Dictionary of Music and Musicians*, 2nd ed., ed. Stanley Sadie and exec. ed. John Tyrrell, 295–97. London: Macmillan, 2001.

———. *Grażyna Bacewicz: Chamber and Orchestral Music.* Polish Music History Series, 3. Los Angeles: University of Southern California, 1985.

Wood, Elizabeth. "Grażyna Bacewicz (1909–69): Form, Syntax, Style." In *The Musical Woman: An International Perspective 1984*, ed. Judith Lang Zaimont, 118–27. Westport, Conn.: Greenwood Press, 1984.

Zierolf, Robert. "Composers of Modern Europe, Australia, and New Zealand." In *Women and Music: A History*, ed. Karin Pendle, 197–99. Bloomington: Indiana University Press, 1991.

Recordings of Sonata II for Piano

Nancy Fierro. Avant AV 1012, Dorchester Classics DRC 1004, and Ars Musica Poloniae 2001.

Ewa Kupiec. Hanssler Classic CD 93.034.

Krystian Zimerman. Muza SX 1510, Olympia OCD 392, and Muza SXL 0977.

JUDITH ROSEN

Sonata II for Piano

Grażyna Bacewicz

JUDITH ROSEN

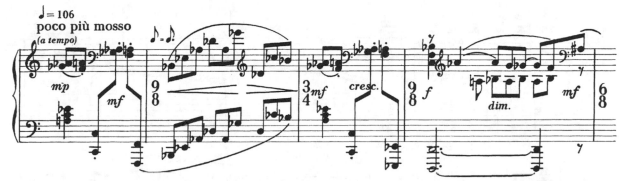

Grażyna Bacewicz   391

JUDITH ROSEN

Poco più mosso

Grażyna Bacewicz

JUDITH ROSEN

Grażyna Bacewicz

395

JUDITH ROSEN

Grażyna Bacewicz

397

JUDITH ROSEN

Toccata

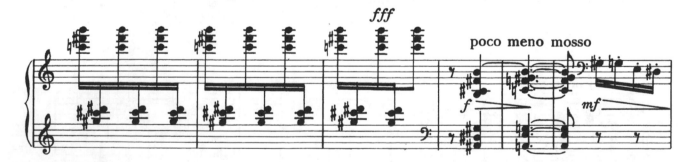

JUDITH ROSEN

Grażyna Bacewicz

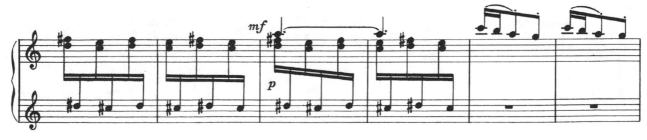

  JUDITH ROSEN

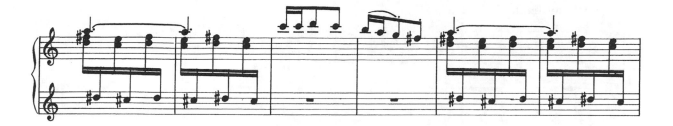

Grażyna Bacewicz

403

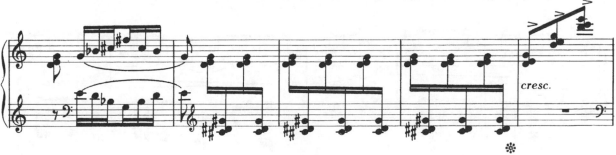

JUDITH ROSEN

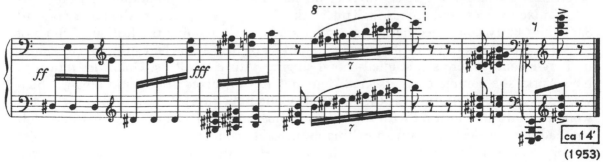

(1953)

Grażyna Bacewicz 407

Julia Amanda Perry
(1924–1979)

ROBERTA LINDSEY

Julia Amanda Perry followed a path established by many American musicians in her musical studies. Born in 1924 in Lexington, Kentucky, she was raised in Akron, Ohio, beginning her study at home. In college she continued her pursuits in New Jersey and New York, and took part in private instruction in Massachusetts as well as in France and Italy. Her family regularly engaged in musical activities at home; her physician father was an amateur pianist, her two older sisters studied violin, and her mother strongly encouraged her children in their musical endeavors. Julia Perry's first instrument was the violin, and she later studied voice and piano. Upon matriculating from Akron High School, Perry attended the Westminster Choir College in Princeton, New Jersey. While there, she focused her attention on conducting and composition while continuing her lessons in applied music. According to Green, Perry was a talented composer, but one who "found conducting to be her most rewarding medium of performance" (Green, 71). The combinations of voice and various instruments allowed her to experiment with a wider range of sonorities within her compositions.

The summer before her senior year at Westminster, Perry traveled to Birmingham, Alabama, and worked with a young choir. By all accounts, this was a very positive experience, with the choir performing one of her compositions. Edward notes, "Perry's early works, mostly songs and choral music, show a strong influence of spirituals" (Edward, Grove Online). This statement echoes Ammer, who stated, "Like Margaret Bonds and Florence Price, Julia Perry arranged some spirituals, and like them she wrote a considerable amount of vocal music" (Ammer, 177).

Perry graduated with a Bachelor of Music (1947) and a Master's in Music (1948) from Westminster Choir College. Her master's thesis was a secular cantata for baritone, narrator, mixed voices, and orchestra. This work, *Chicago*, was based on the poetry of Carl Sandburg. Perry continued her composition studies by attending the Juilliard School of Music in New York in 1948. She spent the summer of 1949 at the Berkshire Music Center in Tanglewood, where she studied choral singing with Hugh Ross. Upon her return to New York, she completed the sacred cantata *Ruth* for mixed voices and organ, which was subsequently performed at the Riverside Church. In 1951, Perry returned to Tanglewood to study composition with the Italian composer Luigi Dallapiccola. That Perry felt she had a great deal to learn from this avant-garde composer is evident in her desire to continue working with him after he returned to Italy. Perry sought and received

Guggenheim Fellowships to study with Dallapiccola in Florence, Italy, in 1952 and again in 1954.

Perry upheld a tradition of European musical instruction, and she found critical acceptance in taking this step. Walker-Hill states that many African-American women traveled and were well received as musicians in Europe during the late 1800s, both as performers and later as composers (Walker-Hill, *Piano Music*, 2). American men had been studying in European conservatories since the 1800s, and the opening of various curricula to women around 1870 in the European conservatories ensured that women were able to learn musical composition. In 1921, with the opening of the American Conservatory of Music at Fontainebleau in France, young American musicians had another opportunity to study with that most remarkable of teachers, Nadia Boulanger. Perry took advantage of her fellowship to take private lessons from Boulanger in 1952, and she also studied with Dallapiccola. Rosenstiel notes that Boulanger considered Perry to be one of her "more gifted black students of the '50s" (Rosentstiel, 370).

Although Perry returned several times to New York, it appears from the secondary source material that she spent the majority of the 1950s in Europe, studying with Dallapiccola, Boulanger, Zecchi, and Galliera, as well as organizing and conducting several concerts sponsored by the United States Information Service. Upon her return to America, Perry moved back to Akron, Ohio, and took an apartment "on the top floor of her father's medical office building" (Green, 73). Here she wrote *Homunculus, C.F.*, the work that appears in this anthology, for celesta and piano, harp, and a series of percussion instruments, consisting of vibraphone, xylophone, wood blocks, bass and snare drums, cymbals of various sizes, and timpani. This is an unusual instrumental combination, but one that corresponds to Perry's sense of experimentation.

This composition incorporates both traditional and experimental treatments, one of Perry's trademarks. First, the use of a C.F. (or Chord of a Fifteenth) represents traditional expanded harmonies found in African-American jazz. The C.F. is a stack of eight notes a third apart, or it may be viewed as a combination of two major-major seventh chords. Second, and, as Green speculates, C.F. could "also stand for Cantus Firmus, a fixed or given melody used as the basis for the work" (Green, 73). This traditional method of using a fixed melody dates back to the late Middle Ages and the beginning of polyphonic musical texture. A third means by which Perry refers to tradition is in subject matter. Homunculus was a "little man" created by Goethe in *Faust*, a work used many times as the basis for other musical compositions.

The experimental nature of *Homunculus, C.F.* is evident in the orchestration, especially in the percussion group mentioned above. The use of a rhythmic motive for the first section of the piece is also somewhat unusual. The "pantonal" nature of the C.F. as a melodic focus demonstrates Perry's absorption of modernist techniques. The motive beginning in the snare drum is played in retrograde to complete the eight-measure phrase.

Homunculus, C.F. is divided into four sections. The first section consists of the nonpitched percussion instruments playing a distinct rhythmic motive. The four-measure motive becomes a rhythmic pattern to create a canon between the snare drum and the wood blocks. In the bass drum, Perry introduces a new rhythm in measure 9 just as the snare drum phrase ends. This new rhythm becomes a counterrhythm for the snare drum and wood blocks. Cymbals (m. 21) close the canon between the snare drum and wood blocks. Perry repeats the first section with some modification.

The composer slowly introduces the C.F. in the timpani in measure 41. This is a transitional point between the strict rhythmic section and the melodic section (section 2) beginning at measure 60. In this section Perry uses the harp, timpani, celesta, and vibraphone to present the various notes of the C.F. At measure 81, she expands the number of notes and increases the tempo. The cymbals and wood blocks create additional rhythmic interest.

Perry's transition into her third section is very short (one measure, 94). This section represents the harmonic possibilities of the C.F. Sustained tones are played on the vibraphone, with layers of notes added by the celesta. Green states, "Perry based this entire section on E^7 or E^9 chords which further supports the basis of the composition—the C.F. built on E" (Green, 76). The snare and bass drums play portions of the original rhythmic motive found in section one in section three.

Section four begins at measure 106. Perry builds each musical element to this point, balancing the rhythmic, melodic, and harmonic patterns established in the previous sections. The full chord of a fifteenth finally emerges at measure 177, only three measures before the piece abruptly ends.

In Goethe's *Faust*, the Homunculus is a "little man" created by Wagner within a glass phial. The little man, or spirit as he is sometimes called, is able to levitate the phial in which he lives, to move about, communicate, emit light, and yet he lacks freedom. From the time of its inception in the drama (II.ii.2), the Homunculus seeks activity. Slowly at first, the Homunculus stirs and then flies off into the night in his glass phial, bearing Faust to a clearing. It reappears later in act 2, but this time speaks of freedom. "From place to place I flit and hover, and wish that in the best sense I might be. My glass I long impatiently to shatter" (Goethe, 269).

As previously noted, Perry wrote her composition while living in her apartment located in her father's medical building. Green believes that "These clinical surrounding evoked memories of the medieval laboratory where Wagner, youthful apprentice to Faust, made a successful alchemy experiment, fashioning and bringing to life a creature he called homunculus" (Green, 73). It is possible to speculate that this composition represents one of Perry's musical manifestations of the turmoil surrounding the civil rights movement of the late 1950s and early 1960s, and the African-American's increasing desire to achieve freedom from societal constraints. Another work that supports this speculation is Perry's setting of the spiritual "Free at Last."

In 1971 and 1973 Perry suffered paralytic strokes that affected her right side. She taught herself to write with her left hand and continued composing, completing symphonies 5 through 12. Her total oeuvre consists of twelve symphonies, two concertos, three operas, and numerous instrumental chamber and solo works, cantatas, songs, and choral pieces. She wrote her last compositions in 1976 (Edward, Grove Online). Julia Perry passed away in Akron, Ohio, on 29 April 1979.

Further Reading

Ammer, Christine. *Unsung: A History of Women in American Music.* Portland, Ore.: Amadeus Press, 2001.

Campbell, Don G. *Master Teacher: Nadia Boulanger.* Washington, D.C.: The Pastoral Press, 1984.

Edward, J. Michele. "Perry, Julia." In *The New Grove Dictionary of Music* Online, ed. L. Macy. http://www.grovemusic.com. Accessed February 2003.

Goethe, Johann Wolfgang von. *Faust.* Trans. George Madison Priest. Franklin Center, Pa.: The Franklin Library, 1981.

Green, Mildred Denby. *Black Women Composer: A Genesis.* Boston: Twayne Publishers, 1983.

Rosenstiel, Léonie. *Nadia Boulanger: A Life in Music.* New York: W.W. Norton & Company, 1982.

Southern, Eileen. *The Music of Black Americans: A History.* New York: W.W. Norton & Company, 1983.

Walker-Hill, Helen. "Music by Black Women Composers at the AMRC." *American Music Research Center Journal* 2 (1992): 44.

———. *Piano Music by Black Women Composers: A Catalog of Solo and Ensemble Works.* Westport, Conn.: Greenwood Press, 1992.

Homunculus, C. F.

Julia Amanda Perry

*) Xylophone is not transposed

ROBERTA LINDSEY

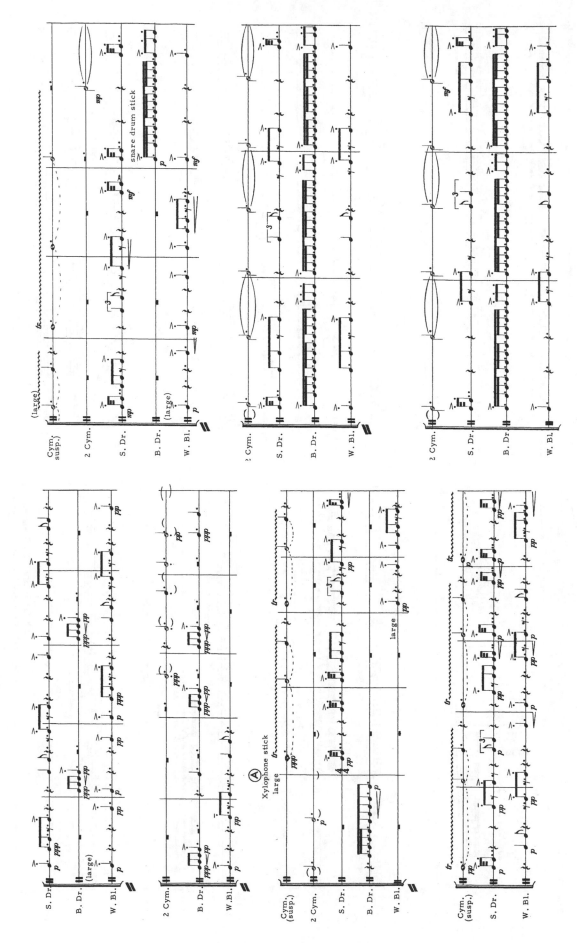

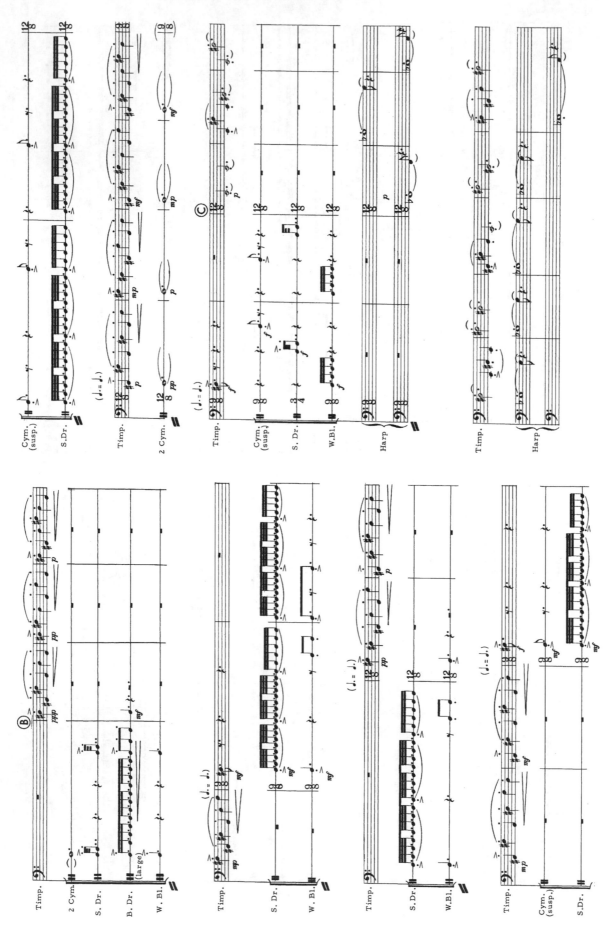

ROBERTA LINDSEY

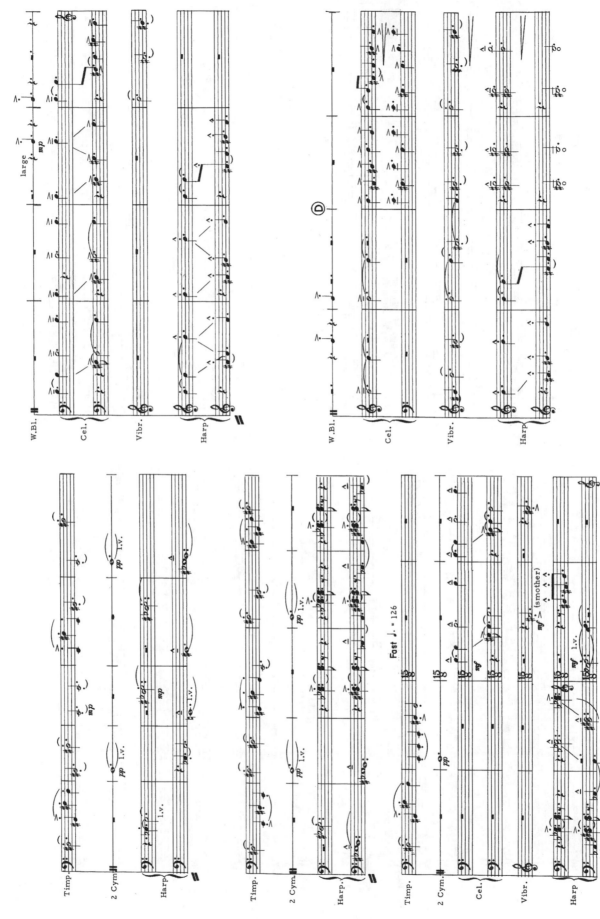

Julia Amanda Perry

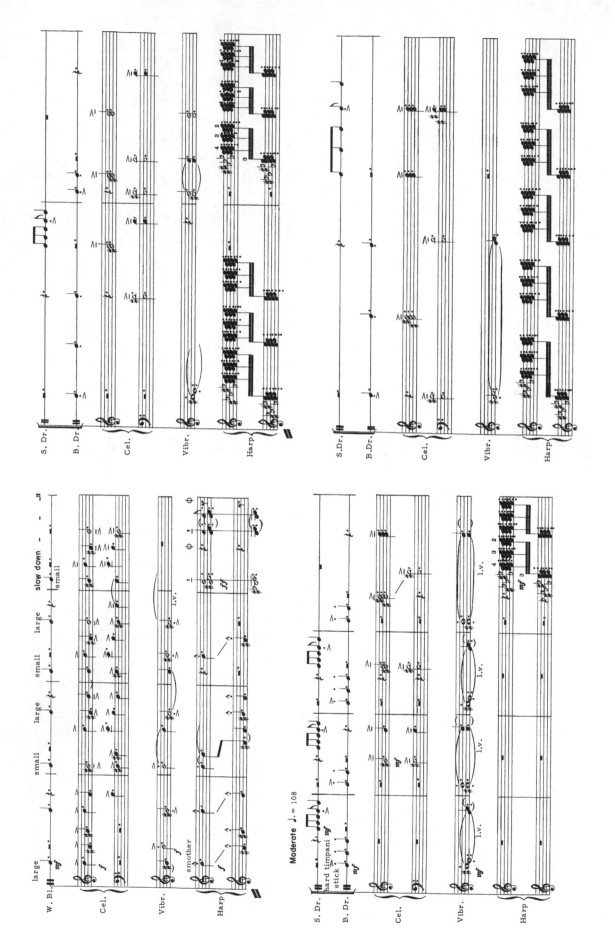

ROBERTA LINDSEY

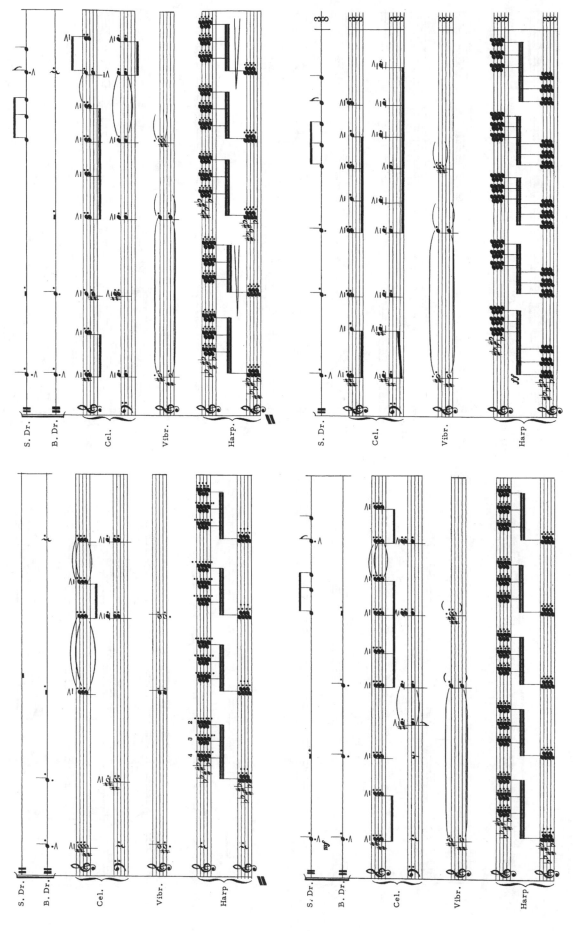

Julia Amanda Perry   417

418   ROBERTA LINDSEY

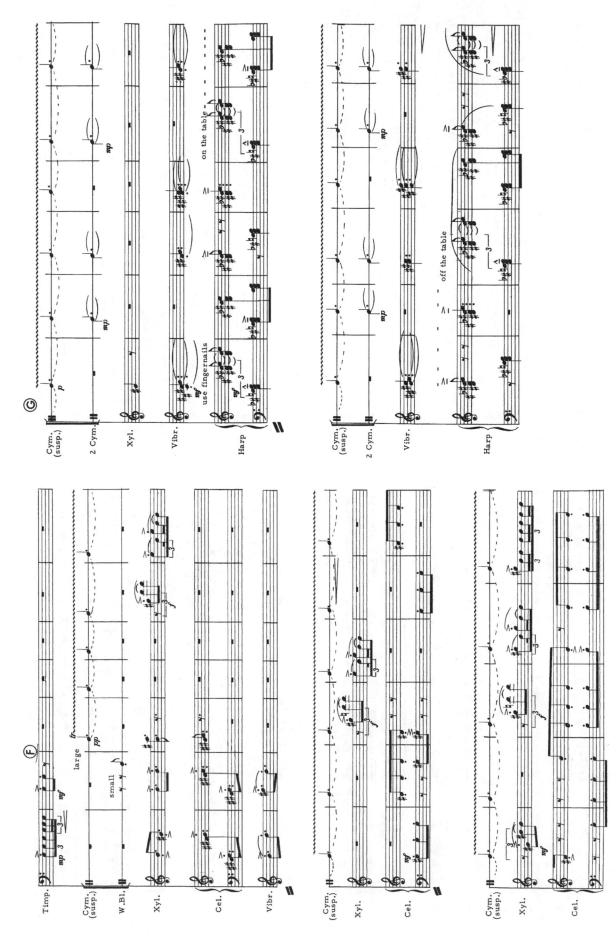

Julia Amanda Perry

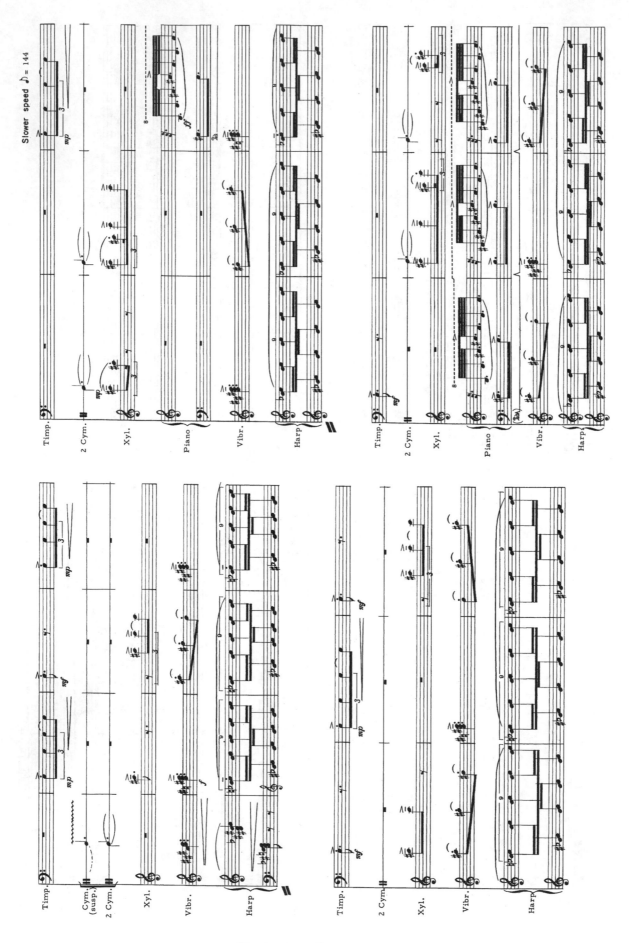

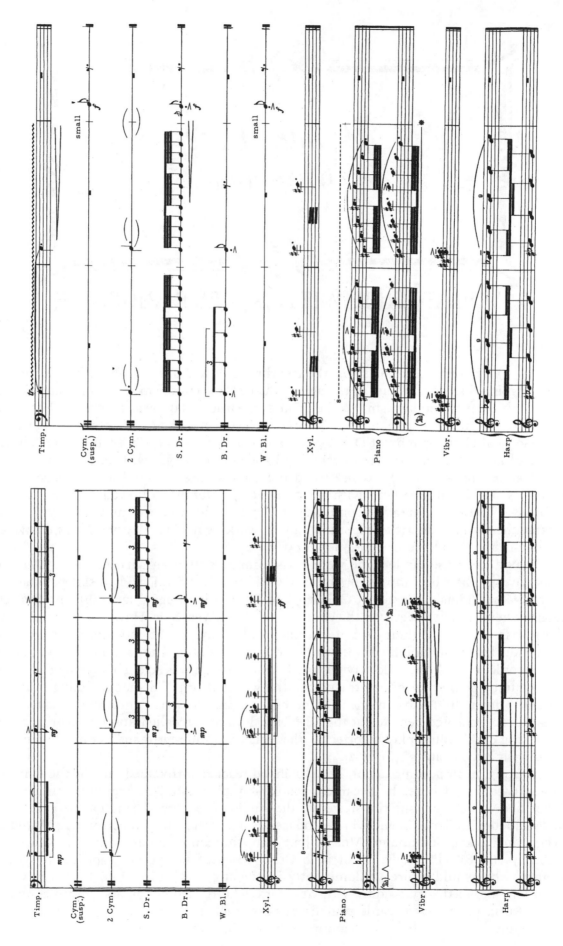

Julia Amanda Perry

421

Vivian Fine
(1913–2000)

VIVIAN FINE WITH JAMES R. BRISCOE

Vivian Fine's music spans the last three-quarters of the twentieth century. She was born in Chicago, Illinois, as the age of musical Romanticism was fading and that of twentieth-century modernism was beginning in earnest. The year before her birth, the Ballets russes under Diaghilev with Nijinski as lead dancer had scandalized Paris with a hypersensual choreography of Debussy's *Prélude à l'après-midi d'un faune,* and Schoenberg had launched total chromaticism and Expressionist *angst* with *Pierrot Lunaire.* In the year of Fine's birth, Stravinsky and the Ballets russes would again enrage some Parisians but inflame others with *Le sacre du printemps,* followed in just days by Debussy's subtle but equally "confusing" ballet *Jeux.* In America, meanwhile, Ives had cleared the path to American experimentalism, working in obscurity on *The Unanswered Question* (1908) and the *Concord Sonata* (1909–1915).

David and Rose Finder Fine were Jewish immigrants from Latvia and the Ukraine, respectively. Their beginnings in America were humble, with David working at the box office of the Yiddish Theater of Chicago, and Rose, beginning at age fourteen, as a secretary. They lived in poverty in the ghetto of the Near West Side. However, both followed the Jewish heritage in their love of learning, read avidly, and attended lectures. In time, their industry would notably improve their economic status. They soon had three daughters: in order of age, Adelaide, Vivian, and Eleanor. Vivian was so enchanted by the sound of her aunt's piano that at age three she "threw a tantrum"—a shock coming from the normally quiet child—to convince her mother to permit lessons. A neighborhood teacher, Miss Rosen, accepted her even at that age. Fine, however, recalled Rosen's severity: when the young child would play incorrectly, the teacher would reprimand her by "hitting my hand with a fly swatter" (Cody 2).

Noting an important talent, her childhood teacher introduced Fine at the Chicago Musical College, where she became a scholarship piano student beginning at age five. When she was eleven, she transferred to the studio of Madame Djane Lavoie-Herz, who had studied with Scriabin and who introduced Fine to "the whole repertoire. . . . I studied everything, Bach, Schumann, Mozart [but also] the contemporary music of the time, Debussy and Ravel" (Cody, 4). In 1924 Herz presented her young pupil to the young woman who would figure predominantly in shaping Fine's direction, Ruth Crawford. Soon Fine began theory studies with Crawford, who turned her sights toward composition: "Ruth was an avant-garde composer as my teacher. . . . it made me feel that it was completely natural to be a woman and to be writing adventurous music" (Cody, 5). So entranced did Fine become with the new world of music that she quit school at age fourteen and never earned a high school diploma.

Between the introduction to Crawford and leaving Chicago in 1931, Vivian Fine immersed herself in the discipline of the classics as a pianist, but also the study of the avant-garde as a composer. She met and much admired the Scriabin student and modernist Dane Rudhyar, but she was perhaps most encouraged by the Hungarian Imre Weisshaus, who took a great interest in Fine's independent atonal compositions. Henry Cowell arranged for her debut as a composer when Fine was sixteen, programming her "Solo for Oboe," and he later would supervise her first publication, *Four Songs*, in the *New Music Edition* in 1933. In 1929, she had her compositions performed in New York at the Pan-American Association of Composers and at Dessau, Germany, at the International Society of Contemporary Composers.

Upon moving to New York in 1931 at age eighteen, Fine began what Cody sees as her first creative cycle, lasting until about 1946 and resulting in fifty-four compositions. She studied composition classically with Roger Sessions beginning in 1934, his fee waived because she played his music so well in concerts, but continued following the avant-gardist advice of Henry Cowell. In this early New York phase, she studied piano with Abby Whiteside. Equally vital to her development was her association with Copland, Rudhyar, Antheil, and others in the self-styled "Young Composers Group." In 1932 Arthur Berger, likewise a young modern, singled out a performance of her *Polyphonic Piano Pieces* as "most successful. While the musical fabric in its contrapuntal complexity might conceivably pass for Schoenberg, the nervousness of the rhythm is American in character" (Cody, 11).

Fine had to gain a living only by hard work in the depths of the Great Depression, and became accompanist and composer for dance companies that emphasized contemporary choreography, including those works set by Doris Humphrey, Charles Weidman, and Hanya Hol. Her father had lost his job in Chicago, and her parents had joined her in New York. Fine had already gained renown for her ability as a pianist and sight-reader of modern scores, and indeed she fell immediately to writing music based on the modern dance enacted by the new choreographers: "I had a knack for catching in music the characteristics of the dance. . . . Not everybody can do it, to watch movement then write music" (Cody, 12).

By 1934 Fine's music, previously highly dissonant, turned to an expanded tonality. Whether, like Copland, she saw the times as right for greater accessibility can only be speculated, but by this time her compositional achievements allowed her to speak more simply. Regarding the 1937 *Race for Life* for the choreographer Doris Humphrey, and other works of the period, Fine observed, "There was something less original about the compositions that I wrote when I began to write tonal music, but it enabled me to have a mastery of writing eventually" (Cody, 14). The tonal period of her composition peaked in 1944 with the *Concertante for Piano and Orchestra*, her first major work for orchestra. Not coincidentally, she spent that year under the tutelage of the conductor George Szell for orchestration, a brief but also important influence on her writing.

In 1934 she met the sculptor Benjamin Karp, and they married the next year. In 1942 the Karps had their first child, Peggy, and six years later their second, Nina. Although this mid-life interlude as young wife and mother saw a lessening of composition, Fine noted that she was able to envision herself anew: she recognized that composing for orchestra had broken through as a major idiom. Moreover, after the war, she left traditional tonality behind.

The family left New York and its modernist intensities in 1948—and its financial insecurities as well—when Ben Karp accepted a position in Montclair, New Jersey. In 1951 the Karps moved to New Paltz, New York, for another academic position at the state college. Fine composed regularly, although the number of works declined. "In our town we have a comparatively quiet village life," she admitted to one interviewer (Cody, 18). She nonetheless found time to direct the Rothschild Music Foundation and perform at its concerts, traveling to New York City two or three times weekly.

The fellow experimenter Wallingford Riegger wrote an important précis of Fine's creativity, listed below. He saw three creative periods: a youthful and atonal period to age twenty-four, a "more diatonic period" from 1937 to 1944, and a "return to atonality, tempered occasionally by key impressions," in 1958.

In the view of Judith Cody, Fine experienced a "second creative explosion" in 1964, when Bennington College in Vermont approached her regarding a position in composition and piano. Although she regretted the long drive from New Paltz, she found a "very lively scene" at the department of music that was much to her liking. One advantage, recalling Haydn at Esterhaza, was hearing her compositions performed quite regularly; when Ben Karp retired in 1969, she assumed a full-time position at Bennington and the couple moved there. Works composed for this setting included the *Missa Brevis, Concerto for Piano, Strings, and Percussion for One Performer*, and *Meeting for Equal Rights 1866*. Vivian Fine was one of the founders of the American Composers Alliance and was its vice president from 1961 to 1965. She also held teaching assignments at New York University, the Juilliard School of Music, and the New York State University at Potsdam. In 1980 she received a Guggenheim Fellowship and was elected to the American Academy and Institute of Arts and Letters.

Later compositions written on commission included *Drama for Orchestra*, requested by the San Francisco Symphony and premiered in 1983; *Ode to Purcell*, commissioned by the Elizabeth Sprague Coolidge Foundation and performed at the Library of Congress in 1985; *Poetic Fires*, by the Koussevitsky Music Foundation and performed in 1985 by the American Composers Orchestra, with the composer as piano soloist and Gunther Schuller as conductor; and *Songs for Saint Cecelia's Day*, requested by Trinity College and performed in 1985. Vivian Fine composed two operas, *The Women in the Garden* (1977) and *The Memoirs of Uliana Rooney* (1993). In 1987 she retired from Bennington College. But, as late as 1993, Fine at last witnessed the premiere of her opera *Uliana Rooney* at the University of Richmond, Virginia. In her libretto Sonya Friedman creates Rooney as a fictional Hollywood composer, a loose cannonball who marries ten times in the course of his life. Elements of the autobiographical are present in the libretto: Rooney also is of Russian Jewish heritage, and he, too, seems to have encountered the formative impressions of *Le sacre du printemps* and *Pierrot Lunaire*.

On 20 March 2000, Vivian and her older sister Adelaide were in a serious car accident in Bennington. Adelaide lived three days, but Vivian died instantly. Benjamin Karp, her husband of sixty-five years, died nine months later after a lengthy illness.

"Dance of Triumph: The Rescue of Alcestis" is the fourth and final section of the ballet suite *Alcestis*. Martha Graham commissioned and performed the ballet by her dance company in 1960; it was Fine's first work in the genre in twenty years. Heretofore the choreography etched out by the dancers had suggested Fine's compositional response, but in the case of *Alcestis* the composer wrote in response to a script by Martha Graham. The Alcestis myth concerns the sacrifice of Alcestis's life for her husband, Admetus, so that he may thereby attain immortality. As the household of Admetus mourns for Alcestis, Hercules arrives. The news of her death is kept from Hercules, and he feasts and drinks in heroic fashion. When he learns from a servant of the death of Alcestis, he seeks out Thanatos (Death) and battles with him for her life. Victorious, Hercules rescues Alcestis and returns her to Admetus.

The movement is marked alla breve, allegro energico, and is scored for woodwinds, brass, timpani, xylophone, piano, harp, and strings. The "Dance of Triumph" begins with a rush of energy that subsides only momentarily at measure 35. The lyric respite is interrupted by strident gestures almost immediately, but legato and the dynamic level of piano in the strings returns at measure 50. Although a fortissimo brings a sharp contrast at measure 71, it is relaxed only for a moment in the next measure, but then it is re-energized by a fortissimo as the "Dance of Triumph" concludes.

Here, as in general in her music, Vivian Fine writes in a freely atonal style, projecting sharply etched motives and driving rhythms. Her expressionist idiom perhaps most closely resembles that of Miriam Gideon among American women, although Fine's atonality is virtually complete and the expressionism more intense. Heidi von Gunden recalls the score explanation: "[The work is] an attempt to depict the dramatic and emotional impact of the myth . . . [that] avoids descriptive or representational writing" (67).

In the course of section 4, Fine builds energy largely through the strident nature of disjunct intervals in each part ranged horizontally, such as one hears in the trumpet line at the outset. The tension between lines also suggests the power of the triumph of Alcestis over Death, such as the outburst of dissonance at the structural articulation of measure 20, *forte* C-sharp and A-sharp in the strings against A and G in the winds. The movement is in essence through-composed, building progressively to the triumphant conclusion. Fine nonetheless suggests an inner architecture by alternating lesser and stronger dynamics, the bright beginning tempo with meno mosso sections, and lyric sections contrasted with brusque passages.

Vivian Fine was a woman of strength and was herself a "Dance of Triumph." By her model career as a woman in composition, to her brilliant pianism for American music, through the importance of her teaching at Bennington College, and by her key advances in American musical modernism she became one of the decisive composers of the century. As Wallingford Riegger observed in 1958, "It is true that we are gradually overcoming our provincial attitude in regard to adulation of anything from abroad at the expense of the American product. Recognition, long overdue, of Vivian Fine's contribution would be another step in this direction" (Riegger, 3).

Further Reading

Cody, Judith. *Vivian Fine: A Bio-bibliography.* Westport, Conn.: Greenwood, 2002.
Riegger, Wallingford, "The Music of Vivian Fine." *American Composers Alliance Bulletin* 8, no. 1 (1958): 2–4.
Von Gunden, Heidi. *The Music of Vivian Fine.* Lanham, Md.: Scarecrow Press, 1999.

Recording

Alcestis. Composers Recordings CRI 145; rereleased as CRI CD 692 (1995).

Dance of Triumph
The Rescue of Alcestis

Vivian Fine

VIVIAN FINE WITH JAMES R. BRISCOE

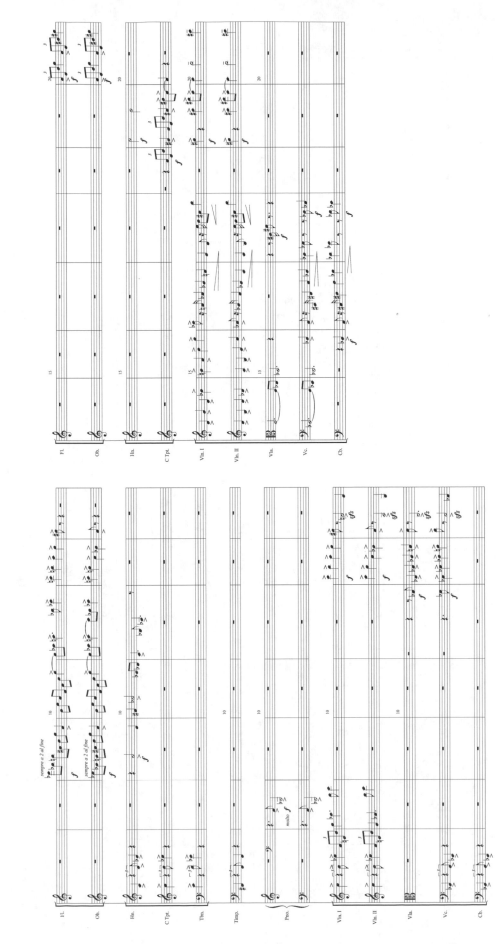

Vivian Fine

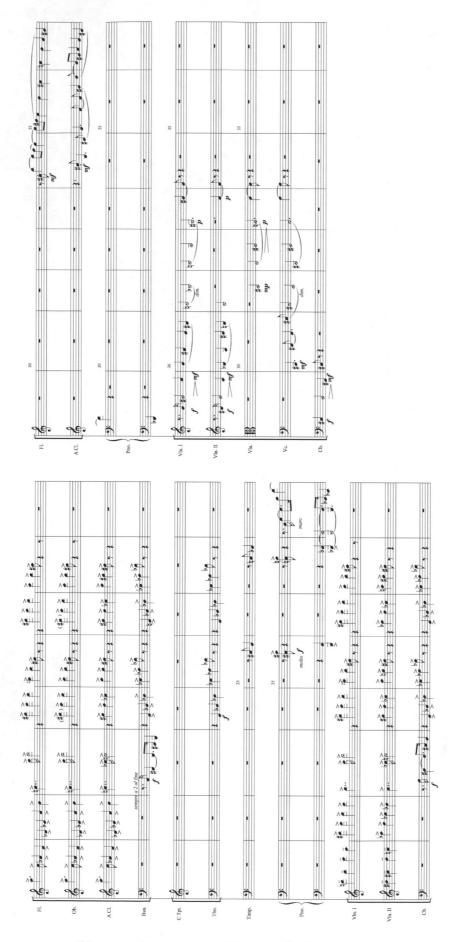

428   VIVIAN FINE WITH JAMES R. BRISCOE

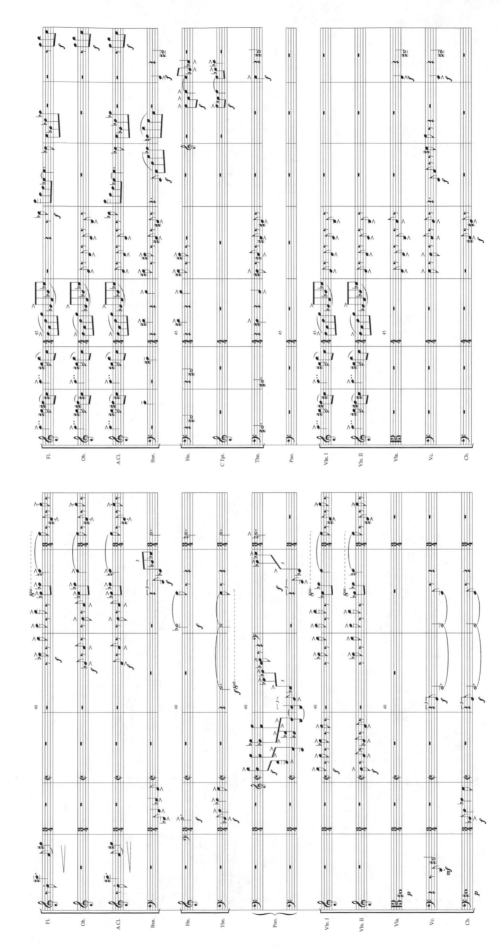

Vivian Fine

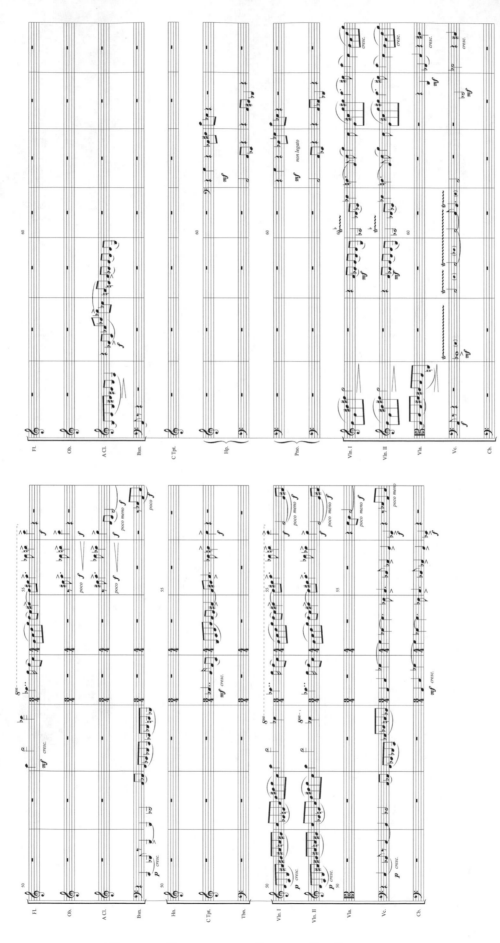

VIVIAN FINE WITH JAMES R. BRISCOE

Vivian Fine

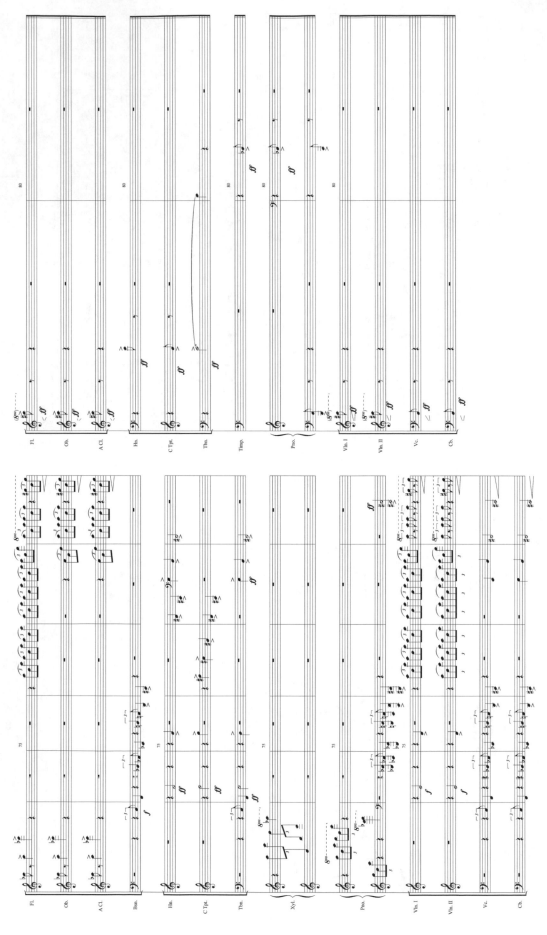

VIVIAN FINE WITH JAMES R. BRISCOE

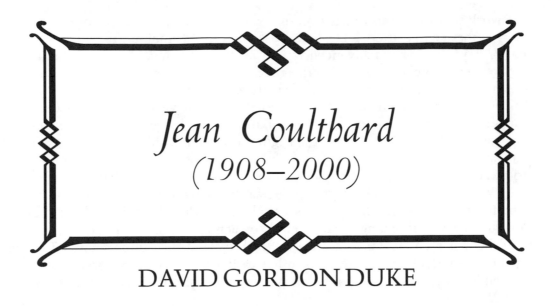

Jean Coulthard
(1908–2000)

DAVID GORDON DUKE

Jean Coulthard began composing while a schoolgirl, helped immeasurably by her mother, one of the few professional musicians in early-twentieth-century Vancouver. By her teens Coulthard was captivated by the harmonies and textures of English and French early modern composers—particularly Debussy, who remained a persistent influence. In her early twenties she studied for a year in London with Ralph Vaughan Williams at the Royal College of Music. She returned to Vancouver filled with an intense personal drive to compose, but knowing her deficiencies in technique and craft.

Coulthard's struggle throughout the 1930s and the years of World War II was to write and to learn the craft of musical composition as a professional. She built a substantial early catalogue of songs, piano works, and a handful of compositions for ensembles, mostly withdrawn in later years. Having no teachers or mentors closer than San Francisco, she went on occasional study trips for "criticism lessons" with Aaron Copland in New York, Darius Milhaud at Mills College in Oakland, California, and Arnold Schoenberg in Los Angeles. Then, during the early years of the war, Coulthard was greatly encouraged by Australian-born composer Arthur Benjamin, then in Vancouver. In 1944–1945, Coulthard went to New York for intensive lessons with Bernard Wagenaar (1894–1971). Wagenaar taught at the Juilliard School, where his pupils included Ned Rorem, William Schuman, and Norman Dello Joio; Coulthard worked with him as a private student in 1944–1945 (and in several subsequent refresher courses in the later 1940s), finally acquiring the technical skills for the type of career she had long envisioned.

By 1945 Jean Coulthard's protracted apprenticeship was over: the advice of some of the twentieth century's most illustrious names and the foundation of skill imparted by Wagenaar gave her the confidence to work in the great forms of the classical tradition. After her second return to her native Vancouver, she began what she habitually called her "parallel career" as a university lecturer in theory and, in time, composition at the University of British Columbia.

Between 1946 and 1948, she was at work on three sonatas for piano, oboe and piano, and cello and piano—works that were, to borrow a phrase from M. F. K. Fisher, a measure of her powers. During the subsequent fifty years of her extraordinarily long and productive career, Coulthard produced solo and duo sonatas for almost all orchestral instruments. The 1946 *Sonata for Cello and Piano* became one of her most popular and frequently performed chamber works; ultimately published by the prestigious British firm Novello, it was performed, broadcast, and recorded by cellists at home and abroad.

The work was audacious for its time and place. The Canadian repertoire to that date had few chamber compositions, let alone works in a modern idiom. In the west coast of Coulthard's day, able cellists advanced were a rarity, and new music by Canadian composers was most unlikely to feature on their occasional recital programs. Publishing, apart from songs and educational works, was scarcely an option.

By contrast, the optimism of the immediate postwar years and the success of the state-supported Canadian Broadcasting Corporation (CBC) helped buoy up the composer. Coulthard sensed that she was in on the beginnings of a new phase of musical development in Canada.

Coulthard intended in her first sonatas to write substantial multimovement works following "traditional" formal designs. Wagenaar had taught her that sonata form could be reconciled with a twentieth-century sensibility, and that the skill to handle motivic variation and harmonic change was a mark of achievement for a serious composer. Coulthard herself seems to have decided to push beyond the "impressionist" or, occasionally, "English" feeling for harmony in her earlier work to an exploration of bonded triads, extended harmonies, and polytonality (not unlike similar idioms used by Milhaud or Copland).

If the first movement of the Cello Sonata was to prove Coulthard's most "composerly" work to date, the second movement appears a more straightforward exploration of contrasting lyrical and dramatic moods. Subtitled "Saraband," it opens with a gentle drift of sonorities in the piano: an implied C-sharp minor triad in the first measure flows to a bonded A major/G minor sonority by measure 3. The cello enters with an unfolding line, narrowly restricted to melodic seconds and thirds before melting into the A major triad component of the bonded sonority. Thereafter the piano extends this melodic line as the cello adds a descant extending into the instrument's upper register. A second phrase continues in a similar manner, incorporating further bonded sonorities. The first section of the movement concludes in measure 13 with a modal cadence, D minor, with an added major seventh, resolving to E major, strongly flavored with parallel fifths in the cello.

Just before measure 14, the cello surges forward to begin a contrasting drammatico section, at once extroverted and passionate. The new materials develop and intensify until an unexpectedly stark two-part passage in measures 28–30. The dramatic core of the movement follows at once, an even more impassioned section with double stops (often fifths) in the cello, insistent sixteenth-note seconds and thirds, and sweeping thirty-second-note arpeggios in the piano.

A short cadenza link for the cello leads to a modified return of the opening material in measure 42. Here the piano part is altered to incorporate open fifths (which unambiguously confirm the opening C-sharp minor sonority), while the cello brings forward a fragment of the initial melodic line, a free stretto of originally discrete melodic and harmonic ideas. Thereafter the bonded triads (first heard in measure 3) are transformed into a rippling, sextuplet figurations that subtly throw the duple cello lines into a delicate rhythmic relief. By measure 47, the movement appears to be ebbing to a peaceful conclusion, but instead rises to a final dramatic outburst as a fragment of the initial cello theme is presented in a dramatic unison (measures 53–54). Then elements from the beginning of the first drammatico section in measure 13 and the note arpeggio figure first heard in measure 35 are fused together. The movement's closing bars begin just before measure 56 with a return of material first heard in measures 7 and 8; thereafter the cello and the piano exchange material as both sink into their lower registers with concluding A major/G minor cadence chords.

Many listeners will perceive the Saraband as a rather free blend of contrasting elements. Closer inspection reveals how the composer has created coherence out of economically restricted material: the interval focus on seconds and thirds established in the cello's opening line becomes a harmonic focus in the climatic sixteenth notes in the middle section; the consistent use of modal cadences; the interest in revising and combining materials in new contexts. Though much of Coulthard's work uses complex, even extravagantly rich textures (which the composer felt might be a representation of the lush intensity of the British Columbia coastal rain forests), in this movement moments of particular importance are highlighted by lean two-part or even unison writing.

The Cello Sonata should be viewed as a work marking Coulthard's emergence as a mature composer. Despite the Sonata's authority and quality, one doubts that the newly confident composer would herself have imagined a career encompassing five further decades of activity and the production of similar works for nearly all orchestral instruments, not to mention symphonies, concerti, a full-length opera, and hundreds of choral, vocal, and keyboard pieces.

Throughout her career, Coulthard was never (and never wished to be) an innovator: she early developed a vision view of herself as an artist concerned with quality and self-expression, not with advanced technique or stylish idioms. The *Sonata for Cello and Piano* unmistakably defines the moment this artist found her voice.

Sarabande
from Sonata for Cello and Piano

Jean Coulthard

David Gordon Duke

Jean Coulthard

437

DAVID GORDON DUKE

Violet Archer
(1913–2000)

ROBERT WEBER WITH JAMES R. BRISCOE

Violet Archer was both a widely performed composer and a dedicated, influential educator. Admirers of her music point to its melodic vigor and seamless craftsmanship, while her former students credit her with nurturing in them both a formidable technique and an inquiring musical mind. This, together with her tireless promotion of Canadian music, long made her a prominent participant in Canada's musical life.

Violet Balestreri Archer was born in Montreal to an Italian immigrant family. She and her family legally adopted the anglicized name Archer in 1940. Her own musical life began early, for she was composing seriously for the piano before she was out of her teens. In 1930 she entered the Conservatory of Music at McGill University, where her teachers included Claude Champagne and Douglas Clarke. To pay her way though school, she took jobs as a chamber musician, accompanist, church organist, and music teacher. Working prevented her from receiving her Bachelor of Music degree and Teacher's Licenciate in piano until 1936, but it gave her varied and valuable experience of practical musical activities.

Eventually desiring further study, Violet Archer spent the summer of 1942 in New York as a pupil of Béla Bartók. Bartók's lessons brought a new discipline and economy to her writing, as well as a more sympathetic approach to folk materials. During the period 1940–1947, she played percussion in the Montreal Women's Symphony Orchestra. She began to appear as a composer of distinction in 1942, when Sir Adrian Boult selected her *Britannia, a Joyful Overture* in 1941 for performance with the British Broadcasting Corporation (BBC). In 1947, Archer began to study with Paul Hindemith at Yale University. Along with his usual emphasis on the practical aspects of composing and music making, Hindemith honed her technique and taught her how to organize her music better. Both Bartók and Hindemith had a profound impact on Violet Archer, and she considered them "the greatest musical minds of this century."

After Yale granted Archer a Master of Music degree in 1949, her academic career began. For the next thirteen years she taught at North Texas State College and the University of Oklahoma. She returned to Canada in 1962, to the fledgling music department of the University of Alberta in Edmonton. Through the efforts of Archer and her colleagues, the department was soon flourishing. Today, many of her former students are successful and active composers both in Canada and abroad. Even though she retired from the university in 1978, her interest in teaching never flagged, and she remained active in music education virtually until the end of her life. Upon her retirement, she was awarded the Queen's Silver Jubilee Medal for long and distinguished service to music.

Violet Archer's creative output is both prodigious and diverse. Her catalogue numbers well over 220 works for many media—from solo flute to full orchestra and chorus. Solo song and choral cycles form an important part of her oeuvre, and she has also written two operas, *Sganarelle* (1973) and *The Meal* (1983). From her own powerful style, as influenced by Hindemith and Bartók, she has forged a musical language marked by forceful counterpoint, soaring melodic lines, and traditional forms, which has lately been modified by more stringent Expressionist techniques.

Archer's music has been performed worldwide, and among her many awards are an Honorary Doctorate from McGill University (1971), an Honorary Fellowship in the Royal Canadian College of Organists (1985), the Order of Canada (1984), and an Honorary Membership in Sigma Alpha Iota.

The *Sonata for Alto Saxophone and Piano* is one of Archer's most popular chamber works. It was commissioned in 1971, through the Canadian Broadcasting Company (CBC), by Paul Brodie, who also recorded the work. The *Sonata* was premiered in 1972 by Eugene Rousseau at the World Saxophone Congress in Toronto. The saxophone and the piano are equal partners in this piece, which exploits the lyrical quality and wide range of the saxophone. The movements are entitled Preamble (reproduced here), Interlude, Valsette, and Rondo.

The Preamble is cast in sonata form. The first theme appears immediately. Two notes in the first measure of the saxophone part—D–D-sharp—reappear at the start of each of the following movements and form a unifying element. The brief second theme (m. 30) contrasts with the first through its slower rhythmic movement, although tight structure is maintained by subtle references to the original motive in the left hand. The following development section (m. 55) is drawn largely from the first theme. A dialogue between the saxophone and piano forms the recapitulation (m. 105), and a short coda completes the movement.

The Interlude is in ternary form and projects a blues feeling through its "swinging" dotted eighth notes and the Gershwinesque parallel chords in the piano. The middle section begins with three notes taken from the climax of the opening theme.

The opening phrase of the Valsette expands the D–D-sharp motif from a semitone to an augmented octave. This charming movement is formally quite strict, based solidly on the eighteenth-century minuet.

The opening figure of the Rondo borrows both the D–D-sharp motif and the rhythmic figure from the Preamble. Following the opening statement, the Rondo goes through two digressions, the first animated and the second lyrical. Both are derived from the main theme, as are the transitional materials between the sections. A register shift in the last return of the theme heightens the tension moving into the final cadence and serves as a coda.

Further Reading

Archer, Violet. "Making Music." In *Our Own Agendas: Autobiographical Essays by Women Associated with McGill University*, ed. M. Gillett and A. Beer, 76–82. Montreal: McGill-Queen's University Press, 1995.

Dalen, B. "The Composer's Voice: What Women Can Do." *Canadian University Music Review* XVI, no. 1 (1995): 14–40.

Whittle, J. "Violet Archer's Formative Years: A Bibliographical Catalogue of Her Compositions." *Canadian University Music Review* XVI, no. 1 (1995): 145–95.

Recording

Sonata for Alto Saxophone and Piano. Paul Brodie, saxophone; George Brough, piano. Radio Canada International. RCI 412.

Preamble
from Sonata for Alto Saxophone and Piano

Violet Archer

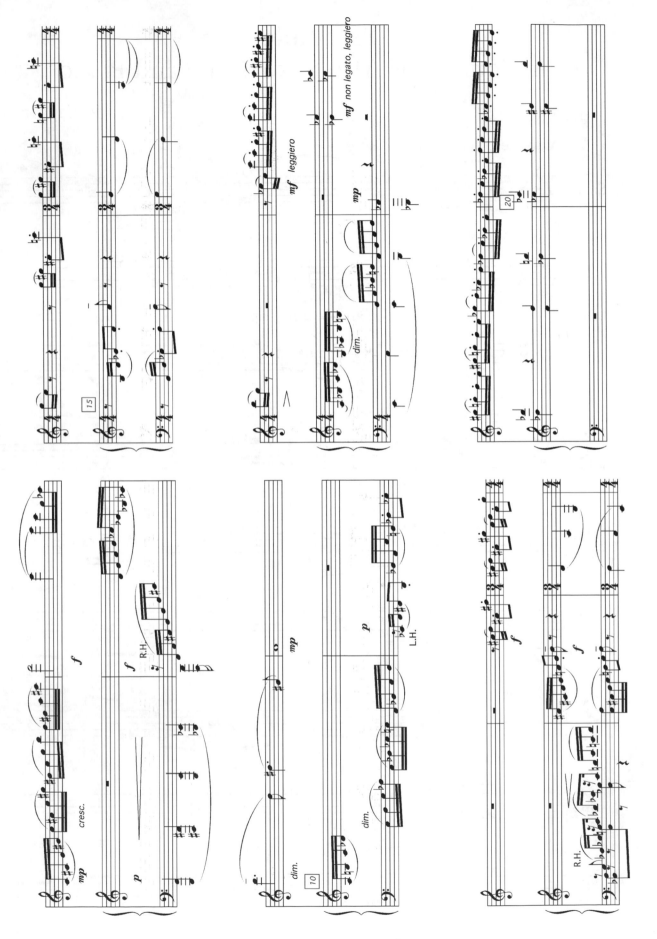

ROBERT WEBER WITH JAMES R. BRISCOE

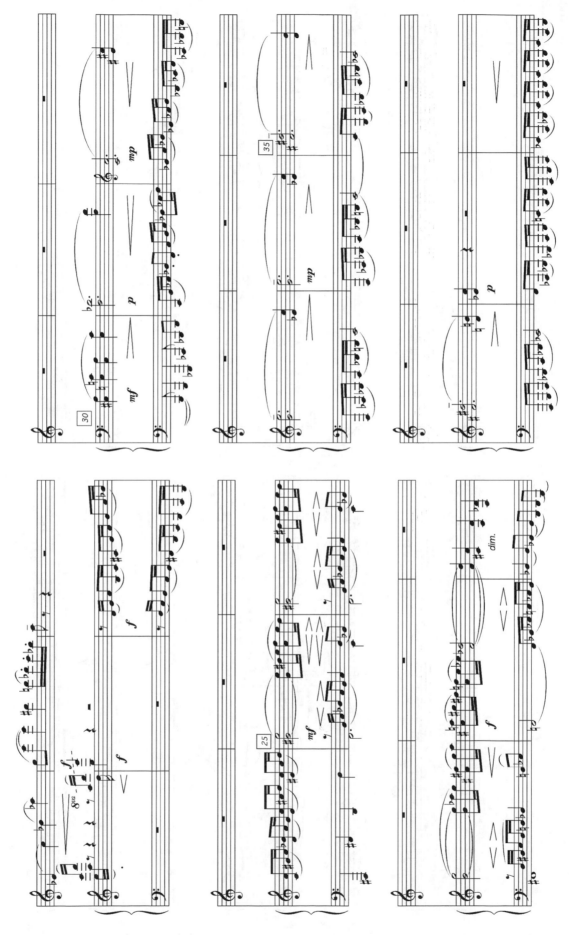

Violet Archer

445

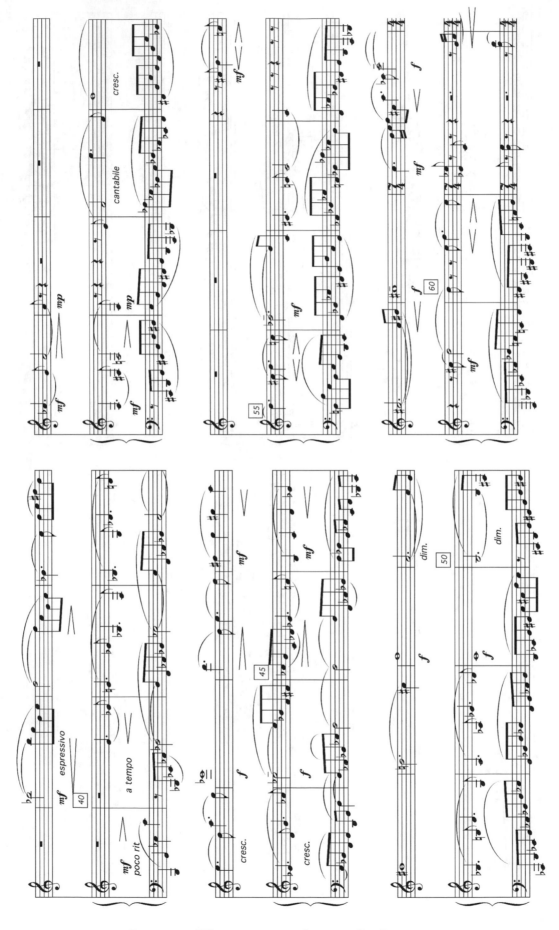

ROBERT WEBER WITH JAMES R. BRISCOE

Violet Archer

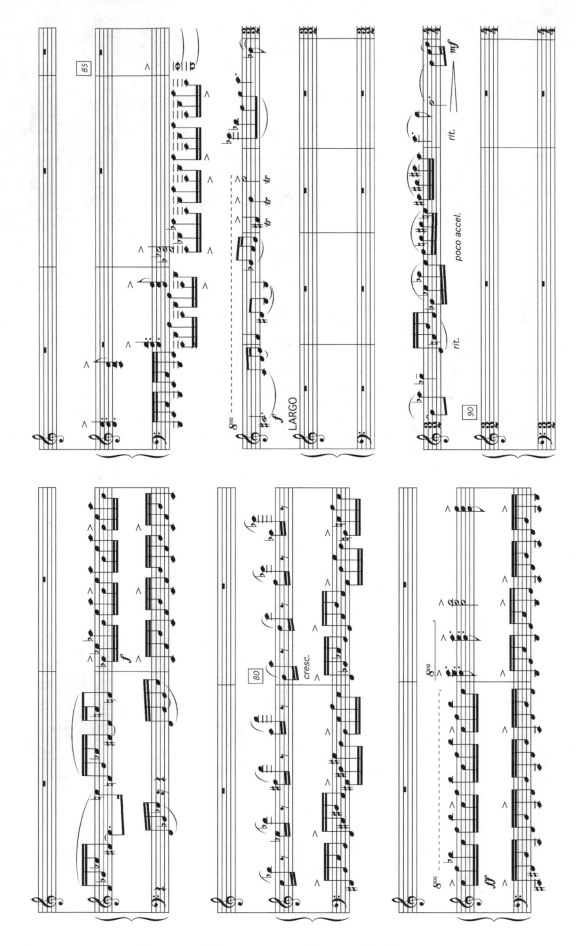

Robert Weber with James R. Briscoe

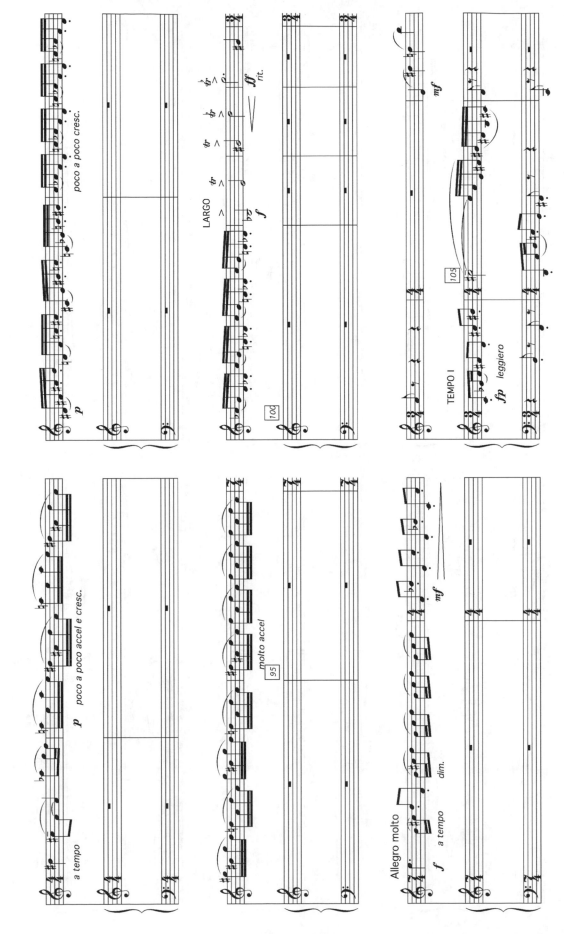

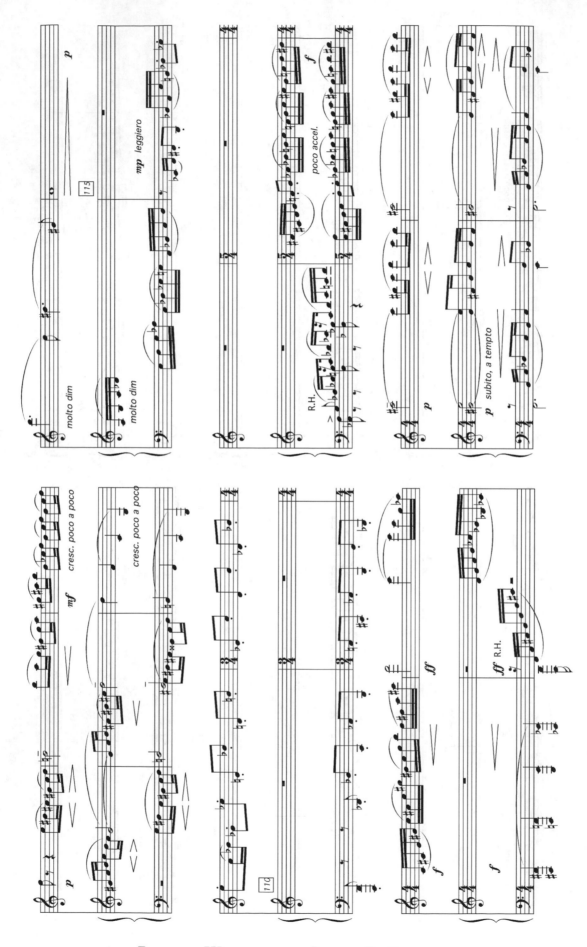

ROBERT WEBER WITH JAMES R. BRISCOE

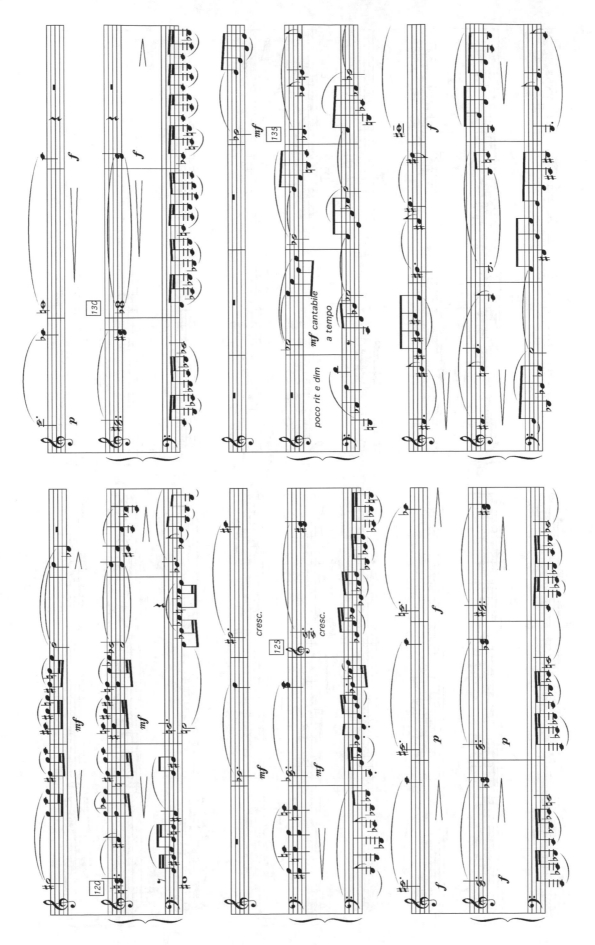

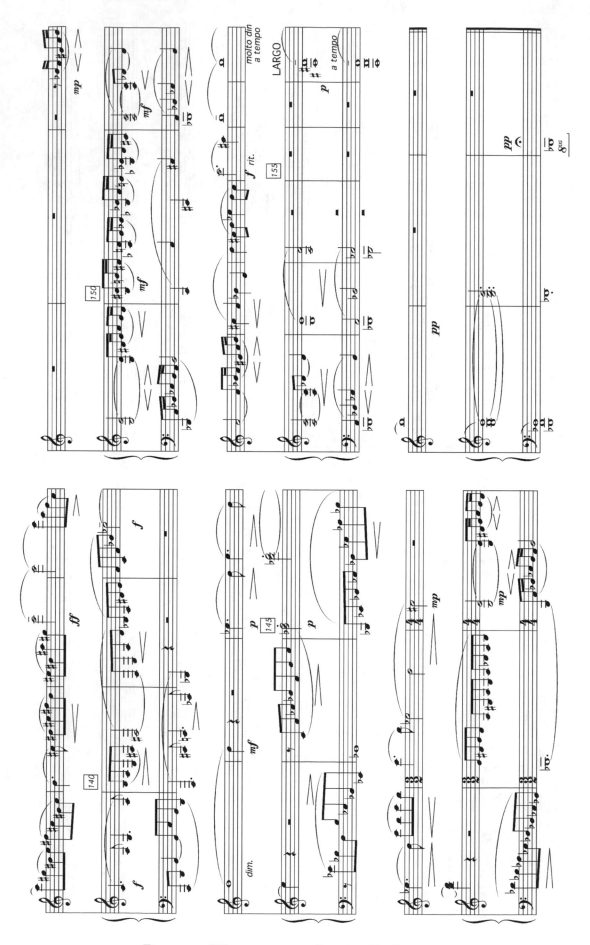

Pauline Oliveros
(born 1932)

ROBERTA LINDSEY

LISTEN! What do you hear? Do you hear the sound the air makes as the fan moves it around the room? Do you hear the blood traveling through your circulatory system? What do you hear? These questions might be posed by Pauline Oliveros. The composer John Adams wrote, "In her life and work, Pauline Oliveros practices an extremely difficult discipline: 'Always to listen' " (Adams, 32). Listening may encompass more than just hearing music, or television, or radio. To Oliveros, the term "listen" takes on additional meanings. She is interested and involved in the concept of "Deep Listening," investigating sounds that abound all around us every day and night. Some sounds can only be sensed; their normal frequency is above that of the ordinary individual's hearing. Some sounds are blocked out as irritants and are termed "noise." But are they really noise?

Oliveros's love of sound began when she was a young girl. Born in Texas in 1932, Oliveros grew up surrounded by both traditional and nontraditional music. Her mother and grandmother taught her how to play the piano, her grandfather collected musical instruments, and her brother played the accordion (Pendle, 228). Oliveros also learned how to play the accordion, as well as the tuba and French horn. All of these instruments represented traditional music culture to the young woman. Yet Oliveros frequently experimented with her grandfather's radio, tuning it to the "static sounds" (von Gunden, 3). The sounds she heard are considered to be a type of nontraditional music.

After graduating from San Francisco State College in 1957, Oliveros began to write her own experimental music. She became interested in manipulating traditional music by means of electronic equipment and tape, and helped to establish the San Francisco Tape Center. In 1966 she was appointed director of the Tape Music Center at Mills College, and the following year she began teaching electronic music at the University of California at San Diego (UCSD), where she later became director of the Center for Music Experiment and remained until 1981 (Ammer, 244).

Oliveros's music from her early period includes writing down her "slowed-down improvisation" (von Gunden, 11). She began to investigate various Asian influences, such as the poetic structure of a haiku. Oliveros also incorporated the sounds of her surroundings into her music. One such example of this technique appears in "An Interlude of Rare Beauty," where the vocal line imitates the motions of a swimming seal.

Oliveros assisted in starting the Project for Music Experiment and Related Research (PME), but she realized there had to be something more. "It was my good fortune to be one of the first faculty [from UCSD] with release time from teaching for a quarter to conduct a research project at PME" (Oliveros, *Roots*, vii). She expanded her investigations into various studies in conscious and active awareness as well as other types of Asian philosophy; T'ai Chi, karate, rituals, dreams, ceremonies, mandalas, and meditation. "The major and enduring shift in her work came in the mid-1970s when her studies of Native American cultures and Eastern religions led to a kind of meditative improvisation as a way of teaching people to recognize their own musicality" (Taylor, Grove Online).

It was through this study, release time, and funding from the Guggenheim Foundation that Oliveros developed a series of meditations. The term "meditations" caused several difficulties for her. When asked pointblank by Gagne what the term "meditation" meant to her, she replied that it was just a word, a term used

> in a lot of different ways. There are different meditational structures and forms—just examine traditional religions for their meditational practices. I'll take two examples, one is yoga and one is Zen. In yoga, the high practitioner is generating large-amplitude alpha waves in a meditative state, and if you introduce a stimulus, there'll be no response; the alpha wave will stay with the same amplitude. If you do the same thing to a Zen practitioner who is just as accomplished in generating high-amplitude alpha, the brain wave changes to beta instantaneously and then goes back. That's a very large difference: The Zen practitioner is balanced between inner and outer, and the yoga shuts down the outside world. These are profound differences in structure. If you analyze these different pieces, the Sonic Meditations and Deep Listening Pieces (which is another collection of them, about 30 pieces), each one has different uses and different forms. One piece might require a yogiclike state, another one might require a Zenlike state, another one might require going from one to the other. So it's exercising these faculties we have. But the overall use of the term meditation means for me to stay with it, whatever it is. (Gagne, 220–21)

In another article, Oliveros discussed the problematic nature of the term "meditation." She explored both the religious and nonreligious perspectives and found that "all meditation (both secular [non-religious] and religious) is similar in that it employs attention, awareness, concentration, openness and repetition" (Oliveros, "On Sonic Meditation," 138). Her *Sonic Meditations* are a series of instructions or "word-scores" for performers to focus their listening and "sounding" skills (Kingman, 577).

Composed in 1971, *Sonic Meditations* consists of twenty-five pieces. According to Introduction II of the score, "Each Sonic Meditation is a special procedure for the following: 1. Actually making sounds, 2. Actively imagining sounds, 3. Listening to present sounds, [and] 4. Remembering sounds" (Oliveros, *Sonic Meditations*, [2]). Three of the *Sonic Meditations* are included in this anthology. The first, Meditation I, is entitled "Teach Yourself to Fly."

> Any number of persons sit in a circle facing the center. Illuminate the space with dim blue light. Begin by simply observing your own breathing. Always be an observer. Gradually allow your breathing to become audible. Then gradually introduce your voice. Allow your vocal cords to vibrate in any mode which occurs naturally. Allow the intensity to increase very slowly. Continue as long as possible naturally, and until all others are quiet, always observing your own breath cycle.

> Variation: Translate voice to an instrument.

This is one of the simplest of the meditations to perform. The pieces become gradually more difficult as you progress through the process. By the time you reach the next set of instructions for the example in this anthology, you will have experienced expanding spatial awareness, sustained tones, increased mental stimulus, and visualization.

Meditation XIV
"Tumbling Song"

Make any vocal sound, but always go downward in pitch from the initial attack. The initial attack may begin at any pitch level. Go downward in a glissando or in discrete steps continuously. Go any distance in range, at any speed, dynamic or quality, but the breath determines the maximum time length of any downward gesture.

In this performance/meditation Oliveros is having the group again focus on their breathing, but has added another component—that of producing a recognized musical sound, a glissando, or steady stream of notes, in a downward motion. Unlike the first meditation or the next one, however, Oliveros does not provide for any variations in the performance.

Meditation XV
"Zina's Circle"

Stand together in a circle, with eyes closed facing the center. One person is designated, the transmitter. After observing the breathing cycle, individually, gradually join hands. Then slowly move back so that all arms are stretched out and the size of the circle increased. Next stretch the arms toward center and move in slowly. Finally move back to the normal sized circle, with hands still joined, standing so that arms are relaxed at sides. Return attention to breath. When the time seems right, the transmitter starts a pulse that travels around the circle, by using the right hand to squeeze the left hand of the person next to her. The squeeze should be quickly and sharply made, to resemble a light jolt of electricity. The squeeze must be passed from left hand to right hand and on to the next person as quickly as possible. The action should become so quick that it happens as a reflex, before the person has time to consciously direct the squeeze. Simultaneously with the squeeze, each person must shout hah. This shout must come up from the center of the body (somewhere a little below the navel) before passing through the throat. There must be complete abdominal support for the voice. When the first cycle is complete, the transmitter waits for a long time to begin the next cycle. When the reaction time around the circle has become extremely short, the transmitter makes the cycles begin closer and closer together until a new transmission coincides with the end of a cycle, then continue trying to speed up the reaction time. If attention and awareness are maintained, the circle depending on its size, should be shouting almost simultaneously.

Variations:
1. Reverse the direction of the pulse using the left hand to transmit and the right hand to receive.
2. Reverse the direction of each cycle.
3. Each person chooses which direction to send the pulse. The transmitter continues to control the beginning and ending of a cycle.

Heidi von Gunden, in her study of Oliveros's music, provides a detailed index of the following points of concentration that should be observed for each meditation (von

Gunden, 108–109). In Meditation I, "Teach Yourself to Fly," the participant should have "focal and global attention tuned to breathing resulting in involuntary sounds." Meditation XIV, "Tumbling Song," also includes both nonlinear, sensory, imaged, and remember information (global attention) with single or sequential and linear material (focal attention). The focal attention in this second example has shifted from breathing to the vocal sound, while the global attention is on the descending gesture of the glissandi. Upon reaching Meditation XV, "Zina's Circle," the focal attention has again shifted back to the breathing. Global attention now is tuned to the trigger. For all the meditations, one person should act as the leader.

Oliveros notes that this compositional experience was necessary for her growth as a musician. "I learned to compose at a different level. Instead of composing the content, I was composing the outside form and giving people tools to participate in the creative process. And that felt good to me, and it also sharpened my own tools" (Gagne, 221).

The citations from *Sonic Meditations* are quoted by permission of Sylvia Smith, Smith Publications.

Further Reading

Adams, John Luther. " 'Winter Music': A Composer's Journal." In *Reflections on American Music: The Twentieth Century and the New Millennium*, ed. James R. Heintz and Michael Saffle. CMS Monographs and Bibliographies in American Music no. 16. New York: Pendragon Press, 2000.

Ammer, Christine. *Unsung: A History of Women in American Music*. Portland, Ore.: Amadeus Press, 2001.

Gagne, Cole. *Soundpieces 2: Interviews with American Composers*. Metuchen, N.J.: Scarecrow Press, 1993.

Kingman, Daniel. *American Music: A Panorama*. New York: Schirmer Books, a division of Macmillan Press, 1990.

Oliveros, Pauline. *Sonic Meditations*. Baltimore, Md.: Smith Publications, 1974.

———. "On Sonic Meditation." In *Software for People: Collected Writings 1963–80*. Baltimore. Md.: Smith Publications, 1984.

———. *Roots of the Moment*. New York: Drogue Press, 1998.

Pendle, Karin, ed. *Women and Music*. Bloomington: Indiana University Press, 1991.

Schwartz, Elliott. "The American Century: Remembering the Past, Contemplating the Future." In *Reflections on American Music: The Twentieth Century and the New Millennium*, ed. James R. Heintz and Michael Saffle. CMS Monographs and Bibliographies in American Music no. 16. New York: Pendragon Press, 2000.

Tawa, Nicholas. *American Composers and Their Public: A Critical Look*. Metuchen, N.J.: Scarecrow Press, 1995.

Taylor, Timothy D. "Oliveros, Pauline." In *The New Grove Dictionary of Music* Online, ed. L. Macy. http://www.grovemusic.com. Accessed February 2003.

von Gunden, Heidi. *The Music of Pauline Oliveros*. Metuchen, N.J.: Scarecrow Press, 1983.

Zimmerman, Walter. *Desert Plants: Conversations with 23 American Musicians*. Vancouver, B.C.: Aesthetic Research Centre of Canada, 1976.

Thea Musgrave
(born 1928)

JAMES R. BRISCOE

The composer and conductor Thea Musgrave was born in Barnton, Midlothian, Scotland. After graduation from Edinburgh University, she studied composition in Paris with Nadia Boulanger from 1950 to 1954. Many of her early works were composed on commission and were of an expanded diatonic idiom. These include *Suite o'Bairnsangs*, written for the British Broadcasting Corporation, and the chamber opera *The Abbot of Drimock*.

After her return from Paris, Musgrave's style turned toward chromaticism and abstraction in form, as seen in her Piano Sonata and String Quartet. By the end of the 1950s, Musgrave had adopted serialism, and she had come to represent fully the mainstream of British composition in that regard and in her disavowal of the experimental avant-garde.

Her opera *The Decision* was staged by the New Opera Company in 1967. According to *The New Grove Dictionary of Music and Musicians* (second edition), this work "forced an extroversion which her earlier works generally lacked, and the benefit is apparent in most of Musgrave's subsequent work." The 1960s saw a spate of commissions for major works, such as the *Clarinet Concerto*, for the Royal Philharmonic Society, and the *Viola Concerto*, for the BBC, first performed by her husband, Peter Mark. Musgrave has explained her concept of "dramatic-abstract" procedures in certain innovative instrumental compositions of the 1960s as "dramatic in presentation and abstract because of the absence of a program . . . a kind of extension of the concerto principle." One such work is *From One to Another*, which uses a prerecorded tape in conjunction with a solo viola.

The joint commission of *Harriet, the Woman Called Moses* (1985) by the Royal Opera and Virginia Opera and *Simón Bolívar* (1995) by the Los Angeles Music Center Opera and Scottish Opera confirm her status as one of today's foremost composers. Thea Musgrave has received major awards from the Koussevitzky Foundation and twice from the Guggenheim Foundation. Glasgow University conferred the Honorary Doctorate of Music in 1995. Other major compositions of the 1990s include "On gratitude, love, and madness" for chorus in 1992, "The Strange and the Exotic" for chorus in 1994, the Oboe Concerto "Helios," and the orchestral work *Phoenix Rising* of 1998 for the BBC Symphony Orchestra.

Musgrave became a resident of the United States in 1972. Increasingly active as a conductor of her own works, she conducted her opera *Mary, Queen of Scots* at its premier in August 1977 at the Edinburgh International Festival and again in 1979 at the Spring

Opera Theater in San Francisco. *Mary, Queen of Scots* was first performed in the United States by the Virginia Opera Association, and it has had subsequent performances in New York, Chicago, London, and Stuttgart. In his review for *The Spectator* concerning the Edinburgh premiere, Rodney Milnes stated:

> Against all odds it has a better chance of becoming established in the repertory than any new work seen here in the last ten years. . . . Musgrave's musical language, vaguely post-Britten, eschews the angular declamation that has been so depressing a characteristic of contemporary opera. . . . This is a twentieth-century grand opera, and it works.

Andrew Porter in *The New Yorker* added his accolades following the U.S. premiere:

> I found myself forgetting the careful planning, the parallels, the influences, and instead caring very much about Mary herself—move by move, event by event—and being at the same time rapt in the music, intent on the movement of the melodic lines, calmed or excited by the shifting patterns of harmonic tension, and stirred by the colors of the score. There is a visionary quality in Mary.

As with Wagner's operas, the remarkable dramatic force of *Mary, Queen of Scots* derives largely from a single authorship of both music and libretto. Musgrave based the latter on the play *Moray* by Emilia Elguera:

> Writing my own libretto has given me a heightened sensitivity to the perennial question of balance between musical and dramatic elements in opera: I wanted my opera to have vitality and depth; and I needed to find the right delicate balance between them. To achieve this I worked in the following way. After making the initial outline and sketching out a complete draft, I decided to leave detailed working out until I came to write the music. Thus the libretto could reflect the demands made by the music and vice versa. . . . In fact I was rewriting the libretto right up to the day the opera was finished.

Mary Stuart (1542–1587) was aptly called by her cousin Elizabeth I "the daughter of debate." The rightful heir to the throne of Scotland, Mary grew up in France and married the boy king François II. She returned to Scotland at age nineteen, already a widow. As a Roman Catholic she was unwelcome to many, Scotland having been led toward Protestantism by the forceful preacher John Knox. She first married the widely hated Lord Darnley; following his murder, she married her cousin Henry Stuart. The Scottish nobles imprisoned Mary, but she escaped to England. There, however, Elizabeth feared her as second in line to the throne, placed her in confinement for eighteen years, and finally had her executed. In the composer's words,

> The whole work revolves around Mary, her personality expressed through the situations in which she finds herself. There is her marriage to Darnley, which goes wrong so soon; her stormy relationship with Bothwell; and all the confrontations with her brother James, each vying to gain . . . ultimate power and control. It is a struggle to the death. Mary is a tragic figure yet vitally alive.

The excerpt given here represents Mary at her most determined moment, when she vows to rely on her inner resources and to reign without the aid of her presumed allies, who have deceived her at every turn. While some relate her idiom to that of Benjamin Britten, that "easy" comparison is not altogether helpful. Extended tonality does not revert to more simplistic tonality as it does in Britten. A penchant for the strong setting of English with all its angularity in Britten becomes more lyric in Musgrave, and a brilliant orchestral palette is made personal by Musgrave's frequent call on brass "power blasts." Here are the elements of quite an innovative imagination.

Monologue of Mary
from *Mary, Queen of Scots*

Thea Musgrave

James R. Briscoe

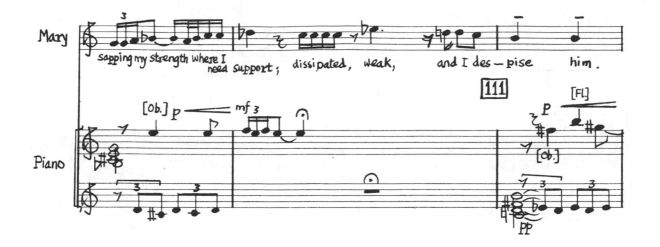

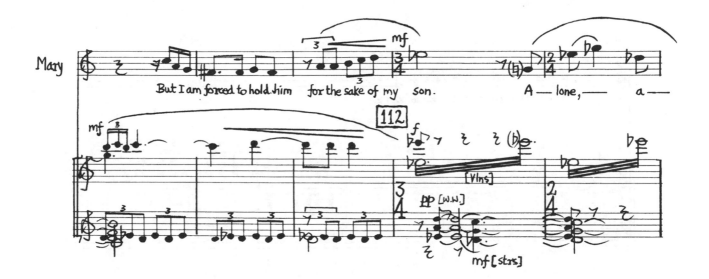

Shall I send for Bothwell?

He is a strong man and could protect me.

But can I trust him? Or does he, like my brother, wait in the dark to make me a prisoner?

JAMES R. BRISCOE

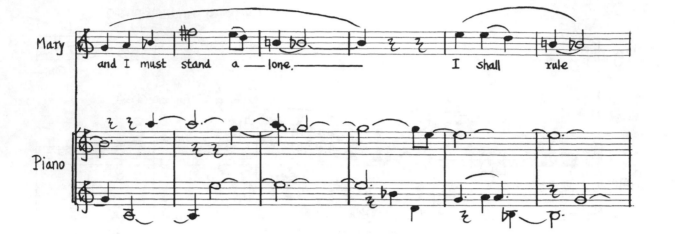

　　　James R. Briscoe

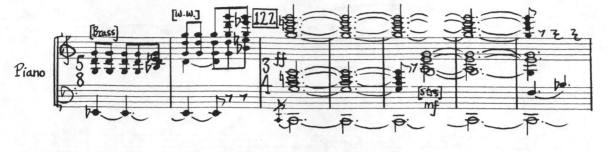

JAMES R. BRISCOE

Ellen Taaffe Zwilich
(b. 1939)

CRAIG B. PARKER

Ellen Taaffe Zwilich was born 30 April 1939 in Miami, Florida, and ranks among the most performed and popular living American composers. She has composed works in all media except opera, and her compositions have been commissioned and performed by numerous major orchestras, chamber ensembles, and soloists in the United States and abroad. Her entry in *Baker's* states: "In her music, Zwilich has succeeded in combining technical expertise with a distinct power of communication. Her idiomatic writing is ably complemented by a poetic element found in her handling of melody, harmony, and counterpoint" (*Baker's*, 4046).

Zwilich was educated at Florida State University (B.M. in theory, 1960; M.M. in composition, 1962) and the Juilliard School (where she became the first woman to earn a D.M.A. in composition in 1975). Her main composition teachers were John Boda, Elliott Carter, and Roger Sessions. She also studied violin with Richard Burgin and Ivan Galamian, and was a violinist in the American Symphony Orchestra under Leopold Stokowski from 1965 until 1972. Zwilich is the recipient of numerous awards, most notably the 1983 Pulitzer Prize in Music. Other significant honors included the Elizabeth Sprague Coolidge Chamber Music Prize (1974), a gold medal in the twenty-sixth annual Competition "G. B. Viotti" (1975), grants from the Martha Baird Rockefeller Fund (1977, 1979, and 1982), a Guggenheim Fellowship (1980–1981), a Norlin Foundation Fellowship for residence at the MacDowell Colony (1980), the Ernst von Dohnányi Citation from Florida State University (1981), honorary life membership in Local 802 of the American Federation of Musicians (1983), an Academy Award from the American Academy of Arts and Letters (1984), residency at the American Academy in Rome (1990), the Alfred I. Dupont Award (1991), election to the American Academy of Arts and Letters (1992) and the Florida Artists Hall of Fame (1994), the NPR and WNYC Gotham Award for contribution to the musical life of New York City (1998), and the Miami Performing Arts Center Award (1999). During 1995–1999, Zwilich held the first Composer's Chair at Carnegie Hall and hosted "Making Music," an imaginative concert and interview series devoted to living composers. She was named Musical America's Composer of the Year in 1999, and was appointed Frances Eppes Distinguished Professor of Music at Florida State University in 2000. She received honorary doctorates from Oberlin (1987), Manhattanville College (1991), Converse College (1994), and Mannes/New School (1995). In conjunction with the 22 September 2000 premiere of her Millenium Fantasy, the mayor of Cincinnati proclaimed an "Ellen Taaffe Zwilich Day" and awarded her a

Key to the City. She was also twice mentioned by Charles M. Schulz in the *Peanuts* cartoon strip.

Primarily known as a composer of instrumental music, Zwilich has completed more than two dozen orchestral works, including four symphonies for orchestra (1981–1982, 1985 [*Cello Symphony*], 1992, 1999 [*The Gardens*]). Her extensive concerto output contains some of her most inventive music. Her solo concertos include works for flute (1989), oboe (1990), clarinet (2001–2002), bassoon (1992), trumpet (*Concerto for Trumpet and Five Players* [1984] and *American Concerto* [1994]), horn (1993), trombone (1988), bass trombone (1989), violin (*Romance* [1993], Violin Concerto [1997], and *Partita* [2000]), and piano (*Piano Concerto* [1986], *Peanuts Gallery* [1996], and *Millennium Fantasy* [2002]). She also wrote several works in the concerto grosso tradition: *Images* for two pianos and orchestra (1988), *Concerto* for violin, violoncello, and orchestra (1991), *Triple Concerto* for violin, violoncello, piano, and orchestra (1995), and *Rituals* for percussion and chamber orchestra (2003). Other Zwilich orchestral pieces include *Symposium* (1973), *Prologue and Variations* for strings (1983), *Celebration* (1984), *Concerto Grosso* (1985), *Tanzspiel* (a ballet, 1987), *Symbolon* (1988), *Fantasy* (1993), *Jubilation* (1996), *Upbeat!* (1998), and *Openings* (2001). Her other instrumental works include *Ceremonies* for band (1988), *Sonata in Three Movements* for violin and piano (1973–1974), two string quartets (1974 and 1998), *Clarino Quartet* for four trumpets or four clarinets (1977), *Chamber Symphony* for flute, clarinet, violin, viola, cello, and piano (1979), *String Trio* (1982), *Divertimento* for flute, clarinet, violin, and cello (1983), *Fantasy* for harpsichord (1983), *Intrada* for flute, clarinet, violin, cello, and piano (1983), *Double Quartet* for strings (1984), *Trio* for piano, violin, and cello (1987), *Praeludium* for organ (1987), *Quintet* for clarinet and strings (1990), *Romance* for violin and piano (1993), *Lament* for piano (1999), and *Lament* for cello and piano (2000). Zwilich's solo vocal works include *Einsame Nacht* (song cycle for baritone and piano, 1971), *Im Nebel* for contralto and piano (1972), and *Trompeten* for soprano and piano (1974), *Emlékezet* for soprano and piano (1978), and *Passages* for soprano, flute, clarinet, violin, viola, cello, piano, and percussion or soprano with chamber orchestra (1982). Her choral works include *Thanksgiving Song* (1986), *Immigrant Voices* for chorus, brass, timpani, and strings (1991), and *A Simple Magnificat* (1994).

Thematic transformation, continuous variation, and cyclic procedures characterize much of Zwilich's music. Most of her music, although essentially chromatic, is based around a tonal axis, which is often established by ostinatos or pedal points. Large-scale chromatic bass movement permeates her compositions. Simultaneous sounding of major and minor triads with the same root is a common Zwilich harmonic device. Angular melodic lines are often comprised primarily of seconds, thirds, and their octave displacements. Motto themes and motivic development abound, as do propulsive rhythms. Zwilich's works exhibit a mastery of orchestration, without reliance on unusual effects. Bell-like sonorities are prevalent in all families of the orchestra. Zwilich demonstrates her confidence in every section of the orchestra with her virtuosic writing for all players.

Zwilich's *Symphony No. 1* (*Three Movements for Orchestra*), movement 1, is presented here. It is the best-known of her symphonies, and is one of her most performed works. She began this piece while in residence at the MacDowell Colony in 1981, but she interrupted work on it to write *Passages* for soprano and chamber ensemble on commission by the Boston Musica Viva. By the time she returned to her orchestral piece, Zwilich had been commissioned by the American Composers Orchestra and the National Endowment for the Arts, so she knew *Symphony No. 1* would be played, with Gunther Schuller as conductor. She recalled,

It was played very, very soon after it was finished, which is why the confusion of the title. The program went to print, I think, six weeks before the program, and I finished the piece three weeks before the program. They called me and said, "We can't wait any longer for a title." I said, "Well, it's in three movements and it's for orchestra," so they said, "OK, *Three Movements for Orchestra.*" I often write a piece and then think about what I'm going to call it. I really didn't want to grapple at that point with the issue of is this a symphony, and what is a symphony, what does it mean if I call it that. So, for the first performance, the program read *Three Movements for Orchestra.* But I felt it was a symphony and so did Gunther, and we just called it that. (Zwilich interviewed by the author, 23 April 1987)

As with all her mature works, Zwilich sketched the first symphony directly onto full score. As she remarked,

Part of my thinking is orchestral. One of my unwritten rules is that there are no second-class citizens in the orchestra. There's a big terribly difficult tuba solo in the second movement and I figure a tuba player is as much a virtuoso as a concertmaster in your ideal orchestra. . . . I really like to have the sense that there are no second violins, that everybody in the orchestra is a virtuoso, and part of my orchestral writing is writing that gives everyone something they can sink their teeth into. (Zwilich, master class at Kansas State University, 23 April 1987)

As is her usual procedure, Zwilich developed the generative motive, in this case an accelerating ascending minor third enriched with fifths. Countless sketches, similar to what a serialist would do with regard to aggregates, followed, as she explored the possibilities of her material. Then all sketches were abandoned and she just wrote.

The first performance of *Three Movements for Orchestra* took place on 5 May 1982, by the American Composers Orchestra, with Schuller conducting, at Alice Tully Hall in New York. Among the many words of praise regarding this work printed following its first performance were these in *The New Yorker:* "It is an unabashedly romantic composition, lushly Straussian in sound, enjoyable to hear" (Porter, 88). The *New York Times* review of the premier stated, "The new score by Miss Zwilich also made a strong impression. An assertive, colorful essay, it possessed a sense of direction and coherence that, combined with an innate vitality, sustained the flow of events in a remarkably absorbing way. The expressiveness of the solo writing was particularly appealing" (Libbey, C8).

In April 1983, this work was selected over seventy-nine others as winner of the Pulitzer Prize in Music. Zwilich became the first woman to win this award, which was instituted in 1943. This recognition catapulted her into the musical spotlight, and made her a national spokesperson for women composers. In November 1984, John Nelson and the Indianapolis Symphony recorded three Zwilich works, including her first symphony, for New World Records. This recording brought Zwilich her first Grammy nomination in 1987, in the category of "best symphonic composition." That recording won the 1987 Arturo Toscanini Music Critics Award, as voted on by writers throughout the United States and Canada. The *New York Times* review of the first all-Zwilich orchestral recording contained the following assessments:

Mrs. Zwilich's harmonic palette seldom ventures beyond Bartók's or Shostakovich's. Strong contrasts in rhythm, harmony and sonority, growing out of a continuous-variation form, anchor the symphony in the late 20th century. The music rises and falls with ease and grace, yet with tension too, and Mrs. Zwilich's ear for color assures beautiful surfaces for her framework.

What is most striking about the symphony, though, is the particular emotion that rises to the surface. It is a consoling loneliness, again echoing Mahler. This mood permeates not just the symphony but also the shorter, equally fine Prologue and Variations and Celebration which fill out the disk. . . . The recorded sound is a bit weak and distant, favoring the winds, but otherwise this is a disk to cherish. (Pincus, 23)

Ellen Taaffe Zwilich   469

Symphony No. 1: Three Movements for Orchestra is built around a tonal axis, in this case the pitch class A. The symphony's first fifteen measures contain the basic melodic and harmonic implications for the entire piece, and are dominated by the motto of an ascending, accelerating minor third. This generates a constant intensification of the opening "Andante" until the "Allegro" is reached in measure 78. Following the climactic point in measure 199, the movement's intensity diminishes until it recalls the tranquility of the opening bars. The principle of developing variation shapes the entire first movement together with the following two movements.

The lyrical second movement employs a traditional song form, in which complex harmonic structures characterize the more dramatic middle section. The agitated final movement of this symphony utilizes an adapted rondo form. Quotations and paraphrases of material presented in the opening movement appear regularly in the final two.

Throughout this symphony, octave displacements of seconds and thirds create jagged melodic lines. Harmonies are usually derived from the stacking of thirds, both major and minor. Metric changes, ostinatos, imitation, inversion, and augmentation abound. Structural high points are marked by either complex harmonic structures, resonating bell tones, or dramatic use of silence. Root movement by major or minor second is common, with pedal points often determining the tonal axis. In *Symphony No. 1: Three Movements for Orchestra*, Zwilich's adept transformations of the opening motto theme and all the subsequent material generated from it, combined with her always skillful orchestration, yield a masterwork deserving of the numerous accolades and performances it has received.

Further Reading

Baker's Biographical Dictionary of Musicians. Centennial Edition. Farmington Hills, Mich.: Schirmer, 2000.

Duncan, Scott. "Ellen Taaffe Zwilich: Emerging from the Mythos." In *The Musical Woman: An International Perspective*, vol. III: *1986–1990*, ed. Judith Lang Zaimont, 410–38. New York: Greenwood Press, 1991.

Gunn, Nancy. "Organicism, Motivic Development, and Formal Design in Ellen Taaffe Zwilich's Symphony No. 1." Ph.D. diss., City University of New York, 1993.

Hauptman, Fred. Review of Ellen Taaffe Zwilich's Symphony No. 1; Prologue and Variations; Celebration (New World Records NW 336). *American Music* 5, No. 3 (Fall 1987): 352–4.

Libbey, Theodore W., Jr. "Music: Schuller Conducts." *New York Times*, 7 May 1982, C8.

Page, Tim. "The Music of Ellen Zwilich." *New York Times Magazine*, 14 July 1985, 26, 28–31.

Pincus, Andrew. L. "High Emotion from a Prize Symphony." *New York Times*, 12 October 1986, Sect. II, 23.

Porter, Andrew. "Musical Events: Athenian Pursuits." *The New Yorker*, 31 May 1982, 86–88. Reprinted in Andrew Porter, *Musical Events: A Chronicle, 1980–1983*, 258. New York: Summit Books, 1987.

Rockwell, John. "Ellen Zwilich Considers Pulitzer Double Victory." *New York Times*, 4 May 1983, C17.

Rubinsky, Jane. "Ellen Taaffe Zwilich's Upbeat Road to the Pulitzer." *Keynote* 8, no. 9 (November 1984): 16, 18–19.

Schnepel, Julie. "Ellen Taaffe Zwilich's Symphony No. 1: Developing Variation in the 1980s." *Indiana Theory Review* 10 (1989): 1–19.

Recording

Symphony No. 1: Three Movements for Orchestra, Prologue and Variations, and Celebration for Orchestra. Indianapolis Symphony Orchestra, John Nelson, conductor. Liner notes by Richard Dyer. New World Records NW 336 (LP) and 80336-2 (CD).

Symphony No. 1, movement 1

Ellen Taaffe Zwilich

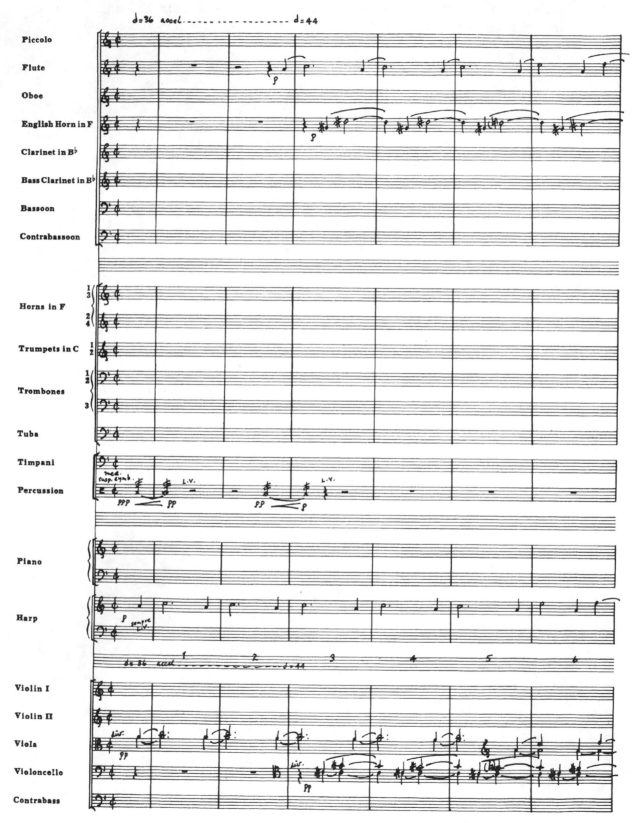

CRAIG B. PARKER

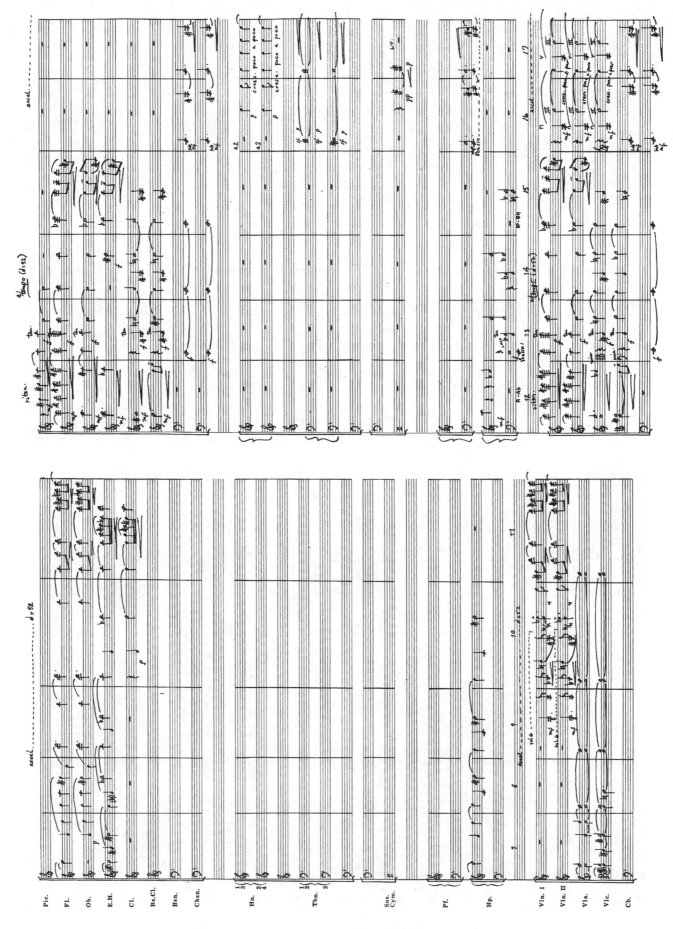

Ellen Taaffe Zwilich

473

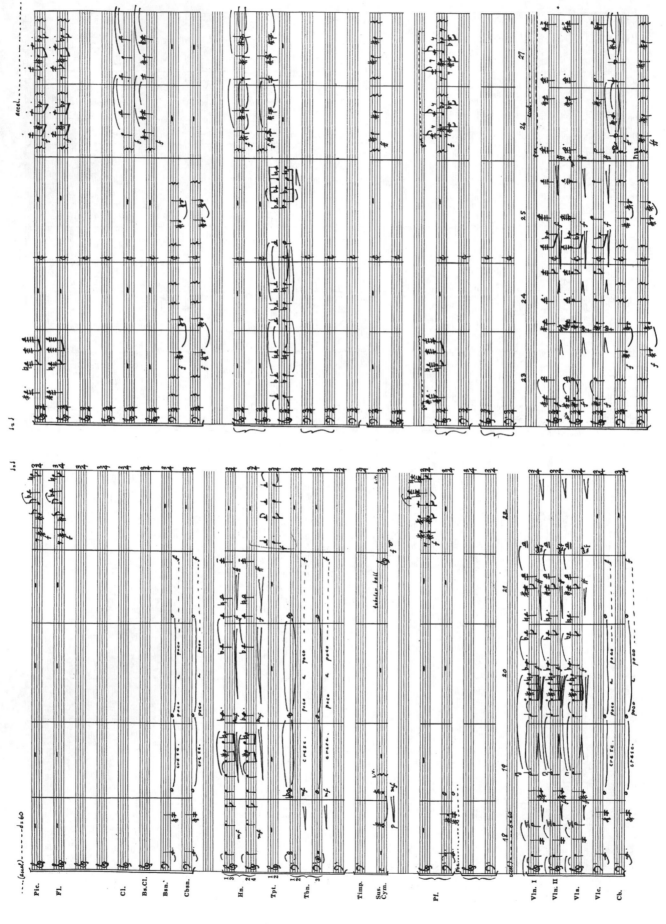

CRAIG B. PARKER

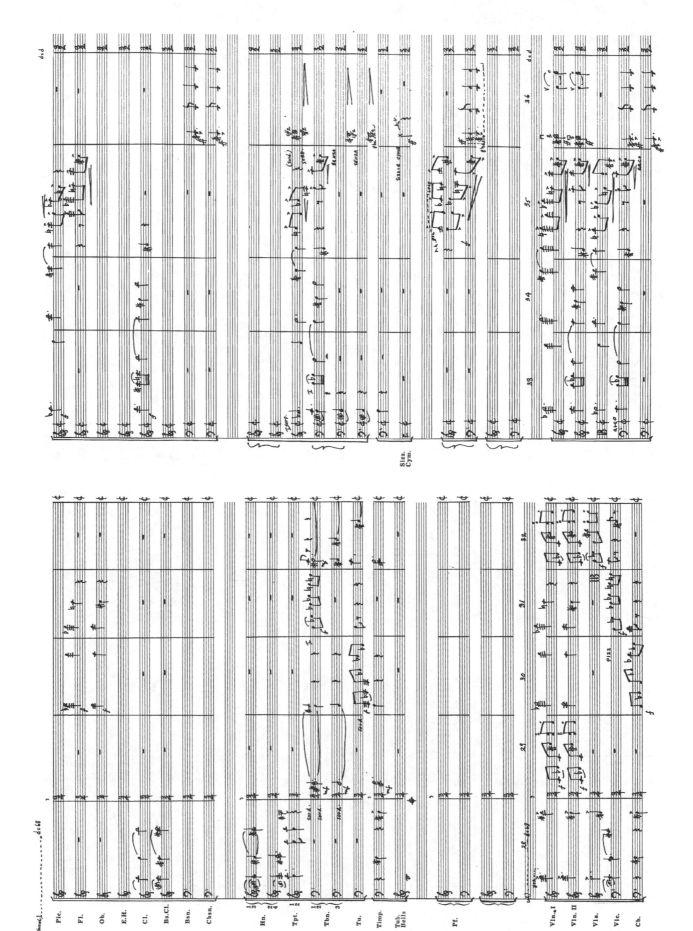

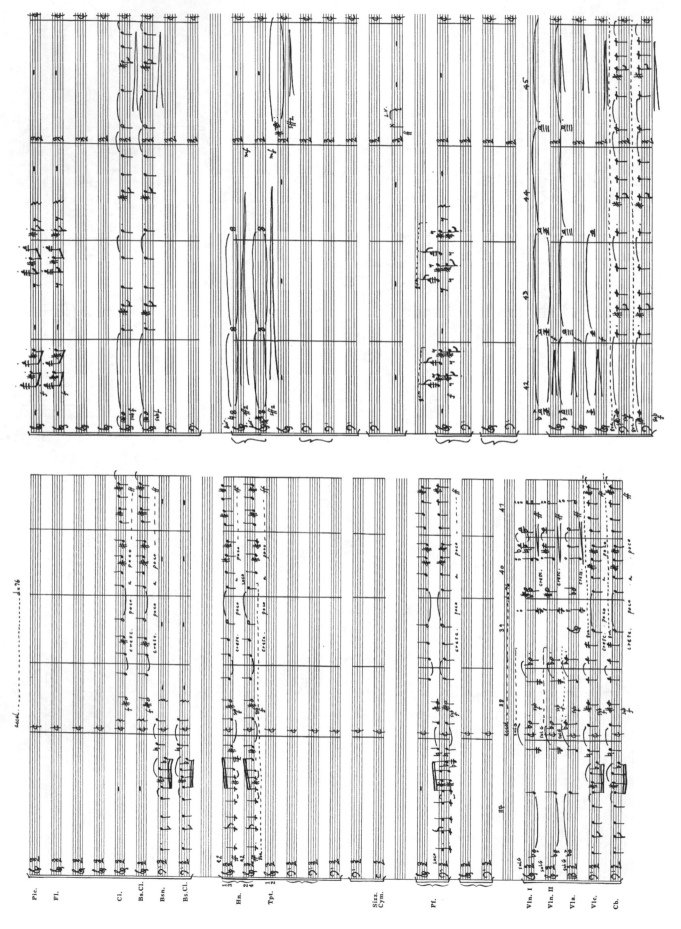

Craig B. Parker

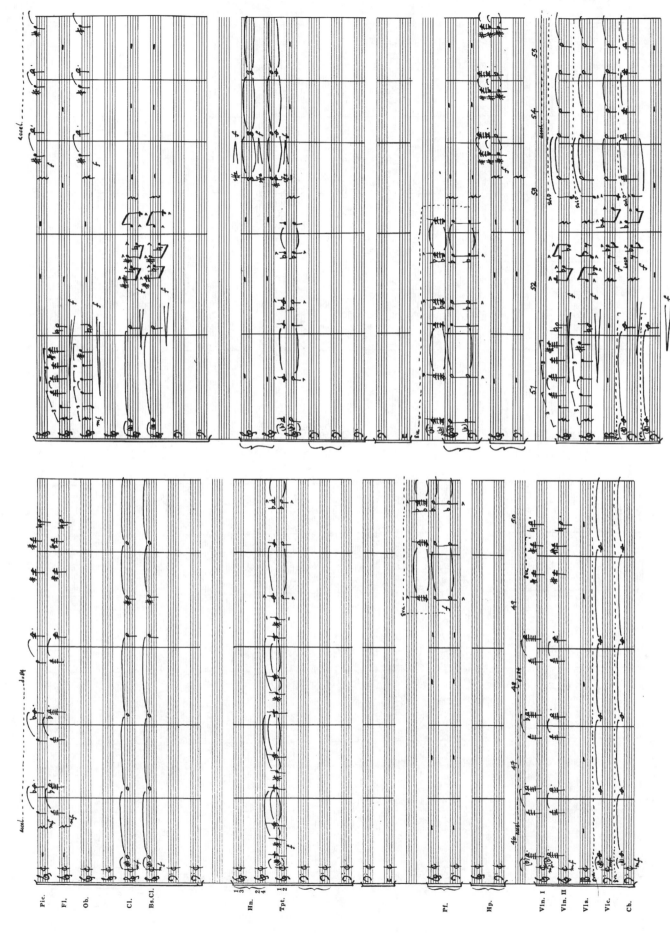

Ellen Taaffe Zwilich

477

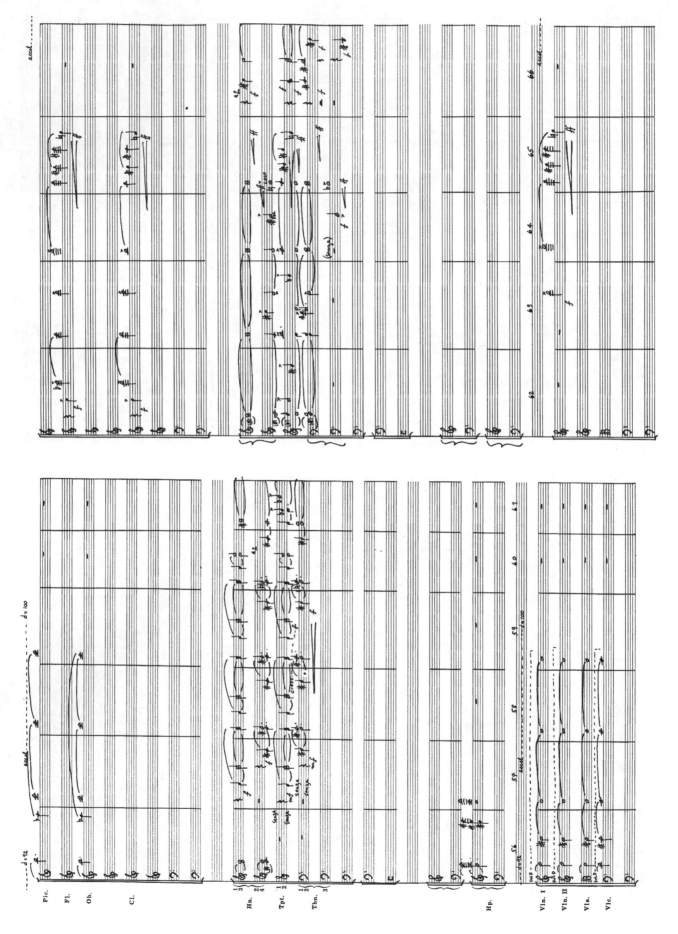

CRAIG B. PARKER

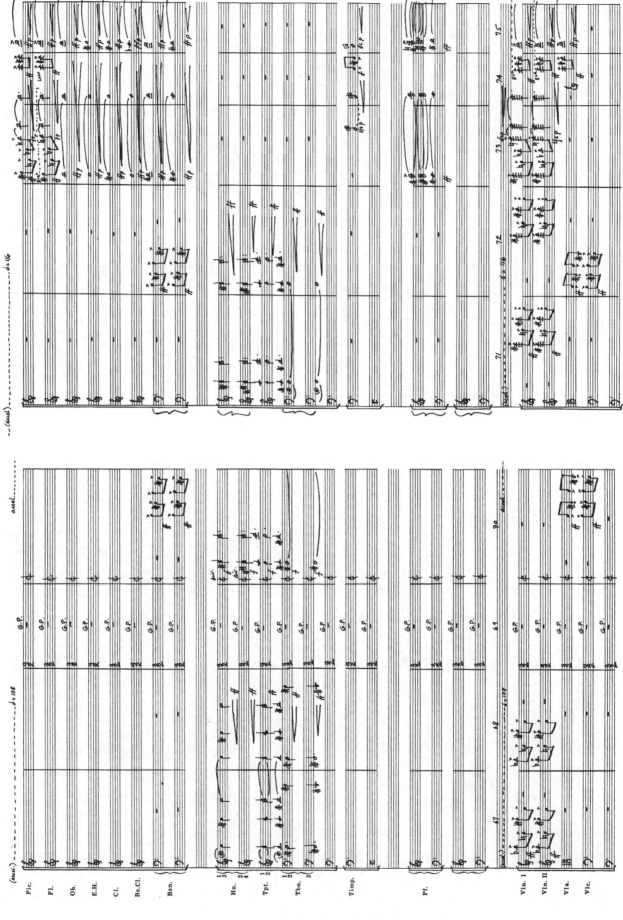

Ellen Taaffe Zwilich

479

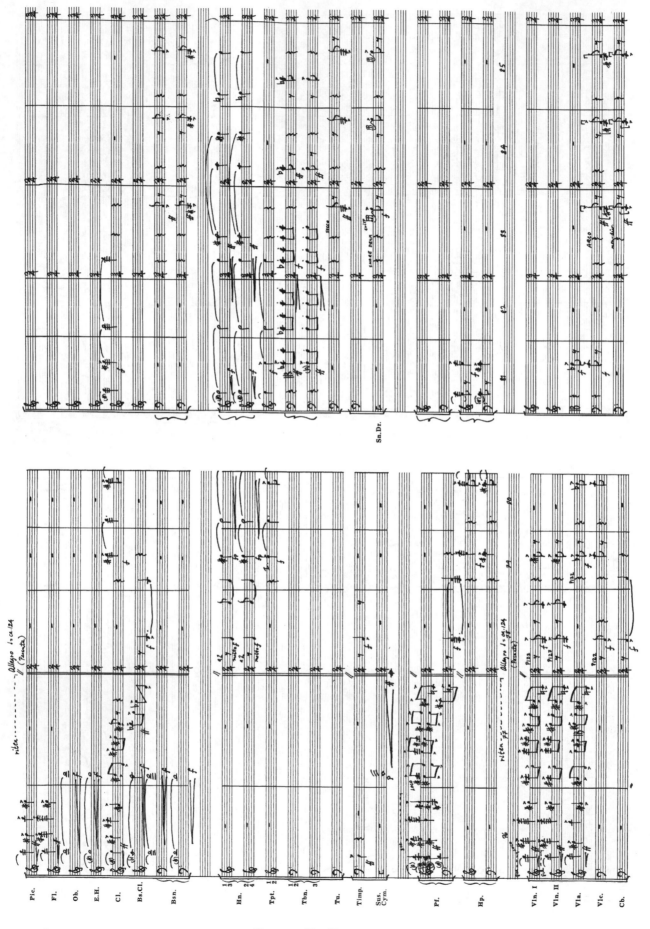

Pic. Fl. Ob. E.H. Cl. Bs.Cl. Bsn. Hn. Tpt. Tbn. Tu. Timp. Sus. Cym. Pf. Hp. Vln. I Vln. II Vla. Vlc. Cb.

Sn. Dr.

Craig B. Parker

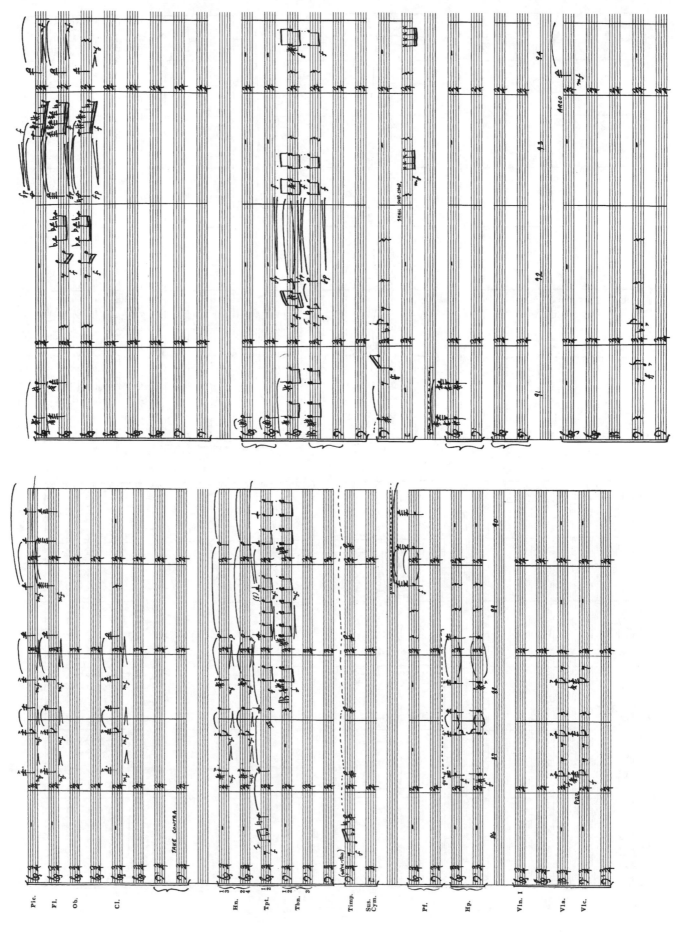

Ellen Taaffe Zwilich

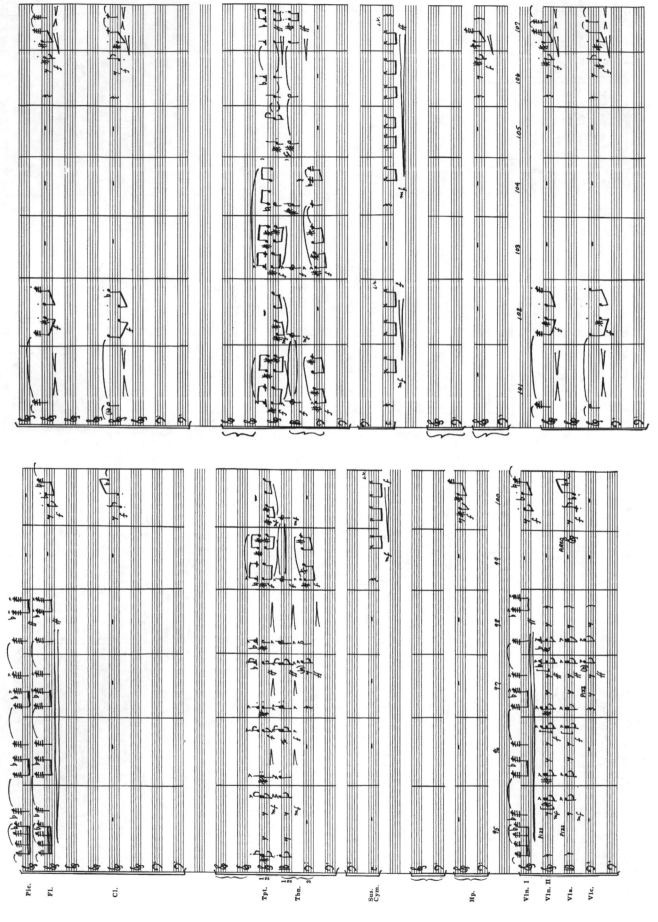

CRAIG B. PARKER

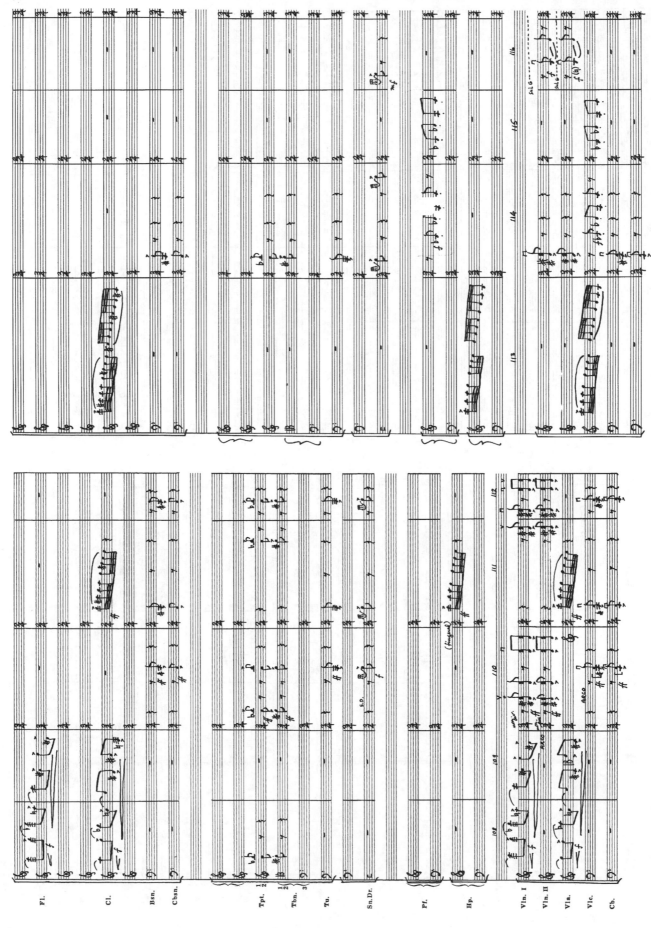

Ellen Taaffe Zwilich

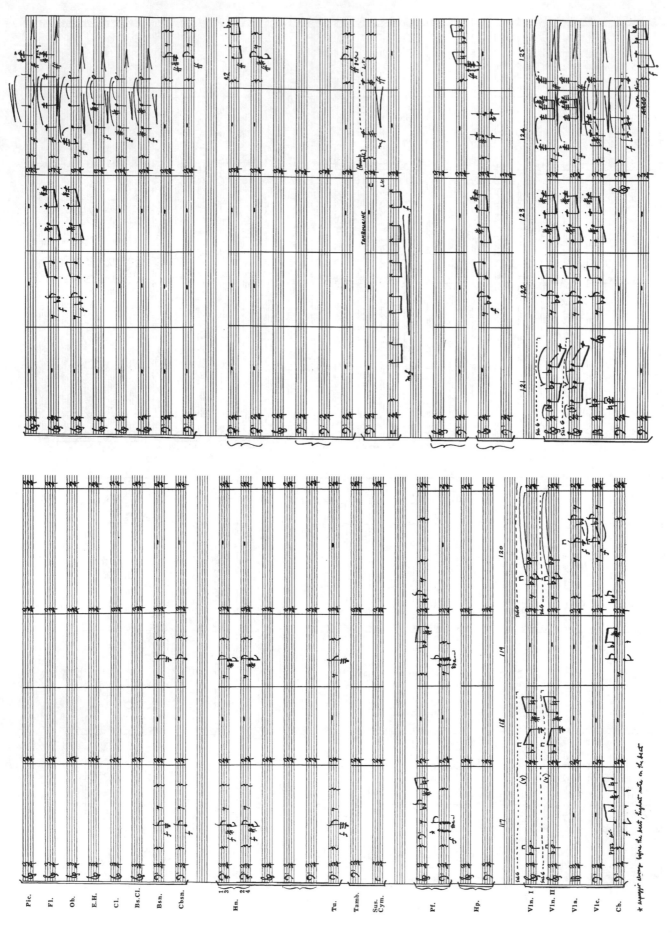

484   CRAIG B. PARKER

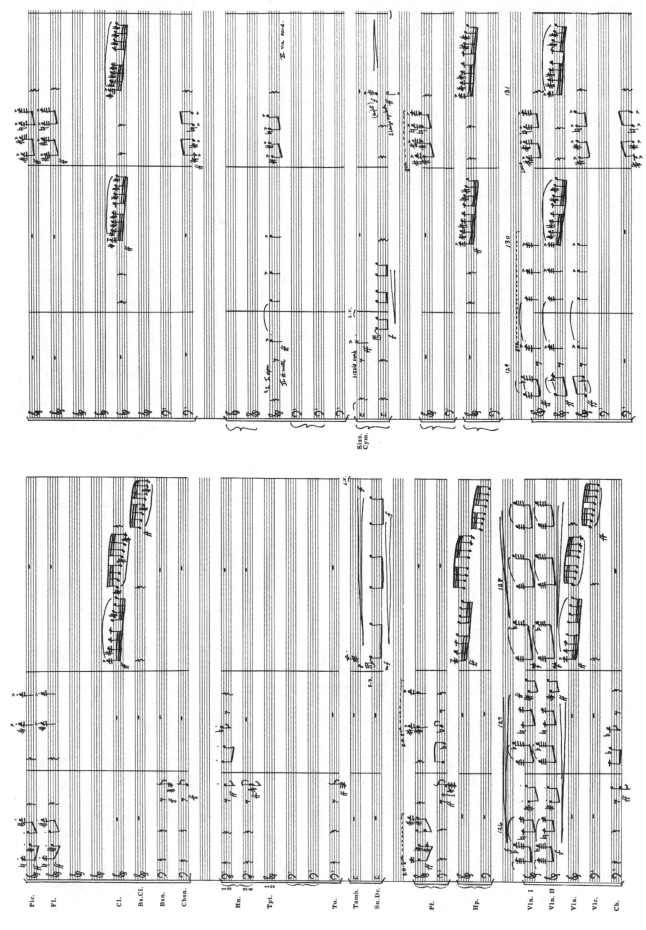

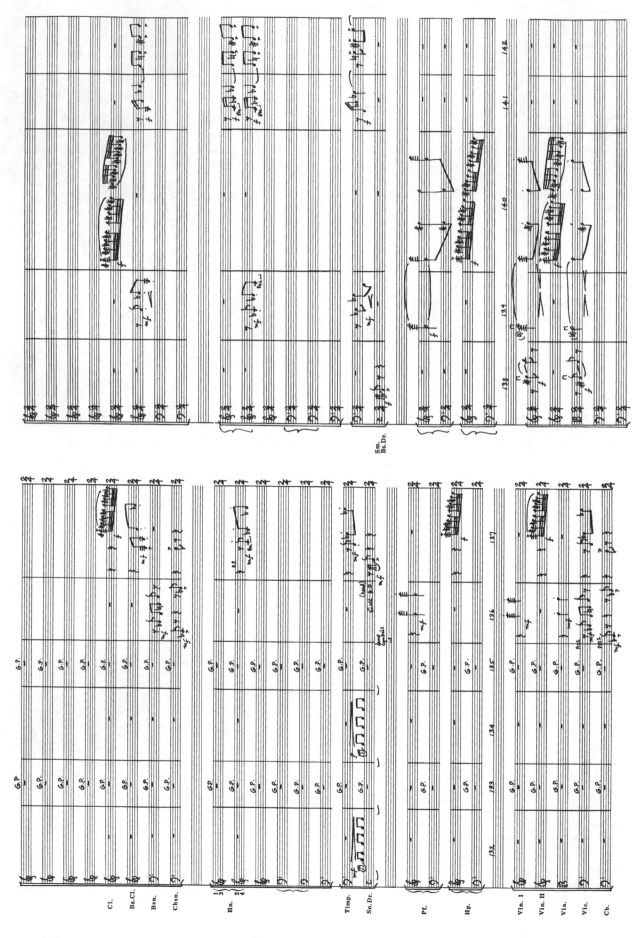

CRAIG B. PARKER

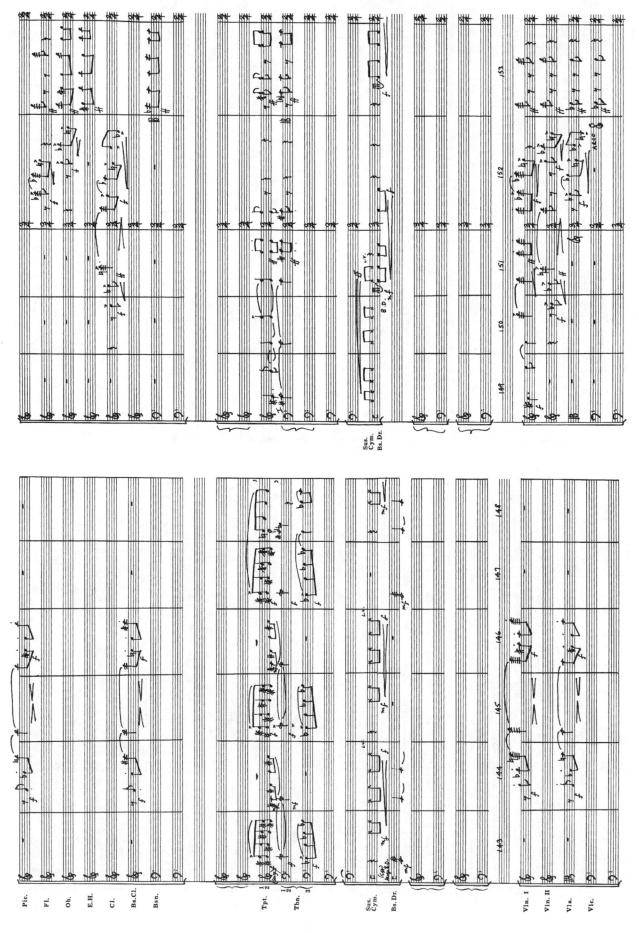

Ellen Taaffe Zwilich

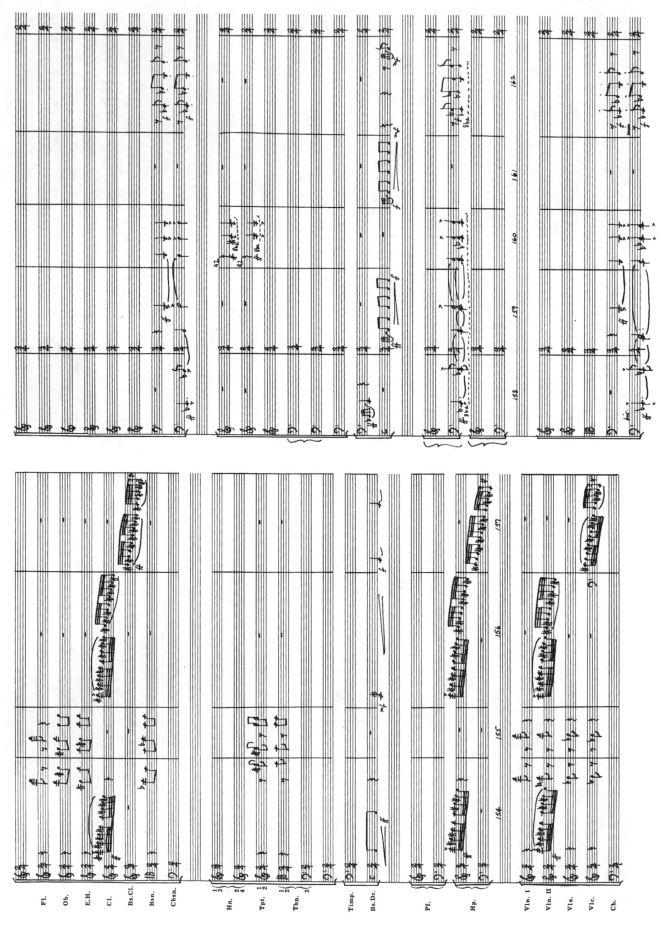

CRAIG B. PARKER

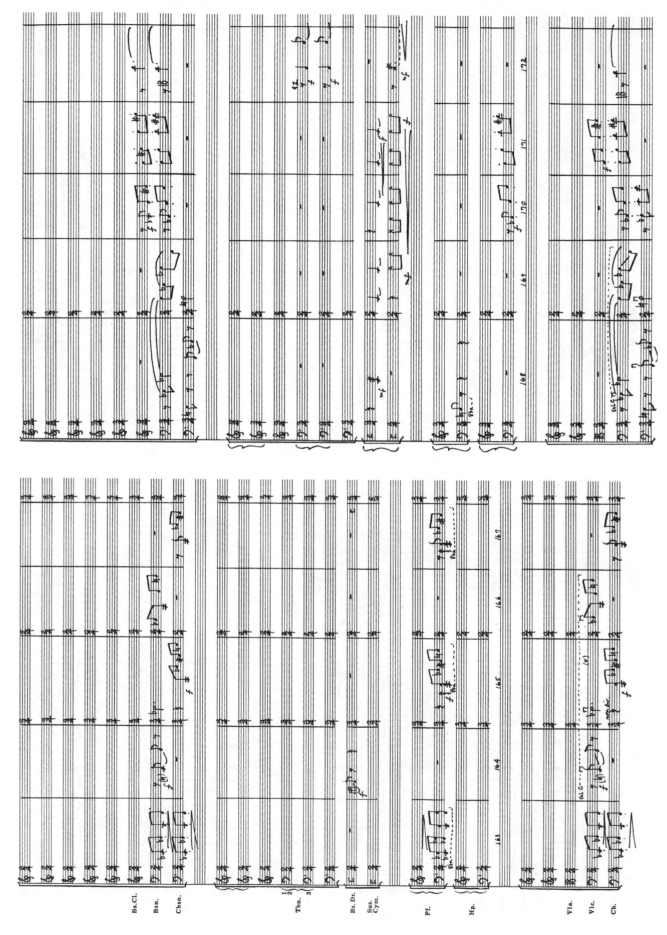

Ellen Taaffe Zwilich

489

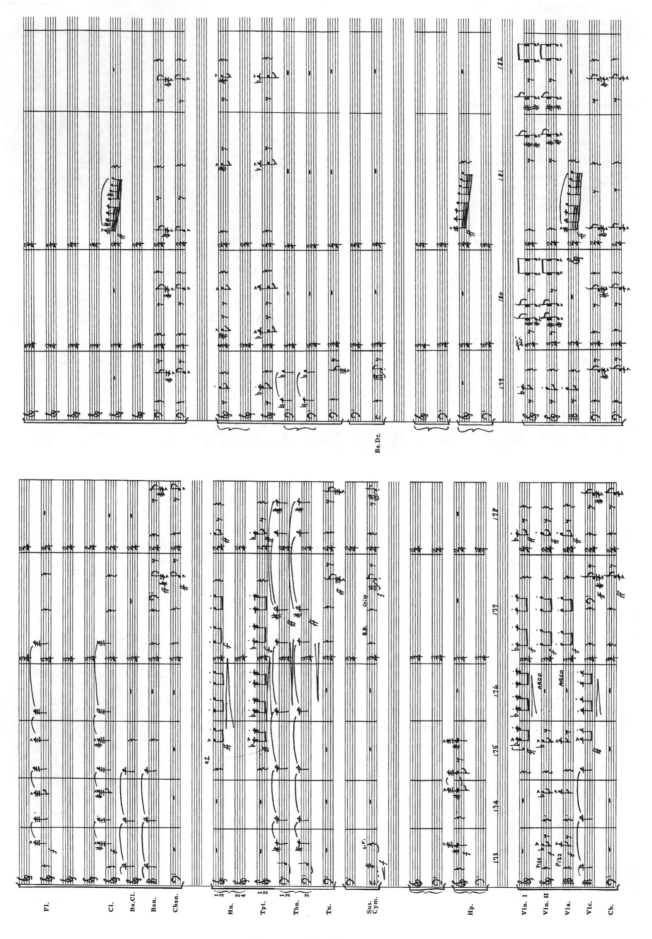

CRAIG B. PARKER

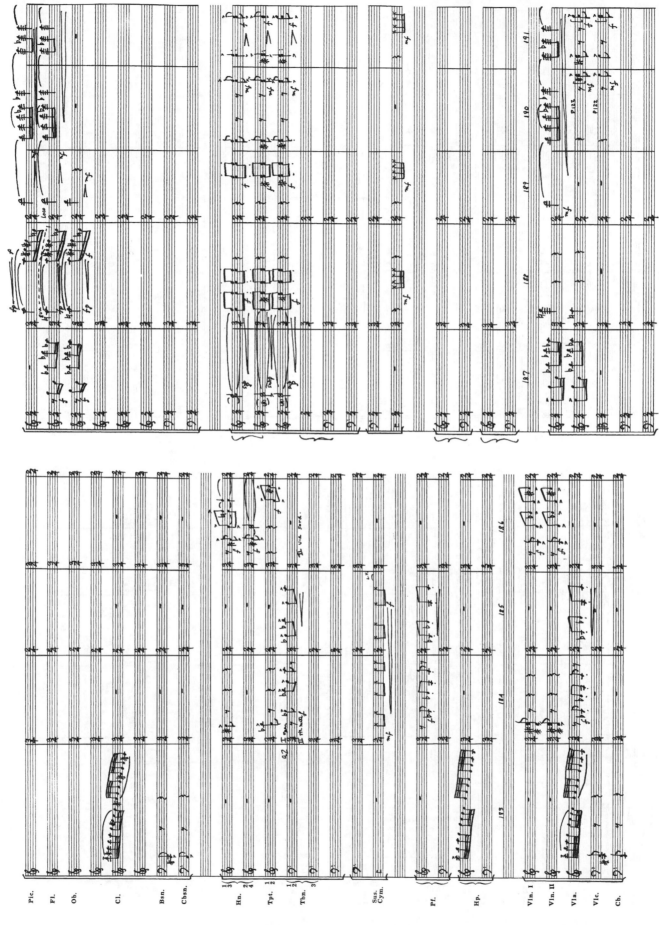

Ellen Taaffe Zwilich

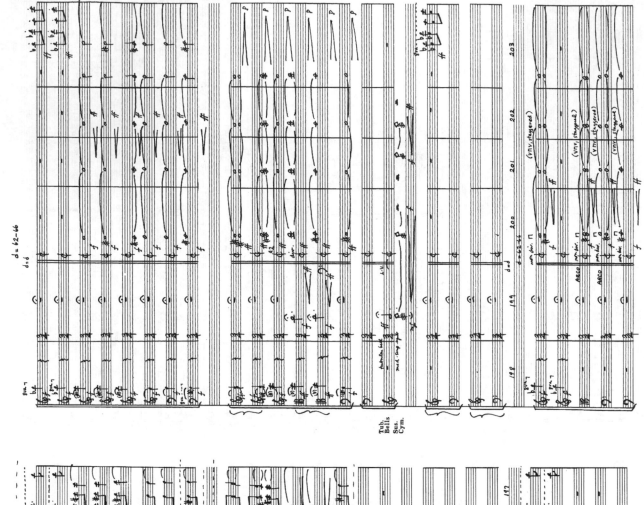

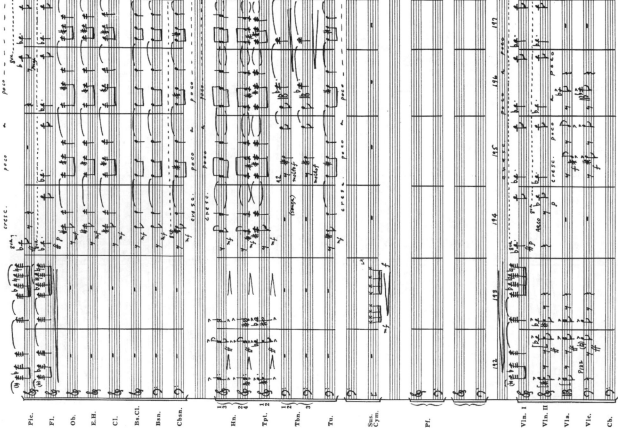

CRAIG B. PARKER

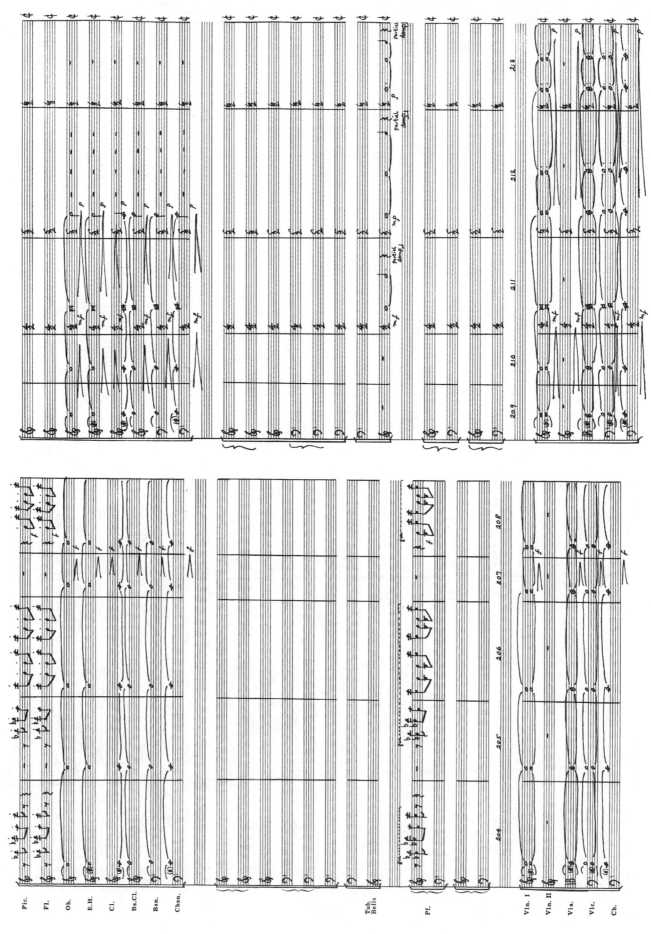

Ellen Taaffe Zwilich

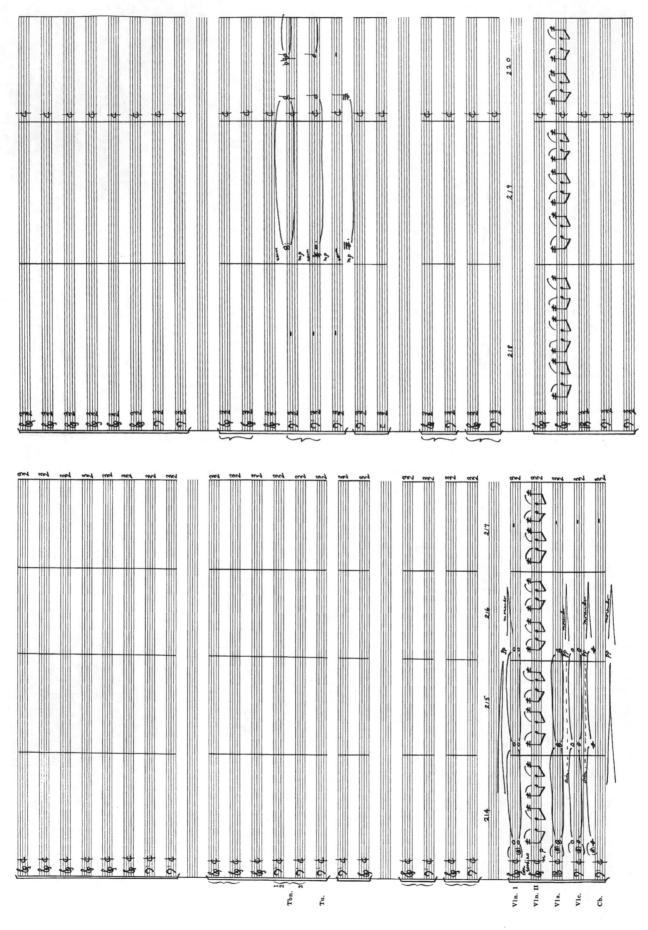

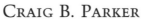

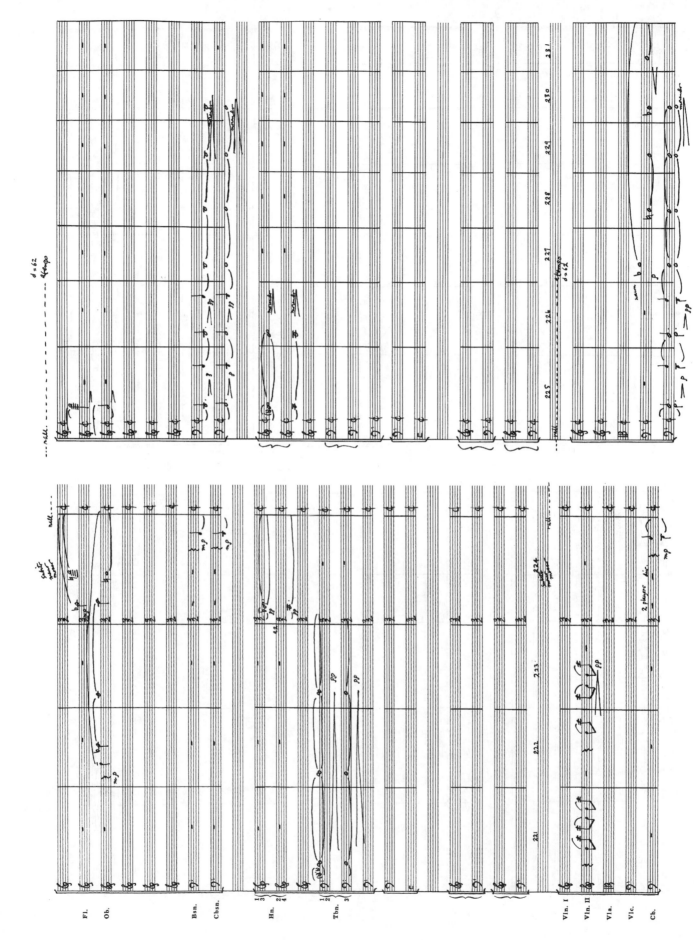

Ellen Taaffe Zwilich

495

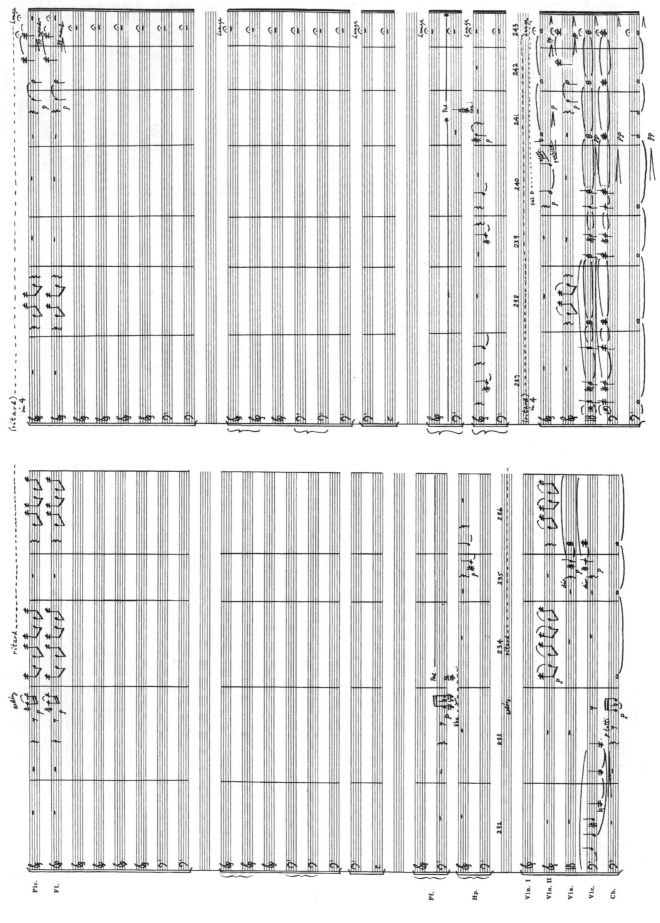

CRAIG B. PARKER

Augusta Read Thomas
(b. 1964)

JAMES R. BRISCOE

Writing about Augusta Read Thomas, the critic John von Rhein of the *Chicago Tribune* observed that "Thomas's music, particularly her orchestral music, fairly explodes with an extroverted boldness of utterance audiences and musicians alike find challenging yet immediate. It's music that doesn't sound like anybody else's—music that insists you pay attention." Performances by Pierre Boulez directing the Chicago Symphony, Esa-Pekka Salonen directing the Los Angeles Philharmonic, the San Francisco Women's Philharmonic, and Markus Stenz directing the Orchestre Philharmonique de Radio France received brilliant critical and audience acclaim, confirming von Rhein's estimation. And, yet, Thomas does not sacrifice her high-reaching motivations for quick success. As Philip Kennicott wrote in the *Washington Post*, "She is in favor of musical independence and does not look to musical schlock and pop tunes for redemption in the concert hall. More power to her. [She does not] dip into the treacly reservoir of familiar habits and melodic ideas for inspiration. Her *Concerto for Orchestra: 'Orbital Beacons,'* was dedicated to the arch-modernist Pierre Boulez, premiered by him and, it seems, influenced by his aesthetic as well."

Augusta Read Thomas has received commissions for ensembles and festivals worldwide, from the choral and orchestral work *Daylight Divine*, sung by the Indianapolis Children's Choir at the Festival St. Denis in Paris, to *Blizzard in Paradise* for the eight cellos of the National Symphony of Washington, D.C., under Leonard Slatkin, to *Aurora: Concerto for Piano and Orchestra* requested by the Berlin Philharmonic. In all, the reception by critics emphasizes her craft, artistic instinct, and sincere yet not condescending connection with listeners. As Robert Maycock of *The Independent* in London put it, "Thomas shows an unmistakable air of knowing what she wants to say and how to say it. Balances work, blends succeed. There is a powerful lyrical instinct at work."

Augusta Read Thomas was born in Glen Cove, New York, and educated at Northwestern University, where she studied with Alan Stout and Bill Karlins; at Yale University, where she studied with Jacob Druckman; and at the Royal Academy of Music in London. She served on the composition faculty at the Eastman School of Music from 1993 to 2001 and then became professor of composition at Northwestern University.

She composed the opera *Ligeia*, with the libretto by Leslie Dunton-Downer based on a short story by Poe. It was awarded the prestigious International Orpheus Prize and performed in Spoleto, Italy. Thomas continued work on two additional operas with Dunton-Downer as librettist, *Dreams in the Cave of Eros* and *Kashgar*. Many of her works have been recorded, including *Love Songs* and *The Rub of Love* for chorus recorded by Chanticleer, and *Meditation* for trombone and orchestra recorded with Christian Lindberg as soloist. Prizes, awards, and fellowships are particularly numerous, and they demonstrate that she is among the most acclaimed composers in contemporary music at the beginning of the Third Millennium.

Seth Brodsky wrote for her exclusive publisher, G. Schirmer, that "While her structural sense is undeniably more Germanic, the sensual lineage of her musical language is more specifically French: its gestural clarity seems possessed by the best of Debussy's pianism." Brodsky attributes to Messiaen and early Boulez an infectious dance rhythm, and to Varèse an admiring nod. Her music never ceases to be elegant, graced, and refined. Although it is emotionally moving, French subtlety is maintained.

Brodsky asks, "What then is that 'some one scene, some one adventure, some one picture' that rules Thomas's creative life? Although Thomas is adamantly not a 'programmatic' composer—her music actually moves in quite the contrary direction, toward a kind of vigorous abstraction—four images do indeed dominate: the Voice, the Bell, the Sun, the Spirit."

. . . circle around the sun . . . for piano, violin, and cello, included in this anthology, was composed in 1999 on commission from the Children's Memorial Foundation in honor of George D. Kennedy. It was premiered by the Amelia Trio. With its use of bells to represent the sun, it takes orchestral bells, or carillon, as a point of departure. Her piano concerto, *Aurora*, incorporates the bell and the voice for its central sonorities, while the sketches for *Aurora* indicate that the piano is "like the Sun, giving energy which gets magnified by the ensemble." Referring again to Seth Brodsky, one notes that Thomas herself proclaims the sun as her greatest muse. Thomas has even noted, "I feel as if the sun writes my music." The work for children's chorus, soprano, and orchestra, *Daylight Divine*, seeks to realize her long-standing dream, to write music "without matter and only energy."

The structure of *. . . circle around the sun . . .* might be heard as a continuing double variation. That is, two ideas are stated in succession and varied without recapitulating the beginning (or only indirectly). The composer begins with the "bell" idea, and thereafter it recurs in sustained or unadorned tones. The second idea is a halo (or "aureole" or "reverberation"), seen as a bright and light arpeggio or rapid repetition first in measure 3 and more typically in measure 5. Augusta Read Thomas appears to understand the bell tone as the sun, emitting a halo of light and spirited neighbor tones—planets, if you will—that are at once complementary but separate bodies.

Movement I immediately develops the two central gestures after stating them. Idea 1, the sun tone G, is joined by the secondary sun B flat as measure 1 ends. The halo of idea 2 bursts out in an atmosphere of expansion ("Bright," "expansive," "radiant," "earnest"). By the end of movement I, the secondary bell tone B-flat predominates. The halo is expanding as well; Thomas displays the brightly fragmented neighbor tones increasingly profusely.

Movement I ends with a modified half cadence on D, the dominant of the sun G. Movement II begins attacca and impresses the second bell tone, B-flat, and its secondary D in a triadic kinship with the primary G that began Movement I. As usual, the movement of the bell or sun tones is "majestic and grand," while that of the shooting meteors is "light, but energized," "spirited," "soaring," and "thrusting." By measure 32, the main bell has become the variant D (albeit in the structural G minor triad of the sun tone), and it expands quickly by adding the seventh of the Gmin7 triad, F. The bell tone group expands to F-sharp at measure 38. In an unpredictable outburst, the halo idea 2 expands through the indications "rubato," "rit. freely," moving to subito piano and fortissimo. At times the rhapsodic outburst of bodies neighboring the sun might "jab" or be "playful" or "cantabile." The celestial creation seems a delightful adventure! After measure 56, the bell tones persist alongside the spinning halo of idea 2, but idea 1 now has reached a state of continual outgrowth: by measure 62 the sun G has evolved to its chromatic, circling kin F-sharp and G-sharp.

The fundamental bell B-flat is regained by its enharmonic A-sharp in measure 67, and G returns at measure 69. But these are only memories of the original sun, which has itself evolved as continuously as its halo. The climax of energy occurs at measure 87, in a near-Golden Mean proportion of .641 to 1 in this composition of 137 measures. Here the tension is at its height, and the mere hint of the G sun is encircled by the powerful tones A and F. At this moment, the "Circle around the Sun" is perfected, even by referring to the ancient Greek proportion.

Both the bell and its halo evolve nearly to the end, until the Sun breaks through the vast reverberating tones. The Sun in its single G purity, sustained at measures 131–34, is only a memory of creation's beginning and of its former self. Creation starts anew in both bell and halo at measure 135. Suggesting the perpetual renewal of the cosmos, all tones but G are present at the ending of the work.

Further Reading

Brodsky, Seth. " 'Seeking the Spheres to Connect Them . . .': The Music of Augusta Read Thomas." November 2001. Available online at http://www.augustareadthomas .com.brodsky.

...a circle around the sun...
Trio for piano, violin, and cello

Augusta Read Thomas

I

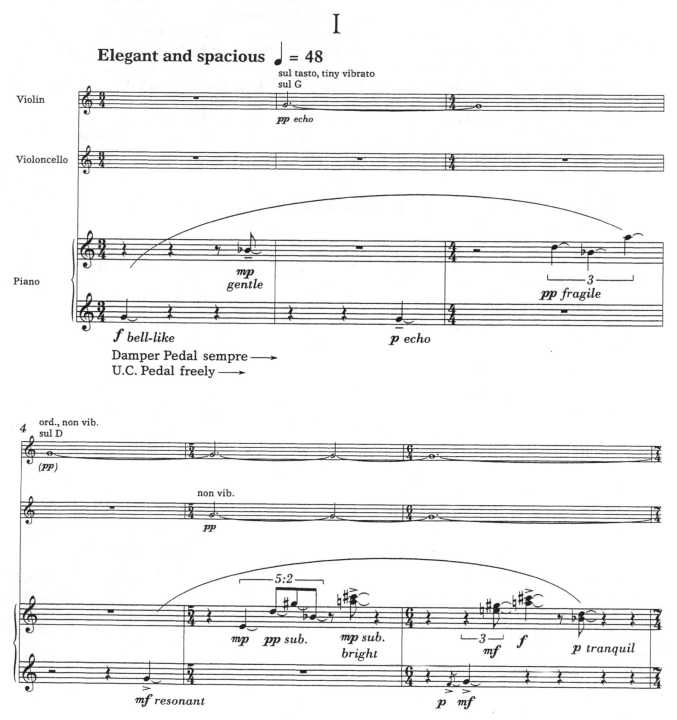

James R. Briscoe

II

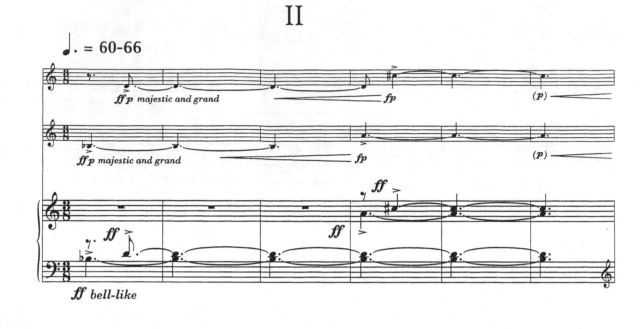

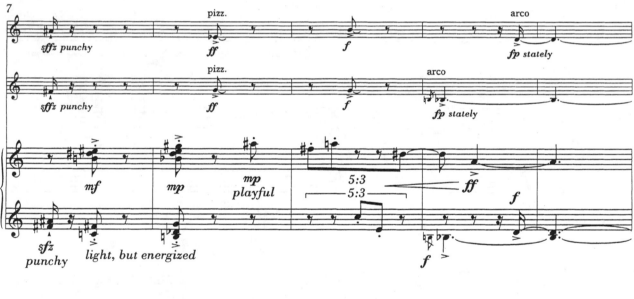

James R. Briscoe

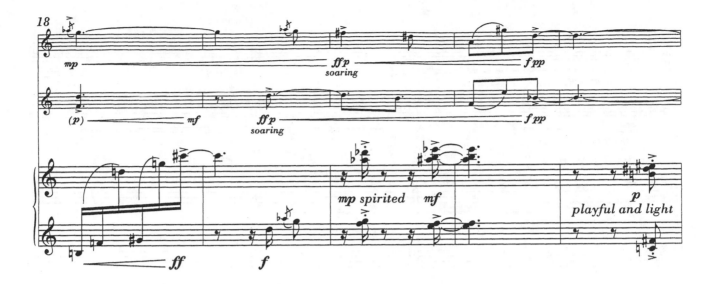

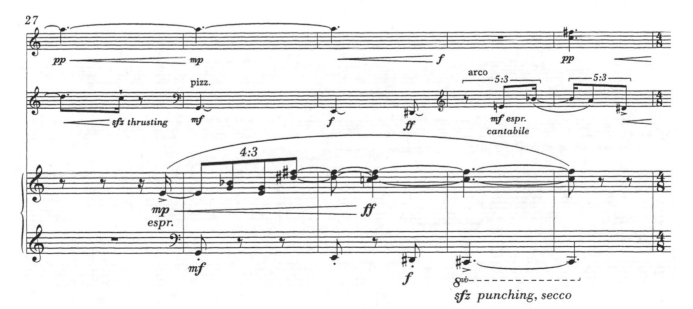

Augusta Read Thomas

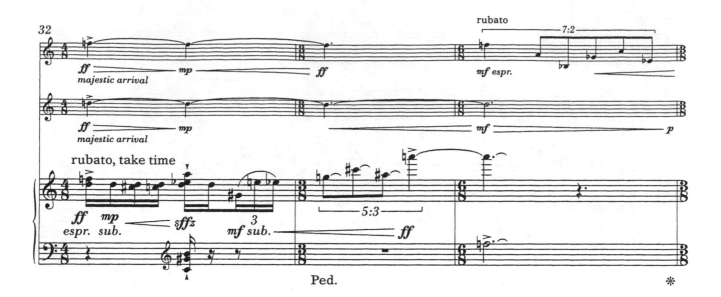

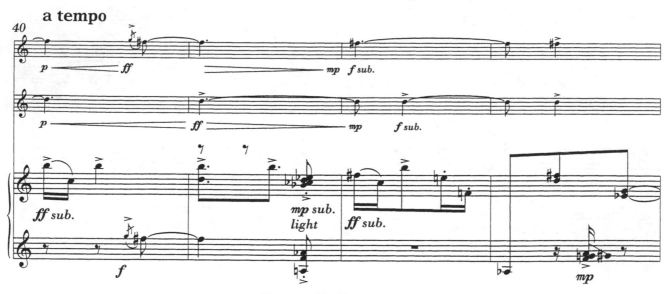

JAMES R. BRISCOE

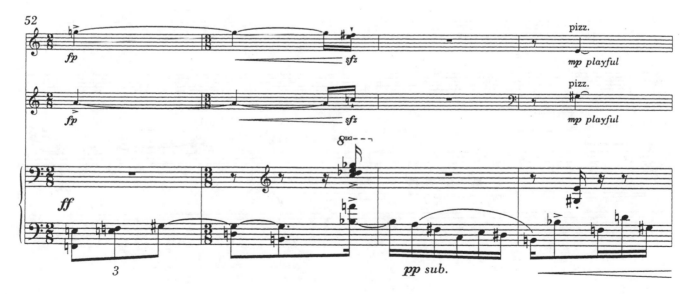

Augusta Read Thomas

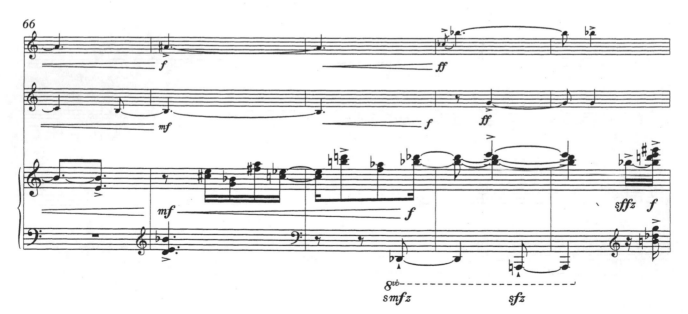

JAMES R. BRISCOE

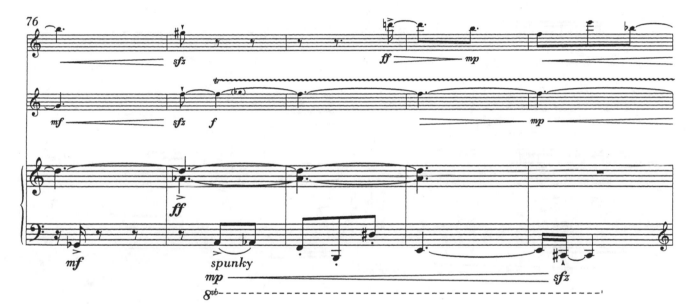

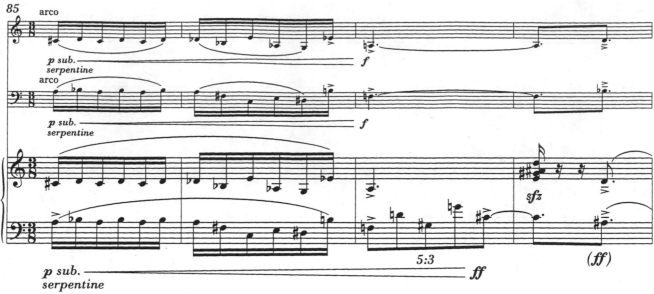

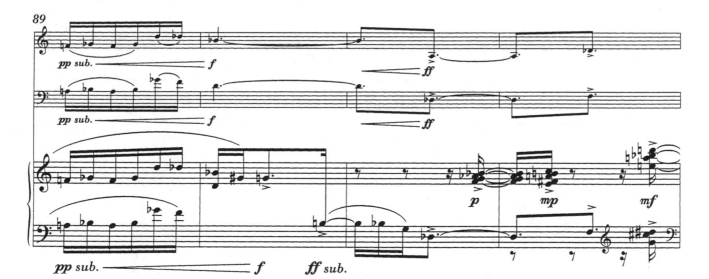

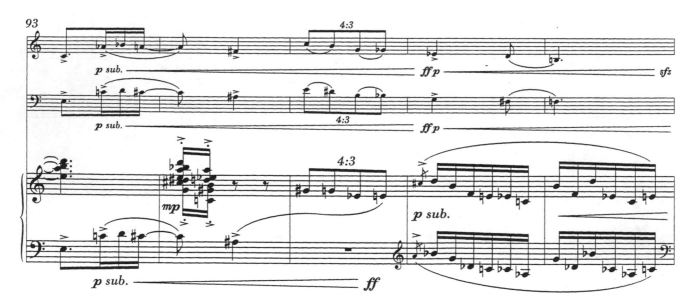

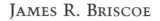

JAMES R. BRISCOE

Augusta Read Thomas

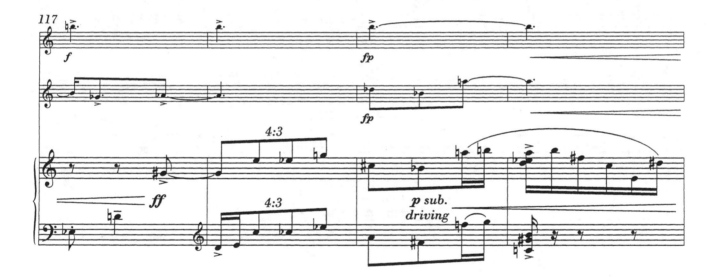

JAMES R. BRISCOE

General Bibliography

Adkins Chiti, Patricia. *Donne in Musica*. Rome: Armando, 1996.

Ammer, Christine. *Unsung: A History of Women in American Music*. Westport, Conn.: Greenwood Press, 1980.

Baroncelli, Nilcéia Cleide da Silva. *Mulheres compositoras*. São Paulo: R. Kempf Editores, 1987.

Blume, Friedrich, ed. *Die Musik in Geschichte und Gegenwart*. 14 vols. Kassel: Bärenreiter, 1949–1968. Supplements in 2 vols., 1973, 1979. Index, 1986.

Boenke, Heidi M. *Flute Music by Women Composers: An Annotated Catalog*. New York: Greenwood Press, 1988.

Bowers, Jane, and Judith Tick, eds. *Women Making Music: The Western Art Tradition, 1150–1950*. Urbana: University of Illinois Press, 1986.

Claghorn, Charles Eugene. *Women Composers and Hymnists: A Concise Biographical Dictionary*. Metuchen, N.J.: Scarecrow Press, 1984.

Cohen, Aaron I. *International Discography of Women Composers*. Westport, Conn.: Greenwood Press, 1984.

———. *International Encyclopedia of Women Composers*. New York: Books & Music USA, 1987.

Dees, Pamela Youngdahl. *A Guide to Piano Music by Women Composers*. Westport, Conn.: Greenwood Press, 2002.

Fuller, Sophie. *The Pandora Guide to Women Composers: Britain and the United States*. London and San Francisco: Pandora, 1994.

Glickman, Sylvia, and Martha Furman Schleifer. *From Convent to Concert Hall: A Guide to Women Composers*. Westport, Conn.: Greenwood Press, 2003.

Grattan, Virginia L. *American Women Songwriters: A Biographical Dictionary*. Westport, Conn.: Greenwood Press, 1993.

Green, Mildred Denby. *Black Women Composers: A Genesis*. Boston: Twayne Publishers, 1983.

Heinrich, Adel. *Organ and Harpsichord Music by Women Composers: An Annotated Catalog*. New York: Greenwood Press, 1991.

International Alliance for Women in Music. *IAWM Directory*. Norman, Okla.: IAWM, 1995.

International Congress on Women in Music. *Female Music Rush Hour: 9th International Congress on Women in Music*. Kassel: Furore Verlag, 1995.

International League of Women Composers. *ILWC Journal*. Framingham, Mass.: International League of Women Composers, 1989.

Jackson, Barbara Garvey. *Say Can You Deny Me: A Guide to Surviving Music by Women from the 16th through 18th Centuries*. Fayetteville: University of Arkansas Press, 1994.

Jezic, Diane. *Women Composers: The Lost Tradition Found*. New York: Feminist Press at The City University of New York, 1994.

Johnson, Rose-Marie. *Violin Music by Women Composers: A Bio-bibliographical Guide*. New York: Greenwood Press, 1989.

LePage, Jane Weiner. *Women Composers, Conductors, and Musicians of the Twentieth Century*. Metuchen, N.J.: Scarecrow Press, 1988.

Marshall, Kimberly. *Rediscovering the Muses: Women's Musical Traditions.* Boston: Northeastern University Press, 1993.

Marx, Eva. *210 Osterreichische Komponistinnen.* Salzburg: Residenz, 2001.

Mayer, Clara. *Komponistinnen im Musikvertag: Katalog Lieferbarer Musikalien.* Kassel: Furore Vig, 1996.

Neuls-Bates, Carol. *Women in Music: An Anthology of Source Readings from the Middle Ages to the Present.* Rev. ed. Boston: Northeastern University Press, 1996.

Nichols, Janet. *Women Music Makers: An Introduction to Women Composers.* New York: Walker, 1992.

Nies, Christel. *Unerhortes Entdecken: Komponistennen und ihr Werk.* Kassel and New York: Barenreiter, 1995.

Nopp, Regina. *Frau und Musik: Komponistinnen zur Zeit der Wiener Klassik.* Linz: R. Trauner, 1995.

Olivier, Antje, ed. *Komponistinnen: Eine Bestandsaufnahme: die Sammlung des Europäischen Frauenmusikarchivs.* Düsseldorf: Tokkata-Verlag für Frauenforschung, 1990.

Olivier, Braun. *Komponistinnen aus 800 Jahren.* Kamen: Sequentia, 1996.

Pendle, Karin. *Women and Music: A History.* Rev. ed. Bloomington: Indiana University Press, 2001.

Placksin, Sally. *American Women in Jazz, 1900 to the Present: Their Words, Lives, and Music.* New York: Seaview Books, 1982.

Rieger, Eva. *Frau and Musik.* Kassel: Furore-Verlag, 1990.

Sadie, Julie Anne, and Rhian Samuel. *The Norton Grove Dictionary of Women Composers.* New York and London: W.W. Norton, 1994.

Sadie, Stanley, and John Tyrrell, eds. *The New Grove Dictionary of Music and Musicians.* 2nd ed. London: Macmillan, 2001. Also available online at <http://www.grove online.com>.

Schleifer, Martha Furman, and Sylvia Glickman. *Women Composers: Music through the Ages.* Vols. 1–6 and ongoing (composers born before 1599–1899 to date). New York: G. K. Hall/Gale Group, 1996.

Slonimsky, Nicholas, ed. *Baker's Biographical Dictionary of Musicians Centennial Edition.* New York: Schirmer Reference, 2000.

Sperber, Roswitha. *Women Composers in Germany.* Bonn: InterNationes, 1996.

Straus, Joseph N. *Music by Women for Study and Analysis.* Englewood Cliffs, N.J.: Prentice Hall, 1993.

Tick, Judith. *American Women Composers before 1870.* Rochester, N.Y.: University of Rochester Press, 1996.

Walker-Hill, Helen. *From Spirituals to Symphonies: African-American Women Composers and Their Music.* Westport, Conn.: Greenwood Press, 2002.

———. *Music by Black Women Composers: A Bibliography of Available Scores.* Chicago: Center for Black Music Research, Columbia College, 1995.

———. *Piano Music by Black Women Composers: A Catalog of Solo and Ensemble Works.* New York: Greenwood Press, 1992.

Weissweiler, Eva. *Komponistinnen vom Mittelalter Bis Zur Gegenwart: eine Kultur- und Wirkungsgeschichte in Biographien une Werksbeispielen.* München: Deutsche Taschenbuch Verlag, 1999.

Contributors

Elizabeth Aubrey has published widely on medieval secular monophony, including *The Music of the Troubadours* (Indiana University Press, 1996). She was co-author and editor of *Songs of the Women Trouvères* (2001) and is Professor of Musicology at the University of Iowa.

Laura Barceló-Lastra was born in Temuco, Chile. She holds a bachelor's and master's in violin performance, and currently is completing the Master of Music History degree at Butler University. She has begun a major documentation of the life and music of Juan Orrego-Salas, now in his eighties, and she plans to interpret these materials as a doctoral thesis.

Melissa Blakesly is a Ph.D. candidate at the University of Cincinnati. Her dissertation currently is in progress and is focusing on gender and sexual representations in operas composed by women in eighteenth-century France and Italy.

Adrienne Fried Block wrote the award-winning biography *Amy Beach, Passionate Victorian* in 1999. With John Graziano, Block co-directs Music in Gotham: The New York Scene 1862–1875. Funded by the National Endowment for the Humanities, the project is based at the Graduate Center of the City University of New York. It documents musical life in that city.

James R. Briscoe, Professor of Musicology at Butler University, is a specialist in French music, the works of Claude Debussy, and women's music. He has received research and teaching grants from the French government, the National Endowment for the Humanities, and the Mellon Foundation. In addition to writing numerous articles, critical editions, and books, he is the editor of *Contemporary Anthology of Music by Women* (Indiana University Press, 1997).

Marcia J. Citron is Lovett Distinguished Professor of Musicology at Rie University. She has written the award-winning books *Gender and the Musical Canon; Letters of Fanny Hensel to Felix Mendelssohn; Cécile Chaminade: A Bio-bibliography;* and *Opera on Screen.*

Suzanne Cusick is Professor of Music at New York University, having joined that faculty recently after ten years at the University of Virginia as department head. Cusick is notable for feminist criticism and has published in the collections *Musicology and Difference* and *Queering the Pitch.* She is completing a monograph on Francesca Caccini for the University of Chicago Press.

David Gordon Duke heads the Music School at Vancouver Community College. Born in Vancouver, he studied theory and composition with Jean Coulthard, about whom he now writes. He received graduate degrees from the Universities of North Carolina and Victoria. A writer on several aspects of Canadian music, and a speaker on Canadian radio, he researched music of the first peoples of the British Columbia coast.

Susan Erickson works extensively on Baroque performance practice and women composers. She taught on these topics at the University of Sydney, Australia, and at the University of California, Davis. Recently she and the violinist Robert Samson Bloch recorded La Guerre's violin and harpsichord sonatas of 1707. La Guerre, on whom she now writes, is her specialty.

Mark Everist is Professor of Music at the University of Southampton. He has published books on the nineteenth-century motet (1994) and on nineteenth-century French stage music (2002). He is editor of the *Magnus liber organi* (2001–2003).

Jill Munroe Fankhauser was born in New York City, and she holds degrees from Cornell and Johns Hopkins Universities and from the University of Cincinnati College Conservatory. She edited "Three Arias" from *Talestri, regina delle amazzoni* by Maria Antonia Walpurgis (2002).

Annegret Fauser is Professor of Musicology at the University of North Carolina at Chapel Hill.

Nancy Fierro is a noted concert pianist, recording artist, and educator. She performs internationally on women composers and has performed many premieres of their works. She is on the music faculty of Mount St. Mary's College in Los Angeles.

Susan M. Filler published *Gustav and Alma Mahler: A Guide to Research,* soon to be reissued in a revised edition. She edited two songs by Alma Mahler for the first time by Hildegard Publishing, and has edited Alma's *Vier Lieder* in *Women Composers: Music through the Ages.* A book on music source readings during the Third Reich is forthcoming from Indiana University Press.

Christin Heitmann earned a Ph.D. at the University of Oldenburg with a dissertation on the orchestral and chamber music of Louise Farrenc. Heitmann is co-editor of the composer's orchestra, chamber, and piano works for the *Kritische Ausgabe,* Wilhelmshaven 1998–2003, and serves on the Sophie-Drinker-Institut in Bremen.

Barbara Garvey Jackson is Professor Emerita of Music at the University of Arkansas. She has served the discipline of musicology well through her many publications on women composers, and she established ClarNan Editions, dedicated to publishing their music.

Bryony Jones read music at the University of York and completed a master's degree at the University of Liverpool, where she currently is researching the music of Rebecca Clarke. Her book *The Music of Lord Berners (1883–1950): "The Versatile Peer"* was published in 2003.

Michael Klaper was born in 1970 in Bietigheim-Bissingen near Stuttgart. He studied musicology, medieval German literature, and art history at the Universities of Tubingen and Erlangen; he received his Ph.D. from the latter in 2002. Since then he has served as Assistant Lecturer in Musicology at Erlangen.

Carolynn A. Lindeman served as President of the Music Educators National Conference and on the Advisory Board of the Kennedy Center for the Performing Arts. She has published in various areas of music education, including, recently, on May Frances Aufderheide in *Women Composers: Music through the Ages.* She is Professor of Music at San Francisco State University.

Roberta Lindsey is Professor of Musicology at Indiana University–Indianapolis, where she has pioneered music appreciation study online. Her master's from Butler University concerned Copland's piano music, and her doctorate at Ohio State University dealt with his early ballet *Grogh*. She has presented papers at the American Musicological Society and the Society for American Music, and has received major fellowships for study at the Library of Congress.

Thomas J. Mathiesen is Distinguished Professor and David H. Jacobs Chair in Music at Indiana University. A specialist in the music and music theory of antiquity and the Middle Ages, he is also Director of the Center for the History of Music Theory and Literature at Indiana University.

Hidemi Matsushita earned his Ph.D. in musicology at Brigham Young University. He wrote his dissertation on Maria Theresia von Paradis, edited and published several of her works, and contributed articles on her in various journals and encyclopedias. He is co-ordinator of music at Arapahoe Community College in Littleton, Colorado.

Sharon Mirchandani is Associate Professor of Music History and Theory at Westminster Choir College, Rider University. She has published on Marga Richter, U. U. Church, Anne and Nancy Wilson, and feminist theory and musicology. She has read papers for the American Musicological Society, the Society for American Music, and the College Music Society. She is an editor for the *Journal for the International Alliance for Women in Music*.

Craig B. Parker is Professor of Musicology at Kansas State University, Manhattan.

Karin Pendle is Professor of Musicology at the College-Conservatory of Music, the University of Cincinnati. She is editor and an author of *Women and Music* (Indiana University Press), which is in its second edition.

Beatrice Pescerelli teaches courses on early music at the University of Bologna. She published a major study and critical edition, *I madrigali di Maddalena Casulana*, with the publisher Leo Olschki (Firenze, 1979). More recently, Pescerelli has written on the medieval document *Speculum Musice* in *Studi Musicale* no. 1 (1991).

Barbara A. Petersen is Assistant Vice President for Classical Administration at Broadcast Music, Inc. She has chaired New York Women Composers since 1985 and serves on the board of the American Music Center. Petersen has written a book on the lieder of Richard Strauss and articles in the *New American Grove* and *Grove Dictionary of Opera*. She earned a bachelor's at Carleton College and a master's and doctorate in musicology at New York University.

Martin Picker received his Ph.D. in musicology from the University of California at Berkeley, taught at the University of Illinois for a short time, and served at Rutgers University until retiring in 1997. He is a scholar of the music of the Renaissance, publishing *The Chanson Albums of Marguerite of Austria* (1965); *The Motet Books of Andrea Antico* (1987); and volume 16 of the *New Josquin Edition*. He has retired to Charlottesville, Virginia.

Janet Pollack received her M.A. and Ph.D. in musicology from Duke University. She now teaches music history, theory, and world music as Assistant Professor at the University of Puget Sound. She contributes regularly to the *Renaissance Quarterly* and wrote "Princess Elizabeth Stuart as Musician and Muse" for *Many Headed Melodies.*

Caroline Potter is Senior Lecturer in Music at Kingston University, United Kingdom. She wrote the book *Henri Dutilleux* (1997) and numerous articles on French music since Debussy. She is co-editor with Richard Langham Smith of the forthcoming *French Music since Berlioz,* and is writing a book on Nadia and Lili Boulanger.

Nancy Reich has served on the faculties of Manhattanville College and New York University, and has been visiting professor at Bard College and Williams College. Reich's award-winning biography of 1985, *Clara Schumann: The Artist and the Woman,* was hailed widely by critics and has been translated into German, Japanese, and Chinese. It was published in a revised edition in 2001. The City of Zwickau awarded her the Robert Schumann Prize in 1996, on the centennial of Clara Schumann's death.

Ellen Rosand, Professor of Music at Yale University, wrote the first modern study of Barbara Strozzi and her music (1978). A specialist in Baroque opera, she is the author of the book *Opera in Seventeenth-Century Venice* and of articles on Monteverdi and Handel.

Judith Rosen has written on women composers in *High Fidelity/Musical America; The Musical Woman* (vols. 1 and 2); *New Grove Dictionary of American Music and Musicians;* and in the present connection the book *Grażyna Bacewicz: Her Life and Works.* For the latter she received the Amicus Poloniae badge of Poland. Rosen was founding President of the Board, the Arnold Schoenberg Institute, is on the Advisory Board of the Los Angeles Chamber Orchestra, and is a consultant for the San Francisco-based Women's Philharmonic.

Diane Touliatos-Miles is Professor of Musicology and Director of the Center for the Humanities at the University of Missouri at St. Louis. She is well known as a scholar in Byzantine and Western medieval music, Ancient Greek music, and women composers. The Byzantine nun Kassia has been a particular emphasis in her work.